D0992072

REVOLUTIONARY LIVES

REVOLUTIONARY LIVES

Anna Strunsky & William English Walling

James Boylan

UNIVERSITY OF MASSACHUSETTS PRESS · Amherst

Copyright © 1998 by
The University of Massachusetts Press
All rights reserved
Printed in the United States of America
Designed by Mary Mendell
Set in Trump Medieval with Kolloss display type
by Keystone Typesetting, Inc.
Printed and bound by BookCrafters
Library of Congress Cataloging-in-Publication Data
Boylan, James R.
Revolutionary lives : Anna Strunsky and William
English Walling /
James Boylan.
p. cm.
Includes bibliographical references (p.   ) and index.
ISBN 1-55849-164-3 (cloth : alk. paper)
1. Walling, Anna Strunsky, 1879–   . 2. Walling, William English,
1877–1936. 3. Socialists—United States—Biography. I. Title.
HX84.W26B69   1999
335.'.0092'273—dc21
[B]   98-26696 CIP
British Library Cataloguing in Publication data are available.

Contents

REVOLUTIONARY LIVES

Introduction

"This Aspiring and Questing World"

In the years before the Great War, William English Walling and Anna Strunsky were among the most glorious of the American left's Beautiful People: "millionaire Socialists," rivaled only by the Lincolnesque James Graham Phelps Stokes and his immigrant journalist bride, Rose Pastor.[1] English and Anna were striking individuals—on the platform, under bylines, or as (frequently) reported in the Sunday supplements. As seen in the press, they were almost caricatures: he slim and imperious, the Southern aristocrat; she warm, passionate, voluble, a touch of something foreign in her voice.

They were seen, and saw themselves, as destiny's couple, plunging always toward the heart of their times—revolution, pogrom, labor war, racial violence, radical controversy. Freed by affluence to choose his roles, he played the controversialist, the journalist *engagé,* the publicist in the old sense of that term: the writer who minds the world's business. She was a novelist by aspiration, a reluctant but moving orator, and ever the idealist. Their influence on their era was not inconsiderable: They fed American sympathy for the Russian revolution of 1905, struck the initial spark for the founding of the National Association for the Advancement of Colored People, and rode the tide of prewar American socialism when it seemed capable of transforming American politics and society.

Yet their names are today known chiefly to specialists, and the world of radicalism that they inhabited can seem more remote than, say, the first Elizabethan era. Their present obscurity is to a degree deserved, for they never fully won the conventional attributes of fame: achievement, enduring reputation, or power. By the time other members of their generation were rising to eminence with the New Deal, they had all but vanished from public view. The coin in which they traded before the war had become all but worthless.

The title *Revolutionary Lives*—taken from that of an unpublished book by Anna Strunsky—is to a degree ironic; Anna and English Walling were self-styled revolutionaries whose radicalism was ultimately played out in bourgeois settings. Yet for forty years they *did* lead revolutionary lives, in the sense that they continually discarded old identities for new, old issues for new; like their contemporary Hutchins Hapgood, they were exemplars of Victorians seeking to emerge into the modern world.[2]

Moreover, they led adventurous lives, marked with episodes of physical and intellectual daring, even recklessness, and a restlessness that led them always to believe that their lifework was incomplete. Not the least of their struggles, in the end, was the conflict in their own household, centering on increasingly divergent views of humanity and society, peace and war. Their remarkably variegated pilgrimage, their largely untold story, I am persuaded, enriches our understanding of that era—"this aspiring and questing world," as Anna's cousin Simeon Strunsky called it—of American radicalism before 1914, and its extinction in the Great War.[3]

Where twenty or thirty years ago I, like many of my contemporaries, might have dismissed half of the tale—Anna's half—as irrelevant or inconsequential, it is now possible to study the two of them on equal terms, and justifiably so. We can explore more freely now the links between domestic and public spheres, between personal acts and social consequences. In this perspective, Anna and English have equal salience.

If the tale proceeds more through her eyes than his, it is not only because he habitually concealed his inner self but because she left such rich if sometimes enigmatic resources. She clearly hoped that her papers would one day be used by historians, and I have tried to employ them in the spirit that she prescribed during her literary apprenticeship, when she defended W. E. Henley's critical biography of Robert Louis Stevenson: "There are . . . two manifestations of the principle of loyalty—that of the fanatic, eager, superlative, puerile, bent only on seating the little god of its making on a throne in a drama of one night's running, and that of the lover in whose love something of the iron has entered, but who feels that to posterity it were a gain to have the picture true."[4]

PART ONE

Anna: Love and Work,

1877–1905

1 *"Miss Annie"*

The San Francisco of a hundred years ago—"The City That Was," as Will Irwin named it after its destruction in 1906—spawned an energetic, informal, sometimes amateur artistic-literary-journalistic culture. Less daunting than the more commercial New York, it offered aspirants easy access and ready encouragement. It did not matter a great deal if one had not yet achieved much; nobody had. What mattered was one's ability to create and play a congenial role.[1]

The representative institution, if it can be called an institution, was "the Crowd," a floating alliance of the left and the literary that gathered at the restaurants on the old Montgomery Block and later spread out to scenic Piedmont, overlooking the bay from behind Oakland, and southward to Carmel, "the seacoast of Bohemia."[2]

This Bohemia was peopled with vivid if evanescent figures: Gelett Burgess, an outcast from academic life, founder of a short-lived magazine of aesthetics called *The Lark,* author of a quatrain called "The Purple Cow," a work he had already come to rue. Arnold Genthe, portrait and documentary photographer. Xavier Martinez ("Marty"), painter of Aztec heritage and Parisian airs, dressed always in corduroys and flowing red ties, creator of the famous frieze of black cats at Coppa's, the Crowd's hangout. George Sterling, a minor poet whose darker side caused the suicide of two women associated with him; ultimately, he killed himself as well.[3]

A warm, striking, voluble, attractively disheveled young woman can be glimpsed in the Crowd—holding forth at Coppa's; turning out reviews for the latest little literary periodical; showing up to hear, and to be seen hearing, such visiting celebrities as William Butler Yeats; performing in amateur theatricals at the outpost in Carmel. Activist, intellectual, writer-in-gestation, she played these roles so grandly that the reverberations were still inspiring literary excesses years later: "Anna Strunsky! It is fifteen years since that dark, flashing, warmly radiant girl leaned across a table in Coppa's old restaurant, or darted up the stairs to Martinez' attic studio, but the fragrance of her memory still hangs over tales of old San Francisco. No one who met Anna Strunsky ever forgets her, they say."[4]

She first won celebrity in 1896, when William Randolph Hearst's *San Francisco Examiner* dubbed her the "Girl Socialist of San Francisco." The fascinated reporter found in her face the "beauty of intelligence" rather than prettiness and noted her "pleading, sorrowful voice." He referred to her as Russian by birth but clearly identified her as Jewish with references to "Oriental" aspects of her appearance. He also recorded that she had difficulty answering questions from the floor. From that time forward, the press found her, as her friend Jack London pointed out, "exceptionally good copy."[5]

Yet to a degree the bohemianism was a facade and the flamboyant Anna Strunsky who appeared in the Hearst newspapers was in part a reportorial concoction. Sexual overtones always lingered between the lines, yet Anna Strunsky remained part of a conventional immigrant family that had striven to make itself part of the American middle class, and she remained determinedly Victorian in her personal conduct. Moreover, behind the apparent self-confidence lay not only uncertainty about her own abilities but a lingering conviction that she was surrounded by and destined for death.

In her later years, Anna Strunsky rarely mentioned in writing the first nine years of her life, in Russia. As a woman of forty, she offered a fragment:

> The only recollection of Russia for me [was] of a long village street and barefoot children and rambling hovels. I remembered myself a little child standing in a patch of sunlight and poking my fingers into a wall and finding it soft as sand. I dug and dug and let the fine red dust slip into my fist and laughed to think I had the stuff of which houses were made,— weak, powdery stuff, unstable as water.[6]

The only trace of Russia that she bore as an adult was a faint accent that enriched her expressive and precise English.

Her early years, before California, must be inferred from family tradition and fragile newspaper clippings.[7] The Strunsky family came from a rural place, Babinots, in western Russia, within the czarist pale of Jewish settlement. Her father, Elias Strunsky, was a worldly Jew and businessman who had learned Russian. Her mother, Anna Horowitz, came from a religious family that arranged her first marriage, to a young seminary student with acne. Rather than consummate the marriage, the sixteen-year-old bride took refuge with her parents, who bought her a divorce. After nine months, she was permitted to marry Elias.

In the mid-1880s, Elias Strunsky, inspired to look toward America by reading Tocqueville in Russian translation, decided to emigrate. He took his five children and pregnant wife out through Germany, thence to England. A family story says that because Anna was small at nine her parents misstated her age to get a cheaper ticket, hence much subsequent confusion over her real birthdate, which was March 21, 1877.[8] Family tradition also says that they crossed the Atlantic on the *Egypt*, which sailed from Liverpool on September 8, 1886, and entered New York harbor eleven days later, sailing past the Statue of Liberty, just rising on her pedestal.[9]

The Strunskys came to America carrying little beyond the family feather-beds and copperware. Like other hundreds of thousands, they made their first home on New York's Lower East Side, crowded into a tenement on Madison Street with the toilet in the backyard. The three boys, ranging in age roughly from ten to fifteen, worked at home sewing shirts, while their father delivered them to the sweater, the wholesaler. They found larger quarters a few blocks away on Cherry Street, probably on the "Penitentiary Row" described sourly by the reporter Jacob A. Riis, then collecting material for *How the Other Half Lives*: "It has become peopled wholly with Hebrews, the over-flow from Jewtown adjoining, pedlars and tailors, all of them."[10]

The last child, Morris, was born on Cherry Street. The three older brothers continued to make shirts, assisted by young radical exiles whose political expertise exceeded their sewing skills; Albert, the oldest brother, had to redo socialist needlework late at night. Not surprisingly, the brothers became so interested in socialism that their Uncle Isadore warned their father to keep an eye on them.

About 1888, the family left the Lower East Side for a marginally easier life at 326 East Thirty-ninth Street. The older brothers went to work at a nearby steam-operated shirt factory. One day their mother decided to take the boys a hot lunch, but in the factory she almost fainted in the noise and heat. Back home, she cried and demanded that her husband go back into business on his own and let the children resume their education. Albert entered the family business with his father—first wholesale groceries, then liquor—while Hyman and Max went to school, as did Anna, her sister, Rose, six years younger, and the youngest, Morris.

Anna took easily to American education. By the time she was fifteen, six years in America, she was perceived as the brightest student at P.S. 49 and was rewarded with a short feature and a crude line portrait, drawn from a photograph, in the *New York Herald*. Her teachers praised "Miss Annie" for her scholarship, her fluency in languages, her writing (she had already been published in a magazine), and her sweet temper. Her mother recalled: "My two small daughters were pretty and intelligent and had good brains. . . . When I used to go upstairs and look at them and think that they will have a college education and will have professions, one can imagine how I felt as a mother."[11]

Elias Strunsky left New York for his health in 1893 and started a new liquor business in San Francisco. He sent for his family and moved them into a big house at 901 Golden Gate Avenue. It was a warm, bookish, and loqua-cious household. Himself a mediator rather than a combatant, Elias Strunsky always insisted on providing food and wine for an evening of argument. The

Strunskys welcomed a flow of participants in the world at large, among whom the anarchist Emma Goldman was the most celebrated. Anna recalled: "The memory of the men and women that came and went throughout the years is perhaps the most romantic and the most precious memory of my life. This was my best school and from these personalities I got more than I ever got out of books or halls of learning. Here were truly formative forces—meeting people in intellectual councils; budding genius, refugees, revolutionists; broken lives and strong lives, all made welcome, all met with reverence and with warmth."[12]

With such models before her, Anna was bound to become politically active herself, nor could there be doubt as to her commitment. The exiles who visited the Strunskys were messengers of the revolutionary socialism that they hoped one day to carry home to Russia. Many of them had found an American base in the Socialist Labor Party, tiny in membership but a rallying point of radicalism in America. Its leading figure was Daniel DeLeon, who ran a weekly called *The People*. DeLeon laid out an almost Calvinist kind of Marxism, demanding that its readers ignore all interim betterment in favor of the ultimate goal of pure socialism. The party was less forbidding in its local branches, and the San Francisco branch was notable for its advocacy of women's rights. Anna's emerging identities—Russian immigrant, woman-to-be, aspiring intellectual—all impelled her toward the party.[13]

Characteristically, she made an instant and wholehearted choice. Still "hardly more than a child," perhaps sixteen, Anna joined the "American branch"—the term used to distinguish a nonimmigrant local—of San Francisco's Socialist Labor Party. Her father, who had inspired her interest in politics, disagreed with her decision and they clashed—"not because he grudged me to a great cause, but because he felt there was something amiss with the cause with which I had become infatuated." Despite her father's doubts, socialism proved an enduring commitment.[14]

In a time when fewer than ten thousand women a year entered American higher education, the two Strunsky sisters went to college. Anna finished Lowell High School in San Francisco and in 1896, at the age of nineteen, went to study thirty miles to the south at the handsome new sandstone quadrangle of the university named for Leland Stanford Jr., late son of the railroad magnate. She listed her "proposed calling" as writer and lecturer. Even with the minimal tuition, the burden on her family of living expenses, residence fees, and books must have been substantial, but was borne without complaint.[15]

Stanford, under the presidency of the ambitious ichthyologist David Starr Jordan, was part of a new wave of universities, Johns Hopkins and Chicago among them, that were nurturing the reformers-to-be of the Progressive Era. Anna Strunsky took a class from one such reformer-teacher, the economist and sociologist Edward A. Ross. Ross remembered years later that she had been his student, but if he noted her at the time he must have regarded her coldly, for he was convinced that people of origins such as Anna Strunsky's threatened to drag America down into a genetic hell. Eventually, Ross was fired after he called publicly for shooting at any ship bearing Japanese toward California.[16]

Stanford in 1896 was a rough Arcadia, set in the unmarred fields and hills beyond the lights of San Francisco. When William James came to lecture in 1898, he described the hills as "bathed in ether, milk and sunshine." Anna recalled that she impressed the eminent psychologist by arguing in a seminar that conversion from faith to free thought could be a religious experience; afterward, he asked for a copy of her paper, but she never sent it.[17]

Instructors and students were thrown together in democratic closeness, and Anna formed strong friendships among the faculty. Her correspondence with Melville Best Anderson, a professor of literature, lasted decades. But her first confidante was a history teacher, Mary Sheldon Barnes; she remembered "how tenderly and greatly Mrs. Barnes loved me, how when I was a mere child, a mere crude little laggard, she ennobled my days and fired my heart." Her intense attachment to Mrs. Barnes is clear in a letter she wrote to "Madonna Marie" at the start of her sophomore year:

> I thank you, I thank you, friend, sweetheart, mother! I shall thank you forever for discovering your soul to me so that I may love you. . . . Do you know that you save me from being a coward? Many a night have I looked up at the stars only to be paralyzed with the vastness and grandeur of it all—a kind of shrinking before immensity, a fear of life, a painful wonder at the meaning of it; a realizing what supreme living is, and, finally, a death-bringing conviction that strength was not given me to meet the Universe! But always have I felt that hand in hand with *another* I might be a force such as has never been.

Mary Sheldon Barnes died as Anna was starting her junior year; for years afterward, Anna planned a memorial monograph but she did not write it.[18]

Grief may have affected Anna's academic work in the fall of 1898, but her transcript reveals trouble developing earlier. An English major, she did well enough in literature courses, but in ethics and sociology (perhaps Ross's course) she earned only Stanford's "conditioned" grade—neither pass nor fail, and sometimes remediable; and she failed zoology. Although she recalled later only that she had a "condition" in history and an unfinished Shakespeare paper, in fact the record of the fall semester of her junior year reveals full-blown collapse: only one course, history of the French Revolution, passed; three "conditions"; and three grades marked "def," perhaps for "deferred." A note is appended: "Suspended from Univ. Dec 27 98 (Scholarship Com.)."[19]

Probably there was more to her downfall than grades. Anna later hinted in a letter to her New York confidante, Dr. Katherine Maryson (whom she called "Katia") of deeper controversy: "Did I ever tell you how they tortured me at Stanford? . . . All my Stanford memories are poisoned, every step there is inquisitorial." A year after her suspension, her new friend Jack London wrote to her that she had nothing to be ashamed of in her failure to be "an intellectual machine." But he went on to suggest more: "Believe me, I do know the suffering entailed, and I do also know that I have not the moral bravery to face the music as you are doing."[20]

In her memoirs, Emma Goldman wrote that Anna had been suspended "because she had received a male visitor in her room instead of in her parlour." But it may be that Emma Goldman was trying too hard to cast Anna in her own nonconformist image, for in a later edition she retracted the whole story, no doubt at Anna's prompting. It is true enough that Stanford, while paying lip service to student independence and individual responsibility, remained rigid in matters of "good morals and decency"; it also seems probable, however, that if Anna had other than academic troubles they were more likely political than moral.[21]

Even as an undergraduate, Anna had become a formidable platform presence. She was chosen for the Stanford team in the important debate against Berkeley. (This may have been the occasion of a family telegram to her: "Congratulations [to] you, Stanford has chosen the best. Your People.") She also placed her talents at the disposal of the Socialist Labor Party, and probably gave it too much time, considering her academic difficulties. Much later, she recalled, "I did endless drudgery like being secretary of the Central Committee for 2½ years, and on other committees to which I gave my precious time—time for which my soul and my young fiery senses had other uses altogether."[22]

A surviving paper, "Specialization of Vocation under Capitalism," reveals the socialist Anna Strunsky at twenty, just before her sophomore year at Stanford. Delivered to the Bay Area's Karl Marx Club in August 1897, the lecture already contains her characteristic blend of slightly ostentatious learning and fervent emotion. More substantially, she enunciated a standard for her own life-to-be, no doubt with little inkling of how hard it would be for her to meet it: "Goethe called the matter of personal relations 'the little world' and the question of work 'the larger world,' and he claimed that the little world is the heart of the larger world, for indeed the two problems are most closely interrelated. In order to live highly in either it is necessary to live highly in both."[23]

The Stanford records do not make clear what happened to her academically after her suspension in December 1898. The best guess is that she continued in an unmatriculated status to finish the uncompleted work in her junior courses, for she maintained a Stanford address through the following year. And the resumption of study is suggested in a later diary entry: "I who was tost out of here, whose life was embittered coming back." For a time, she was registered as a nondegree student at the University of California, Berkeley. No record survives of further completed academic work at either place.[24]

Despite the turbulence, Stanford did its work, authenticating Anna as an intellectual, a relatively elevated status in loosely drawn San Francisco circles. She now moved capaciously and comfortably in its Anglo-American literary culture, less a foreigner than a slightly exotic Californian-American. She spoke and wrote fluently, if elaborately, and was seen to be a rising literary and political presence.

Yet her private meditations show that she did not truly believe herself flashing, or warmly radiant. An Anna Strunsky not seen in public felt herself gripped by uncertainty, ignorant rather than cultured, doubtful of her ability to undertake and complete her "work," and obsessed with death. "Death, love, work," she wrote on the first page of her first notebook. "Death called me 'Love,'" she wrote in a poem she had worked on since she was at Stanford, "And kissed my lips & hair." Even before real death began pay to its calls, she was prepared with an obsessive sense of mortality—or morbidity.[25]

2 *"Comrades!"*

Late in 1899, the local section, American branch, of the Socialist Labor Party sponsored a commemoration of that brief candle, the Paris Commune of 1871, at San Francisco's Turk Street Temple. Years later, Anna Strunsky invoked the scene:

> [We] had climbed the dusty stairs and had sat in the garish hall lighted by flickering gas-jets. [We] had looked about . . . at the red-draped speaker's stand, the pictures on the walls of Marx, Engels, Liebknecht, Lassalle, at the black letters on white stretched across the platform: "Workers unite! You have only your chains to lose, you have a world to gain!" . . .
>
> We had listened to the eloquence of the speaker, Austin Lewis, a London University man who brought something of an old-world culture to our Western movement. It was as if we were there in that Paris which we had never seen, in a time before we were born. We were by the side of the Communards on those barricades. In that hour we re-lived those days and nights of conflict and tragedy. . . . The speaking over, we rose and sang the *Marseillaise* and the *International.*"[1]

She remembered an incident at the end of the evening: "He was there that night. . . . He rose from a seat well towards the front and walked towards the platform. I too was on the way to the speaker." They were probably introduced by Frank Strawn-Hamilton, a tousled socialist philosopher: "Do you want to meet him[?] . . . he is Jack London, a Comrade who has been speaking in the street in Oakland. He has been to the Klondyke and he writes short stories for a living." They shook hands and talked: "He was proud, he said, that we had men like Austin Lewis with us. Already some of the best and finest had crossed the barriers of class to side with the people. Then he hurried away to catch the last ferry for Oakland where he lived with his mother."[2]

Jack London was twenty-three; she, a year younger. She recalled, embroidering the memory: "he seemed at once younger and older than his years. There was that about him that made one feel that one would always remember him. He seemed the incarnation of the Platonic ideal of man, the body of the athlete and the mind of the thinker." She recast the meeting in epic terms, claiming that she felt at the time "as if I were meeting in their youth, Las[s]alle, Karl Marx, or Byron, so instantly did I feel that I was in the presence of a historical character."[3]

It may have seemed a fated match—the meeting of two of the party's emerging stars. It was strange if in fact they had not heard of each other, for the Bay Area's socialist and literary circles were not large. But he had been inaccessible—away in the Klondike and then in isolation to teach himself to be a writer. She may have been away as well, clinging to Stanford.

Their first conversation was clearly more extensive than a how-do-you-do. The air of excitement—a sense of circling and appraising each other—can be inferred in the letter he wrote a few days later: "My dear Miss Strunsky," he began. "Seems as if I have known you for an age—you and your Mr. Browning." He added, to assure her that he competed at her level: "I shall certainly have to re-read him."

She had identified herself as a writer, for he offered, in his role as "economic man," to tell her how to sell writing to "the silent sullen peoples who run the magazines," a paraphrase from "The White Man's Burden," by Rudyard Kipling, his favorite poet. Daringly, he plunged into an aggressive but prophetic appraisal: "as I sat there listening to you, I seemed to sum you up somewhat in this way: A woman to whom it is given to feel the deeps and the heights of emotion in an extraordinary degree; who can grasp the intensity of transcendental feeling, the dramatic force of situation, as few women, or men either, can. But, this question at once arose: Has she expression? By this I mean simply the literary technique. And again, supposing that she has not, has she the 'dig,' the quality of application, so that she might attain it?"[4]

He had come close to the mark, but also had come close to overstepping. Next day she replied in a letter that remarked: "Somehow it is a new note to me, that of being seen as 'aimless, helpless, hopeless.'" In his reply, he back-pedaled, insisting that he had used no such words, and had merely been speculating. In fact, she was gently showing him up, because the quotation was not from his letter, as he supposed, but from the Browning he claimed to have read:[5]

> What had I on earth to do
> With the slothful, with the mawkish, the unmanly?
> Like the aimless, helpless, hopeless, did I drivel
> —Being—who?
> (Epilogue to "Asolando")

By way of implied apology, he claimed that he was too rough a character, too bruised by life, to observe niceties, and launched himself into near-poesy: "Take me this way: a stray guest, a bird of passage, splashing with salt-rimed wings through a brief moment of your life—a rude and blundering bird, used to large airs and great spaces, unaccustomed to the amenities of confined existence." Still, he had been invited for Saturday evening, and accepted.[6]

At the Strunskys' fireside that December weekend, Jack London looked even more pleasing: "The light played on his face. He had large blue eyes, dark lashes, a broad forehead over which a lock of brown hair fell and which he often brushed aside with his small, finely shaped hand. He was deep-chested, wide shouldered." She omitted mentioning, although she noted it elsewhere, that he was missing a tooth or two. The evening followed his agenda: "Jack picked up a copy of Rudyard Kipling's *Seven Seas,* recently published, turned to the 'Song of the English' and read it aloud. The Anglo-Saxons were the salt of the earth, he declared. He forgave Kipling his imperialism because he wrote of the poor, the ignorant, the submerged, of the soldier and sailor in their own language."[7]

Then: "We read Swinburne. By the light of the fire he copied in a little black notebook the lines he printed ten years later in the last chapter of *Martin Eden.* 'From too much love of living / From hope and fear set free' ["The Garden of Proserpine" (1866)]. . . . We looked at the lights reflected in the glistening side-walks. Then he went away. I watched his quick half running walk, his rolling sailor's gait, until he turned the corner."[8]

Thus, on zephyrs of late Victorian poets, she was being drawn, not unwillingly, into the orbit of a powerful personality, one already practiced in capturing satellites male and female. Not that Jack London yet had the potency of celebrity or riches. He had had a brief flutter of publicity as the "Boy Socialist" in Oakland, much as Anna had been dubbed San Francisco's "Girl Socialist." Now he was a still impoverished and industrious apprentice writer, with only odds and ends published. But he was on the verge of recognition, with a story due out in the *Atlantic Monthly* and a collection of stories, *The Son of the Wolf,* accepted at the *Atlantic*'s adjunct publisher, Houghton Mifflin of Boston. Most important, he had learned how to make himself into an untiring producer, from the same fiber that had already transformed him from an uneducated roughneck into a passable man of letters.[9]

Now, it appeared, he had decided to test his self-developed intellectual muscle on Anna Strunsky, partly to see if he could match her literary fluency, but also, clearly, to attract her. In his effort to impress he stumbled again. He sent for her criticism a piece of writing containing a portrayal of a Jewish couple; she rebuked him: "Only not all Jews haggle and bargain." Again, he pleaded the clod. He restored his status as friend with a long, comforting letter as she left Stanford. On January 21, 1900, he started his letter with the usual, "Dear Miss Strunsky," but stopped and wrote: "O Pshaw! Dear Anna"; she did not follow suit until the next month.[10]

His campaign intensified. She recalled that he sent her something—a letter, a note, a clipping, a poem—every day, sometimes signed only "Wolf." He sent flowers, books. They met often, to read Wordsworth, Swinburne, or Browning. They hiked the hills surrounding the Bay. He joined her at sessions of an informal debating society led by Gelett Burgess. They showed up at Coppa's, although he felt uncomfortable in the Crowd. When Anna and her brothers went to the theater, he came along, especially for Shakespeare or Ibsen.[11]

In February 1900, two months after their meeting, she accepted his offer of literary mentorship, which he couched in terminology that was heavily humorous: "I shall stand over you with a whip of scorpions and drive you to your daily toil. Like Pharaoh of old, I shall hold you in bondage." He submitted to her a box of his rejected or abandoned manuscripts, she recalled, "to encourage [me] and in doing this he was like a beggar exposing his sores." One of her memoirs, written in the third person, recalls them as an oddly matched couple: "They had approached each other across what gulfs of difference! He was a doer and she was a dreamer. He was ambitious for her." Already the doer had planted in the dreamer a notion that was hard to erase— that she would somehow emulate him as a writer.[12]

By March, their partnership was no longer purely literary; she believed that she was being courted: "He had known her several months and had wooed her." The critical moment, for her, arrived on a day she remembered as April 4, 1900. She recalled it years later in the third person, in novelistic terms:

> On a certain Wednesday they had climbed the slopes, slippery with pine needles and sun-parched grass, still warm to the touch. The first star shone. The bicycle which had brought him from Piedmont had been left standing against one of the walls of North [Gate] Hall [Berkeley]. . . . They would remember that day, the clear sky, the breeze stirring the leaves of the red-wood under which they sat, with the book open to the chapter on Kant with which her review in class would deal the following morning—The Categorical Imperative. . . . There was a feeling of crisis between them—of something nearer, sweeter about to be born.

She recalled being unintentionally defensive:

> . . . his hands straying over her loosened hair, she threw a vista of distance and struggle between them, and made the lovely moment stagger off and away. . . . For her soul followed the fashion and was wrapt securely from her own view and his in many impenetrable patchings of indirection and over-elaborateness. She had taken refuge in a remark about going to Russia, fearing that she had been overbold, fearing that she might feel she had made some demand upon him. Youth says one

thing and means another. . . . She feared he might think that she was wooing him, that she was "invading his personality," a phrase she had learned from her Anarchist friends. He must be convinced that the fluttering of her hand as it lay in his, the color racing her cheeks, the voice breaking with eager happiness, had nothing to do with him. Heaven forbid he should think it concerned him!

If he had asked her to marry him, sitting there on that knoll, the book on her lap, she might have thrown her young arms around his neck, pressing her head against his shoulder which it hardly reached. He did not ask her . . .[13]

She blamed her own diffidence for chilling this tender episode; perhaps it did. Jack could have been testing whether their fervent acquaintanceship of three months had transformed itself into love; her elusiveness may have persuaded him it had not. On the other hand, her diffidence may have had little effect, for he had another sufficient reason for holding back.

A few days later, she recalled, "[I] had his letter lying in its accustomed place on the little mahogany table that stood in the window looking out upon a garden of iris and flag—the same square envelope which had come daily . . . for months." This letter seemed calculatedly impersonal. He wrote: "It was rather sudden. I always do things that way. I have been so rushed that I have forgotten whether you were on the list of those I did write to, or did not."[14]

On April 7, 1900—one day after he wrote to Anna—Jack London married Bessie Mae Maddern, a cousin of the theater's Minnie Maddern Fiske. Bessie Maddern was a woman, Anna recalled, "to whom he had only once referred in a casual way." In fact, Jack had known Bess for four years; she had tutored him before his brief enrollment at Berkeley, and she had been engaged to a friend of Jack's, now dead. Anna remembered being surprised—and yet the chronology is jumbled, for the letter she remembered as revealing the marriage in fact thanked her for her congratulations. But such distinctions are too fine to maintain across the years. What counted was the shock. She had not tried to claim Jack and now he had placed himself out of reach.[15]

Three weeks later Jack returned, by himself, to the Strunskys' fireside:

There was a fire in the grate and its light played on his face. He spoke of his marriage. He had acted with directness and conviction perhaps only because he had needed to be convinced. He had acted through what might be called defense psychology. He had arrived at some idea that it would be easy to trick his imagination, to harness his fancies. One had a purpose in marrying. One married for qualities. He would found his marriage on that friendship in which love resolves itself. It was as if he was saying he could be happy without happiness—this romantic youth. . . . [He] explained how he had worked it out—there was to be freedom within the frame of marriage. . . . He thought it something new, modern, not realizing that he was being old-fashioned and living like the majority who do not aspire to the luxury of love.[16]

For a time his letters—he continued to write—concentrated on literary business. He played the agent, saying that he had sent a story of hers to the *Atlantic*, but that she should not expect to have it accepted (it was not), and the mentor, planting ever more firmly in her mind the notion that she, like he, must become a writer: "O Anna, don't disappoint me. You have got everything; all you need is to work and work, and to work with the greatest care." He added briskly that she should learn to use a typewriter. As the summer of 1900 took hold, she heard from him less often.[17]

Abruptly, on July 31, came an outburst in his most elevated style. She had not, after all, utterly mistaken his intensity:

> Comrades! And surely it seems so. For all the petty surface turmoil which marked our coming to know each other, really, deep down, there was no confusion at all. Did you not notice it? To me, while I said "You do not understand," I none the less felt the happiness of satisfaction— how shall I say?—felt, rather, that there was no inner conflict; that we were attuned somehow; that a real unity underlaid everything. The ship, new-launched, rushes to the sea; the sliding-ways rebel in weakling creaks and groans; but sea and ship hear them not; so with us when we rushed into each other's lives—we, the real we, were undisturbed. Comrades! Ay, world without end!"

But he concluded less as comrade than taskmaster: "O, Anna, if you will only put your flashing soul with its protean moods on paper!" He remained ambitious for her, but could she be ambitious for herself?[18]

If Jack London's call to comradeship brought Anna back into his orbit, she could hardly say so, given his new marriage. On the other hand, she did not recoil; she became a kind of a friend of the family, visiting the newlyweds at their home on East Fifteenth Street in Oakland and sailing with them on Jack's boat. The three of them—Jack, Anna, and Bess—were becalmed aboard the *Spray* near the end of a late-summer day when he unveiled his strategy:

> He was speaking of eugenics. He was saying that love was a madness, a fever that passes, a trick. One should marry for qualities and not for love. Before marrying one should make sure one is not in love. Love is the danger signal. . . . Jack proposed that we write a book together on eugenics and romantic love. The moon rose, paled, and faded from the sky. Then the night came awake and our sails filled. Before we landed we had our plot, a novel in letter form in which Jack was to be an American, an economist, Herbert Wace, and I an Englishman, a poet, Dane Kempton, who stood in relation to him of father to son.[1]

They also decided the method of collaboration—a real exchange of letters between her home in San Francisco and his across the bay in Oakland. Neither of them stated outright the underlying proposition, nor was there a hint of what Bessie thought of it: that Anna would be attacking the loveless basis of his marriage, and he defending it, a possibly cataclysmic scenario.

Within weeks she sent him her first letters as Dane Kempton, and he promised a reply the next day. The writing soon fell into a pattern. He praised ("over-praised," she recalled) her drafts and edited them gently. He pronounced himself fumbling and despairing as he wrote his own letters as Herbert Wace. It appeared that he had deliberately cast himself in the less empathetic role. She fell comfortably into writing as a character who outwardly resembled her almost not at all—elderly, male, a Londoner, an Anglo-Saxon—but the idea of playing a teacher of literature and Victorian moralist clearly appealed to her, as perhaps did the possibility of gaining an upper hand over Jack.[2]

In October 1900, Jack unveiled the project, and his friendship with Anna, to his constant correspondent Cloudesley Johns: "Didn't I explain my volume of letters? Well, it's this way: A young Russian Jewess of San Francisco and myself have often quarrelled over our conceptions of love. She happens to be a genius. She is also a materialist by philosophy, and an idealist by innate preference, and is constantly being forced to twist all the facts of the universe in order to reconcile herself with her self. So, finally, we decided that the only way to argue the question out would be by letter."[3]

A few months later, he praised her in a letter to another friend as if he were showing off an exotic trophy: "I should like to have you meet Miss Anna Strunsky some time. She is well worth meeting. . . . She has her exoteric circles and her esoteric circles—by this I mean the more intimate and the less intimate. One may pass from one to the other if deemed worthy. . . . She loves Browning. She is deep, subtle, and psychological. She is neither stiff nor formal. Very adaptive. Knows a great deal. Is a joy and delight to her friends. She is a Russian, and a Jewess, who has absorbed the Western culture, and who warms it with a certain oriental leaven."[4]

The terms with which he chose to identify Anna—"Russian Jewess," "subtle," and "oriental"—were revealing; not conventionally anti-Semitic, he nonetheless explained Anna to friends, and perhaps to himself, first of all as a Jew, and thus an intellectual. Less overtly, the identification was sexual as well; he implied the daring of discussing love in the abstract with a formidably desirable woman. Even if Anna did not think of their relationship as sexual—and it was not, in any literal sense—Jack was already giving signals to the world to interpret it as such.[5]

Initially, the enterprise went badly. A few weeks into it, Anna was angered by something Jack had written or said, as Herbert Wace or as himself—possibly his public declaration that he had determined the inferiority of women by observing their timidity about going into the water at the Piedmont public baths. She complained to him that he had called woman "the creature of a lower evolution, weaker, inferior, unfit," and that he had offered an "insult to every woman in the world." A chill crept over their exchanges.[6]

Yet they were not out of touch. Jack wrote to confess crying as he finished Thomas Hardy's new novel, *Jude the Obscure*; he first wrote "Jack the Obscure" and crossed it out. He started to write her a Christmas greeting and finished it three days later in his literary mode: "A white beautiful friendship?—between a man and a woman?—the world cannot imagine such a thing, would deem it as inconceivable as infinity or non-infinity[.]"[7]

He invited her to come to his twenty-fifth birthday party on January 12, 1901, and confided that he was praying that his first child would be a boy. His daughter Joan was born three days after his birthday.[8]

Early in 1901, Anna turned to the work that she hoped would authenticate her as a woman of letters—a first novel. Her initial step had a rote quality, as if Jack had ordered her to get a notebook and start jotting down ideas. She found a little unused 1900 diary and wrote on the title page: "Anna Strunsky, San Francisco. Book of Ideas." On the first page, she crossed out the printed date and wrote in "February 19, 1901."

On the second page she began fragmentary notes: "Chap. I John Torrence at 12. Fury then gentleness. Oakland—selling papers. Incident of the candy. Chap II the student—First poem The old woman died next door death, love, work. Intense interest of the growing mind. Chap. III Poverty, poetry." She put down other chapter headings, characters' names, plots and fragments of plots. She seemed to be planning a story that incorporated the impoverished childhood of Jack London.[9]

But the first word in the notebook, ahead of all the notes, was "Windlestraws." In all her subsequent outlines, drafts, and fragments, Anna repeated the term almost as an incantation, but she did not indicate outright where she had found the word, or why she chose this obscure term for the title of her novel. "Strewing the pool of time with windlestraws of effort," she wrote.

Centuries before, the term had been used by farmers in Ireland, Scotland, and the north of England: A windlestraw was "a stalk of withered grass," or a stalk "such as is left standing after the flower or seed is shed," and figuratively "anything light, trifling, or flimsy." Or, as Anna's favorite, Browning, would have put it, anything "aimless, helpless, hopeless."[10]

The actual source for her choice lay close at hand. The previous Christmas a socialist friend, Jane A. Roulston, had given her a volume of poems by W. E. Henley, the poet noted for "Invictus" and his biography of Robert Louis Stevenson. The final page contained a short poem, "Epigraph," dated July 1897, in which Henley mourned his daughter, dead three years. He alluded to the memories of her—her "little, exquisite Ghost"—as:

> *Poor windlestraws*
> *On the great, sullen, roaring pool of Time*
> *And Chance and Change . . .*[11]

Here then was not only the word "windlestraws," but the "pool of time." Anna, already obsessed with death, must have been drawn to a poem—even one that in the end is sentimental and trivial—about the death of a child. But she reshaped the windlestraws: no longer, as in Henley, fragmentary memories but scraps of futile work, wasted effort.

In March 1901, resuming work as Dane Kempton, she sent Jack a new letter. Jack responded that he was going back to the beginning to redo everything he had written as Herbert Wace. He sent samples of the letters to *McClure's Magazine* and they came back rejected. "The letter from them is very amusing," he remarked. "It puts us on our mettle. We must do something big with those letters for spite."[12]

In the back of her "Book of Ideas" Anna scribbled notes for their work:

Suggestions for Jack (Letter VII.) Attempt on part of Herbert to create impression of emotion by narrating incidents, such as, a sudden trip to see Hester [Herbert's fiancée], a walk with her, a long silence (Would that be true to this life?) . . .

Dane must be steadier, less emotional. There must be flashes in a night of storm. . . . "Give all to love; / Obey thy heart; / Friends, kindred, days, / Estate, good fame, / Plans, credit, and the Muse,— / Nothing refuse." [Ralph Waldo Emerson, "Give All to Love." These lines eventually appeared on the title page of *The Kempton-Wace Letters*.]

On May 12, 1901, she wrote in her notebook, truthfully but perhaps coyly: "Love letters written by J.L. and me. Real, spontaneous letters between two young literary persons. Fictitious, of course, since we are not lovers."[13]

Although she must have appeared to friends in this time to be busy, creative, and productive, throughout 1901 Anna was passing through a mysteriously dark passage of her life. The notebook is redolent of death; she sketched out a series of stories called "Studies in Suicide."[14]

Part of the turbulence in her life may have arisen from the process of releasing herself from an unwanted suitor. She wrote to Jack enclosing a letter; although she had deleted the name, Jack recognized the writer instantly as a fellow socialist. It could have been Cameron King, a lawyer who had attended Stanford with Anna and had been infatuated ever since. She wrote: "I did not play with this man's soul. I was too careful of it. I wished to strengthen him, to help him. . . . And I did wish to do good by this boy. I pledged myself that since we served the same cause and our work lay together I would make him love the things I loved." Jack argued: "Your growth has been greater than his—why, in his very letter he quotes your Browning, your phrases. . . . he says, Behold! the star! You dare not, cannot, do else than remain the star." Jack's letter evinced a tone of avuncular disinterest, yet he must have known that he was hardly a neutral party.[15]

Early in 1902, at Jack's urging, Anna acquired a typewriter but found it contrary. Jack counseled her to apply oil, then to get a new ribbon, or ultimately to take it back. He returned to her three Dane Kempton letters in longhand and commanded: "Exercise your dire & shaking fist on the machine & in counting up the words."[1]

He cheered her support of W. E. Henley's controversial new biography of Stevenson and her decision to speak on Henley to the San Francisco Woman's Press Association. When they listed her for a speech on Tolstoy, he urged her to stick to Henley. She did and then turned the speech into an energetic article for a local quarterly, *Impressions,* defending the right of biographers not to flatter their subjects. Jack praised the article heartily.[2]

Earnest as he was as a mentor, at the same time Jack was steadily intensifying his correspondence with Anna, by implication proposing himself for another, more intimate role. At this point, he might not have conceded to himself that their joint novel was a stratagem to permit him to resume courting Anna, but as they corresponded about the book, there was a change in the temper of his letters, less avuncular, less professional. One sign was the salutation, "Dear You," or "Dear, Dear You." He acknowledged distance but implied closeness: "As I sit here, I wonder how you are over there, & try to conjure up you & your room." Increasingly, what he wrote seemed to be a code for tides of feeling flowing between them. If she had visualized the grand scenario of the Kempton-Wace letters as the triumph of romantic love over calculation, she had now brought it close to being played out in life.[3]

Curiously, they were apparently drawn together by the intensity of a disagreement over Jack's insistence on witnessing a hanging at the San Quentin prison. She opposed his going; he tried to explain his position but "stuttered & failed." Finally, he wrote a long, aggressive letter asserting that those who are protected by the justice system should not shrink from viewing its consequences.[4]

After twelve such paragraphs in full flight, he stopped and added in longhand: "I went astray somehow. I wished to meet your sweetness with sweetness, and instead have called upon all that was harsh & unlovable in my nature." But he did not back down: "I would rather go, and then, to make it easier for you, never see you again, than to not go & have your favor showered upon me a thousand-fold." A week later he wrote a "Dear Anna" letter saying that her reply had worried him. Yet the threat of a permanent break passed and his letters returned to "Dear, Dear You." Somehow the bitterness of the dispute had reminded them of the importance each placed upon the other.[5]

Late in February 1902 Anna went to the balmy little resort town of San Rafael, on upper San Francisco Bay, the first of the retreats to solitary work that she found so desirable in the abstract—and so unbearable. There she labored not only on the final Dane Kempton letters but on her novel, which she had been sketching for almost a year. From his newly rented bungalow in Piedmont, the artists' colony in the hills above Oakland, Jack now could see as far as Marin County, Mount Tamalpais, and San Rafael: "Day by day I look out across the bay to a nook in the Marin shore where I know San Rafael clusters, and I wonder how it fares with you and how you are doing." It was her birthday, and he wrote that he hoped that she would have a full year: "And may it be an empty one, too—empty of the heartache, and soul sickness, and the many trials which have been yours in the past twelve months." He did not elaborate.[6]

They seemed at last to be approaching the end of their project and a climax in their relationship; the end of the work raised the question of what would come after. He was initially exuberant: "I have just finished reading your last letter, Dane Kempton. . . . And before replying, I must tell you that I feel the letters will *go! Go! Go!*" Hearing from her that she was finding it hard to work in San Rafael, he pressed her to come live with him and Bessie during final revisions. After she returned to San Francisco, she put him off, but ultimately accepted and arrived in Piedmont late in April or the first week of May.[7]

It was a momentous visit. Not long after she arrived—she recalled the date as May 3, 1902—he tried to cancel out the diffidence they had shown each other two years before on the hillside above Berkeley, to persuade her to throw in her lot with him. Remembering herself in the third person, she later wrote:

> Alone together in his house, he told her that his marriage was dissolved, as it would have been if he had never seen her or if she had never been born. He asked her to marry him. It was one thing to be in love with him when he was free like herself; it was quite different when he had become the husband of another and the father of her child . . . but when he spoke and urged her to accept his love, there was a tumult of joy in her heart and she promised to marry him.[8]

But she contemplated such a future only briefly. In an interview late in life, she recalled that she had talked the matter over with her mother. Her mother never dictated to her, but in this instance asked her to imagine what her life would be like with a Jack divorced and tainted with scandal. Anna took the reminder to heart: "within two weeks [I] crossed the S.F. Bay to tell him: 'I do not love you enough to be your wife.' He had done nothing to make me break my promise. I did not feel I loved him enough—but I loved him deeply. I was afraid to take my happiness at the expense of his wife and baby."[9]

Bess, with a wife's antennae, could scarcely have been oblivious to the turbulence under her roof, however little she may have dreamed that Jack had already proposed to their house guest and however "circumspect" (as Anna later characterized it) Jack's behavior may have appeared to outsiders. In an interview two years later, when these details had become grist for the press, Anna recalled the visit in decorous terms:

> During the first few days of my stay Mrs. London was very cordial and manifested great interest in our work, but, after a stay of five days, I became convinced that, for some reason, Mrs. London had begun to dislike me. She said nothing of any importance to make me feel out of place, but, judging from several little occurrences, I decided it was best for me to leave the London home. I carried out my resolve and left Piedmont, much against Mr. London's will, and, apparently, Mrs. London's also. Both husband and wife accompanied me to the train, and the farewell between Mrs. London and myself was that of two acquaintances between whom existed a mutual liking.[10]

Not surprisingly, the chronology of this sequence is unclear. Anna may have understated the length of her visit; she was still at the Bungalow nine days after the date she remembered for Jack's proposal. She may have been there as long as three weeks, or for more than one visit. But certainly she stayed long enough for Bess London to sense or to see that much was amiss, for she provided bitter recollections a year later in her divorce complaint.

There was the allegation—repeated in nearly every account of the matter over the next nine decades—that she, Bess, had found Anna sitting on Jack's lap. But other details were more damning: that Anna and Jack would rise "at the unusually early hour of half-past four in the morning and [would] retire to [Jack's] study where they remained until breakfast time; . . . immediately after breakfast they would wander off into adjacent woods, to remain away all day, leaving [Bessie] to the pursuit of her household cares and duties." And that, no doubt most galling, Anna stepped forward to say good night to dinner guests, as if she were the mistress of the house. After Anna left, Bessie claimed, Jack told her that he and Anna loved each other and wanted to marry.[11]

Jack took Anna's rejection—if it was rejection, for she acknowledged that she still loved him—as merely the opening of the negotiation. Certainly there was no severance. His letters hint that he was receiving letters from her that reciprocated his intensity. When he wrote to her early in June, he adopted a new role embodied in a Kiplingesque signature, "Sahib," which he seemed to use not only in the customary sense of "master" or "mentor" but as "friend" or even, standing it on its head, "slave." Borrowed as it was from Kipling's India, "sahib" hinted of racial difference or superiority. On June 6, 1902, he was her "very miserable Sahib." Four days later, "The Sahib" declared himself "sick with love for you and need of you."[12]

In July, he was definitely interrupted when he left on the Overland Limited for New York, thinking that he was bound for an assignment in South Africa. Anna excused herself from his departure. He wrote from the train, asking her to thank her friend Cameron King for coming to see him off. He enclosed tearsheets of letters by a European noblewoman that the *Atlantic* was publishing, and commented, "Ours are so very, very much better, We've done something, little one, you & I."[13]

On arriving in New York, Jack found that his assignment had collapsed and he quickly assembled a new project, "some writing of the London slums." He heard from Anna on July 29, while he was staying at the New York Press Club, and replied in a single hasty sentence: "Just to say that I received your ink-beteared letter, that I sail to-morrow . . . & that I love you." He wrote further from the *Majestic,* wishing her luck in a lecture at Pacific Grove that day. He wrote again two weeks later to complain that he had been in London nine days and had heard nothing, and sounded the same grievance five days later.[14]

On August 25, deep into his exhausting undercover stay in the East End slums, he finally received two letters from Anna. One, which he referred to as "the W.C.T.U. letter," was routine. He "plunged into the other, and [was] brought up, innocently, unexpectedly, and all in a heap at the quick, sharp rise to the climax."[15]

Anna recalled later her temper when she wrote: "She had tried to write indifferently of this and that, and in the middle of a page came her words like a torrent of tears, stormy as her heart." Her book of ideas contains a passage, near a date of August 14, 1902, after she sent the letter: "It does not help to think that his heart was perhaps as laden as mine . . . I drive back tears. All day long it is a fight to suppress sobs, to hide twitching lips. Oh, mourn, my lost friend, my own."[16]

When she wrote, the last word she had received from him was the terse note sent the day before he sailed, and she responded bitterly: "Your letter was cold enough and long enough in arriving to enlighten me of itself, & I beg your pardon for having been so impetuous in my letters. It wrung that last 'I love you' from you." She now complained that he had lied to her about the failure of his marriage. Since his departure, she had found out that Bessie London was within weeks of bearing a child and had indeed been pregnant when Jack proposed to her. Yes, he replied, a child was to be born but, he insisted, he had not lied to her, either about the pregnancy or about his sexual relations with his wife.[17]

Her letter said, "Do not fear, I shall not speak of this again." He responded: "I could only say that to a person whom I wished wantonly to insult. I could never say it to you. Yet you say it to me, & I can only smile and say to myself that it [was] written by a very cruel woman, by a woman who is as cruel as she is tender & soft, who is as harsh as she is sensitive, who can wound others in degree equal only to her own capacity for being wounded. And the Sahib is dead, and forgiven as the dead are forgiven. Poor devil of a Sahib! He should have been all soft, or all hard; as it is he makes a mess of his life and of other lives."

Nearly two weeks later, he received her next letter, three weeks in transit and written before she could have received his response. She wrote as if she had forgotten her denunciation. His reply was acid: "Your letter of August 19th. has just arrived and it has made me quite happy to hear from you.—Shall I go on in the above vein? For in such a way does your letter begin & go on. I suppose it's sending me the 'news.' . . . If you are unable to send more than the 'news,' why, really, I don't care for the 'news.' "[18]

Before the end of the month he had recovered himself. He had not only finished his reporting but had completed a draft of sixty-three thousand words for the book that was later published as *The People of the Abyss*. He was able to address Anna with equanimity and finality: "You have never had the advantage of seeing a prizefighter knocked out. . . . But should you have seen such a man, panting, exhausted, dazed, bewildered, terrific blows landing on him from above, below, and everyside, and his own arms flying out madly, blindly, threshing the air crazily,—then you would understand my condition when I received that frightful letter from you. My arms flew out madly, blindly, that is all. And I am sorry. I should have taken the knock-out clean & not put up any defense. And now it is all over and done with. So be it. Henceforth I shall dream romances for other people and transmute them into bread & butter." He was leaving in a week for his first tour of Europe. Before he returned home, his second daughter, Bess, was born.[19]

In her third-person mode, she expressed second thoughts years later: "She would of course realize her cruelty later and be overwhelmed with remorse. She would never again write anything to anybody in criticism. Letters would be kind. She would be able to reconcile his statement that all was over between himself and his wife, and the coming of this child." Whatever the issue was that had prompted her to write, she had misunderstood it.[20]

But the letter had done its work, and what had passed between them had now burned away. Left standing was an unfinished framework, the manuscript of the Kempton-Wace letters, now less a metaphor for their love than a piece of work to be completed.

Despite the distances, emotional and geographical, that now lay between them, Anna's literary partnership with Jack London was destined to continue until the Kempton-Wace letters found their way into print. Before he went abroad, Jack had sent the manuscript to Boston, hoping for serial publication in the *Atlantic,* and while he was in England he received an opaque rejection stating that "the prevalence of epistolary fiction makes us fear that your manuscript, despite its undeniable power and charm, is not very well adapted to magazine publication."[1]

Jack had instructed the *Atlantic* to forward the manuscript to the Macmillan Company in New York. Macmillan gave it to its reader George Rice Carpenter, a professor of literature at Columbia University. Carpenter proved unsympathetic: "I am astonished at Jack London's novel. In general, I think you ought to have his next book, whatever it is; but this is one of those *letter* things, without a plot. . . . Now this is brilliant writing—but mere essay-writing. People like letter-novels nowadays, and this will be talked about and will have a sufficient little sale, I suppose; but it is merely a stage, a quickly passing stage, in the development of the author's young genius. It is rather a pity that he hadn't sown this sort of literary wild oats before, and come to you only when he was ready for a real novel, with plot & character in it."[2]

Carpenter had no inkling that Jack had had a collaborator, for George P. Brett, the president of Macmillan, had not told him of one. And perhaps Brett did not know either. Jack later insisted to Anna that he had told Brett that the novel was a joint effort, but that Brett had forgotten. But in fact, Jack's letters to Brett referred to the novel as his, or ambiguously, so Brett was probably not aware of Anna's role until after he made his decision about the book.[3]

Despite his negativity, Carpenter had grudgingly supported publication. On September 16, 1902, Brett wrote to say that Macmillan would publish the novel. In the same letter from England late in September in which he declared their love "over and done with," Jack informed Anna that Macmillan—"one of the largest, most widely known, & reputable publishing houses in the world" (as indeed it was)—had accepted their book. The novel still lacked its conclusion: "I should advise you to plug right in, and get over the difficulty of those last two letters. As you love me, do not put it off till the eleventh hour. I know it is dispiriting to tackle, but the Macmillan seal of approval should at least balance it off. . . . Of course, advantage or disadvantage, blunder or happy stroke, will be shared equally between us." On the next day, he wrote to Brett pushing the notion that the book might "make a hit."[4]

After finishing a draft of *The People of the Abyss*, Jack traveled in Europe on his own into the fall of 1902. He wrote to Anna—using the old "Dear You" salutation—from Rome, with a rambling account of his encounters with closet socialists. The letter caught up with her in Denver, where she was visiting family friends. She was on her way to New York.[5]

Early in November, before Anna arrived there, Jack paused in New York, looked in on Brett, picked up his mail, and collected a check advancing him $150 on royalties. He did not read the mail until his train had reached Texas, and in it he found a letter from Anna saying that she was en route eastward. The timing of her departure in relation to his return may have struck him as other than coincidental, but he went no further than calling it "an unlucky mischance."[6]

At once, he wrote to Brett saying that Anna—whom he designated (or, more probably, revealed) as his collaborator—would call: "I am sure you will find her charming. She is a young Russian-Jewess, brilliant, a college-woman, etc." To Anna he wrote an avuncular letter: "Now, dear you, do not be disheartened when you meet this Mr. Brett and hear him speak of the *Letters* just incidentally. Remember that he publishes more books each month than he has time to read, that he is saturated in books. . . . The thing for you to do when you see Mr. Brett, is to inspire him with confidence in the letters, as I know you to be well able to do."[7]

Before going to see Brett, Anna settled herself in the New York she had not seen since she was sixteen years old. She had an offer from the publisher-impresario (and fellow Californian) Gaylord Wilshire of a desk and work at the New York headquarters of his socialist magazine, *Wilshire's*. (The magazine had another office in Toronto to circumvent the restrictions of the United States Post Office; *Wilshire's* had been banned from the domestic mail in a crackdown on radical publications after McKinley's assassination in 1901.) She stayed for a time with an uncle, then rented lodging uptown on Manhattan Avenue, a street now vanished, near the new Columbia University campus. Later she moved into Whittier Hall at Columbia's Teachers College, on Amsterdam Avenue.[8]

Now that she was in New York she became the more visible author of the Kempton-Wace letters and Jack permitted her to make a variety of small decisions: how their names might appear and whether the title should be *Kempton-Wace* or *Wace-Kempton*, or something else livelier.[9] She wanted to add to the Kempton-Wace debate a batch of the fiancée's—Hester Stebbins's—

love letters, which she saw as remedying the book's failure to illuminate "the third great side of this question, the woman's side." Jack insisted that the book was "letters on Love. . . . It is not Love Letters." But for loyalty's sake at least he argued to Brett in favor of Hester Stebbins's letters as a prologue: "Miss Strunsky has written me that she is about starting to work to add about fifteen thousand words from the woman, Hester Stebbins. I am thoroughly in accord with this plan of hers. It is excellent."[10]

Brett accordingly urged her to go ahead, and she wrote to Brett on December 21 that she had "had a good time" writing the prologue and would deliver it on December 24. On that date, she placed in his hands thirty-seven pages of longhand—only a fraction of the fifteen thousand words promised—comprising nine relatively brief letters from Hester Stebbins to Herbert Wace, purporting to be written from Anna's old dormitory at Stanford, Robles Hall.[11]

Brett, on a scouting trip to California, had Anna's prologue with him when he called on Jack. Brett had written at the top: "I am very doubtful about this prologue." Jack wrote to Anna on January 7 that both he and Brett were against using the prologue because it would delay the true opening of the book. In her later years, Anna professed herself to be relieved in the long term rather than disappointed because the prologue "would have spoiled the book."[12]

Indeed, the prologue was no masterpiece. Writing on her own as Hester Stebbins, Anna showed little of the discipline and elegance that she had revealed, under Jack's tutelage, as Dane Kempton. Even the two letters in which Hester Stebbins survived, at the end of the book, were superior to the Hester of the prologue: The prologue's Hester is tremulous and petitioning; the conclusion's Hester shows her iron in spurning Herbert.

Ultimately, Jack proved to be proprietary about the book—partly, perhaps, because completing it was one of his obligations under a broad agreement he signed with Macmillan specifying that he had to deliver five books over the next two years. During January 1903, he revised all the letters, his and hers, and forwarded them to her, leaving to her the option of accepting or rejecting each "suggestion" he had penciled on the Kempton portions. He accepted Brett's idea that the book should be published anonymously, so as to create a degree of mystery and perhaps to shield him as well. Through all, Jack was scrupulous about the business arrangements, seeing to it that Anna got a separate contract with Macmillan and requiring that royalties be split equally.[13]

Although the correspondence about these transactions was businesslike, mixed in were still biting sparks. Jack could not refrain from striking at her, playing his worldliness against her naïveté, his self-discipline against her vacillation. In December 1902, he wrote, metaphorically: "I am fifty years old to-day. The mystery of man & woman is behind me. I am deep in the mystery of father & daughter. You do not understand this. You are about seventeen to-day. And between seventeen & twenty-seven you will linger until you die. You will never get beyond the man-and-woman mystery." Even more hurtfully, he slandered her Jewishness: "You epitomize your race, as I epitomize mine. You are subjective, in the last analysis; I am objective. You toy with phantasmagoria; I grasp the living facts. You pursue mirages, unsubstantialities, subtleties that are vain & worthless; I seize upon realities and hammer blindly through to results."[14]

He was close to brutal in an exchange that began in a petty misunderstanding the next month. She sent him for his twenty-seventh birthday a prized book: the volume of W. E. Henley's poems she had received from Jane Roulston in which she had discovered "windlestraws." Anna wrote in it, perhaps seeking an armistice: "I love this book and the woman who gave it to me. I recall every hour, at night in my room, in the day on the San Rafael hilltops, when my soul read in it. I recall and I honor yet other times when others who were close read with me. Let it therefore carry my birthday greetings to you, dear Jack. Anna."[15]

In the book Jack found two slips of paper; he assumed they marked passages commenting on their estrangement. She denied that she had placed the slips. He seemingly accepted her explanation and apologized; but then, although he knew that she had just heard of the death of her sister-in-law, he could not suppress his own grievance. He remarked that he had heard "all kinds of flattering news" about her activities in New York: "[I] know that you are glowing & rampant, living always at the pitch of life as is your way, pleasuring in your sorrows as ardently as in your joys, carelessly austere, critically wanton, getting more living out of hours & minutes than we colder mortals, God pity us, get out of months & years. Child, how one envies you." She did not reply for so long that he wrote to wonder whether she would ever write again.[16]

In fact, she had been passing through another dark time, and his scornful characterization of her as thoughtless and "rampant" must have added to her depression. Only a month or so in New York, she had made notes for a story: "Girl away from home. Accidental death by escaping gas." At the end of January, she received the news of the death of her sister-in-law Mary (Hyman's wife); she stopped working and probably would have returned to San Francisco, still owing revisions of the last two letters for the novel, had she not herself been bedridden "with a tenacious kind of influenza." She convalesced at her cousin Simeon Strunsky's home in Hoboken, and did not resume work until March.[17]

The necessities of the book eventually put Anna back in touch with Jack. She worked furiously and delivered the final batch of proofs to Macmillan in mid-April. There was a last-minute flurry when the poetry excerpts that were supposed to preface the book disappeared at the printer's; the book went to press without them.[18]

Macmillan brought out *The Kempton-Wace Letters* early in May 1903. Wilshire, who had the power to arrange such things, saw to it that Anna was given a literary coming-out, a luncheon at the Astor House on lower Broadway studded with the eminent: William Dean Howells, Richard Watson Gilder of the *Century*, Norman Hapgood of *Collier's Weekly*, Leonard Abbott of *Literary Digest*. Jack wrote to her near the end of May, warning her not to place great weight on the reviews; she "must be prepared for all kinds of rot adverse and eulogistic." But within three weeks he wrote to Brett, ostensibly cheered by the first newspaper notices and urging a big promotional campaign.[19]

Despite Jack's boosting, *Kempton-Wace* did not catch on. Brett wrote to him at the first that a thousand copies had been sold; but two months after publication he conceded that the grand total to that date was 975, despite Macmillan's having put two thousand dollars into advertisements.[20]

Years afterward, Joseph Noel, a San Francisco journalist who knew both Jack and Anna, looked at the book as less a collaboration than two different books laid into a single binding. As to Jack's portion, Noel agreed implicitly with Jack's friend George Sterling, who said that for Jack this book was "a spiritual misprint, a typographical error half a volume long." In becoming Herbert Wace, said Noel, Jack had reduced himself to a term-paper level and deprived himself of all the strengths of his writing.[21]

But Noel argued that on Anna's side the book was not merely a diversion but eventually her chef d'oeuvre. He praised her contribution: "Courage, devotion, the power to hope largely, to dream bravely, are in her pages. The simplicity of faith in life and life's processes gives dignity and beauty to nearly all she writes under the name of Dane Kempton."[22]

Despite Jack's management of the project and his suppression of her prologue, the book still emerged more hers than his, both in words and in spirit. Wace, a boor from the beginning, fades. Voluble and argumentative for two-thirds of the way, he falls almost silent at the end, while Kempton (and Hester Stebbins, in the small part that remained to her) gain strength.

Anna's writing, stiffly ornate in the first letters, settled into a mode of restrained passion, which can be read not only within the structure of the book but as a reflection of what she had learned in her complicated transactions with Jack London. In the end, he acquiesced in a conclusion that confounded all his arguments: Marriage for the sake of genetics, marriage as a part of a man's career plans, lost out; Hester Stebbins, speaking through Anna, broke her engagement to Herbert Wace.

Anna's voice seems to speak directly to Jack in Hester's final lines, written after the rest of the book and echoing back to more than three years before, to the time when they met, when she had denied being "aimless, helpless, hopeless":

> You must know it of me that before everything else in the world I pray that knowledge of love come to the man over whom the love of my girlhood was spilled.
>
> Do you ask me what is left me, dear friend? Work and tears and the intact dream. Believe me, I am not pitiable.[23]

In June 1903, after publication of *The Kempton-Wace Letters*, Anna retrieved the manuscript from Macmillan and left it with her friends the doctors Katia and Jay Maryson, who lived on the Lower East Side of Manhattan. Eventually she forgot where it was and assumed for years that it had disappeared in the San Francisco earthquake. She did not recover it until 1958.[1]

She may have been in a whirl at the time: early in July, she was due in Boston to board the S.S. *Canadian* for Europe. George Brett of Macmillan advanced her $500 for the trip, noting that the payment was only just; her co-author, Jack London, had already been collecting royalties. Apparently, this was her only payment from Macmillan for *The Kempton-Wace Letters*. She departed with a farewell note to Brett:

> [The advance] enables me to take a long looked-for trip to the Old World and I am very happy. While in London I shall call on Kropotkin and others. I may be able to incarnate an echo from the International Revolutionary movement into a book which will be the Uncle Tom's Cabin of the capitalist regime. Could I do this I would not so much care what became of my life, could I write the book that would serve the Cause and the Muse at the same time. And believe me, Mr. Brett, none loves life better than I, and none is more joyous than I.[2]

This might have seemed extravagant, unguarded talk to parade before a staid representative of the capitalist regime, but Brett refused to be alarmed by even the most radical propositions from authors, and he merely observed to Anna that her "second novel"—he was crediting *Kempton-Wace* as the first—"is the one on which it seems to me a great reputation might be made." For him, a salable manuscript always outweighed politics, hence Macmillan's standing as the era's leading publisher of writers of the left.[3]

The trip was Anna's equivalent of the Grand Tour, and conceivably could also have been encouraged by her family to divert her from regrets over Jack London. Her companions were an old San Francisco friend, the whimsical Gelett Burgess, known as "Frank," and his sister, Ellie. A few days out, Anna wrote to Katia in excellent humor: "We are beside ourselves with happiness and bonhommie. . . . Mr. Burgess tantalizes the Captain (a simple but sentimental soul) by writing him amorous and unsigned verses. The Captain, much to my embarrassment, believes that it is I who am making these immodest advances to him. He was sitting by me and sighing like the unhappy swain he is a minute ago."[4]

Once in London, she started a new notebook, in which she listed the tombs in Westminster Abbey. She viewed the Roman wall at Chester, and visited Anne Hathaway's cottage in Stratford-upon-Avon. At Oxford, she and the Burgesses called on the self-exiled American poet, Louise Imogen Guiney, who subsequently wrote to a San Francisco friend: "who should turn up in Oxford, about 10 o'clock one rainy evening, but the old Lupe [Burgess], looking far blither than ever I saw him, with his pretty sister and a delightful young rough-shod radical of a Russo-American, whose name I forget, though it would be a dull business to forget her."[5]

Before the end of July they moved on to Paris. Anna scribbled: "The love of life laid firm hand on me when I looked from my balcony upon the night at Paris. . . . I choose to live on rue Jacob, Quartier Latin, Paris, 4eme etage on a level with the chimney-studded roofs. I choose to live where I can look the night in the eyes and press my tenderness upon her." She noted, or embellished, a visit to the city's great graveyard and its memorial to Héloïse and Abélard:

> This I saw in the Cimetiere Pere Lachaise. Rachel of the subtle face and heart of flame passing barefoot with shroud in [word illegible] the tomb of Heloise, laying her hand upon the iron realizing and seizing with her sweet eyes upon the most-veiled moon above. Rachel studying the part of Heloise, reading her lines from the stars and the moon and the mist and from the tomb-crowded street.[6]

The party traveled south by rail in August: Dijon, Lyons, Tarascon, Nîmes, and Les Baux, the village clinging to a hill alongside a dead medieval city. She was buoyed by Genoa, but grew pensive as they approached Florence: "Our compartment was dark. I leaned out of the window a long time and wondered, wondered about truth and love and death. Truth and love and death—I am finding them all. The Trinity surrounds me. . . . I left the window and sat down close to Frank in the dark."[7]

She started another notebook as they made a chilly voyage down the Rhine and returned to London. On September 23, they called on Peter Kropotkin, the aging Russian anarchist-in-exile. Anna noted "the warmth of his hand and the embrace of his look," but wondered afterward: "Why does he not ask me about the movement in America? Does he not know I know?"[8]

The final days of the trip turned sour. The publisher Gaylord Wilshire, who had given her a publication fête in New York, was in London and scheduled a lunch for her at the Liberal Club. But he neglected to invite Anna's traveling companions, and Burgess made such a to-do that Anna herself had to decline; she commented: "He would not have interfered had he been a friend."[9]

Returning through New York early in November, she paused at the elegant Brevoort on lower Fifth Avenue and entrained, "escorted by a host of friends, real friends." She made notes for "Windlestraws" on the way: "Yes I will dedicate my book to one dead. He will know how strongly I have wrought and with how much weakness, how I have burned and loved, how I have done battle with a world of slaughter and smugness. The dead now above will know." Her notes do not make clear whether she was referring to a dead man or, metaphorically, to Jack.[10]

Again in San Francisco after a year, Anna reported a "sad homecoming" to Katia: her mother was ill and the memory of her sister-in-law's death was still fresh. Her notebook again turned morbid: "Standing over Mary's grave you see how easy a thing it is to get down below with her, to lie stretched out by her side in her grave as I lay by her side in life." Self-pityingly, she observed to Katia that when she and Rose went to the Ruskin Club they were "all to turn in written definitions of happiness. Think of it, Katia—a written definition of happiness, we who have missed it so often!"[11]

Inevitably, Jack, whom she had not seen since his departure for England fifteen months before, reappeared. He had written her a short letter while she was in Europe; it is not clear when it caught up with her. "How you must be enjoying yourself!" he exclaimed, with a touch of scorn. He added that he had no idea how "Our Book" was selling, but injected a warning about poor sales, picking up a cue from Brett: "It is a good book, a big book, and, as we anticipated, too good & too big to be popular." Nonetheless, Macmillan was issuing another edition with their names together on the title page.[12]

The revelation that she was the coauthor of *The Kempton-Wace Letters* led to a round of excess in the San Francisco press. One story appeared under the heading: "The Divine Anna": "Miss Anna Strunsky, the poet of the 'Kempton-Wace Letters,' who defended lyric love so lyrically against the biological onslaughts of the scientific Jack London, is home again in San Francisco from her trip to Europe, penning enthusiastically a novel with a purpose for the Macmillan Company. Miss Strunsky is of the land that produced Turgenev and Tolstoi, and of the race that produced the Book of Job and The Song of Songs."[13]

Anna learned that Jack had called on her parents—he sometimes called them his "love family"—and was gone on a long sailing trip with his friend Cloudesley Johns aboard the *Spray*. She also heard, before her return, that Jack had abruptly left the family bungalow in Piedmont and had moved back, alone, to Oakland. Rumors were circulating that she had caused the separation. Brett wrote to Jack asking him about a story in a New York paper with a headline suggesting that the *Kempton-Wace* collaboration was pointing him to a divorce. Jack wrote back coolly: "As the reporters could not ascertain the real reason, they dug one out of the book, that is all. So far as the public is concerned I have no statement to make except that the *Kempton-Wace Letters* play no part whatever in the separation."[14]

This was a highly selective response: In fact, Jack was now permitting Anna to be cast in the role of homewrecker—a role that she had unwittingly invited. When Anna first heard of Jack's separation, months before, she wrote to him from Europe, consolingly: "Cameron [King] sent me a newspaper clipping some weeks ago. I am sorry for all the unhappiness, and I am strong in my faith. You never meant to do anything but the right and the good—poor, ever dear, dreamer! You will never do wrong. I cried over the news, half in gratitude for your strength and half in sorrow, perhaps all in sorrow, for all the sadness with which you are weighted." She might have been less forgiving had she known that Jack quoted these very words to his new love, Charmian Kittredge, as an assurance that Anna would not make trouble for them and, implicitly, that he would let Anna take the blame for the separation of which Charmian was the real cause.[15]

Despite her break with Jack, Anna still saw herself in the image—that of a fiction writer—that he had carved in her psyche. On her return to San Francisco, she moved from the family home on Golden Gate Avenue to quarters on Sutter Street, in the same building where her brother Max, the physician, had opened a new office. Intending to isolate herself to work on "Windlestraws," she wrote to Brett that when he visited in January she would show him "my nieces and my manuscript."[16]

But she found again that she could not bear lonely scribbling. She emerged to visit Stanford, where Rose was in her second year, for what proved to be a visit of reconciliation. The women students who lived at Robles Hall (including Rose) invited her to appear at a campus event, and she found herself sitting next to President Jordan. Her diary entry suggests that Stanford had decided to let academic bygones be bygones:

> [Dr. Jordan said:] "There is a book for you in my office which has been yours a long time." "But there was a condition, Dr. Jordan," I stammered. "I remember of no condition regarding you." Oh, what a beautiful evening it has become! I shall make a return for this happiness. And yet I am happy only through past bitterness. I . . . a credit to the university that was unwilling to keep me.

Just what the "book" was is not clear, for Stanford made no record of it. It probably was not a diploma; perhaps it was a prize. It meant, in any case, the alleviation of a terrible defeat.[17]

At the start of 1904, Jack rushed for a moment back into her life. Russia and Japan stood close to war in the Far East, and Jack, with no moorings at home, was dickering with three or four periodicals and syndicates to assign him to cover the war, if it should happen (as it did, near the end of January). Abruptly Anna too began to negotiate with San Francisco newspapers to hire her as a war correspondent. Her plan was already well advanced when Jack and Brett of Macmillan dined at her home on January 2, 1904. Brett thought the idea foolish, that she would be "shot or maimed or wrecked nervously," as she reported it.[18]

There was more than a touch of light-headedness in her sudden willingness to drop her work on "Windlestraws," to abandon her family again so soon after returning home, and, most recklessly, to set out for Tokyo and beyond on the same boat as Jack. On January 3, she wrote breathlessly to Katia:

> If war is declared I leave Thursday for Japan as War Correspondent for the S.F. Bulletin. Steamer Siberia, Captain Smith, via Honolulu and Yokohama. Do not get frightened, dearest, it is a splendid opportunity from every standpoint and I hope to do some good work. It will delay Windlestraw a bit but I hope not very long. My engagement with The Bulletin may not last over three months.
>
> St. George and the Bulletin, Katia! I shall be the best war correspondent in the United States. . . . Even Mamma is glad. My salary is not yet fixed. I will write what it is and all the details when I come to know. All this is out in the contingency that war is declared within the week. . . .
>
> Jack goes Thursday for the Hearst Syndicate on the same steamer. He gets $2000 a week and all expenses free and I expect only $200 a week and expenses. There's equity for you.

There was a brief entry in her notebook—"Jan 7, 1904—the Siberia for Japan. The war correspondent"—followed by several addresses.[19]

But before the *Siberia* sailed with Jack aboard, she wrote to confess to Katia: "War is not declared and I am not going. . . . I made a prodigious blunder about Jack's salary. He gets less than half of what I said a month rather than a week. . . . The Bulletin was anxious to have me go, but I asked a ridiculously enormous salary—I am ashamed to tell you how much. The joke is on me."[20]

The episode could have been viewed—and later was, in rumor—as a last attempt, now that Jack was separated from his wife, to recapture him. (She had no knowledge at this time of the energetic affair between Jack and Charmian Kittredge.) But her letters to Katia about the matter are open and innocent; she wrote enthusiastically of being a professional and competing. Underlying this impulse was surely another: that of flight, to escape from a novel that she doubted that she could complete, a career she doubted that she could attain, or attain in a manner that would fulfill the expectations that she had raised among her "tyrants," the friends among whom she had played the role of rising literary star.[21]

Late February found her, with her adolescent brother, Morris, at another hideaway, Los Gatos, three hours south of San Francisco on the eastern slope of the Santa Cruz Mountains. At first, she was in high spirits. "How my life spirals!" she exclaimed to Katia. "I constantly seek the world through (Oh, Shame!) a publisher." The faithful Cameron King assigned himself to bring her a supply of a thousand sheets of paper and set for her a stint of covering thirty pages a day.[22]

She reported to Katia that she had heard that Jack had ruptured a tendon in a leap on the *Siberia*. To her notebook she mused: "Sometime in life I will find him again and he me, sometime when we are both old, in the barren years when there will be nothing to gain! How ashamed we will be before each other at our shameful renunciation! Will we stop and make apologies?" Jack was still on her mind, and seemed likely to stay there forever.[23]

By March 15, she was working through a draft of a thirteenth chapter of "Windlestraws," a total production, in her estimate, of twenty-five thousand words. Near the end of the month she wrote to Katia that she was leaving her "Eden." Her brother was a little bored, and her mother wanted her home for Passover. But she planned to return early in April: "I have never before worked so steadily or so well. I have a good grip on the novel. . . . By the end of June I should be through and then for a play that's in my mind."[24]

In a later fragment of memoir, she reflected on her retreats: "My father could not understand why I should leave a comfortable home to live quite by myself in this way, far from friends and family, to whom I was devoted. He was perhaps right. I achieved very little in these long pilgrimages and suffered from loneliness. It was not natural for a young girl to live alone. But I wanted to feel that I could. Do one hard thing a day to stiffen your fibre. So I chose a manner of life that was hard for the social girl I was, hard but beautiful and rewarding."[25]

In the end, she decided not to return to Los Gatos at all. To Katia, she complained of the isolation and rationalized, "One should learn to work and live with people." Early in June she confessed: "I have done nothing towards Windlestraws for six weeks and shall take it up again on Sunday."[26]

There is no evidence that she took it up again then, or ever. The surviving pages make it clear why she did not submit the novel to Jack, to Brett of Macmillan, or even to a typist, for it never jelled. Names and situations changed in midstream; the scrawled pages were strewn with false starts and lapses. In patches, the prose was as elegant and literate, even in draft, as the letters of Dane Kempton; but it was similarly laden with Victorian locution and romantic convention. Only when she described the travails of the Socialist Labor Party as it campaigned to establish free speech on city streets did she break through to a kind of journalistic realism. But she did not view her task as reportage; she tried rather to enter the inner life of her characters. Traces of her own preoccupations are interwoven: a young writer's struggle to satisfy both literature and politics, the love of a young woman student for a writer, a prolonged hospital scene that echoes what she must have known of Mary Strunsky's death. Convincing only in patches, "Windlestraws" was never to become a novel; its remains are little more than the bare stems of its title.

Jack London returned from the Far East at the end of June 1904, long before the end of the war between Japan and Russia, frustrated by his inability to get close enough to the fighting to write about it. A day or two before he landed, Bessie London, having already placed a restraining order on his assets, filed for divorce. Anna Strunsky was named in the petition as having alienated Jack's affections.[1]

The accusation was accurate enough in substance, for Jack had declared his readiness to leave Bess while Anna was staying at the bungalow in Piedmont. But it was false in its implication of adultery, and doubly false because Anna now had to endure public blame in the place of the true, or successor, correspondent, Charmian Kittredge. All but conclusive evidence that it had remained an affair of the mind can be seen in the last paragraph of the frantic letter that Jack wrote from London two years before. He had asked why, if he did not love her, he had "spent months building up a wonderful tissue of lies." He went on: "Only one other significance could attach itself to this wonderful tissue of lies, and as I did not seek that thing, the months & years were truly purposeless and wasted." "That thing," seduction, he would not have dared to state thus to her had the case been otherwise.[2]

A coarser corroboration can be found in the memoir of Joseph Noel, an Oakland reporter who knew them both. He was certain that there had been no sexual affair between Jack and Anna, for he recalled Jack as saying, "It would have to be marriage if anyone went after Anna. . . . You know what a hell of a fuss these little intellectuals make about their virginity."[3]

Given only Bess's accusation, the press fastened on the theme of a flamboyant, exotic Anna as the transgressor, often with only glancing attention to verifiable fact. A *New York World* story, for example, penalized Anna for her short-lived plan to go the Far East by erroneously reporting that she had in fact sailed on the *Siberia* with Jack, implying that she had been cohabiting with him across the Pacific. However, readers were spared Bessie's allegation that Jack had returned from his European trip infected with gonorrhea.[4]

Seeking Anna's response, a reporter from the *San Francisco Chronicle* called on her in her quarters at 974 Sutter Street and found her a thoroughgoing Bohemian, ensconced in a "bizarrely furnished apartment, with framed pictures of Maurice Maeterlinck"—the Belgian playwright then in vogue among socialists—"and [a] number of the young Californian novelist's [Jack's] photographs in his customary sweaters and Byronic collar effects." Anna looked "worn and wearied," and complained that the scandal had reduced her mother "almost to the stage of nervous prostration." But she covered loyally, condemning "the silly little stories about lovemaking that went on before Mrs. London's eyes." She added: "His behavior was most circumspect toward me and always has been. . . . He was blindly in love with his wife." Jack's statement to the press was equally bland: "Outside of the time that we were thrown together as collaborators on the 'Kempton-Wace Letters,' I have seen very little of Miss Strunsky, as she and I have been away from San Francisco a great deal. We have not even corresponded, except on matters relating to our book."[5]

Anna came to believe later that she was a pawn in a plan initially designed by Bessie London's lawyer to make a divorce impossible. The papers accusing Anna were to be held in a "sealed" file, and when Jack returned from the Far East, he was to be told that he could have a divorce—but only at the cost of injuring Anna. But the story became public almost at once and that part of the plan, if such it was, fell apart. Yet Bessie's complaint was not merely strategic, for her charges do not have the ring of fabrications; despite Jack's assurance that he was in love with a woman that Bess did not know, she clearly believed that Anna was the offender. For his part, Jack saw Bess's strategy as aimed at staking a claim to his money and property. After he agreed to build a house for her and to make alimony and support payments, her complaint was amended to desertion and that was the basis of the divorce as granted three months later. Anna's name was removed, but only after she had been battered in the newspapers for more than a month.[6]

In midstream, late in July, Jack wrote to her, responding to two letters from her and another from her friend Cameron King, who was purporting to act on her behalf. King had apparently inquired about an impending marriage; Jack wrote to Anna, either dishonestly or self-deceptively: "Either he imagined it, or you imagined it, or else he has some outside information which is news to me & which I should like to hear." He added a tepid apology: "I do most earnestly hope that your name will not be linked any more with my troubles. It will soon die away, I believe. And so it goes. I wander through my life delivering hurts to all that know me." Finally, as if they were still playing their Kempton-Wace roles, he asked: "Unspoilt in your idealism? And think of me as unsaved in my materialism. And why should we forget each other yet awhile? Why should we not always remember & know each other?"[7]

A few days later, he wrote again, in answer to another letter from her, that he was glad that she intended to finish the novel, and asked if he could read what she had done—"if it's typed." (It was not; it never was.) In none of these exchanges with her did he mention Charmian Kittredge, with whom he had commenced his affair more than a year before, about the time that he moved out; she had now been placed out of sight of the press, with relatives in Iowa.[8]

Anna and her mother retreated in September to Agua Caliente, a resort at Calistoga, north of San Francisco. Still ignorant of the circumference of Jack's circle of women and assessing the change of circumstance now that he was divorced, Anna wrote one of her most confiding letters to Katia:

> Jack has his divorce.
>
> There hasn't been much more unpleasantness for me though what there was was hard enough to bear. It was a plain case of black mail. The divorce was obtained by his wife on the grounds of desertion. I am very glad he has his freedom at last. He has suffered bitterly. Further, I do not know.
>
> I hide nothing from you dearest. I think we do not love each other but I may be slandering a supreme feeling in thinking so. I am too breathless from the race for happiness and do not know. After all, I have not raced very hard.
>
> I have the Semitic temperament that gives up over readily and I have ever had a genius for giving up. I must be fought for gallantly to be won and I think Jack would rather wait than fight. He, too, is tired. He is a pessimist and what has a pessimist to do with love? So, dearest, you know all.

This letter seemed to mark her concession that Jack was now beyond reach.[9]

At the start of 1905, Anna again went into seclusion, on Kings Mountain, in the hills above Stanford. It was an unpleasant season, with constant rain and impassable clay roads. Alone, she contemplated her first twenty-seven years. At a later point, she recalled of this time:

> I chose a mountain near my university and from its heights I considered the world and myself, paused to note the meagre achievement of the years and resolved to begin life over again for myself, as if I had indeed entered upon a new day. . . . And from my mountain height I resolved upon a broader scope. My thoughts that in the city had been arranged and settled here broke out afresh. They left the work I was engaged in and betook themselves to spinning a web of the mysteries of love and death and to locking them within the fates of a far-away burial ground, called Pere Lachaise.[10]

Thus she marked the start of a second novel, with the first left unfinished. The idea originated in her visit to Père Lachaise in 1903 and centered on a girl growing up at the edge of the great cemetery, a symbolic representation, one could suppose, of her own sense of closeness to death. Such a work might be better designed than "Windlestraws" to answer her obsession with mortality but it was light-years from the great socialist novel that she had promised to Brett.

In her isolation, Anna kept a daily journal. On January 20, she braved the weather for a hike that frightened her: "I thought I realized for the first time what the sensations of an explorer must be. . . . Not one human being in all my miles of tramping. I lay down in the road once, too weary to choose a better place and I wanted so badly to sleep, but it was getting dark and I dared not for fear I should not wake before a long time." Ultimately, she found her way back to the cabin, only to venture out again the next day to hike five miles to the base of the mountain, and struggle back for fourteen miles because she lost the road in a thunderstorm. Warm and in bed, she contemplated photographic proofs that had just arrived: "I would make some changes in my face . . . although it is a comely face, mainly eyes and sadness! There is one picture that has gaiety and much sweetness, the look I suppose I wear when I've written a chapter a morning."[11]

The next day, she wrote and dedicated to Jack London on his birthday a poem called "The Road" (a title that he happened to use two years later for a book about life as a tramp):

> The way was long and you were at its ending,
>   Night fell and still it stretched before me
> The sea leaped up and mocked me for my feebleness
>   It was a bitter war and hard, my love!
> Oh baffled heart when turnings grew too sinuous,
>   Oh wild despair when stony trail misled!
> My soul grew sick and shrieked to all the hills around
>   That I must live and reach you, O my love!
>
> Oh dearest love, this gray gulch swayed and beckoned me
>   The trackless forest lured me to its rest.
> The swollen river pledged me dreadful promises
>   To lay me like a gift before my love!
>
> Then the road died and fast I reached the trysting-place
>   You were not there, O much besought and dear
> I turned my face and took the bitter length again
>   And groped my way, forgotten by my love.[12]

Three days later, on January 25, 1905, she received a letter from Cameron King. She wrote in her diary:

Revolution in Russia! This ought to be the happiest day of life and . . . my heart is full of dread and misgiving. . . . If I could speak Russian I would go there if I had to walk—I could go in a semi-literary way.

Oh my comrades, it is a better thing to be an onlooker. "It is good to live now," says Cameron in his letter to-day. "It were good to die too if we were in St. Petersburg. . . . But here? Well, we . . . need not be too sure that the day will never come when the Cause will not demand our blood. And we will be ready, dear."

She could not yet note the coincidence—that the day that she had marked with an epitaph-poem for Jack London was the opening of the first Russian revolution, a date to be known in history as "Bloody Sunday." It was the hinge joining past and future.[13]

On January 26, seemingly transformed, Anna walked again to Woodside, but her thoughts were no longer morbid, although it was the second anniversary of Mary Strunsky's death:

I walked about a mile through brush—not lost this time, but experimenting with trails. I am gritty. I used to think I was cowardly, but I am not.

Several times I was like Absolam caught by the hair. I had to crawl, in shrubbery and dead menzonitas. . . . A hundred times I was struck in eyes and face. Then I had to jump into ravines and across ditches, and it would have been bad for me if I had sprained an ankle. Last week a skeleton of a man was found on the mountain—probably (in my opinion) a man who got lost *experimenting* with trails!

I thought of Russia all the way.[14]

PART TWO

English: Searching for a Calling,

1877–1905

Unlike many of his contemporaries, William English Walling never conde-
scended to write an explanatory article called "Why I Am a Socialist." Introspective writing was not his medium. Consequently, how and when he began to think of himself as a socialist, or what kind of socialist he considered
himself, is not clear. There was little in his background that pointed toward
radicalism; he came from an affluent family of traditional Democrats. But he
encountered currents in his youth that pushed him in new directions.[1]

The family's wealth and eminence, later much exaggerated in the press, lay
primarily on his mother's side. It was indicative that he was called not by his
first name but by the maternal family name, "English." Family recollections
assert that his mother, Rosalind English Walling, was the dominant figure in
the lives of her two sons, English and Willoughby George, maintaining private channels of communication with them into their adulthood.[2]

Although the boys were born in Louisville, Kentucky, their father's native
city, the family's life revolved around the English family residences in Indiana, in Indianapolis and at "Englishton," in tiny Lexington, a few miles north
of the Ohio River. When the boys were small, the family moved to Indianapolis from Louisville. Their father, Willoughby Walling—one of Louisville's
leading physicians, educated in Berlin and a professor of anatomy—opened
a pharmaceuticals business under the aegis of his wealthy father-in-law,
William Hayden English.[3]

William English Walling was named for this same man, his maternal
grandfather, whose portraits show the same intensity around the deep-set
eyes as his grandson's. As American statecraft goes, William Hayden English
never reached the top rank, but he was prominent in pre–Civil War politics.
He became a lawyer at eighteen, a state legislator, and a proslavery Democratic member of Congress who believed firmly in the inferiority of the
enslaved; he sponsored a bill that unsuccessfully sought to admit Kansas to
the Union under a proslavery constitution. Eventually a crossroads town in
his district was named for him by his constituents.[4]

After the Civil War, he prospered in banking, at the expense of families he
evicted during the panic of 1873. He and his wife, Emma Jackson of Virginia,
had two children: William Eastin English, whose pursuit of sexual adventure
kept him from rising higher than a seat in the legislature; and Rosalind, who

in 1876 married Dr. Willoughby Walling. William Hayden English returned momentarily to politics as the vice-presidential candidate on the national Democratic ticket in 1880; his acceptance speech was required childhood reading for his grandsons. He was supposed to supply the bankroll for the campaign, but his niggling contributions did not carry even Indiana; state and nation went Republican.[5]

Four years later, when the Democrats won the White House for the first time since the Civil War, William Hayden English had enough influence in the new Cleveland administration to get his son-in-law a consulship. In 1885, the Walling family moved to Edinburgh, and English and his brother were given several years of Scottish education before the Republicans returned to office in 1888. When the family left America, it numbered five; on its return, it was only four, for the boys' little sister, Mary, had died abroad at the age of thirty months.[6]

In 1886, nine-year-old English watched from a hotel window in London as police clashed in Trafalgar Square with the unemployed, led by socialists. His widow depicted the spectacle of this infamous "Black Sunday" as providing an early impetus toward radicalization.[7]

After the family returned to America, the sons, eleven and ten, were enrolled in Trinity Hall, an Episcopal school for boys near Louisville. There they shone; the headmaster, not averse to flattering well-off parents, reported to Dr. Walling: "English acquits himself in his studies with the usual credit, while that boy Willoughby is a constant delight. My laborious & responsible avocation is in the large a thankless & discouraging one, but the burden is always the lighter for such boys as yours."[8]

English started what became a lifelong practice of writing home to report his exploits. He reported that he had a 500 in arithmetic, and "500 is perfect and I am the only boy in school who got perfect in anything." His only blemish, twenty-five demerits, was for being off the grounds without permission. The brothers stayed a year or so at Trinity Hall, then joined the family at its new home on Drexel Boulevard in Chicago. They went to Chicago's Hyde Park High School, not far from their home, English in an advanced placement that permitted him to graduate at the age of sixteen.[9]

A week after his fifteenth birthday, English wrote to the new University of Chicago, which was opening its doors the following fall under president William Rainey Harper, and asked if there were age restrictions on admission. Ultimately he waited until he graduated from high school before he enrolled in the university's second entering class, in the fall of 1893. English thrived on the curriculum, which was so flexible in its requirements as to be known as "Harper's Bazaar."[10]

Because home was so close, English rarely wrote to his parents as an undergraduate, and he was not given later to reminiscences about his campus life. But it is clear that he was a top-ranked student and an enthusiast for fraternities. Harper had wished to establish a residential university, and thought the old-fashioned literary societies would be more conducive to democracy than fraternities. But English pledged Delta Kappa Epsilon and cherished the companionship of "Dekes" during and immediately after his college years.[11]

Academically, he marched straight through, completing several college-level courses even before he left high school and earning many A's. He did particularly well in mathematics, with an A-plus in calculus. He encountered either heavier going or tougher grading in political science and economics. Or perhaps he was already formulating dissenting views that were less likely to earn high grades. He was awarded the bachelor of science degree (the equivalent of a bachelor of arts elsewhere) on April 1, 1897, and immediately enrolled in the university's graduate school. Two years after his graduation, he was elected to Phi Beta Kappa and given a key that he declined to wear.[12]

Midway in his college years, his maternal grandfather died and his two grandsons received a share of the estate. Not coincidentally, their father retired at the age of forty-eight. English received a lump sum large enough for an income of ten thousand dollars a year, but from the start his parents were apprehensive about his ability to manage it. Before or perhaps during a graduation trip to England, he decided to invest part of his inheritance in the Agate Springs Stock Farm, in the almost unsettled northwestern corner of Nebraska. James H. Cook, the proprietor, was much encumbered, and the investment involved English in years of concern over mortgages, loans, and other headaches. Yet the Agate ranch provided him with a summer retreat and a taste of vigorous outdoor life—which he needed, for he was thin, even scrawny. The ranch also initiated what became a lifelong pattern of continual, even compulsive, recreational travel.[13]

The careers of the two brothers moved in parallel for a time, with English, the elder by a year, in the lead. Both graduated from the University of Chicago, and both, in pursuit of their grandfather's profession, went to Harvard Law School, which neither completed. English entered Harvard Law first. Away from home, he resumed in earnest his correspondence with his parents. From the start, the letters were revealing, not because they were necessarily more candid about private matters than most letters to parents, but because they provided an opportunity for him to reveal unabashedly what he usually concealed from friends—the extent and height of his aspirations and his analysis of his faults.

Arriving in Cambridge in September 1897, the twenty-year-old reported dutifully on his social and physical activities. He saw "Aunt Bessie and

Albion"—connections of the English family—and attended a ball given by "Cousin Hannah." He gave a smoker in his quarters at The Dunster, where he served Dekes and other law-school friends milk punch, ale, and rarebit. He walked ten miles, Lincoln to Concord to Walden, with a Miss Cutts, who set such a pace, he said, that "my calves are sore yet." Later, he reported that he was using the Sandow system, promoted by a pioneering bodybuilder, to expand his chest and arms.[14]

He reported dutifully to his parents that he was upholding southern or border-state mores. In an early letter from Cambridge he wrote: "Everything is well except that I may have to leave Memorial. There are three niggers at the only table where I have friends, and dont propose to eat with them all the year round, even though they are nice fellows. After every effort is made to move them, if they dont go, I will board next door to the Hall here." He felt even more uncomfortable with Easterners, as he observed in a letter to his brother: "The more I see of these people the more opposite they seem to those of the south & west. Especially the younger ones, very genteel & dignified, but so terribly cold & stiff socially."[15]

Before long, he revealed doubts about the whole project, his choice of law as a profession. He complained of overconcentration: "I do object to having no time or leisure for anything but law—[I objec]t to it now and expect to object to it all my life." He was disappointed after the law club met in his rooms to practice for moot court: "I had to take issue with the teachings of the law school, though the law itself was on my side." He chafed at the influence of the school's dean and leading scholar, James Barr Ames, proponent of the case method of studying law: "While I failed to convince the court, brought up in the theories of Prof. Ames, they nearly all congratulated me on my argument and I think I might have won before an unbiassed [sic] tribunal."[16]

Before the end of winter, he was backing away: "I am coming nearer to a rational view of the work, and have decided to try to be a little more careful and thorough and not put in quite so many hours." Finally he wrote out for himself a batch of reasons for leaving the law, first of which was: "Law and business are eminently narrowing." He added a list of occupations for which legal education was not essential. At the lower end of the list he wrote: "14. Gentleman of the higher type. 15. Journalism." He was not only discouraged by the demands of the curriculum but also seemed to miss the spirit of inquiry or indirection that he had found at the University of Chicago. He did not return to Harvard for a second year.[17]

The four-month Spanish-American War started about the time he returned home in the spring of 1898. There is no indication that he was deeply stirred by it; in any case, he did not enlist. However, in January 1899, English and his brother sent a note of congratulations to Albert J. Beveridge, the young Republican whose imperialist drum-beating had persuaded the Indiana legislature to elect him to the United States Senate. Beveridge, no doubt aware of the Wallings' political connections, took time in the postelection bustle to acknowledge their note, and to add: "You are fine types of that strong, virile, hopeful, militant and unconquerable young Americans to whom we must look from this moment on." English later took a more jaundiced view of Beveridge.[18]

In the fall of 1898, English returned to the University of Chicago graduate school, concentrating on sociology and economics. Both were new fields of study, institutional in focus and reformist in temper. Elsewhere, sociology was often an academic dumping ground, collecting courses not wanted by other disciplines, but Chicago had created a full-fledged department under Albion Small, hired away from the fountainhead of academic progressivism, Johns Hopkins. Small was the founder and editor of the *American Journal of Sociology*, which began life in 1895 as a periodical of exposure as well as scholarship. Sociology's famed Chicago School had its origins in this period.[19]

In economics, the most visible presence was Thorstein Veblen, just becoming infamous among respectable economists for his crabbed, irreverent *Theory of the Leisure Class*. English was Veblen's student, and there may later have been a touch of Veblen in the detachment and irony in English's writing. More important, Veblen became English's first model for the creation of an American socialism.[20]

English's record in graduate school suggests that his year there was devoted more to searching than to studying. He earned letter grades in only two of his ten courses. This may have been the time when he first began to view himself as a radical critic of American society, and perhaps even began to think of himself as a committed socialist, although he did not affiliate himself until much later with any party or faction. Not that he concentrated on socialism academically; he took a mere "pass" in the course of that title.[21]

By 1899 English had definitively left the track that would have led him into a traditional profession, gravitating instead into Chicago's flourishing network of social work, reform, and socialism. For a time, he moved into a tenement near Hull-House, the pioneering settlement near the Chicago stockyards, founded in the 1880s by Jane Addams, and committed himself to live on the equivalent of the wages of a common laborer.[22]

He also found what remained, until near the end of his life, his only regular job. John Riley Tanner, a conservative downstate Republican who succeeded John Peter Altgeld as governor of Illinois, had recently married Rosalind Walling's cousin Cora. English was prompted to approach Tanner. A family tale relates that Tanner offered to find English a seat in the legislature—Democratic or Republican, it did not matter—until the young man announced himself to be a socialist, whereupon the governor, only momentarily nonplused, settled for making him a factory inspector. English was issued an identification card and worked out of the New Era Building in Chicago. One of his daughters recalls his memory of inspecting a cookie factory and deciding that he would never eat Fig Newtons again.[23]

English just missed working under the formidable Florence Kelley, who had served Altgeld as the state's first chief factory inspector. The new chief, one Louis Arrington from downstate Alton, was no Florence Kelley; in his first report he apologized for his lack of activity and blamed Kelley for his department's shortcomings. In the fall of 1900, English represented Illinois at the fourteenth annual factory inspectors' convention in Indianapolis and, the minutes noted, read "in a very excellent tone of voice" a paper, "The Dangerous Trades," which drew on British sources and his own trip to England for a discussion of occupational hazards and disease. He probably also wrote the detailed essay on child labor that made up the entire text of the Illinois factory inspectors' report for 1900. Both efforts showed diligence in research, with a certain stiffness in presentation.[24]

English did not give up his growing political interests while he was a state employee. He and his brother apparently tried to assemble a student socialist organization of the type that emerged five years later as the Intercollegiate Socialist Society. They sent a circular to Jack London, who replied to Willoughby that he had never identified himself with students, but that he would supply names of two who could help. One was Cameron King; the other was Anna Strunsky: "This young lady has not only been an undergraduate at Stanford, but is now enrolled in the University of California. She was a delegate to the last socialist state convention, and is well up in all things socialistic." He wrote this letter the same day that he wrote his impassioned "Comrades!" letter to Anna: July 31, 1900. There is no evidence that either English or Willoughby pursued this lead.[25]

The factory-inspector appointment did not last past the end of Tanner's administration early in 1901 (Tanner died a few months after he left office), and English was cut adrift. He contemplated a trip to New Mexico with Robert Hunter, a well-off contemporary from Indiana who was working for the Chicago Board of Charities, but he settled for visiting an orange plantation in Florida. A letter to his parents reveals, again, his careless conventionality about race, tempered with goodwill. He wrote:"I have arranged for a coon and alligator hunt and also [am] taking a bright young darkey out of school for a week or so to be my guide in the woods. I'll teach him his lessons meanwhile."[26]

His search for a new challenge led him before the end of 1901 to the work of the Industrial Commission, a joint congressional-presidential body that was about to issue a huge report, more than three years in gestation, designed to describe the new shape of corporate America. More than likely, English was pointed toward the commission by Veblen, who was interested in using its output in his next book, *The Theory of Business Enterprise.* But it is not clear whether English, as a budding socialist, was interested primarily in the commission's policy recommendations on regulation and licensing of corporations—that is, taming the beast—or in the voluminous testimony that condemned industrialists out of their own mouths.[27]

With his brother, he formulated an ambitious, self-financed project: a one-volume summary of the nineteen volumes of testimony before the commission, to be followed by an annual volume on economic affairs. He sought out the insurgent economist John R. Commons, sixteen years his senior and out of work, as was frequently Commons's fate. After losing two academic jobs, Commons had joined the staff of the Industrial Commission. Later he wrote a minority report on trusts for a Democratic member of the commission, who rewarded him with two weeks of great meals. At this point he hooked up with English and Willoughby Walling.[28]

The Wallings gave Commons a free hand with expenses. He opened and staffed a Washington office in the Bliss Building, opposite the Capitol, while English, not content with millions of words of testimony, went about the country commissioning new articles. The young men's confidence and charm were all but irresistible. N. I. Stone, a young Russian immigrant economist who was recruited as staff statistician, recalled: "The two brothers attracted attention wherever they appeared. Both tall, erect, lean, handsome . . . they looked like twins. Both had a lively sense of humor, a smile that lit up their faces and with their lively interest in public affairs, conversation never lagged and was always bright and sparkling."[29]

Despite the glow of apparent success, English was rapidly transforming the ambitious into the unmanageable. Although he had prepared himself by qualifying to join the National Association of Accountants and Bookkeepers, he clearly did not have a grip on the project's finances. One night Stone asked Willoughby and English if they could estimate how much the whole project would cost. English guessed that the first volume would cost twenty-five thousand dollars and that its receipts would pay for subsequent years. Stone put him in touch with the reality: With Commons spending freely, even wildly, expenses could run well into six figures. English disappeared for a few days; when he came back, he announced that the project was dissolved.[30]

The brothers provided generous termination pay for Commons, Stone, and the others, and the only hard feelings were those English felt for himself. Stone recalled that the twenty-five-year-old remarked to him afterward: "You don't know how I envy you . . . that you at your age can command a $2,500 salary. If I had to work for a living, I don't know whether I would be worth three dollars a week to anybody." His brother, Willoughby, wrote to their father, expressing concern over English's state of mind: "English needs a good shaking up and a trip here and a trip there will do him no good. He must do something radical or he won't do anything."[31]

A month later, English wrote to his parents, perhaps unconsciously echoing Willoughby's terminology: "As you may imagine the inward shaking up I have gotten out of my recent experience is still having its effects. I find myself shifting into a very different view of my own future, so different that you may not realize it yet. . . . [M]y outlook on everything is almost inverted and I find myself very much more in harmony with the people around me and things in general. Like every young man, I ought at least to have an ostensible occupation."[32]

Cast adrift when his oversize plan for the economic yearbook foundered, English Walling was thrown a comradely life preserver. In April 1902 he received a letter from Robert Hunter. Hunter, like English, had Indiana roots and socialist inclinations; they had been friends in Chicago when Hunter was working there for the city's Bureau of Charities and managing the municipal flophouse. Now Hunter was in New York, just installed in a prestigious post as head worker at the University Settlement, on the Lower East Side of Manhattan. On his first day in office, Hunter wrote to urge English to consider living in New York: "I wish I might hope to have you come to the Settlement. At present we are overcrowded here but I hope that within a month of so, I shall be able to make arrangements for more room." Hunter understated the matter; he was not only making more room, he was cleaning house.[1]

English no doubt already knew of the University Settlement. Like its London prototype, Toynbee Hall, the University Settlement was founded on the proposition that good would flow from having university graduates live among (but not necessarily with) the poor, partly to set a good example. Fifteen years after the founding of Toynbee Hall, New York and Chicago were now dotted with settlements. Jane Addams's Hull-House was the most famous and was typical of American settlements in having mostly women workers. But the University Settlement, established in 1887, was the oldest in America, regarded affectionately by Toynbee Hall as its "dear and distinguished child." Like Toynbee Hall, the University Settlement had only male residents.[2]

At the end of 1901, the settlement lost its head worker, Samuel Bronson Reynolds, who in seven years had transformed it from a hole in the wall to a mainstream institution allied with the city's municipal reform movement. As a reward, the new reform mayor, Seth Low, appointed Reynolds his secretary. The University Settlement Society's search for a successor quickly settled on Hunter. He came from the family of a prosperous buggy manufacturer in Terre Haute, Indiana, and was a graduate of Indiana University. Although he was only twenty-eight, he had been in charity work off and on for ten years, and had made the requisite pilgrimage to Toynbee Hall. He was a socialist, but this was not regarded as alarming or disqualifying.[3]

Hunter's predecessor, Reynolds, who remained on the governing council, might have expected that so junior a head worker as Hunter might be amenable to guidance. But Hunter jarred Reynolds by terminating most of Reynolds's cohort of residents and bringing in his own. Hence Hunter's invitation to English and an array of other men much like himself generationally, regionally, and politically.[4]

By the fall of 1902, Hunter had most of his spaces filled, but English held back. Hunter wrote a second time in June, while English was rusticating at the Agate Springs Stock Farm in Nebraska: "I wish you were to be in New York permanently, so that I might count upon you for various kinds of advice and assistance." English visited in September, and Hunter tried to entice him by nominating him for the editorship of *Municipal Affairs*, a city-planning journal based in New York. Nothing came of that initiative, and by the end of the month English was back at Agate Springs, enjoying "perfect rest and freedom" and again assuring his parents that his white-elephant investment in the ranch would eventually be profitable. He avoided any direct reference to his own future. But he did not delay a decision long; by November he was back in New York to move in at the settlement.[5]

Where Toynbee Hall had erected in London's East End a cluster of buildings resembling a small college, the University Settlement symbolized itself, and America, with a new five-story building rising among the tenements at Eldridge and Rivington streets on the Lower East Side. It looked like an office building, but an annual report aptly likened it to a palace, functioning both as a public institution and as a residence. The report observed: "The work is done on too large a scale to permit the home-like atmosphere and the personal touch which are so desirable when the conditions render them feasible." But on the inside the Women's Auxiliary sought to accommodate the residents by decorating their quarters in the style of a men's club or fraternity house. The centerpiece was a fifteenth- or sixteenth-century fireplace, "picked up" in Italy by one of the building's architects.[6]

Those architects—John Mead Howells, son of the novelist William Dean Howells, and Isaac Newton Phelps Stokes, an heir to a mining fortune—suggested the institution's ties to gentility and wealth. It was the reputability of the place that English emphasized in writing to his parents: "The Settlement has had or has on its council such men as Low, Schurz, Roosevelt, Speyer, Rockefeller, Stillman, etc. It is really the most fashionable charity or reform (I dont know which) in the city and money has been lavished on it."[7]

English joined half a dozen other new residents at 184 Eldridge Street. Hunter's first recruit had been Leroy Scott, a graduate of Indiana University and more recently a minor editor at the monthly *Woman's Home Compan-*

ion; he was hired as assistant head worker at $100 a month. There were also Howard Brubaker, a would-be writer just out of Indiana University; Ernest Poole, a new Princeton graduate from Chicago, who saw himself as a future novelist of the slums; and S. G. Lindholm, who had worked with English on the economic yearbook.

The last to come, even more belatedly than English, was the one celebrity among Hunter's crop: James Graham Phelps Stokes, brother of the architect, Newton. Graham, as he was known, was a member of one of the city's old and wealthy mercantile families; he had to look after family businesses, but his heart was with New York's social and reform enterprises, which placed him on more boards and committees than he could efficiently serve. The Stokeses were particularly important to the University Settlement; in addition to Newton's role, his sisters were part-time volunteers, and Graham himself was a member of the governing council. Although he had lived at the settlement once before, the press viewed his return as remarkable and somewhat amusing. An out-of-town newspaper poked fun at him: "not even the dinner party among the smart set at Newport last summer, when a trained monkey was the guest of honor, aroused more interest."[8]

Indeed, settlement residents—particularly male residents in a field dominated by women—were in danger of being seen as unmanly, as "exquisites." They were equally vulnerable to the charge of dilettantism, of playing at sharing the lot of the poor while continuing to live in comfort. Few stayed long or became social-work professionals. One wonders whether English had pondered the chilly view his teacher Thorstein Veblen took of settlements as an outpost of leisure-class gentrification: "The solicitude of 'settlements,' . . . is in part directed to enhance the industrial efficiency of the poor and to teach them the more adequate utilization of the means at hand; but it is also no less consistently directed to the inculcation, by precept and example, of certain punctilios of upper-class propriety in manners and customs. The economic substance of these proprieties will commonly be found on scrutiny to be a conspicuous waste of time and goods."[9]

The new group of residents tried to shrug off their reputation as dabblers. They decried the idea that they were setting a good example, and preferred to think of themselves as field sociologists, learning more than they taught. As self-protection, they resorted to unsentimentality. Brubaker recalled that their informal motto was a mocking echo of a phrase used by visiting up-towners: "You are doing a noble work," and that the word "uplifter" was used as a smiling insult. According to his associate Poole, when English received a clipping from an Indiana newspaper sentimentalizing an interview he had given, he called on the settlement boys' octet to hum "Fair Harvard," while he intoned quotations dubiously attributed to him:

"It shall be my aim"—sweet harmony—"to live my life among the lowly"—music still sweeter than before—"and to bring a little sunshine"—more chords—"to those whose lives are full of clouds."[10]

Among Hunter's recruits, English promptly became first among equals. Poole and Brubaker, only slightly younger, regarded English, at twenty-five, as much their senior in worldliness and their superior in intellect. His room, piled high with books and documents (he invited Poole in to admire his library) soon became a place of ferment, echoing with debate on social wrongs and remedies. When he was at the top of his form, English was sometimes light and mocking, sometimes wrathful: "[H]e was of the high-strung sensitive kind, quick to grow indignant or angry, and so truly exciting at such times that when the glad news went down the hall—'Another big argument! Walling is sore!'—we would flock into the room." Just as he had valued the University of Chicago for its freedom of opinion, it was the conception of the settlement as a forum that most appealed to English. By long-established policy, Brubaker recalled, the settlement "opened its rooms to meetings at which anybody could advocate anything—including doctrines which would have pained the financial supporters of the institution." English particularly approved and defended the right of labor unions to convene at the settlement.[11]

The settlement was a strenuous place, with nearly a thousand neighborhood children and adults coming in every day. Besides such direct services as public baths, a credit union, and legal aid, the settlement housed classes and clubs, and every resident had a boys' club or two to manage, either athletic or cultural. Stokes ran a naked exercise class for residents only. English was assigned his share of duties: he lectured (in a series called "Labor and Social Movements"), organized club meetings, greeted visitors, "did what was expected of him." Some duties pained him. Capable of great charm, he was much in demand for the weekly luncheon with wealthy young women and attended, reluctantly. As a man of reputed social standing, he was often invited uptown and finally yielded to an invitation to a dinner dance. Poole remembered that English returned after daybreak and told of dancing away the night with a beautiful young woman. Then he put out his cigarette and said: "I guess that will be plenty," and Poole never again saw him in dress clothes at the settlement.[12]

Nor did he care for intrusive charity workers, overbearing philanthropists, or the Mugwump reformers with whom Samuel Reynolds had been allied. At the first opportunity, he sought to reestablish the settlement's contacts with the local regular Democratic leader, "Little Tim" Sullivan, who had been exiled under the Reynolds regime. His reward was a pair of stories in the *New York Herald* ridiculing his efforts at détente as a waltz pairing tea-sippers and barflies.[13]

Hunter had bigger things in mind for English, whom—perhaps alone among his recruits—he regarded as a social equal. He proposed English for the visibility of a membership in the City Club, a fashionable social organization for reformers. Hunter soon enlisted him as well in his first major campaign as head worker. Hunter had been drafted by an old Chicago colleague, Florence Kelley, now head of the Consumers' League and living at the nearby Henry Street Settlement, to chair a committee of settlement workers on child labor. Hunter parceled out writing assignments to Scott and to Poole, and asked English to take over the chair. But English plunged into the giantism that had killed the economic yearbook; Hunter recalled in his unpublished memoirs that "Walling's immense program of studies and inquiries . . . would have taken years to complete." Mrs. Kelley prevailed on Hunter to resume the chair; English stepped down, having received another lesson in what happened when appetite outruns skill. Poole—less mature, less brilliant in English's eyes, but gifted with an ability to tell heartrending little stories—became the star, widely published and quoted, of the child-labor campaign and of a subsequent campaign against tuberculosis.[14]

English may have felt a twinge of envy and chagrin at Poole's sudden eminence. At the same time Poole's success may have led English to pursue an ambition he had not yet admitted, except at the bottom of that long list of occupations he had written out before he left Harvard. He was surrounded at the settlement by aspiring writers—not only Poole, but almost every other member of Hunter's squad. To this point he had thought of himself as a scholar, a sociologist acting upon social issues. But was not one component—perhaps the most important component—of social action laying it before the public?

To be a journalist—a writer for magazines—had considerable appeal at that moment to young men who had chosen not to enter traditional professions. No other occupation could provide the freedom to travel, to inquire, to explore great issues, to help set the world's agenda. This was an era when one could make oneself heard; there were new, more venturesome magazines supplanting the quiet monthlies of the genteel tradition, and they welcomed new voices. This was indeed the time to be a gentleman journalist.

When English Walling came to the University Settlement late in 1901, he may have had a friendly agreement with the head worker, Robert Hunter, that he did not have to stick close to home. In any case, he began almost at once to test the boundaries, to step away from settlement work to make a name for himself as a writer. His letters home scarcely mentioned the settlement; instead, he reported on his campaign to break into the magazines.

His first important contact, probably through family connections, was Walter Hines Page, a North Carolinian of whom it was said that wherever he hung his hat became the unofficial capital of the New South. Formerly a newspaperman, Page was now Frank Nelson Doubleday's partner in the publisher Doubleday, Page, and editor of a crisp new monthly, *The World's Work.* The contents consisted entirely of nonfiction, generously interlaced with large photographs. As editor, Page shopped for forward-looking but not disturbing economic and social theories, offered portraits and profiles of successful men, and publicized new technologies. He was impatient of fine writing; he was selling up-to-dateness. In essence an apologist for business, he sidestepped the rising tide of muckraking, even when muckraking became profitable.[1]

Although the tone of the magazine scarcely harmonized with English's radical tendencies, he was persuaded at least that Page was open to fresh opinion. The campaign proceeded by stages. English reported to his father in November 1902: "I saw Page again but we have not had our 'long talk' yet." In December: "Mr. Page has written apologizing for his delayed invitation." Matters improved in January: "I have seen Mr. Page three times recently." And five days later: "I have definitely arranged for a series of articles with Page."[2]

The proposed series dwindled to a single article on the building trades unions in New York. The subject was complex: disruptions in construction rising from the chaotic dealings of unions with employers split into thirty trade associations. English took his time, reading and interviewing widely. He paused to turn out an article for *Wilshire's,* the socialist periodical, praising the newspaper impresario William Randolph Hearst as a near socialist.[3]

In March, he left the city for the springtime trek that became a lifetime pattern. He spent Mardi Gras in New Orleans with his parents and went on to California, where his newly married brother and his bride, Frederika Haskell of South Carolina, were lazing in the soft air of Pasadena. While he was in California, his mother sent him a gift, "a first-class April fool," and he responded in terms that his mother no doubt regarded as part of the joke: "I was certainly fearfully disappointed to open a promising jewelry box and find a huge nigger ring."[4]

On his return, English found the University Settlement in crisis. Hunter, the head worker, had become engaged to Graham Stokes's sister Caroline, a volunteer at the settlement. But simultaneously Graham, his brother-in-law-to-be, brought to a head a feud with the old head worker, James Reynolds. At the April meeting of the governing council, Stokes submitted a letter denouncing the "absentee government" of such council members as Reynolds. He resigned from the council and Hunter, about to be a member of Stokes's family, had no choice but to quit as well.[5]

In this schism, English, a Hunter recruit, was perforce a member of the Hunter faction. He and three other residents were ushers at the Hunter-Stokes wedding in Connecticut, which the newspapers, noting that Hunter was from Indiana, treated as a union between a society woman and a backwoodsman. A few days later Hunter and his bride sailed for Europe aboard the *Celtic*.[6]

While they were gone, the *New York Tribune* floated a story that Hunter and all but one or two of the University Settlement residents were going to secede and establish a new settlement. But Graham Stokes soon deflated that scheme in an interview with Rose Harriet Pastor, a reporter for the *Jewish Daily News*. It became apparent that Hunter's recruits at the University Settlement had decided not to jump ship; even Graham Stokes was staying on. Hunter was the odd man out. He abandoned settlement work, set up housekeeping in Connecticut, and devoted himself for the next year to writing *Poverty*, an otherwise important study marred by xenophobia.[7]

Once Hunter's resignation was final, the University Settlement Council found a new head worker. On paper, James H. Hamilton seemed a likely successor. Like Hunter, he had attended Indiana University, where he had studied under John R. Commons. But there was no natural affinity between Hamilton and his new associates. Hamilton was fifteen years older than English and did not like the idea of supervising a peripatetic literary colony. He thought that residents ought to be in residence, and he was increasingly impatient as English, Poole, and others traveled across the country and overseas.[8]

As it happened, when Hamilton arrived at the settlement English was vacationing in the Adirondacks. There he and Graham Stokes and Raymond Ingersoll, a fellow uplifter, got lost climbing Mount Marcy. During this stay,

English's article finally appeared in *World's Work*, more than ninety pages deep into the magazine, between a survey of grading in elementary schools and a profile of Pope Leo XIII.

The presentation was serious rather than engaging, filled with facts and data and showing the scars of struggle and rewriting, an impression confirmed in a letter to his parents: "I entirely agree with Father that the World's Work article was incommensurate with the time put in it. But . . . [i]t was my first and much time was wasted finding the ropes." He was afflicted by Page's insistence on timeliness: "The events discussed were developing every day and had to be waited on." This battery of rationalizations seemed to be offered as much to reassure himself as his parents.[9]

While his article made nowhere near the impression of Poole's work on child labor, he could be satisfied that he had shown himself capable of managing the work. For the moment, every prospect pleased. He wrote that S. S. McClure of *McClure's Magazine* had asked him for an article and *World's Work* wanted several more: "I have decided to stick right to the magazine work and the labor question and am thinking out a systematic series that should give me plenty of work and some public attention."[10]

In the fall of 1903, new residents arrived at the settlement house. The biggest catch was Walter Weyl, a few years older than English, an academically trained labor economist who had been a valuable aide to the miners' union in the great anthracite strike of 1902 and 1903. In Weyl, English immediately found a worthy debating opponent, able to hold him to more literal standards of argument than the more junior Poole or Brubaker.[11]

English, Poole, and Weyl went on the road together in November 1903 to attend the convention of the American Federation of Labor in Boston. On the train up, Poole recalled, Weyl talked nonstop about the coal industry, the miners, and labor, through the night and, after their arrival in Boston, into the next day.

In Boston, English was on a mission that gave him a chance for a new test of his organizing skills. While he was in England in 1897, he had discovered the English Women's Trade Union League. There was no American counterpart and he and the allies he collected decided that there should be one—possibly less in the interest of women's equality, to which he had at that point paid no particular attention, than in the interest of strengthening labor unions and the AFL.[12]

In Boston, English teamed up with Mary Kenney O'Sullivan, a unionist who had been like himself an Illinois factory inspector, and was able to sign on as national officers both Jane Addams of Hull-House and the famed Chicago stockyards social worker Mary McDowell. They held three meetings in Fanueil Hall for AFL delegates (nearly all men) and representatives from

Boston settlements and reform groups (nearly all women). On November 19, 1903, the meeting brought into existence the Women's Trade Union League of America, a hopeful alliance of working women and genteel reformers.[13]

Back in New York, English plunged into organizing a New York branch of the new league. He became secretary of the organization and arranged to have its first meetings at the University Settlement. He recruited two experienced trade unionists, Margaret C. Daly and Leonora O'Reilly, to pull the organization together. But once the league had a structure and offices of its own, he began to lose interest. He resigned formally in March 1905, as he was about to leave the country. So well did he obviate his role that twenty-five years later he had to press an ill-tempered claim to historical recognition when the WTUL incumbents had all but forgotten him in their official histories. In his larger scheme of things, the work that English did on the Trade Women's League was a brief voluntary chore, which nonetheless had the side benefit of making him known to important figures in the labor movement, most notably Samuel Gompers, founding head of the AFL.[14]

As the possibilities of Walter Hines Page and *World's Work* faded, English still sought a patron or mentor. This time he turned to a figure who was more accessible, if slightly less reputable. Arthur Brisbane was a son of the Albert Brisbane who founded Associationism, "a veritable popular front of reform" of the 1840s. As the father had spoken through Horace Greeley's *Tribune,* the son was now editor of William Randolph Hearst's *Evening Journal* and unofficially the ambassador of the politically ambitious Hearst to the reform community. Although he was more of a propagandist than a believer, Brisbane talked and wrote a good enough game to be welcomed as an ally at the University Settlement.[15]

English had already placed a calling card on Brisbane's doorstep with his article in *Wilshire's* proclaiming that the Hearst press, despite its tawdriness, was one of the forces aiding socialism and unionism; Brisbane, he declared, "brilliantly points a moral to the men and events of the day." Brisbane in turn flattered English, who reported to his parents: "I have a strong impression he would back me up if I went into Independent politics here, which might happen—some day when I am wiser. He gave some good ideas about writing, is modest, splendidly educated and a good fellow." A week or two later, he added: "Everything is going beautifully. Brisbane has written me three times since I saw him besides saying some most complimentary things. He is to lunch with me."[16]

Brisbane's friendship was not disinterested. Brisbane's boss, Hearst, not content with his avocation of occupying (when he chose) a seat in Congress, had now set his sights on the presidency. His seven newspapers were of course solidly behind him, but Brisbane had assigned himself the task of consolidating support on the elite left. English wrote to his father in February 1904: "We are all very much interested in the Hearst Campaign. Stokes has come out in an open letter for him and we have all shown our interest in one way or another."[17]

Stokes, it turned out, was the real object of Brisbane's flattery and English found himself a supernumerary. When Brisbane's newspaper, the *Evening Journal*, published Stokes's open letter supporting Hearst, it buttered up Graham with the headline, "Brilliant Record of J.G. Phelps Stokes," and compared him to the sainted Tolstoy. English was not among the guests at "a little dinner party" that Stokes gave that same week, although both Brisbane and Robert Hunter were there.[18]

After February 1904, Brisbane's name did not further appear in English's letters home. Brisbane remained an acquaintance, but if English ever had any hope that Brisbane—or perhaps any other senior sponsor—was going to launch him into the greater world, it now had faded. He finally had to shrug off the idea of being a protégé.

Despite its uncertain beginnings, English Walling's new career as a magazine journalist gradually gained momentum. While his writing lacked fluency or grace, he was industrious, energetic, and productive. Equally important, he found two dependable outlets among smaller opinion magazines.

One was the weekly *Independent*, based in New York, hospitable to diverse views and friendly toward young and inexpensive writers. A Protestant journal founded before the Civil War, the *Independent* had been reinvigorated and secularized under Hamilton Holt, himself a former University Settlement resident, without losing its moral sternness or, for that matter, winning much circulation.

There was also the *World To-Day*, remarkably similar to the *Independent* in tone and stance, published at the University of Chicago. The *World To-Day* had started as a kind of monthly encyclopedia but, under the editorship of the theologian Shailer Mathews, had steered toward current affairs. Like the *Independent*, it was friendly toward lesser-known writers.[1]

English made his first appearance in each magazine in March 1904. The *World To-Day* article was a continuation of his *World's Work* report on the New York construction trades; it may have been rejected by *World's Work*. The article in the *Independent* of March 10, 1904, was a departure for him: a nine-page on-the-scene report on the strike in the silver mines at Cripple Creek, Colorado. The context of the article did not make clear precisely when he had visited Colorado, but it must have been during the winter of 1903–4.[2]

He was clearly pleased with his progress when he wrote to his father at the end of March on returning from a short trip to the Bahamas: "The two articles printed this month in the World To-Day and the Independent both received favorable comment from the press. I am learning how to get more red and yellow in as the World's Work advises without endangering my reputation for fairness." A second *World's Work* article appeared in May 1904. This appearance was to be his last in the magazine. Page may have recognized English's prose could not easily be polished to the right degree of slickness, and English may have decided he did not want to work in the world of the new magazines where editors dictated and writers executed.[3]

By the spring of 1904, English, always competitive, had fixed on a new target for emulation: "I really believe I will pass Ray Stannard Baker one of these days and he is the only man well ahead of me in this work." Baker was a formidable rival. Seven years older than English and light-years farther into his career, Baker was one of the stars at *McClure's Magazine*; he too was writing about organized labor, less out of sympathy at this point than out of a conviction that unions represented still another form of monopoly.[4]

Baker's publisher and editor, S. S. McClure, had declared—in a January 1903 editorial later called the opening fanfare of muckraking—that his magazine was on a mission to expose a new era of lawlessness. Baker's contribution in that issue was an article on the anthracite strike of 1902–3, "The Right to Work: The Story of the Non-striking Miners," given equal billing in the issue with an installment of Ida M. Tarbell's history of the Standard Oil Company, and the Minneapolis exposé in Lincoln Steffens's series, "The Shame of the Cities." Where English and his associates—particularly Walter Weyl—had sympathized with the coal strikers, Baker took the part of the miners who opposed the strike.[5]

English's feelings of rivalry grew from a supposed grievance, of which Baker was no doubt unaware; indeed, he probably remained utterly oblivious of his junior competitor. Baker sometimes visited the University Settlement and gave Ernest Poole, among others, advice about writing. No doubt he also talked with English. In a letter to his father in February 1904, English wrote: "This time I was very careful not to give Mr. Baker any of my detailed facts, but I had a long talk with him, trying to make him see a new point of view with considerable success. His standpoint is so different from mine that he is not likely to look at anything the same way, and of course, I did not give him any of my 'stories.' "[6]

The implication was that after an earlier meeting Baker had helped himself to some of English's material. English did not specify just which work was involved, but in November and December 1903 Baker had published articles on the New York buildings trades unions, the subject both of English's earlier article in *World's Work* and of his subsequent article in the *World To-Day*. English may have concluded that he had talked too much.[7]

This sequence established a pattern that lasted a year, with Baker seemingly dogging English's footsteps or, less frequently, with English trying to catch up with Baker. Every labor story that English wrote for the *Independent* or the *World To-Day* in 1904 had a parallel in a Baker story for *McClure's*, and each one, when English read it, must have been a lesson to him on getting ahead in the big magazines. Not only was Baker given more space, but he was a more skillful reporter and storyteller, more centrist politically, and of course more of a name.

The most direct competition between master and novice occurred over the Cripple Creek strike. The struggle there had begun in earnest in August 1903 when the radical Western Federation of Miners called a strike at Cripple

Creek, which produced two-thirds of Colorado's silver. The strikers faced a coalition of the mine owners, an anti-union Citizens' Alliance, and the Colorado state government. In December, the governor declared the strike a rebellion and proclaimed martial law.[8] English wrote two articles on the strike for the *Independent,* in March and August 1904, while Baker's article, "The Reign of Lawlessness: Anarchy and Despotism in Colorado," was published in *McClure's* for May 1904, midway between the two by English.

In technique if not in substance, English was far outdone. English's first article, "The Great Cripple Creek Strike," was matter-of-fact in tone, impartial while somewhat legitimizing the miners' position, comprehensive in scope but stumbling in presentation; it reflected neither the turbulence nor the passions of the little labor war. Baker's narrative was at the same time more skillful and less direct: positioning himself as a witness passing moral judgment on behalf of the public, he was critical of all parties. He decried the abuses of strikers' civil rights under martial law, but in the end managed to load onto the union the bulk of the blame. English's second article could be read as a response to Baker's; it largely absolved the union and argued that martial law was a strike-breaking device. In fact, martial law did ultimately crush the strike.[9]

Cripple Creek was not yet the end of the contest. English also wrote on the rise of employers' associations and the open-shop movement—both a flatly factual report in *World's Work* and a tract in the *Independent* titled "The Open Shop Means the Destruction of Unions." The latter was so outspoken that he had to reassure his father that he was not subscribing to the heresy of the closed shop—union membership as a condition for being hired. English argued to him: "The Open Shop, while it may also be right and just, is favored by business men not on these grounds but for business reasons. . . . I claim public sympathy should lean toward the men because they are the more important factor."[10]

Inevitably, Baker was on the same track and two months later published in *McClure's* a longer, more skillful—and impeccably neutral—article on the open shop. As a final twist, Baker invaded English's home territory on the Lower East Side for a sympathetic study of unionism in the garment industry. Paradoxically, Baker was moving closer to English's stance on unions and incurring increased resistance at the magazine. *McClure's* killed several of Baker's more sympathetic labor manuscripts and finally moved him off the labor beat entirely.[11]

Although English now no longer needed to worry about having his toes, or heels, trampled, he too moved away from on-site labor reporting. He apparently stopped only briefly in Chicago during the great packinghouse strike of 1904; in any case, he did not write about it. That opportunity was seized upon by his nimble colleague Ernest Poole and, of course, by Upton Sinclair, who used the strike as the basis for his novel *The Jungle.* English stayed at the Nebraska ranch in the summer of 1904, traveled to Cripple Creek for his second *Independent* article, tracked elk and "killed several against the laws of Wyoming." He also finished an essay, "twice as long as expected," on organizing unskilled workers; it later appeared in the monthly *Annals* of the American Academy of Political and Social Science. His discussion remains notable for identifying the schism between trade and industrial unionism that tore open the labor movement thirty years later.[12]

Still in the West in August 1904, English received a twitting letter from the head worker at the settlement. Congratulating him on his Cripple Creek article, Hamilton could not refrain from an implicit reprimand, asking "whether your plans for the next year will keep you out of town as much as this."[13]

Despite such prodding, English, Poole, and Brubaker continued to consider themselves residents, and English returned to the settlement in the fall of 1904. During the summer their colleague Leroy Scott had left to return to magazine work, but maintained a tie to Eldridge Street by marrying Miriam Finn, an immigrant and worker at the settlement. His replacement was Kellogg Durland, who arrived with a worthy record of settlement work in London, Edinburgh, and Boston, lectures at the Sorbonne, a book on Scottish miners, and writing for the *Boston Transcript.* But his recommendations were strangely flawed. and Hamilton wrote that he was hiring Durland "with all his faults." The faults were not specified, but trouble dogged Durland throughout his brief stay.[14]

There was another newcomer. Arthur Bullard, a Missourian, quit Hamilton College in upstate New York after two years to get closer to real reform. When he first came to the city, he did probation work, then a function not of government agencies but of the private New York Prison Association. Bullard and English were soon close friends.[15]

After merely pausing at the settlement, English took flight again. He was in Chicago talking with labor leaders when Theodore Roosevelt was elected president over Judge Alton B. Parker, who had beaten Hearst for the Democratic nomination. On the day after the election, English wrote an analysis of the labor vote for the *Independent* and caught a train with union delegates to the AFL convention in San Francisco. He reported on the convention for the *World To-Day.*[16]

At the end of 1904, English could count his career as a writer a mild success. In a relatively few months, he had established himself as an acceptable analyst of the labor movement and of labor economics, and had displayed both reporting and scholarly credentials. The tacit rivalry with Baker had sharpened his performance and output. He was now in full stride as a freelance writer, not for the money—the fees, if any, were minuscule—but for the placements, for making himself a recognizable voice in the great economic contests—the "class war"—of his time.

Despite his apparent commitment, an underlying restlessness was already showing itself. He could not stay with one subject or in one place for long. Intensively as he might work on the subject at hand, he showed himself always ready to move to something that looked more urgent, more challenging, closer to the heart of the times. And so it was with his labor journalism, which he abandoned early in 1905 for the next thing.

On Monday, January 23, 1905, New York newspapers broke out in headlines about the slaughter before the Winter Palace in St. Petersburg. The *New York Times* story began: "This has been a day of unspeakable horror in St. Petersburg." Thousands, led by a Father Gapon, had sought to petition the czar and had been answered by gunfire; dozens, perhaps hundreds, fell. Both the Russian ambassador in Washington and, curiously, the American ambassador in St. Petersburg tried to explain away the event by blaming the victims. But explainers were lost in the clamor; for the time being, the incident was utterly self-defining.[1]

On the Lower East Side of Manhattan, wild excitement reigned Monday night as the exile branches of rival Russian revolutionary parties debated the significance of the event. Who was Father Gapon? Was this really the start of a revolution? Abraham Cahan, editor of the Yiddish daily, *The Forward*, was sure that it was. The Bund, the Jewish Social Democrats, flocked to headquarters on East Broadway to hear a message from their central committee in Geneva announcing cooperation with the other radical parties. A committee was dispatched to nearby Clinton Hall to offer friendship to the Revolutionary Socialists meeting there. After speeches and the singing of the "Marseillaise," the meeting disbanded. "Few, however, went to their homes," Arthur Bullard reported. "All night long the *cafés* were crowded and over their strong tea and wine cakes excited groups discussed the outlook."[2]

What came to be known as "Bloody Sunday" also had a deep impact at the University Settlement. Bullard had already become treasurer of the New York Society of the Friends of Russian Freedom, which had invited representatives of the revolutionary parties to come to America to raise money. Thanks to introductions by Cahan, Ernest Poole, always first to seize an opportunity, had obtained the first English-language interview with the best-known of these visitors, Katherine Breshkovsky—"Babushka," or Grandmother, as she was known—a daughter of a noble family who turned revolutionary and spent years in Siberian exile. Poole turned out a long, dramatic story for the weekly *Outlook*.[3]

Before the end of the Monday after Bloody Sunday, Poole was contriving to get himself to Russia. He hurried uptown to the offices of the *Outlook*, for which he had covered the Chicago stockyards strike, and prevailed on its editors to designate him their Russian correspondent—never mind that he had never been in Russia and did not know the language. It was enough that he was ready to go.[4]

English Walling stepped into Poole's preparations as a kind of mother hen, clucking over him while Poole arranged passage, interviewed as many exiles as were available in New York, obtained letters of introduction, and packed. On Friday night, January 27, English assembled a farewell party at the Little Hungary Café, and they drank and talked and sang until long after midnight. On Saturday morning, with New York digging out from a blizzard, English hauled his fellow residents out of bed and down to the pier. A representative of the *Outlook* stuck a letter of credit and a passport in Poole's hand; he boarded, and was on his way. English may have had rueful thoughts as he waved good-by. He believed Poole was immature and unprepared, but Poole was bound for Russia and he was not. To have departed in a flurry was simply not English's way.[5]

English had advised Poole to disguise his first article by incorporating it in a fake business letter, starting with enough dull stuff about selling shoes to make the censor nod. It worked well enough, and " 'St. Petersburg Is Quiet' "—a sardonic title—appeared in the *Outlook* in mid-March. Thereafter Poole sent back stories without pause, and English faithfully had them typed, proofread, and sent on to the magazine. Ultimately, Poole produced more than twenty articles from a trip of two months.[6]

English spent the early months of 1905 cleaning up obligations old and new. He gave up his administrative posts in the Women's Trade Union League. He assisted briefly in the planning for the new Intercollegiate Socialist Society, and his name was signed to its organizational call after he left the country. He corresponded with Richard T. Ely, the academic empire builder at the University of Wisconsin, and agreed to ship Ely bundles of socialist literature from Europe. Possibly most important, his first significant theoretical article on socialism appeared in the *International Socialist Review.* "An American Socialism" attempted to wrench the basis of socialism away from Marx and hand it to his old mentor, Veblen. His reward was to be attacked vehemently and at double the article's length by Robert Rives La Monte, the periodical's reigning intellectual, who scoffed at English as equally ignorant of Marx *and* Veblen.[7]

But by the time the attack appeared, English was long since departed. Having swung through Chicago to say good-by to his parents, he was ready to go by the end of April. He may not have planned every step, but at this point he knew at least that he would be gone a long time and that he wanted to reach Russia at the end of the summer. But he did everything at a different pace from Poole; for English, there would be no rush to catch the next ship or to imitate Poole's anecdotal journalism. Poole's later recollection of his expedition to the Caucasus and back as a "glamorous writing adventure" was the antithesis of what English had in mind. The danger, of course, was that he might take so long in preparation that there would be no revolution left when he got there.[8]

His first step was to hook up in London with Poole, just back from Russia. When English arrived, Poole, who had been writing furiously to finish a Russian series for the *Outlook*, was ready for a break. English no doubt arrived laden with news from the settlement, especially the splash made in the press by Graham Stokes, who had just become engaged to Rose Pastor, the poor young reporter for the *Jewish Daily News* who had been sent to interview him two years before.[9]

In June, English and Poole moved on to Paris, and English reported to his parents that he and Poole were going to live just beyond the western terminus of the Metro, "at a little hotel at Neuilly at the corner of the Bois de Boulogne." He dropped a hint, backhandedly, that he was having second thoughts about Poole as a traveling companion: "Ernest is hardly the man friend to lean on [that] Mother desired but he is perhaps better. He looks to me as an older brother and I feel the responsibility. He is 25 and knows less in every way than I did at that age. [English was now twenty-eight.] But we are in entire sympathy. He has a splendid disposition and everybody is interested in his talent. Of course his work is purely literary."[10]

He and Poole paid calls on French socialists, among them Jean Longuet, a grandson of Karl Marx, and they went about with David Graham Phillips, the former journalist whose novel about political corruption, *The Plum Tree*, was selling well in America. "Read it," English advised his parents. "He knows everybody at Washington and has drawn sketches to the life of Hanna, McKinley, Aldrich, Roosevelt and the whole gang. He has no use for any of them but is very moderate in his expressions."[11]

He assured his parents that he was not idling: "Several American friends and periodicals expect me to write or bring back a more accurate, up-to-date and judicial view of social conditions on the continent. I shall not disappoint their expectations." Later in the month he wrote, "Everything goes better and better—I make friends, I learn French."[12]

He said nothing about one new friend. He encountered Anna Berthe Grunspan one evening near her home on the Quai de l'Hôtel de Ville. By her account, he approached her as she and a woman friend were walking, and asked, in stumbling French, whether she was not "Hebrew." She said that she was, and he exclaimed that he was very fond of Hebrew ladies, the brightest and prettiest in the world. He gave her his card and he seemed so pleasant that she went with him to the Fête de Neuilly, an amusement park near his and Poole's hotel. There he spent more money than she was accustomed to seeing and laughed off her protests.[13]

Anna Berthe Grunspan was at the time sixteen or seventeen years old, an immigrant who had arrived in France with her mother and younger brother. Two brothers remained behind in Russian Poland. She recently had left school to become a shopgirl. She lived with her family in quarters so humble that, she recalled later, she tried to keep English from paying a call. He began to see her several times a week, then every night. They entered a sexual liaison that, in his account, began within a few days at his and Poole's rooms in Neuilly. He persuaded her to quit her job, assuring her that he would give her money equivalent to her pay.[14]

At the end of June, friends from the settlement crowd—Arthur Bullard, Howard Brubaker, Poole's elderly roommate, Fred King—turned up, and they went hiking in the Swiss Alps, savoring the long, glorious summer of the traveling classes. English left Anna Berthe Grunspan behind and came along, but quit abruptly. Poole recalled: "I remember vividly a walk that he and I took together, that last afternoon, up a broad winding mountain road, with snow peaks towering high above us. He told what he hoped I would do with my life. He was dreaming of grand new worlds for us all beginning to open far ahead, with summits like those mountain peaks. That evening in our little hotel he asked us not to come to his train. He smiled and said: 'I hate good-byes.'" English may have been expressing his usual abhorrence of sentimentality but was also avoiding explanations, for his good-by to Poole was indeed definitive.[15]

Nor did he tell his companions or his parents where he was going. He was off to eastern Europe, at least in part because, he wrote later to his parents, he "had an offer of company," but he did not identify the companion. His destination was Poland, and his traveling companion was Anna Berthe Grunspan. The trip combined journalism, humanitarianism, and sex. Before leaving Paris, English went to the American embassy for passports, and swore (shakily, by his own later admission) that Grunspan was his wife. His humanitarian mission was to help get her two older brothers past Russian border guards and into the west.[16]

As for journalism, on June 23, Cossacks had attacked and killed Jews at Lodz, Poland; English received letters and cablegrams from Paul Warburg and Jacob Schiff, New York investment bankers who were patrons of the University Settlement, asking him to look into the situation. He benefited from his months of preparation. As he wrote later, "I was armed with confidential letters from New York, London and Paris to Revolutionists of every variety." There might have been danger in carrying such letters across the Russian border into Poland, but he evinced the conviction of invulnerability common to Americans of his class and time, and assured his parents that he was utterly safe.[17]

They stopped overnight in a hotel in Berlin. Later Grunspan was to present a tale of shocked sensibility. After she had gone to bed, he entered her room and made it clear that it was his room, and his bed, as well. She did not protest or cry out, she said, because she assumed that they were engaged and perhaps this was the American way of engagement. For his part, he recalled the night as simply a continuation of what had begun in Paris.[18]

There was an incident at the border as they left Poland, accompanied by Grunspan's two brothers. When the time came to persuade the border guards to let them pass, she recalled, he hung back and she went into the guardroom with the captain and, she said, pleaded emotionally. His account was roughly the same, but carried the innuendo that she might have offered the guard a sexual favor for his cooperation. The four of them went on to Leipzig, then Switzerland. He sent the Grunspans on to Paris and turned to his writing.[19]

On his return, English exuberantly unveiled his adventure—part of it—to his parents: "The trip prolonged itself to three weeks but I have material for two articles and two newspaper letters of the lighter kind (not exactly light though) that you both recommend. In Krakau and Warshaw [sic] I was dined and wined and treated like a prince. . . . I made a hit everywhere and have fine connections when I go again."[20]

Later in the month, he reported to his parents that by dint of "over-work" he had finished five articles, three of them on Poland. Given the slowness of transatlantic mail and of magazine deadlines, the best of these did not appear until more than three months later, in the *Independent*. "Revolution in Poland" drew on his contacts with former socialist exiles who had returned to Poland to support the uprising; he portrayed them as representing a paradox: a moderate political program pursued by extremist means. He referred coolly to the hundreds of executions of czarist police by terrorists. The article had no overt eyewitness component, but it was compact, vivid, and revealing.[21]

As if to compensate for his impulsiveness in rushing to Poland, English carefully plotted out the rest of the year. On July 26 he was going to Basle "to change partners." His new traveling companion was Henry Moskowitz, whom he had met at the University Settlement. Moskowitz, like Poole, was younger than English, but probably seemed older; he already had considerable status not only as a scholar but as an organizer and reformer. An alumnus of the University Settlement's boys' clubs, he had become at nineteen the head resident at the Down Town Ethical Society, sponsored by the Ethical Culture Society, the non-deistic offshoot of Judaism.[22]

English praised Moskowitz, after his fashion, to his parents: "A Roumanian Jew by birth he is among the most genial of that genial people. A pet of the rich and active Ethical Culturists in New York he is full of all that is high-minded and serious." English explained that he would pick up his companion's expenses ("and being raised in poverty they are not much") and that they would travel in Bohemia, Galicia, Roumania, and Hungary ("that is, esp. the Jewish parts") while Moskowitz taught him German and "a few elements of the Jewish dialect that I need."[23]

Although his plans had pointed him toward Russia for half a year, English had done nothing to clarify his status at the University Settlement. Back in New York, James Hamilton, the head worker, decided late in the summer of 1905 that he had had enough of absentee writers. With half of his residents touring Europe, he issued an interdict. He sent English a letter announcing stiffly that he had established new work and residence requirements and that Walling, Poole, and Weyl, the three most frequent absentees, would have to count on finding lodging elsewhere when they were in New York—that they were in effect evicted in favor of "residents who can regularly be relied on." In the margin of the file copy of Hamilton's letter, Albert J. Kennedy, a later head worker and would-be historian of the settlement, wrote: "The poor old headworker & the bright boys. Life from the point of view of a landlord."[24]

English gave no sign in his letters that he took note of his banishment. He was deep into his new role of roving scholar-foreign correspondent, studying, traveling, writing copiously.

The fall passed largely according to plan, once he had addressed the difficult Grunspan matter. He saw her during two weeks he spent in Paris, but she threatened a scene when he left late in the summer. As he later retold the story to himself in preparation for testimony: "I therefore take her to Geneva and tell Bullard the whole situation. He meets her and agrees she has no special charm though sociable as the French are." He had no intention that she should become his permanent companion, but she declined to leave voluntarily. Ultimately, he took her to the station and, with great difficulty, put her on the train back to Paris. He claimed later that he told her at that time that their affair was ended. Later in the year, as a kind of settlement, he paid her way to London for training in English secretarial skills.[25]

English set off with Moskowitz late in August. In Bohemia, part of the Austro-Hungarian Empire, they met Alice Masaryk and her brother Jan, destined to become, after the Great War, the president of Czechoslovakia. They attended the Socialist Congress at Jena: "We sat on a platform with [Masaryk] while he addressed 25,000 people for universal suffrage and against monarchy and aristocracy." English shipped bundles of socialist literature back to Professor Ely at Wisconsin and, from time to time, notified his parents of his whereabouts and assured them of his brilliant prospects. From Roumania: "I shall, with my improved French & German, write some very interesting articles on conditions in these countries. Gompers has begged me for more and Everybody's [a popular muckraking monthly] has also approached me."[26]

At the end of September, Moskowitz went off to his university and English informed his parents that he was changing his "*ethical* for an *esthetic* companion": Oden Por, a Hungarian exile. From the Grand Hotel Hungaria in Budapest he reported that Oden Por was translating his article on universal suffrage for a Hungarian magazine: "It is a hot one. I show that our shortcomings are due to the trusts, corporations and other 'business' elements and not to our democracy." A week later, he wrote to his mother from Agram (later Zagreb), Croatia, that he had sent off the family Christmas presents, adding, with the ethnic slanginess he used in writing to his parents: "Tell Father we 'jewed' the Turks down to beat the band—leaving the store, etc."[27]

He did not confide fully one important component of his plans for the fall. He mentioned that some of his New York friends had turned up in Switzerland, but the senior Wallings were not immediately made aware that his purpose was to establish a base in Geneva for a syndicate to supply news about the Russian revolution to America. Arthur Bullard, who had left the settlement and arrived in July, was put in charge and was designated to study Russian. "God help him," English remarked. As for himself, he was now fixed on going to the center of revolution, St. Petersburg.[28]

PART THREE

Converging on the Revolution,

1905–1906

Late in the winter of 1905, Anna Strunsky's yearning to go to Russia seemed idle, simply another dream that would remain unfulfilled. But the revolution at least pulled her out of isolation as a struggling novelist, and she resumed her old role as an orator and agitator. A few days after she heard about Bloody Sunday, a couple named Maievsky, Russian exiles, came to her retreat on Kings Mountain and proposed that she join them and several Berkeley academics in a magazine, "Russian Review," designed to provide discussion of the revolution. That idea faded, but she eventually kept a promise to start a chapter of the Friends of Russian Freedom when she returned to San Francisco.[1]

The revolution, or the thought of playing a role in the revolution, raised her emotions to a high pitch. She wrote to her confidante Katia:

> I cry, Long live the Revolution, and would gladly shed my blood in the field. Would that it could be, sweet sister! . . .
>
> Ah, Katia, I am hungry for you all! I want more, more of this world. I want to rush to it, away from myself! The peace and beauty of this mountain are not enough to content me, my work is not enough, nor the love I get or give. I am a clamorous thing, "a seething bit of ferment," as Jack would say. I know that I am spilling heavy drops from the wondrous cup, and I cannot break it, I who have broken much.
>
> Well, dearest, do not distress yourself for me. I am thought young and gifted, on the threshold of a great career and in the heart of a great love.

But at this point, she suggested ruefully, there was no great love.[2]

Days later, she came down from the mountain to the Stanford campus, and descended into her old morbidity. When the residents of Robles Hall sang "The Spanish Cavalier," she remembered that it was the favorite song of her sister-in-law, Mary, dead two years. On February 18, she received word of another death: "February 8, 1905 Wednesday, in Brooklyn, by accidental gas asphyxiation, Robert Wilson, age 36," she wrote in her diary. "I wish I had died before this news came to me." She plunged into a frenzy of soliloquized grieving that lasted weeks and was not exorcised until a memorial service more than a month later. She returned to Kings Mountain and poured page after page of self-recrimination into her diary.[3]

Wilson, a few years older than she, was a friend from childhood who had eventually offered himself, perhaps at the time she was most deeply involved with Jack London. She berated herself: "I refused myself to him. I was blind with worldliness. I chose the more fortunate, the gayer and they in turn refused me, so that we suffered together and in the same way, my lover and I." She assured herself frantically that he had been her real love and promised that she would be his in another life, only to remember that she did not believe in a hereafter.[4]

Possibly all this rage for grief was a displacement of her other disappointments, but two years later and thousands of miles away she still recalled Wilson's death as a time in her life that "I did awaken to true love"—true perhaps because impossible. Even in her display of grief, however, she could write more candidly to Katia of her other loss: "The heart is gone out of me since I have deserted Jack. There is not a thought for him, not a clinging regret. Well, so be it!"[5]

She paused in her mourning for Wilson to announce to Katia that she had completed a draft of her new novel: "I have finished my book of Violette of Pere Lachaise. I need only revise and type it now." She added, as if surprised, "And curiously it is all about death." When Anna returned from Kings Mountain late in February, she found a letter waiting from George Brett of Macmillan. He said that he had seen a clipping announcing that the novel she had once promised him, "The Cause," was nearly ready for publication, and reminded her that he had been promised a reading. She put him off with a promise to send a short story, and he responded in a disappointed tone that he would of course be interested in anything she wrote. Anna told Katia early in May: "Surely in two weeks Violette will be in Mr. Brett's hands." Brett wrote again to say that he hoped that she would soon be on a train East to deliver her manuscript. But she did not send it and many more drafts, and more deaths, lay ahead before "Père Lachaise" was truly finished.[6]

By May Anna was deep into organizing the Friends of Russian Freedom. She became chairman, Maievsky became secretary, and her own little circle of socialist friends—including two who had been or were in love with her—became the executive committee: Cameron King, Austin Lewis, George Sterling, Jack London himself. The committee's first brochure called for "sympathy and help" for the Russian people, and democratic reforms.[7]

Mailed to New York, this brochure triggered a spark—a critical spark, for it caught the eye of, among others, English Walling. Just before he left for Europe, English wrote to Anna, addressing her as "Miss Strunsky": "I almost shouted with delight at the dash with which you have under taken your Russian movement. Your leaflet is the best yet."

In his letter, English offered congratulations "on the promise of your book"—perhaps the same chimerical novel of which Brett had inquired—

"and to Jack London for his." The latter was a reference to *The War of the Classes*, a book of radical essays that Macmillan had reluctantly published to please its popular young author. He closed, "Hastily (& more) Wm English Walling."[8]

The letter did not come out of the blue. They knew each other, to a degree. Five years before, Jack London had called her to English's attention when English and Willoughby were organizing campus socialists. They had met at least briefly in New York while she was working at *Wilshire's*, perhaps when he wrote his article on Hearst for the magazine. Later the same year, English and Willoughby had attended a meeting of the Ruskin Club in San Francisco with, among others, Anna's sister, Rose, and Jack London; Jack mentioned "the Wallings" in a letter to her. A year and half later, while English was in San Francisco, they were thrown together at a young socialists' Thanksgiving picnic on Mare Island in the bay. The two of them, both voluble, became so engrossed in their words that they talked far into the night and let twenty-four trains pass through the Vallejo station.[9]

What Anna knew about English probably did not extend much beyond knowing that he was a socialist, intelligent, handsome, and well-off. On his part, however, English could hardly have been unaware of the cloud of rumor surrounding *The Kempton-Wace Letters* and Jack London's divorce. Between the lines, there lay the inference that English thought that she and Jack were still linked.

She heard from English again after he arrived in Switzerland. This time he sent a connected portfolio of postcards, views of the Swiss Alps. On the back he announced that he and Bullard had started a bureau "for sending revolutionary news to America." He said that he would send her their weekly bulletin if she would delay distributing it so as not to hinder sales to newspapers. At the end, he opened a glorious, impossible idea: "With your tremendous enthusiasm you ought to be here at Geneva." Then he seemed to turn away and said that perhaps she could merely supply ideas about placing their stories. He added, in response to something she must have written: "Now I'm so glad you are to be free. Hadnt . . ." The rest is missing.[10]

For the time being, Anna continued to speak and organize in San Francisco. She wrote an article on the women of the Russian revolutionary movement for *California Woman's Magazine*, but complained to Katia: "They have butchered it." She was more pleased with her splash in the Sunday *San Francisco Bulletin*, an article headed by a photo portrait of her almost a foot high and surrounded by vignettes of the revolution. The prose was theatrical: "The executioner is hard worked. Gaunt scaffolds outnumber the churches of that pious land, and stand at twilight, heavy with death, obscene mockeries of the laws of God and man." To Katia, Anna boasted that the article "acted as if a bomb had been exploded in S.F. I wish I had made it longer." But notices among her socialist friends were mixed. Austin Lewis disliked it because he believed the Russian revolution was going nowhere; Jack wrote: "It was *good* newspaper stuff. Why didn't you take longer to write it, and make it literature as well?"[11]

By fall, she had decided to try to go to Europe, then to Russia. She made her intentions known discreetly to friends but concealed them from her parents. On November 1, she confided to Katia: "I am working day and night to get to N.Y. in about a month. . . . I shall be in Russia in a little over two months— unless I fail miserably, which cannot be." She did not explain how this miracle was to take place, but clearly a plan was in formation.[12]

She was much in demand; her diary filled up with notes and dates: Sequoia Club, Ruskin Club, Oakland Socialist Branch, Jewish Council, Socialist German Branch. One high point was the monthly meeting on November 3 of the Ruskin Club; afterward, she wrote to Frederick I. Bamford, the host, to enlist his name on a round-robin calling for international demonstrations on the anniversary of Bloody Sunday. Bamford's widow wrote icily years later: "It is not a pleasant contemplation to know that such an amount of actual Nihilistic work was going on in our midst." Anna finally eased her lecture schedule because, as she wrote to her sister, Rose, at Stanford: "It takes strength and time. I shall speak for money a few times because I need it."[13]

The fall gave her an opportunity to bid a definitive farewell to Jack London. After Anna learned that Charmian Kittredge—whom Jack had chosen to shield while Anna was dragged through the press during his divorce—was to marry Jack, she wrote a strangely oblique letter to Charmian: "I reach for your hand across the sea which rolls between the happy and the unhappy. I find you and wrap you in love. Then I kiss you full on the lips, and say farewell. . . . We [she and Rose] slept under the stars, and all night long I ride a meteor through space. I go zipping along from star to planet. That is my honeymoon, Charmian, but the Milky Way is wide enough for you and Jack too, if you care about it." She signed it with her full name, "Anna Strunsky," both indicating that she did not know Charmian well and suggesting that she considered the letter conventionally affectionate rather than truly intimate.[14]

Many years later, Elsie Whitaker, daughter of a member of the San Francisco socialist circle, remembered seeing Anna at the coastal colony of Carmel about this time. Elsie, who must have been a waspish teenager, knew more of the gossip about Jack than did Anna, who may have closed her ears to it: "The awful part of it—I must say that I shocked Anna then by telling her a few things. When I told her about the girls Jack had been going to marry she was horribly shocked."[15]

Anna's plans took on urgency and form in November. Answering a letter in which she must have confirmed her availability, English wrote: "Indeed I hope you come immediately to Geneva! . . . Geneva is your fate, your bridge, & your best means of livelihood." As for himself, he wrote, he was leaving for St. Petersburg later in the month to "preach [in American publications] the necessity in Russia of (1) The stirring of the masses to revolt—of the lowers, to the utmost (2) Widespread battle against Cossacks and police & execution of bureaucrats (3) The most complete *political* revolution, perhaps a republic." At the end, he demanded: "Are you with us."[16]

But it was a cablegram from English (often referred to but apparently lost) that suddenly speeded her preparations. As a magazine writer retold it, Anna's revelation of the cable at Coppa's—"a little bomb of her own"— was greeted with consternation. But once it was understood that there was no stopping her, there began a hastily arranged round of farewells for her—and for Rose, because her sister was now going too. Rose's chaperonage was the price their parents demanded for letting Anna go at all—and not to Russia, they believed, but merely to Switzerland.[17]

The plans put Rose in a state of agitation, not only over the trip but over its personal consequences. Rose had endured an isolated adolescence, all but confined to her room for five years to correct a spinal distortion. She recalled, "I went almost directly from my couch to the University." To go with Anna meant that she had to leave Stanford only months before graduation—and she would have to interrupt her first real romance. She wrote to Anna from Stanford that she did not really want to go: "Oh, you throbbing great-souled thing, you understand all, sister-mine, don't you? He was here to-day. I am a woman of twenty-three years, but a child of three as to the world. I have always held it wrong for a girl who has lived in a nunnery all her life, (that is what college has been to me) to go out and marry the first man she meets. I have received a bomb of love every day for three months."[18]

She did not refer to this admirer by name but called him the "Vagabond." He was Xavier Martinez, thirteen years older than she, the talented and flamboyant Mexican-born painter whose studio was a hangout for the Crowd. The romance had unfolded while Martinez was painting Rose's portrait the summer before, and he had come down to Stanford to visit her almost every week since. When they were apart, he illustrated each daily letter with an exquisite little painting.[19]

Once Anna received her urgent summons (and had assured Rose that they would be gone only two or three months), Rose relented: "I have caught the Geneva fever from you. I am crazy to go. I would like to go without promising anything to the Vagabond and if after I have been away from his influence I still feel as I do then what a great, trusting love I shall have for him! . . . But Anna, great sister of my heart—I must go to [*sic*] you to Geneva at any cost. I must. What a wonderful glorious life God is giving me!"[20]

The Ruskin Club staged a handsome formal farewell. On November 23, thirty or so members and friends gathered at its clubhouse in Piedmont. There was music, a roundtable on public and private revolutions, a bundle of tributes, and "an eloquent and impassioned address" by Anna. Jack London, of course, was not there. He had resigned from the club when he moved upcountry to Glen Ellen, and besides he was far away: four days before he had married Charmian Kittredge in Chicago.[21]

On November 24, there was another, cozier party at Anna's quarters on Sutter Street, when Anna entertained what a local magazine called "a number of her Bohemian friends." Jack London's crony George Sterling was there and presented a farewell poem that started:

> O heart of fire! the star that is thy soul
> And with our spirits sang as star by star,
> Departing leaves a silence.[22]

Anna and Rose took the train for New York on November 28. They were seen off by Royal Freeman Nash, a socialist who had wanted to accompany them to Europe but wavered, and Anna's constant admirer Cameron King. The sisters heard later that another admirer, Rose's Vagabond, had drafted a letter advising Rose against going to Russia and declining to go there with her even should she go, because "his art was more important than what contribution he might make to revolution" and he was aware of an artist "whose head was blown off in the first assault on the barricades." A friend told Martinez that the letter contained prudent advice but was not very romantic. It was never sent; in any case, Rose never resumed their romance.[23]

A day after they left, an interview with Anna appeared in the *Bulletin*, designed, she said, to quiet sensational rumors that she and Rose were off to join the revolution as participants or even terrorists. Anna claimed that she was by no means "heroically immolating her young life on the altar of patriotism, but . . . going away to earn a good salary." She explained that she and Rose "go as journalists, just as other correspondents do," and that they would work for the syndicate while perhaps studying at the university in Geneva.[24]

This cool presentation may also have been aimed at shoring up the reassurances they had given their father; the newspaper account of the Ruskin Club dinner had more than hinted that they intended to go to Russia. Anna recalled years later that it was their mother who made it possible for them to go, and that she may even have known their secret—that they were bound for St. Petersburg: "She was always so sure that what her child wished to do could not be but right and good and that nothing but good could come from it! So she sent Rose and me from San Francisco to Russia when we wished to go, gave us her blessing, herself packed our trunks, refused to listen to all the misgivings of our friends and relatives." But the men in the family clearly did not know and, had they known, would have disapproved as much as the other doubting males in the sisters' circle.[25]

This was indeed Anna's farewell to San Francisco, to Jack London, and the Crowd. She did not see San Francisco again for decades, when the old city had been destroyed and she was a widow.

Assuming that his parents believed him to be in harm's way, English offered such sedulous reassurances as he traveled eastward from Switzerland in November 1905 that they must have been all the more alarmed. By November 28 (the day Anna and Rose Strunsky left San Francisco) he was in Poland, and he wrote to his mother: "I shall not run the slightest risks in Russia—even if I had the morbid curiosity to see the rioting I should not satisfy it as I consider myself a sort of plenipotentiary to get a truly sympathetic, deep and broadminded view of the Revolution into our press."[1]

On December 3, he was still in Warsaw. In his letter to his parents he started to describe the situation there and broke off impatiently: "There is no use going further in this. Read my coming article in the Independent." He envisioned a veritable flood of writing: "I shall begin by articles for the Independent, The World To-Day and the Federationist (in all of which I can speak freely—I may also write some N.Y. Journal editorials). Later I may try something for Everybody's or the Atlantic Monthly."[2]

On the night of December 3, seven months after he left New York, he finally took the train for Russia.

In St. Petersburg five days later, he wrote back to Chicago almost as if he were on vacation: "I have two friends in the Hotel, have met several Americans outside who have invited me to their homes as well as English correspondents. I am also in touch with most of the Russian newspapers and reviews, have a safety-box at the Credit Lyonnais and have made friends with the porter (my man for 1 rouble—50 cents). . . . There are no disturbances whatever just now—the tactics of the revolutionists even more than those of the conservatives being against it. . . . The streets are gayer than Vienna and almost as gay as Paris. It has not even *frozen* yet."[3]

He must have been exhilarated and titillated, for St. Petersburg, even in the midst of a revolution, had much to offer an American with a taste for the first class. John Dos Passos offered a succulent view of the life of Paxton Hibben, a young Indianian then serving as third secretary in the American embassy:

> St. Petersburg was a young dude's romance:
>   goldencrusted spires under a platinum sky,

the icegray Neva flowing swift and deep under bridges that jingled with sleighbells; . . .

white snow, white tablecloths, white sheets,

Kakhetian wine, vodka fresh as newmownhay, Astrakhan caviar, sturgeon, Finnish salmon, Lapland ptarmigan, and the most beautiful women in the world.[4]

English, of course, did not dwell on such pleasures when he wrote home. He was there on business: to set up his news bureau, to flood American newspapers and magazines with news favorable to the revolution, and if possible to keep American credit from being extended to the czarist government, deep in debt from its unsuccessful war with Japan. "As far as I can find out," he asserted, "I am the only English speaking person here who is even trying to understand the revolution." In a few days he had a functioning office, with two men to translate newspapers and documents, and a young Russian journalist to act as an "intellectual guide."[5]

In mid-December, he wrote again, to boast that he was going to have interviews with Gorky, the revolution's most notable literary personage; Witte, the prime minister; and Tolstoy. He was about to dictate articles for the *Independent* to a stenographer borrowed from the New York Life Insurance Company. In midletter, uncharacteristically, he gave way to apocalyptic excitement: "We are on the verge of another 1848. All Europe will be shaken. . . . I have visited the manager of N.Y. Life and the American Consul. They think we are to have the bloodiest revolution of history and that all institutions will be leveled down to the ground. So do I."[6]

There was an additional bit of swagger when he wrote nine days later to predict an armed uprising: "Moscow has been heard from. The devil will break loose here also to-night or to-morrow but I am a favorite of his." He wrote in a similar vein to Anna Berthe Grunspan, emphasizing rather than downplaying the peril: " 'Tis passing dangerous here. Soon the revolutionists will be in the ascendency [sic], and I delight in that thought. Soon the Czar's blood will run, but not until every gutter has been turned into a river of gore. Yet I, I am not afeared. I have here the most important business of my life, to make America and the rest of the world understand the revolution."[7]

In fact, English—and Arthur Bullard, who joined him in mid-December—had arrived in time to see the revolution's dying gasps. Two months before, a general strike had forced the czarist government to grant the rights that led to the "Days of Liberty," an interval when government authority weakened and Russians for the first time began to enjoy civil liberties taken for granted in other European societies. Yet at the same time there occurred a premonitory wave of sanctioned mob violence against radicals and Jews.[8]

Not long after English arrived, the government abruptly arrested the leadership of the St. Petersburg Soviet, the workers' council directing the resistance. The Soviet's new leadership called for an armed general uprising, but real fighting developed only in Moscow, where a general strike was called for December 20. In short order a ring of barricades rose in the center of the city and the czar's governor-general in Moscow called for infantry reinforcements. English again reassured his parents from St. Petersburg: "I shall not visit the scene of the trouble. Bullard is doing that." Bullard, who himself had never seen a shot fired in earnest, set off for Moscow.[9]

In the meantime English initiated the bureau's output by shipping two stories to the *Independent*, which printed the first in its issue of January 18, 1906. The magazine introduced the unsigned article as "written by a gentleman who is now acting as our special correspondent in Russia, and in whom we have the greatest confidence." In the four pages, the inherent drama of the situation—an account of secret meetings at the start of the new general strike—overcame English's usual stiffness. In his second article, published the following week, he retreated into dry analysis, and this tendency was even more marked in a third article appearing in mid-March.[10]

By contrast, Bullard's reporting from Moscow was dramatic. Slight and bespectacled, seemingly always in fragile health, Bullard was twenty-five years old, with scanty journalism experience and rudimentary Russian. But he transformed himself instantly into a combat correspondent. When he reached Moscow on the second day of the eight-day insurrection, he interviewed the revolutionaries who had kidnapped and shot the local chief of the secret police, and eventually made his way into the besieged Prokoroff textile plant, heart of the uprising. He was inside when a regiment of Cossacks reached Moscow and trained its artillery on the factory. When the final attack began, he was detailed to carry a message out through the surrounding troops, and he left with "Vera," a Socialist Revolutionary he had met in Paris.

He described their flight: "After two hours of trying to find a hole in the cordon of troops, we decided on a dash across the frozen river. As we scurried across we had the individual attention of two companies of infantry. I have decided that the only way in which to be safe from Russian troops is to get them to fire at you. Of all the fusillade only one bullet came anywhere near us. That dug up some ice a dozen yards in front of us."[11]

Despite the collapse of the revolt in Moscow, English declined to view the revolution as a failure. He stayed on to witness what he believed was a continuing national social upheaval rather than a mere military struggle against the czar. As he surveyed his personal prospects at the end of 1905, he believed that his post in St. Petersburg gave him a unique opportunity: "At last I am in a position to achieve not only some reputation but even a business success. The demand for our material comes from so many directions, magazines, weeklies and newspapers, that I could easily stay here and make it a business." He quickly added: "I am not going to make anything." Rather more daringly than usual, he went on to give his parents a short political lecture, commending America for making headway against the trusts but adding: "I do not think it is possible to take a single important step until we have done away with our old misrable [*sic*] worm eaten constitution."[12]

During the first weekend in December, about the time English left Warsaw for St. Petersburg, Anna and Rose Strunsky arrived in New York. Anna's notebook filled with appointments. There was lunch with Gaylord Wilshire, who was interested in helping out financially, and who set up an appointment for her at Hearst's *New York American.* She also met Ellery Sedgwick of the *American Illustrated Magazine,* who gave her a note to Frederick T. Birchall, an editor at the *Times:* "The bearer, Miss Strunsky . . . now is on her way to Geneva where she is to handle syndicate stories dealing with the Russian revolution. She is exceptionally bright & capable." There were visits to cousins, to the University Settlement, and to Martha Bensley, who was helping to set up a chic new cooperative, the A Club, at 3 Fifth Avenue. The notebook also filled with details on ship and train fares and schedules, not excluding fares from Geneva to St. Petersburg.[13]

On December 13, at dawn, Anna and Rose sailed in second class on the White Star Line's *Baltic,* bound for Liverpool, with still another admirer, an architect from San Francisco, seeing them off and worrying, he recalled, about "you two 'little girls' on board that huge monster." Anna wrote to Katia en route: "I have resolved never to travel second class again. We do not quite like the attitude of the men. . . . I am sending the article for The World from Queenstown." Poor Cameron King, back in San Francisco, was writing more and more fretsome letters. "Dearest," he wrote, "I think you & Rose had better get passports. All this hullabaloo of the papers about your going to Russia as revolutionists may cause you some inconvenience without definite proofs of your American citizenship." It is doubtful that his letters caught up with Anna en route; in any case, he received no response for weeks, even months.[14]

Anna and Rose paused in London where, on paying an expensive hotel bill, Anna returned to Jack London's favorite, Kipling, for a parody: "If pounds be the price of foolishness Lord God, we've paid them in!"[15] On December 23, they went to Geneva, armed with a list of addresses of exiles, but found on their arrival that nearly all of the revolutionaries had returned to Russia. The next day Anna wrote to her brother Max, maintaining the fiction that they planned to remain in Switzerland: "I am sure I can make a success of the magazine work. We will return perhaps with assured careers, and it ought to be soon, because a thing like this is successful from the beginning or not at all."[16]

In a letter a few days later to her father she talked of settling in Geneva and added: "When my book comes out I am going to give myself the happiness of buying you a wonderful Genevan watch." Next day she wrote again, enclosing repayment of her father's loan of $250, and added: "I promise you it is *not* the last money I shall take from you." She reported: "Mr. Walling sent me by telegram 1000 roubles to-day, which made $506" to be applied to bureau expenses. She asked her father to send them $25 a month until magazine payments began to arrive regularly.[17]

In her notebook on December 29, she sketched writing projects, at the same time describing her own venture: "Note for article on the effect of the Russian Revolution on the spirit of contemporary literature. 1) Incoming of the R. Rev. International effect. polit. social. literary. 2.) Democratic idea in lit. . . . 3.) The rush of literary spirits to the scene."[18]

Early in 1906, Kellogg Durland arrived in St. Petersburg from New York, still trailing his comet's-tail of trouble. He had resigned from his position at the University Settlement the previous spring, and months later the head worker felt called upon to deny the "malicious and wicked newspaper reports" (nature unspecified) that had accompanied his departure. Durland's problem appeared to be a certain aggressiveness, even gratuitous recklessness. As he approached Russia on the train from Berlin, he took the proper precaution of removing the binding of a volume of Kropotkin and wrapping the pages around his body under his clothing. But then he agreed to carry another passenger's bags at the border customs station; the man later opened the bags and showed him that they were full of hand grenades, explosives, and revolvers.[19]

Nonetheless, English found Durland invaluable. He reported to his parents: "[Durland] is a professional newspaper writer, a good interviewer, speaks several languages, is very diplomatic, knows the world and the American magazines. Since he arrived everything has been clear sailing and I have been able to do a days work every day."[20]

Unfortunately for English, Durland did not intend to stay in St. Petersburg shuffling paper. Only a week or so after his arrival, he promoted an invitation from a "gentleman of the court" to put on a uniform and tour the Caucasus with a group of fourteen Cossack officers. The daring of it appealed to him; he could see the depredations of the Cossacks "as it were, from the inside." He left that night.[21]

With Bullard also on the road, bureau communication thereafter was mostly by letter. Durland reported back adventure at almost every step: "About midway to the station we met a company of soldiers. At the command of an officer five of them stopped my carriage while a fifth [*sic*] leveled a bayonet at my breast, so close that when I threw forward my bourka to reach into my jacket it struck the bayonet point." Bullard wrote more analytically. From "the worst smelling train in Russia," he opined: "I hazard the prophecy (a very shaky one) that there will be no peasant disorders of sufficient gravity to cripple the government or to interest American editors."[22]

English was not to wait long for reinforcements. In his letter of January 3, 1906, he told his parents, perhaps with studied casualness, that he was expecting "the Misses Strunski [sic] here soon, the clever California girls." As he wrote, they were already on the way from Geneva.[23]

Anna and Rose Strunsky spent ten days at the now idle revolutionary news bureau headquarters at 27 Avenue du Mail, Geneva. Almost with the new year came another message from English Walling, a telegram reading, apparently in response to qualms: "Come some way need have no fear whatever nothing doing elsewhere get better advice." However marginally comprehensible, Anna took it as a summons to St. Petersburg.[1]

A day or two into the new year, Anna and Rose boarded a train for Berlin. There they paused to obtain American passports by falsely affirming that their father and they had been born in America; then they went to the Russian consulate, where they were issued visas. They boarded a train to the east, and as they crossed the Russian frontier they looked so harmless or so charming that the guards did not even examine their baggage.[2]

Anna recalled: "I sat in the train on the way to St. Petersburg and strained to catch every word spoken around me. . . . I drank in the language even as I drank in the winter scene; the young birches with their slender trunks gleaming as white in the sun as the snow in which they were half sunk. . . . Groups of recruits at the railroad stations, and again the scattered villages and the lonely peasant huts dotting the scene,—here were the Russian people whose rising was that moment making history."[3]

The train plodded through the night and at dawn approached St. Petersburg, on the Russian Christmas Eve. In her diary, Anna recalled: "He met us at the train, dressed in a big Russian coat and an *astrakhan* cap. I kissed him."[4]

For Anna, St. Petersburg was before all else the city described by her father where, as a Jew, twenty years before, he was stripped of his passport: "That we should be here, our father's daughters, that we should have returned with our thoughts and our dreams distilled in us for the purposes of taking part in the great reconstruction!"[5]

But she also found St. Petersburg to be a great bazaar of the revolution, in the last flowering of the Days of Liberty:

> On the streets, they were selling pamphlets, the covers of which were decorated with the portraits of Karl Marx, Bakunin, Kropotkin. In the windows of book shops were displayed photographs of Sophi Perovski,

who was executed for taking part in the assassination of Alexander II; of Vera Zassulich, the first to commit a deed of violence for political reasons in modern Russia; of Vera Figner, whose resurrection from the Fortress of Schlüsselburg had just taken place. . . . More astounding . . . were the cartoons which appeared several times a day and were bought as quickly as they could be had—cartoons portraying the Czar swimming in a sea of blood, mice gnawing away the foundation of the throne. . . . Was I dreaming? . . . Free press, free speech, free assemblage in Russia?[6]

She and Rose were immediately drawn into English's perfervid schedule. They visited halls where new laws were being debated, and stood at the edge of mass meetings of university students. There were constant visits: "All day long and every evening, we were seeing people, going together in a little sleigh from one end of St. Petersburg to the other. When we did not go to them, they came to us. In one room, we would have as guest some man of authority who came to shake his head over the deeds that were being done . . . while those who were committing them were holding a meeting in another room of our hotel apartment."[7]

Yet they enjoyed their strange "American immunity," which in retrospect she found to be tied less to nationality than to class: "We were not suspected of anything more than an objective interest in the Revolution because we were living as prosperous people everywhere live. The internationalism of the classes is at least as much of a fact—far more of a fact perhaps—than the internationalism of the masses; and land owners, bureaucrats and military or official potentates could well hope for sympathy and support from well-to-do Americans."[8]

Ordinary communication from St. Petersburg back to America was slow; an exchange of letters could consume more than a month. Cable was available for urgent news, but was too terse for nuances or explanations. The sisters no doubt persuaded themselves that they were too busy or too preoccupied to write at once. They were of course reluctant to let their father know that they had violated his injunction not to go beyond Geneva.

As of January 20, two weeks after their daughters reached Russia, the Strunskys in San Francisco had received only their letters from Geneva, concerning one of which their brother Morris commented, "You know Rosie always writes some news, but not this time." Anna had written to her father on December 28, if not duplicitously at least opaquely: "Dearest heart, I shall write you longer and better when I am more settled." Only a few days after these letters arrived, Cameron King received a letter that Anna had written at the frontier station, bound eastward from Germany into Russia.[9]

After that, three weeks passed without letters, and the family imagined the worst. The brother to whom Anna was closest, Hyman, complained later: "I could tell you of letters that mother sent me long before she suspected that you are in Russia in which she was telling me of horrible fancies she was having of smooth-tongued spies, . . . when she used to see little Rose in chains." Nor were such fears unjustified; the Strunskys had little reason to believe that the Russian government would treat their daughters as American citizens, rather than as Russians and Jews. After the family learned secondhand— perhaps from Cameron King—that the sisters had indeed gone to Russia, King complained to Anna that he had "to go up to your house every few days now and jolly your mother about Petersburg being safer than San Francisco."[10]

It was two weeks before Anna brought herself to write to her father, to reveal how she had come to be in St. Petersburg despite her promises. But that interval of two weeks had been tumultuous and fateful. A city brimming with apprehension and excitement and danger, the headiness of a great cause—all this would have affected the most blasé. For Anna, an excitable newcomer, it must have been overwhelming. Unexpectedly, it was powerful enough to sweep aside English's deep reserve as well. Mutual recognition came so swiftly, so abruptly that it was clear that the possibility must have been embedded in their minds as soon as she left San Francisco.

Their great revelation came a little more than a week after her arrival. On New Year's Eve (January 12 in the West), Anna, English, Rose, and another man—probably Bullard, passing through after covering the fighting in Moscow—went to a restaurant where a large holiday celebration was in progress. Anna recalled that the crowd rose to sing "God save the Czar!"—all but one young man in a student's uniform, sitting with his mother and fiancée. An officer at a nearby table walked over and commanded him to rise. The student refused and the officer screamed, "I shall shoot you!" "Shoot then," the student replied. At this point, friends dragged the officer away. The Americans became apprehensive: "Was this not a battlefield, too, we asked, as dangerous as that which had raged only a week before on the barricaded streets of Moscow?"

There were two shots; the band stopped. Anna saw a chair raised to strike; she and English pushed past chairs and tables, against a tide of people rushing to the exits. They thought that there had been an assassination attempt. Instead, they found the officer standing over the body of the student. They hurried back to their table and out into the cold night. They took several detours on the way back to the hotel, their sense of danger increased by the fact that the two men were carrying revolvers in their pockets, not for use but to help out revolutionary friends who were expecting to be searched. The shooting was in the papers; the Americans heard that the officer was held four days in jail and released.[11]

It may not have been a coincidence that three days later a report reached the United States that English had been arrested, the word reaching the American press through the editor of the *Forward*, Abraham Cahan. In Indiana, Captain William E. English—Uncle Will—professed himself to be not at all surprised, but said that nonetheless he was telegraphing the president, the vice president, and the family's friend Senator Beveridge. Stories in the Chicago newspapers reached the length of obituaries, and even referred to English in the past tense. On January 19, Paxton Hibben, at the embassy, telegraphed that he had called on English at his hotel and determined that there had been no arrest and that English was in no danger. The newspapers of January 20 cleared the whole thing up.[12]

But the atmosphere of danger and death had worked on them. Anna recalled her strangeness of mood in this interval—the long twilights, after only two hours of daylight, "at once real and unreal." And the curious, perverse joy that rose out of the death of the student: "We could not understand why or whence this joy came that almost oppressed the heart. We were basking in the effulgence; the Russian spirit so fixed on freeing itself, and were receiving as from the source of all inspiration a new faith. We were being born again!"[13]

Anna wrote later to her father that the incident at the restaurant "perhaps was the occasion which forced our love to our eyes and lips." To her brother Hyman she was more outspoken: "Then New Year's Eve we saw a student shot to death in a café for refusing to sing the national hymn, and our love which had been filling our hearts from the hour of our meeting suddenly burst into speech. It was baptised in blood you see, as was fitting for a love born in Russia."[14]

English would long since have "succumbed," he subsequently told his parents, but he had not ascertained that Anna was free of Jack London until she reached Russia: "The moment I discovered this I knew what to do—and—well she is no more given to promises and 'contracts' than I, but when I told her very simply and without any embroidery, in the presence of her sister, how I felt, she was quite speechless for an hour. Her sister says I spent this time talking to her about Anna—I dont remember. But directly she managed to show that she had heard and felt as I did—So—that's all."[15]

Anna described the declaration later to English's mother: "For a little while we refused to believe our hearts, and we were making a fine stand against ourselves and each other when English decided that the Russian Revolution was for the time being not the most important thing in the world!"[16]

There followed playful, empty days, with bureau work languishing and Rose trying to ignore the kittenish behavior of the new couple. Rose remarked to a friend later that everybody thought Anna was English's mistress because they kissed so much and were so jolly.[17]

Eventually the time came to let the world know. Anna's letter to her father thirteen days after their arrival was, like English's later announcement to his parents, an artful arrangement of priorities. First, she had to disclose that they were indeed in St. Petersburg, then explain why they had left Geneva, and finally she had to reveal her love:

Dearest papa,

We are in the city where you have spent so many happy and so many bitter years. At every step, I remember this; my every act is a spiritual vengeance and reward for this.

We staid [sic] in Geneva ten days then, on Mr. Walling's request, came to St. Petersburg to take up my work in the Bureau. I could have done absolutely nothing in Geneva. . . .

Oh, it is all a great dream, and I cannot speak of it yet!

I found Russia in the same hour that I found love. It was fated. Russia had stood for quite other things, but the man I love and who loves me, so tenderly, dear, as tenderly as mother, and as deeply has opened vistas before me and changed the face of things forever.[18]

Three days later she wrote again. Her previous letter could not have arrived, but it is possible that some other word had reached her parents and that they had cabled, for she defended her actions in greater detail: "If Mr. Walling had not cabled to San Francisco two months ago, but had written[,] he would have said definitely that in the end the Bureau would have to leave Geneva for Russia. I am so grateful to Fate that he thought there was not time for a letter for if we had known his plans you would not have let us go and I would not have undertaken to join him against your wish."[19]

This was at the least a rationalization, for Anna's friends knew before she left San Francisco that she was bound for Russia. By the time she wrote, her family must have known too. Not only had Cameron King, who visited the Strunskys regularly, received her letter from the Russian frontier but on January 21 the *New York World* published her article saying that she was in Russia.[20]

English wrote *his* artful letter about a week later. At the start, he maintained the impersonal tone: "I shall write on Witte, the Army, the Cost of the Revolution, the League of Russian Men, the Russian Revolution & America, etc, etc." Then he introduced his main theme: "But the thing I am really writing this about is quite another—a really very serious heart affair—my 'finish' we all believe. You know I am not 'easy' and never have been given in the least to illusions on this matter."

He went on to describe Anna: "She is considered by Mr. Brett the manager of Macmillans as nothing less than a genius in her work as writer. She is the most known speaker on the Coast. She is loved, sometimes too much, by everybody that knows her—literary men, Settlement people, Socialists. All my friends know her. She is young (26) and very healthy and strong." (In fact, Anna was twenty-eight years old, just a week younger than English.)

He saved a final revelation for almost the end: "Of course she is a Jewess and her name is Anna Strunsky (but I hope to improve that—at least in private life—but we haven't spoken much of such things)."[21]

Behind the facade of ebullience, Anna spoke to her diary of apprehension: "Henceforth I am no longer alone. I am more afraid of this than a sick child alone in the dark."[22]

The new couple's preoccupation with each other was broken near the end of January 1906 when word reached St. Petersburg of a slaughter of Jews in Homel (Gomel), a small city nearly five hundred miles to the south. Fighting had erupted between a mob—probably mobilized by the ferociously anti-Semitic Black Hundreds organization—and members of the Jewish resistance, the Bund. The mob brushed aside the Bundists and demolished or burned more than a hundred Jewish stores and dwellings, while Cossacks kept firefighters and police at bay and joined in indiscriminate beating and shooting. Fires were still burning as a regular army unit restored order days later.[1]

The incident at Homel did not differ much in scale from hundreds of others in the previous five months; the Days of Liberty had unleashed anti-Semitic mobs along with the forces of political liberation. But this was the first major outbreak since the arrival of the American revolutionary news bureau in St. Petersburg. Given the nature of the event, the story probably would have gone to Bullard, the designated combat correspondent, but he may have been covering repression in the Baltic states. The next candidate, Kellogg Durland, who had lingered in St. Petersburg only long enough to meet the Strunsky sisters and to be somewhat charmed by Anna, had left for derring-do in the Caucasus.[2]

That left Anna, who must have insisted that she be sent, and sent alone. She was the one who could speak the victims' language, Yiddish, and she may have wanted to demonstrate to English that he had not been mistaken—in the professional sense—in summoning her to St. Petersburg, that she would not be only his lover but his colleague. For his part, although he may have been deeply reluctant to expose his new love to danger (particularly after all the assurances he had given his parents that he was protecting himself), he consented. English gave her leather document cases for her papers and primed her on how to act the objective journalist, the shield that allowed the bureau access to nonrevolutionary sources.

On February 1 she set out unaccompanied for Homel. She wrote English back a wistful note from the train: "My heart has watched you and Rose all the way back to the Hotel. I have even slipped my hand in yours and gone up with you to your room. . . . I remember everything you told me and I shall obey absolutely. I shall return stronger than when I went away and happier, if possible."[3]

She was pursued by a rueful letter from Rose. English, she wrote, "never will get used to Slavonic indolence with Anglo-Saxon intentions. That is me. Oh dear Lord, see that I become Anglo-Saxon this week, aye, even Bostonian[—]anything, for English Walling's sake I beg it Amen." She fretted: "Dearest heart, are you happy? That beautiful sweet compartment. . . . I thought I would never, never, never be away from you a minute on this European trip. Are you safe sweetheart."[4]

After a long day and night on a train crossing wintry Russia, Anna reached Vilna, more than halfway to Homel. She checked into a hotel and began her work. She bought newspapers, read about the massacre in a local Yiddish journal, and hastened to the newspaper's offices, where "in less than an hour I found myself holding audience with everybody worth knowing." She spent five hours interviewing sources the newspaper staff rounded up for her. She also encountered the wife of N. I. Stone, the economist who had helped English on the economic yearbook project five years before; she, too, had returned to Russia for the revolution and was destined to leave the country with the police on her trail. Then Anna met the newspaper's Homel correspondent: "We compared notes on objective journalism."

That evening, she wrote to Rose and to English. She offered a few tender sentiments but mostly discussed such problems as whether to stop in Minsk on the way to Homel, how to get access to the police chief, and how to catch up with General Orlov, whose Cossacks had abetted or joined the massacre: "I missed him in Homel by two days. . . . They tell me his movements are easily learned in St.P. . . . I may be able to overtake him. He will enjoy having to talk with me." But the excitement broke through: "Such a beautiful, full day! Not better, but as good as the full empty days when our love was young. . . . I returned to the hotel an hour ago famished, but glowing. It was so good to be really at work, in Russia, so right and sane. I never felt more at home in life, English."[5]

The next day she boarded the train, got off at Minsk for half a day, and pressed on. Her letters and telegrams were brisk and brave but she felt trepidation as the train approached Homel. Perhaps it was when she paused in Minsk that she sent back a telegram that arrived garbled: "LOVE AND KISSES FOR KOSE ENGLISH FLOM OJECTIVE JOURNALIST=ANNA." She wondered (she recalled much later) whether her unaccustomed creed of objectivity would not lead her to make evil banal: "I feared that the spell which lies in reality might take me by the throat and force me to my knees before it. . . . I feared that I would make room in the universe for the massacre. . . . I might wander among the stricken and perhaps open my mouth to speak puny words. I might exclaim, 'So that is how it was!' the mystery of cruelty and wantonness forever dispelled."[6]

She reached Homel on February 6, ten days after the battle. At the hospital, she spoke with victims—a woman bayoneted, with a leg amputated; a girl with a bandaged face, an eye gone. In a ward across the hall were fifteen men: a youth of twenty bravely talking revolution; a shoemaker scoffing, "He is a Jew and he talks of hitting back!"; a dying boy of twelve; a man with fourteen saber wounds who had been robbed of his watch by Cossacks; a Turk mistaken for a Jew. Her *isvochik*, sleigh-driver, waited outside, but she lingered an hour. Saying farewell, she clumsily offered her hand to David, whose hands had been mutilated: "It was a cruel mistake. My arms passed around his shoulders, for a moment my wet cheek lay against his."

She emerged into a snowstorm and directed the *isvochik* to drive her to The Hole, an infamous slum rising on a marsh where the displaced from the pogrom would have to live. "Let me drive you to America instead," he responded, not as a joke but in reference to a nickname for a richer part of the city. But she insisted on seeing The Hole:

> The snow was covered with an eczema of dark hovels close together, leading downwards into fouler and fouler pits. Between them hills of debris polluted the air despite the merciful frost. Women rushed out of the huts at the sound of our sleigh. . . . Hundreds of human faces I saw in the doorways or pressed against the rag-stuffed holes which served for windows.

She could go no deeper into misery. The moon emerged; she dined and returned to the hotel carrying three bullets that had been given her at the restaurant by women who had learned of her presence.[7]

She wrote to Rose that night about the trial of being objective: "I just had a farewell visit from a Russian advocate & correspondent of 'Nasha Zhizn.'[8] He called last night. I had altogether a terrible time with him because he is a rev and he wanted me to be one, too, and I had established the idea that I was not and was bound to sustain it. God, how I hate lies!! and such difficult lies!" A fragment, perhaps separated from the same letter, goes on with the same anger: "The sister of charity, by the way, knew of the plan to kill the Jews Friday night, but was too good a Christian to give warning. However, she now squares her account with god by making bandages."[9]

Later, she looked out into the street, imagining for herself the death of the victims: "If they should come here tonight—in certain parts of the city they were still breaking windows, robbing and violating—if they should come and scatter me over the room, limb by limb, I would float out to death on a black, tossing sea of fear, forget the face of my love and the cause in which my soul believed, as if they had never been."[10]

The next day she made her rounds again: the hospital, the newspaper offices, photographers. She obtained prints showing the dead—a row of a dozen or more covered bodies with heads visible, stretching away from the camera, surrounded by a black-clad crowd so close that feet are touching the shrouds; a woman and a boy laid head to foot on a single litter, again the anxious somber faces crowding close and bearing witness.[11]

Contrary to what she had heard, she found General Orlov still in Homel, with headquarters at the railroad depot, and was able to arrange to interview him. As she passed the sentries and the anterooms, she was certain that she was being inspected as a prostitute. The general—"a fat, short personage glittering in lace and medals"—apologized for not seeing her earlier and asked why she was interested in so small a pogrom. She replied that the government must know better than the victims why it happened. Orlov pointed to a pile of papers on the table and said: "The Jews burnt the city to get fire insurance. If not for the Cossacks and police not a house would have been left standing in Homel."

He directed her to write, "It was the Jews that burnt their houses," and she wrote. He spoke of open barrels of petroleum and the absence of a crowd in the streets, proof that there had been advance knowledge; moreover, there had been bomb-throwing. "Laughter was strangling me," she wrote later, but she restrained herself: "My role was to be seen credulous and overcome by the clinking presence of the General. . . . They were to assume I was wax in their hands." She fought to retain control: "My arms trembled, my eyes swam. My pen began streaming ink over my notebooks." At the end, he asked for the name of her hotel, so he could send his photograph.[12]

She had hoped to leave immediately, but found that she had missed the last train, and would spend another night in Homel. The next day, February 8, she sat in the railroad station's dining room. At a side table sat General Savitch, an officer with a subcabinet post whom she had met the day before; he had tried to persuade her that he, unlike Orlov, was a liberal. The room and the platforms were crowded with Jews hoping to flee the city, and they surrounded her, asking questions, giving her further details, inquiring how they might go to America:

> I dropped my role of objective journalist. I felt I was seeing these people for the last time, and for the last time I belonged to them. . . . I made an attempt to sustain political respectability by addressing the General, whom I had met the evening before.
>
> "Do not speak with her!" the Jews nervously urged one another. "Do

not compromise her. They are suspicious." . . . When the train pulled up they let me board it alone, not daring to draw further attention to me.

On the train, she recalled, she interrogated herself as to whether her visit had been merely an intrusion: "and as before, the mystery of the horror eluded me. My eyes wandered from the spectacle, my heart shut itself against sorrow, my soul fled the dreadful night."[13]

She wrote to Katia, revealing to her that she was in Russia, and was in love, and that she had been a week on the road: "Dear friend, I am too broken up by what I saw and heard to tell you about it. Read my articles. I have in my bag some bullets that were brought to me by a committee of Jews in gratitude for my interest! My heart is pierced."[14]

Back in St. Petersburg, she was again enveloped in the new focus of her life. For a time, her letters mentioned Homel and urged the recipients to read her articles. But the references to Homel died out; no article appeared Nor was anything else, as the weeks slipped past, published under her name.[15]

Anna and English eventually began to hear reverberations from the news they had sent to America. After Anna's parents received her letter about English, they set aside any displeasure over her duplicity in going to Russia, and cabled their congratulations and best wishes for her marriage. English composed a cable in response ("I hope to deserve her") but because he and Anna had not explicitly agreed on marriage, Anna blushingly rejected that wording and English retreated: "Only a question of time with Anna and me." On the same day that they cabled, Anna's parents wrote, her mother in Yiddish: "I thank God for taking you so far across a great distance to bring you happiness."[1]

Her father painstakingly composed his letter in English to permit Anna to share it: "If he is the best and noblest man in the world, I am sure he is the luckiest . . . and knowing that he is beloved by you my darling I too adore him and love him with all my heart and he is dear to me, I place him in my heart where he will find room enough to be there in the same nest with all my children." The next day, he sent two hundred rubles ($103.50) for a gift to English and asked for his photo.[2]

But on the other side there was a miscommunication or tacit resistance that took weeks to unravel. About the time that Anna heard from her family, English, having heard nothing from his parents, sent them a cable about Anna. The reply from his father was startling and ambivalent: "Surprised and anxious haste always dangerous your happiness ours."[3]

The problem—and English commented that if "the matter were not so serious this would be the greatest laugh that ever occurred on any mortal man"—was that for his father the cable had come out of the blue. Dr. Walling had not yet seen the letter about Anna that English wrote at the end of January. The news that his son was in love and engaged to someone he had heard of only as one of "those clever Strunski girls" was an utter surprise. His mother wrote from New Orleans, where they were staying: "The sudden news of your cable was a great shock to your papa & he hasn't been very strong of late." His mother was at least partly responsible for the shock, for she had received English's letter and withheld it: "I may tell him (but I don't know yet that I will) that I got your letter, while he was ill."[4]

Taken aback when he received his father's cable, English replied: "Nothing done or will be done hastily why distressed." After another unsatisfactory exchange English wrote impatiently:

> Had your two cablegrams. Dont understand them. I love Anna Strunsky and she loves me. . . . Of course we shall be married.
> We are in no haste. But of course I couldn't possibly subject her to your possible veto. . . .
> What distresses you?
> You have made it absolutely necessary that we marry before our return—for fear you might have some objection.[5]

Anna took charge of soothing the senior Wallings with a letter to English's mother. She half-apologized for surprising them and acknowledged that "it was a queer time to fall in love just when English was so occupied with all kinds of princely and ministerial interviews and had plans for scores of articles and when I had come all the way from San Francisco to show what I could do." The letter must have been reassuring, both as to tone and as to Anna's compatibility, for the Wallings' anxiety abated.[6]

English too took a share in calming his parents, arguing that Anna would be good for him and his shortcomings, which he analyzed rather shrewdly:

> Now, Mother, I haven't been a fool about women at all. I've been as fond of their company as Willoughby, Father, or Uncle Will. But I've never let the romance obscure just plain friendship and common sense. That is why I have never dared to love before. . . .
> I've met a nature that I feel is quite larger than my own. That is not a new experience for me with men or with older women. In a young woman it is not to be resisted.
> Her ideas of life are mine, her ambition is mine, her friends even are mine. My faults of disposition—temper, coldness, hardness she is totally without. Her limitations are only those that must go with such a warm-hearted, high-minded character.[7]

English certainly tested Anna's warm-heartedness if, as they both claimed later, he told her around this time about Anna Berthe Grunspan. In any case, he wrote Grunspan a letter seeking to terminate the relationship. She wrote back: "Thank you for that *wicked, cruel* letter that I have just received. People are right when they say 'out of sight, out of mind.' It is so with you." She hinted that she might commit suicide, but she did not.[8]

The other irreconcilable was Cameron King, Anna's disappointed suitor in San Francisco, and he struck back harshly. For two weeks, then three, he heard nothing after Anna's letter from the frontier. Finally he sent a cable and received in response only a terse, "Everything [all?] right." At once, he suspected the worst and demanded: "Tell me exactly the whole truth about why you have not written me for more than three—now nearly four weeks. Why you have not written your mother for an almost equal time. Has it been simply perfidy or something of serious import to you?"[9]

At last he received two letters from her. In response to the first he sent an angry cable and after the second he wrote a long, sour letter complaining that not only she but her family had kept him in the dark. He conceded his selfishness ("I wanted you for my wife") but admitted that she had never given him hope. He went on, exposing some truths she may not have wanted to hear: "If you love him for himself—not because he made Petersburg possible for you, not because he has become unwarrantably confused with the romance of the struggle for freedom, not because you are lonely and he is the only friend within 5000 miles—... why then what question can there be that you have done well?"[10]

When he finally received an explanation, he reproached her for giving up her independence in exchange for money: "You write of fearing 'vitally to displease him in the end.'... And since he has been domineering enough to convert you to opportunism... it is perfectly evident that you are submissive enough in love to honor and *obey*." He even quoted her poet to her:"How goes Browning's poem / I will speak thy speech love / Think thy thought[.]"[11]

Later, he asked her to destroy the most bitter letters, but fragments survived, notably one aimed at a most vulnerable point: "I ought to be satisfied to hear that you are alive and in love once in a couple months. At least refer me to some magazines where your articles have been published. Or frankly acknowledge that you have failed to make good and are a literary bankrupt."[12]

Months later, Anna received reassurance about King from her old friend Jane Roulston: "As to Cammie, you know of what conservative, bourgeois blood he comes—but even then I think you do him wrong—he is not incapable of understanding your love—but it takes a *great* mind to find much beauty in that which gives him pain.... Cameron will find his equilibrium again soon."[13]

Although Anna and English did more planning, or woolgathering, than writing in these giddy days, their revolutionary correspondents remained busy. Kellogg Durland, who remained unaware of developments in St. Petersburg, wrote a friendly letter to Anna hinting that he would like to know her better and help with her writing. To English, he reported early in March that he was happy rocketing about the Caucasus and the Ukraine on his own: "So far as I am concerned I thrive and grow fat on irregularities." But he was worried about Bullard: "If there is anything big doing anywhere of course he wants to be there. But ordinarily, night travel, irregular sleeping and eating render him unfit for good work. After a couple of nights on trains he looks like a roué at the end of a New York spree—and feels like it." Bullard agreed that he needed a respite; he wanted to hole up in Moscow, where he could resume his study of Russian and reestablish contact with the revolutionaries whose uprising he had covered.[14]

Early in April, six of them—Anna, English, Rose, Bullard, Durland, and a Russian photographer named Lubushze—convened in Moscow at the Hotel Slaviansky Bazar, where they remained most of the month. Anna always remembered the early part of this visit as golden; she treasured the snapshots that English took of her on the hotel balcony, perhaps because they appeared to reveal a reborn Anna, strong, smiling, capable, not the doubt-ridden creature of her California diaries.[15]

Yet she remained uncertain of herself. On April 12, she wrote to Katia complaining of "too much excitement, too many calls upon my every energy, too many hopes and fears crowding on me at the same time." She had written nothing but promised "results enough as soon as I get into a quiet place for a couple of months."[16]

But there was more turbulence. Late in April, they heard about the destruction of San Francisco by earthquake and fire, but they could find out nothing about the fate of the Strunsky family. At a Moscow newspaper office, they tried to make themselves understood in German and French, but learned little. They sent cables almost every day: "We can conveniently hasten return if anyone sick or injured cable fully slaviansky bazar Moscow Anna English." "Suspense terrible cable details slaviansky bazar Moscow Anna." In fact, Cameron King and Max Strunsky had sent a cable to St. Petersburg on the day after the quake, but of course Anna and Rose were already in Moscow.[17]

At last, fifteen days after the quake, a cable arrived—by mail—from Katia, who had heard that the Strunskys had escaped uninjured, but that Elias Strunsky's business was destroyed. Two weeks after that, a letter came from Elias himself, written from Santa Cruz on April 29. As Anna reported to her new confidante, Rosalind Walling: "Of all the family he is the chief sufferer, for he is left quite without business or money and he must go to New York and begin at the beginning as if he were thirty instead of nigh on sixty." Max too was going to New York to resume his practice.[18]

With her immediate concerns about the family relieved, she began to hear from friends. Cameron King had retrieved her picture postcards from her old desk on Sutter Street and was sending them; he also sent a vivid account of the disaster. Jack London wrote about the quake for *Collier's Weekly*; to Anna he wrote tersely: "San Francisco is blotted out. I am weary."[19]

"We did not think," Anna wrote to Rosalind Walling, "when we left San Francisco five months ago we would never see it again!"[20]

Through the spring of 1906, Anna and English wrote long letters sketching their future, envisioning what they saw as an ideal socialist married life. Not unlike other couples, they built to a degree upon attractive fictions. Anna's was a vision of perpetual love and perpetual work in a kind of global Eden. After she heard from Jack London—a humdrum letter reporting that he had turned over to Hyman Strunsky six dollars in British royalties from *The Kempton-Wace Letters*—she wrote back, telling Jack about the Russian revolution, Gorky, and English. Then she staked out her future:

> You see, how my love throws me more upon the world than ever. We mean never to have a home, never to belong to a clique, never to prevent life from playing upon us, never to shield each other. This is not a theory, but a fact springing from the heart[?] of the man who loves me. He is far less bourgeois than I and I am not bourgeois. He is my supreme comrade always, heart of my heart. Our lives will show you, friend of mine, how good this love is![1]

She wrote in a similarly expansive vein to her brother Hyman: "We will never have a home—except each others arms—never let our love stand in the way of the world, in the way of any human association. We dedicate ourselves and each other to Life—that is our marriage sacrament." If they had an address at all, she added, it would be the A Club, the socialist cooperative at 3 Fifth Avenue in New York, which she and Rose had visited as they passed through New York. Even that, she made clear, would be merely a stopping place.[2]

To English's mother, she confided: "I adapt myself so easily to conditions that it may be any country could be a home to me. I really feel something like world-citizenship, and provincialism of any kind is distasteful to me, but I am devoted to the future America and I consider that my life belongs to it. English and I see wholly as one in this feeling, as we are on everything that is fundamental and essential."[3]

She saw a life of collaboration and equality. She painstakingly explained to Rosalind Walling that in her first letter she had overstated in speaking of submitting her will to that of English; she did not mean that she meant to dissolve her own personality, but was merely indicating that she would not be willful or contrary: "No, we are equals." In a letter to her family, she noted that English had now put ten thousand dollars into the news bureau, but said that she and he would collaborate to recoup: "English and I will write a book, the first edition of which will pay for the Bureau!"[4]

Yet the same letter ended on a note suggesting something less than equality: "English doesn't trust me to buy the simplest things for myself. (He is going to do all my shopping all our lives!)" And there was just the germ of the organized man's irritation in one of English's letters of praise to his parents: "She cant sew very well, finds my schedules rather difficult and is not exactly masterly in keeping address-books. But I'm used to having chambermaids to do the first, am becoming professional at the second, and will always have a stenographer or secretary of my own."[5]

But for the most part English, still persuading his parents, praised Anna enthusiastically. In a letter on the day after his twenty-ninth birthday, he wrote: "Everyone loves her at once and forever. I study—she writes. I know something of the sciences, she a great deal of literature. She is as democratic as I, as given to sacrificing the present for the future (to her not the future but an ideal). She is as determined to work and to make her work count. She loves the beautiful and scorns luxury. She loves people and is bored by 'society'—in fact like myself has nothing to do with it. She is convinced like myself that we have a right to love and enjoy life only to serve the people and we already know that we know how to succeed at this—*our work*."[6]

He insisted that Anna was already a writer of standing and achievement. In one letter, he reviewed her life, omitting (presumably because Russian censors might read the letter) her country of birth. At Stanford, he said, she had won the "hearts and heads" of students and teachers. The leading publications of the Coast had become interested in her writing and, he added, "Newspaper clippings of her fill a volume."[7]

To counter any gossip his parents might have heard, he scoffed at the notion that the collaboration between Anna and Jack London had been anything but professional and attributed rumors to scandal-hungry editors. Then he described her major work since *Kempton-Wace*: "a marvellous psychological romance—no plot and few characters—a sort of intimate autobiography (largely imaginary) written like a prose poem—every sentence quivering with the most exalted and beautiful feeling." This work—"Père Lachaise"—he considered "as good as published." Anna, he said, "is only 26—in full health and beauty." The account suggested slight shadings in what Anna had told him of herself, notably in pegging her age two or three years under his and in minimizing the seriousness of her entanglement with Jack London—a natural enough tactic for a bride-to-be.[8]

To his future father-in-law, Elias Strunsky, English pledged the equality that Anna desired:

> Anna and I begin to see our lives together in a clearer light. We are talking of our love as much as ever but we begin to speak of our lives too now. This means some very great changes on the part of both. Neither of our lives followed ordinary channels and the adjustment means a great deal. Often it is the woman that does most of the adjusting. With us it is not so. Anna is a personality and a personage in her work and the beautiful and noble influence she must have on the world means as much to me as it does to her. To-day for the first time I have even urged some of her work on her—though I know that must usually be left to her own conscience and inspiration. But I can, must and will help her. I am sufficiently differently constituted to do this and too sympathetic to utter a word that might hinder her in any way.[9]

Gradually, the plans for marriage became more concrete. She wrote to her parents that they planned to marry on the first of June, with the senior Wallings in attendance: "The reason why we want to be married so soon is because we waste so much time in good-byes and greetings."[10]

They insisted that there be no religion in the ceremony. To Rosalind Walling, Anna explained why a religious marriage was impossible, and especially for her—one of the rare occasions on which she discussed the religion of her family:

> Neither English nor I belong to any creed, and a religious ceremony would be farcical to us, at best something less than sincere and beautiful. A greater reason still is that according to the law of Moses I cannot marry English at all, and there is no Rabbi in the world who could listen to our troth without committing sacrilege! From the standpoint of the faith in which I was born I must be stoned to death for what I was about to do. My parents are very liberal yet I have heard them say they would rather see me dead than marry a Gentile. I should not record this at all for their attitude towards English is perfect. . . .
>
> The Jewish religion would unite us only if English became a Jew, and another form of religious marriage is equally impossible for me. It would mean conversion on my part to have even a Unitarian minister officiate, and it would literally kill my mother.

Her mother would not tolerate even a California civil marriage instead of the canopy, she explained, so they would stay in Europe, with the senior Wallings standing up for them before an ambassador or consul.[11]

The elder Wallings decided not to come to Europe, and the wedding date was reset to May 13—that is, May 1 on the Russian calendar. Then they might visit America, English wrote to his parents, but he wanted to be back in Russia by August: "That is full harvest time and monster agricultural disturbances are practically assured. I have notes and photographs and thousands of dollars of value financially and untold worth in my future work. All this will be used. But I must be here for the Crisis even if it comes (or seems about to come) in June or July."[12]

Another argument for getting married promptly and in Europe involved appearances. English conceded to his parents the seeming intimacy of their premarital life: "We are together all day and half the night in the same Hotel. We ought to be married. If we went back to be married it would . . . immediately result in a host of complications, inconveniences, heartburnings, strains and smaller little nuisances that puts it almost quite out of the question." In a postscript, he clarified, at Anna's behest:

> Both of us believe thoroughly in romantic love (one love) in marriage and in all reasonable restraint. We shall marry sensibly and not hastily and we shall not behave as if we were married before we are.
>
> Outwardly we have broken most conventions. We go down the streets hand in hand, we kiss one another in the sleigh[,] we live in one another's sitting rooms and sometimes go into one another's bed-rooms.
>
> Last night being my birth-day and I very tired Anna and Rose came in after I had gone to bed and read me to sleep.[13]

The bureau returned from Moscow in time for the czar's opening of the Duma, Russia's first elected parliament, on May 10. Anna recalled looking out from the window of the Hôtel France, a block from the Winter Palace, "upon that historic procession of equipages with ladies of the royal family and nobility in full court dress, the brilliant uniforms of the ministers and officers and bureaucrats of Russia, some riding, others walking, according to their means; Cossack members, members of the Ukraine and of Poland, who were in national costume, workingmen delegates, and peasants wearing sheepskins and bark boots."[14]

On May 13 Anna sat in the reading room of the Grand Hôtel d'Europe while English was in the barbershop getting shaved, writing to her brother Max and dramatically understating the occasion:

> When he comes down we will go around the corner to the Council [Consul] to be married. . . . We may have to telephone Rose and Arthur Bullard to come over and act as witnesses. . . . I am not "dressed up," no veils or flowers, just a Russian linen street dress and the travelling coat made in dear San Francisco. We read the paper this morning, all the speeches made in the Duma for the Amnesty, and we are really as much

on the way to attend a Labor Conference as we are to the Council. We are anxious to have the marriage over with however, so as to be free to see all that may happen to-day. There is talk of demonstrations.

Later, she resumed in a garden on the Nevsky Prospect:

> English has gone up to interview the Council. He went half an hour ago and found the office still closed. It is 10:30.
>
> So this is our marriage day, and to both of us nothing seems simpler and more beautiful. My heart beats a little loudly as it does just before the Chairman is about to announce me, but that is not because either of us have any fear that the legal tie will make any difference in our love. It is simply that any form one has to go through with however brief and simple is embarrassing. English is a little nervous too. We always feel everything together. . . . (What is keeping English?).

The letter again paused, and resumed the next day, much let down in tone: "We will go to Paris next week and marry as French citizens. The Ambassador here is crazy. He insists on a religious solemnity."[15]

Anna, English, and Rose left Russia in May 1906, but not before they made their pilgrimage, as had so many other foreign admirers, to Yasnaya Polyana to see the aged Tolstoy. Under a tree in an old garden before the white country house, the three Americans sat with Tolstoy, his eldest daughter, one son, a son's wife, and two grandsons while the samovar squealed. Afterward, Anna made cryptic notes in her diary—"The spiritual isolation of the great unfelt by the master, because his soul reaches everywhere." English did notes for the book. Rose all but kept minutes.

First, Rose recalled, there was some unsympathetic banter from the son-in-law about the poor reception the revolutionary writer Gorky was receiving in America. Tolstoy wanted to talk about the new Duma, and said that he had recommended to its leader that he read Henry George on the single tax. Later he commented that Rose was the first American he had met who knew Thoreau's "Civil Disobedience." They walked with him to his room and he predicted that eventually revolution would come: "But I do not speak of it. It will not bring with it what I want." At the end, Rose wrote: "We leave the family smiling and bowing to us from the veranda steps." Anna left them a copy of *The Kempton-Wace Letters.*[1]

They reached Paris on June 2. At first they stayed at a hotel on the Right Bank, but moved out to Enghien-les-Bains, a lakeside spa on the northern outskirts, listed in the era's Baedeker as "a great resort of Jewish families from Paris." From Enghien, English wrote a long, placid letter to his parents, describing their leisurely life in the little suburb—the tiny casino, the open-air restaurants, the boarding house, the sulphur baths, the forest of Montmorency nearby.

Then, engaging in a kind of introspection rare for him, he explored his views—or illusions—about his new emotional life: "Anna and I are coming to a most wonderful and perfect accord. She is as positive as I perhaps and of an even warmer temperament. We have striven with all our strength to lay ourselves bare to one another—an act that consists more in exposing our view of life and work than our own personal needs and habits that are pretty flexible in us both."

He noted seeds of difference: "Through all these months we feel we have never wasted an hour—because we have not forgotten how the other spoke or felt about any of the innumerable aspects of life we have stirred up. Certainly when I have turned myself inside out under a stress of feeling not everything has been good but it has been real. The same thing applies to Anna to a lesser degree—because she carries a great deal more of her self into the ordinary moods than I do."[2]

There was one disturbing incident. As Anna, English, and Rose walked through the Place de l'Opéra on an evening in mid-June Anna noticed a bitterly hostile stare from a woman she had never seen before. English told her that it was a woman who had been asking him for money, and Anna urged English to go talk with her. English approached Anna Berthe Grunspan and they set off on foot. Soon they caught a cab and, he recalled, Grunspan clutched at him, and he did not free himself for an hour. Grunspan later claimed that English had told her he was marrying Anna Strunsky only "for her Socialistic ideas" and that "[Anna] had been living with a man for six or seven years. I couldn't love her." However tendentious, Grunspan's account has a certain ring of authenticity—the note struck by a man who had not effectively terminated a previous commitment. When English returned at last from the carriage ride, he was obliged to fill in for Anna whatever details about the relationship that he may have omitted previously.[3]

In mid-June, the American newspapers received word of the engagement and they responded with a splash of sensation, interlaced with the usual soupçon of casual inaccuracy. A story in Hearst's *Chicago American* invoked the "famous Stokes-Pastor Romance"—the marriage the previous summer of Graham Stokes and Rose Pastor—as well as the marriage of Leroy Scott, a University Settlement resident, to Miriam Finn, another Russian Jewish immigrant. The paper promised the "Inside Story of the Romance of Two Settlement Workers." (Anna had never worked in a settlement.) Another headline announced: "Socialism Finds Bride for a Rich Yankee in Russia." (English would have bridled at being called a Yankee.) The San Francisco papers depicted Anna as a familiar local figure and English as a stranger—the *Call* making an accidental pun by calling him "William English Willing." Evoking her old identity, one headline read: "Girl Socialist Wins Millionaire."[4]

Anna provided her absent family a full account of the events of June 28. The three of them—Anna, English, Rose—met their other witness, Jean Longuet, grandson of Karl Marx, and proceeded to the eighteenth-century mansion that served as the city hall of the Ninth Arrondissement:

> There English and I had to sign our names a dozen times on a dozen different papers before a clerk, then we were ushered into a beautiful room and were seated on a long plush bench behind four other benches in which sat other people to be married and their witnesses. An old

white-haired man entered with a big red, white and blue sash tied around his shoulder. . . .

"William English Walling, do you voluntarily take the Mademoiselle Anna Strunsky to be your wife?"

"Yes Monsieur."

"Anna Strunsky, do you take William English Walling to be your husband?"

"Yes, Monsieur," from me.

"You, William English Walling, and Anna Strunsky, are united in marriage."

Then English signs his name in an enormous book as large as the book of life and I in another enormous book. Then I write in his book directly under his name, and he in my book directly under mine and Rose and Jean Longuet and the two others sign their names in both books, and we leave the room, quietly, calmly, relieved to have the little arrangement done with but feeling neither more nor less love [for] each other than before. We considered it of no more importance than getting a passport.

Afterward, the little wedding party lunched at the Palais Royal, then earnestly visited the National Library and the house of Victor Hugo. Longuet departed and the three others drove in the Bois de Boulogne and had dinner at a restaurant there. Still clinging to her doctrine of ordinariness, Anna concluded: "You see it was a regular Paris day for us. We pay no special attention to the fact that English and I have procured the legal right to love each other."[5]

On the day of the ceremony, an official Paris *Livret de famille* (marriage certificate) was issued to them. Anna was recorded as having been born in the United States. Each was listed as an *écrivain*.[6]

From Enghien-les-Bains, eleven days after the marriage, Anna wrote to her brother Max, laying out the ways in which she and English were to be unexceptional and exceptional:

> We got legally married, because we did not believe it best to run in the face of the world on this matter. But now that we have got married we don't talk of it. We don't like to remember that the law gives us a right over each other. Our love is so strong that we are not in the least afraid of being bruised by the legal form or any other bondage the world may lay upon us, but yet it is better not to remember too much the vulgarity and the meaninglessness of the promises we made to each other before the Mayor. (They were in French, and said too quickly, for us to understand.) I had to sign a paper regarding some property of English's and I signed Anna Strunsky Walling, my legal name—but all my other letters and writings I sign Anna Strunsky.

English says he gets a thrill every time he remember[s] or hears that he loves Anna Strunsky. She is a personality to him. But when he hears me addressed as Mrs. Walling, he feels queer—he hears his name with a Mrs. attached to it. It's not nice from any standpoint.[7]

Before and after the ceremony, Anna and English—Anna in particular—insisted that marriage was an incidental, but probably necessary, accompaniment to their real life's business, referred to generically as his, or her, or their, "work." In fact, they felt compelled to devise reasons why the reverse was true at that moment, that for the time being work was incidental to life. Anna explained during the last weeks before they left Russia that of course English did not want either of them ever to write purely for money: "That is why he has refused to let me do journalism. We do not have to hurry and write articles. I have published nothing, because he and I are planning to use our opportunities here in a better, more permanent literary way."[8]

In a long letter to her brother Max, Anna fended off their mother's natural desire to meet her new son-in-law: "His work in Russia is of the utmost importance—momma does not seem to understand this at all, or she would not ask us to return at this point." Then, about herself, or rather herself and English:

I assure you I am going to do some big writing. I have just learned what to write about!! When I was home I knew nothing.

English and I will write a book on the Russian Revolution. We have already begun.

As a favor to English who begged it I am revising Père Lachaise. It will be sent off before we leave Paris, in two weeks.

It was not.[9]

In her letter to her brother Anna praised English as "refined, deep, brilliant, idealistic, rationalistic." Yet only two days later she began in her diary a kind of a subversive monologue, reflecting a realization that the fictions that they had constructed might be flawed. In an entry less than two weeks after the wedding, she noted a canker:

It was an authoritative note in his voice about a trifling matter that has depressed me. Authority only means disrespect and irritation against perceived weakness in another's personality. It is not loving—it is not to be found in the spirit of a comrade. That is why the least trace of it chills me. . . .

My God, writing terrible words, and he is in the room, perhaps feeling that there is at this moment darkness in my soul. . . . He needs me less than I do him, I may be a kind of parasite after all.[10]

Yet, in her letter to her parents-in-law that same month she was ebullient: "Neither English nor I have an axe to grind, a social panacea to propose; we have no dogma that we are aware of. I think, therefore, we shall not miss our mark."[11]

She received a warning of sorts from her new father-in-law. In a long letter of counsel, Dr. Walling complained, prophetically, that English was careless of his own interests, and by implication of hers: "I know that my criticisms of English are severe sometimes—it may seem so to him—but you see he has led me to expect so much of him, I do most earnestly believe in him, I know him to be honorable, upright and correct in his life and true to those who love him. . . . The theme upon which I must dwell in my communings with this child of mine is that he is wasteful of his talents—as possibly of his estate as well—English has never gotten 'value received' for any expenditure of either talent or purse—as I see it—and it is of this that I complain."[12]

Before the end of July, Anna and English hurried back to St. Petersburg, summoned by urgent telegrams from Durland, who had been left in charge there. The czar had dissolved the First Duma, and the sputtering revolution had flared up, with strikes and mutiny in the armed forces. From Russia, Anna reported to her in-laws that they found that "reaction is in full swing now—200 arrests in Petersburg within the last few days." The new prime minister, P. A. Stolypin, was following a shrewd course of severe domestic repression combined with overtures to liberals abroad. A revolutionary they knew (possibly the terrorist Marie Spiridovna) had been jailed, but English was able to do no more for her than give a petty bribe to a guard to let her to come to the prison window for a conversation.[13]

They took a side trip to Finland, still part of imperial Russia. This was the first time, English noted to his parents on a postcard, that they had traveled together without Rose. They paused at Kronstadt, the Russian island naval base in the Gulf of Finland, and went on to Helsingfors (Helsinki), where troops had just suppressed an uprising at Sveaborg, a base in the harbor. Meanwhile, sailors at Kronstadt mutinied and held out for thirty hours.

When they were back in St. Petersburg, English felt obliged to explain to his parents how routine and safe their business in Finland had been, how congenial their rather tame companions, how minimal their contact with the mutinies. He did not mention that their associate, Durland, had gone undercover to Kronstadt days before the mutiny and had participated in a secret revolutionary meeting among the sailors.[14]

Nor did he mention that they were about to leave St. Petersburg on what was chronologically a wedding trip, but was scarcely a honeymoon.

PART FOUR

Achievement and Sorrow,

1906–1908

Late in August 1906, Anna and English traveled from St. Petersburg to Moscow, then north and west more than two hundred miles to Yaroslavl on the upper Volga. There they boarded a riverboat and floated downstream for more than five weeks and more than two thousand miles. It is not clear how many of their associates came along, but sister Rose and Arthur Bullard joined at least part of the journey; Rose recalled that she and Bullard involved themselves in a brief romance that fell flat, for Rose at least, after a few days.[1]

Their mission was to meet and study Russian peasants, the most complex and inaccessible component of the revolution. A wave of unrest in the countryside late in 1905 had sputtered out, only to revive in the summer of 1906 with the threat of famine and the return of defeated veterans of Russia's ill-fated war in the Far East. English hoped to find that his vision of a democratic Russia was taking shape in the villages.[2]

Anna's journal entries as they floated down the great river contained bits of information about the peasants, but predominantly her scrawled notes reflected loneliness and a growing fear that she had committed herself to a relationship that was already becoming unequal. She fretted over her inability to move forward with her writing. She set down pages of notes for articles and stories, only to break into meditations on what she perceived as English's coldness, fault-finding, inaccessibility. Moreover, as she told her daughter years later, theirs was a marriage that remained—that she caused to remain—unconsummated. For her, perhaps, the "white" (in Jack London's sense) romance of the days in St. Petersburg was enough; perhaps there was some physical hindrance. In any case, the references to "love" in her diary carried a restricted meaning.[3]

On the river, at Nizhni Novgorod (later to be renamed for Gorky), her mood swung. One day she was darkly content:

> English is standing at the desk—on which burn two tall candles. He is busy reading the instructions of the peasants to the Duma. The window is open and it lets in a cold San Francisco breeze. From the couch on which I am lying I see a church and beautiful clouds in a twilight sky.
>
> We have both worked to-day. We have both loved each other, and this

hour I am happy. Nothing troubles me. . . . It is only a few times in my life I have been able to feel so greatly about death, and the flight of youth, the failure of hopes, the aborted work. I remember all these things, but the tragedy of them does not reach me to-night where I lie on the bosom of peaceful love.[4]

Farther downstream, she despaired: "I am bankrupt of all ideas, helpless, without work, without aim—if I am simply the good bearer [of] man's light of love, then it is time to realize it, and say so honestly to myself, to him, to the whole world, and then quietly kill myself. What else can we do?"[5]

But at Kazan, four days later, she wrote:

Yesterday I spoke of terrible finalities—to-day, I think only of wonderful beginnings. My spirit is strong again, life has me again by the hands. I am beginning a book—a real document for the international propaganda. So it goes, always following terrible depression is happiness and strength, and following happiness and strength depression.

. . . [T]errible thoughts assail me of my loneliness, of his unfriend-liness . . . we think separately, suffer separately, he and I. . . . Why does he not ask me to speak? And suddenly he does ask, and my heart grows light as a child's. We are together again.[6]

Her lamentations resumed at Simbirsk, two weeks down river:

Every day I discover some new law . . .

To-day, it is this. That a man tires of the woman he loves, that he prefers to be away from her rather than with her. . . .

It is a knife in my heart.

Well, I shall stay away until he wants me, and then stay away again until he has quite rested from the sight of me. . . .

So love, like everything else in life is a half dead thing, half foul. I must cut my heart in two, must starve myself, in order to have a little of him—no full meal on the board, no deep draught. For one hour of his company I must spend two without him. He said he would show the world how a man can love, that I would be well beloved, but do not blame him for what he said in dearest kindness and has not the power to love. He must suffer too.[7]

English no doubt was preoccupied with amassing information for the book that was destined, it was now clear, to be his alone. As late as mid-September Anna was still taking notes "[f]or the book with English," but the notes were haphazard and impressionistic, as if she had no hope that they would be used. English was drawing away from a collaboration—the one stratagem by which, with Jack London, Anna had so far been able to complete work.[8]

Her concentration was broken by new friction. Anna had evidently turned to English for money to help relatives in Warsaw, or perhaps her own now semidestitute family in New York. He made the transaction difficult. She felt that she had betrayed herself:

> He and I are one. Yet I would a thousand times rather take money from my father, from my brothers, from Rose than from my dear love! I have to take from him—and I have needs which I could supply with very little and which torment me day and night. . . .
>
> Well, I tell myself I must work, I must earn—when I earn I shall do what I can. I have no right to what is not my own. And at this point, precisely[,] the pain comes in—I begin to feel estranged from him, distanced by a brutal fact, that he has and I have not, that there is a barrier.
>
> If I were alone I would earn daily bread and help the others—I am forced into a kind of life which under the circumstances of their need, is distasteful to me. I feel almost immoral. Something has happened to my freedom. I am no longer quite myself. I have parted through love which should have opened to doors of a thousand new spiritual worlds to me, with the dearest right to the soul, to be itself.[9]

At last they turned back. By mid-October, they were on their way out of Russia, leaving Rose in St. Petersburg to run the news bureau.

They returned to Paris. Anna meditated on her loss of independence:

> There are two forces swaying any whole nature, one to love and the other to work. I too have a "Cause" as men have driving me from love! absolving me, making love of him a secondary thing in my life, a thing more or less merely personal.
>
> Something clamors in me to stand apart from him and be myself without his aid or counsel, to reach towards him from a mountain-peak, to warm toward him seldom . . . to listen to him as a relaxation as men have listened to women, as he, perhaps, listens to me.
>
> And so the game plays havoc with the love of women as well as men. There can be no difference. . . . For between love and life there is now a gulf. . . .
>
> Within me are all the stored-up feelings created by tradition, by all my reading, by all my dreaming. Within me run springs of all love. . . . Within me is the passion created by my loneliness[,] my futility as well as by my energy, by the height of my endeavor. . . .
>
> These unite in one force which pulls me straight towards him, which awakes me [to] seek him and love him, letting all things else my soul sees wait!
>
> Perhaps it is the same with him, I say again![10]

She added, perhaps as a rebuke, an invocation of Jack London: "I write—and I write not towards him nor in the hope of making the promise of my talent good to him but for the other who praised me, believed in me."[11]

Alone in the Luxembourg Gardens, on October 29, four months and a day after their marriage, she assessed English as she now saw him:

> He is torn with impatience everytime we disagree in the least. He sees everything out of proportion. He can not bring himself to even listen—a fundamental refusal of my point of view, etc.
>
> To me, on the other hand, he often seems like a Freshman in his insistence[?] on *facts.* A date wrong, an . . . ignorance of a detail gives him cause for indescribable rudeness, attack, mockery. And he is so caught up in the elements that he does not take time to generalize philosophically. He . . . leaps to his conclusions, sometimes creeps—he is never a steady deep teacher.[12]

In a way, Anna had produced a sequel to *The Kempton-Wace Letters*—what Hester Stebbins might have written had she decided after all to marry Herbert Wace. But these letters were written to herself; while they lacked the literary gloss and distance she had applied to Dane Kempton and Hester, they were immensely more candid. Anna might have been appalled had she contemplated the possibility that they constituted not merely a reflection on the present but a prophecy.

As to how English regarded his new marriage, one of the few clues is a uniquely introspective undated fragment that could have been written as early as 1906, perhaps later. The reference to her secret writing ("she writes about me even to herself—does not show it") might refer to the journal she kept on the Volga:

> My dear Anna is distressed by our hot and strenuous talks. She calls them angry. I wonder if they are. I am struggling and one struggles against something. Is it against her? I say I am struggling towards her and against the obstacles and through the veils that lie between us. I want to think that. Sometimes I feel it is only against myself I am fighting so hard—not the imperfections in our love but my inability to grasp her. Then comes a conscious fear that she may be beyond my reach. The idea is crushing, humiliating, insupportable.

He described a picture of Anna's mother, her eyes "abstracted" as she held a child:

> So Anna often lies with me and just then it seems to me she is most loving and most herself. She is most herself when she is most loving. But her eyes are off into another world and the being that lies there in her

arms is not a child but a man. And the man is awake—while her eyes are off in another world.

Then I learn what loneliness is. Never before I knew her had I any such experience. . . . And now here comes a being, lies beside me and loves me—oh so wonderfully—how did it happen?—and travels leaps when I least expect it—off into another life. And always with love on every feature. How could I be angry.

Thus they engaged in their silent dialogue of love and disappointment.[13]

Whatever his inner thoughts, English was shaking himself free, both of the brief interruption of his routines when Anna came into his life and of the short-lived notion that he and Anna would collaborate as equals. It was symbolic of his resumption of his own life when the *Independent* for October 18, 1906, printed his first major contribution in six months. The article was the first in a series called "The Peasant's Revolution."

The article carried a Moscow dateline, and concentrated on the activities of the peasant delegates in the dissolved Duma. In the final paragraphs English offered the view that came to form the basis of his book:

Russia's desperate struggle is not a mere reaction against hunger and the Czar. It is a world event of unparalleled significance, a giant effort to win for Russia, and perhaps other nations as well, what no nation has ever yet attained—unrestricted democracy in government and equality in possession of the land—the fulfilment of the French Revolution, the limit of purely democratic evolution, the conquest of the last of the rights of man; at the same time a fierce attack at the roots of private property and the foundation for a Socialist state.[14]

Early in November, English and Anna returned to New York on the *Kronprinz Wilhelm*. English had been gone from America for eighteen months, Anna for almost a year. English sent a telegram to his father: "Beautiful passage neither sick three fifth Ave."[15]

The America to which Anna and English returned in the fall of 1906 was much changed in its attitude toward the Russian revolution. The sympathy that followed Bloody Sunday, twenty-two months before, had cooled. Maxim Gorky's ill-fated visit to New York—during which he was revealed, to the mock horror of the press, to be traveling with a woman not technically his wife—had tainted the revolution in American eyes. English and Arthur Bullard were later blamed for advising Gorky badly, but in fact theirs seems to have been a peripheral role. English's letters reveal no references either to the trip or to its catastrophic consequences, even when, almost a year later, Anna and English encountered Gorky in Italy.[1]

Once back, the first order of business for the newlyweds was primarily personal. They stopped a few days in New York and gave the Strunskys their first chance to meet English. It was also Anna's first opportunity to see them since the earthquake drove the family from San Francisco. They went on to Chicago to display Anna to the Wallings. Concerning this First Encounter, there survives a fragment of a letter from English to Rose saying that Anna had "charmed fathers soul out of his body." As to her mother-in-law, Anna's comment to Katia was a touch ambivalent: "English's mother is a dear beautiful woman. She has a very strong character." On the whole, it must be said, the Wallings responded creditably after their initial surprise. There was never any question of their affection for Anna, which sometimes seemed to surpass their regard for their son.[2]

But, as English remarked in a letter to Rose, the "welcome was not only private." There were interviews in New York with the *World* and with German- and Yiddish-language newspapers. In Chicago, Anna demonstrated that she had not lost her knack for being good copy, and now, married to a family of standing, she had social cachet as well. On November 23, Hearst's *Chicago Examiner* carried a long, serious interview with "Mrs. W. E. Walling, wife of the Chicago sociologist" concerning the prospects for the Russian revolution. Beyond this one identifying reference, English did not appear in the story. "The reporter talked to me," he grumbled mildly, "but didn't mention me."[3]

Possibly because she may have complained about being called "Mrs. W. E. Walling," she was interviewed again. A story appeared in the *Chicago Daily*

News under the headline: "SCORNS THE NAME OF A WIFE / Mrs. Walling Wants to Be Known as Anna Strunsky, Though Married." The opening of the story was tendentious or perhaps sardonic:

> Shocked Chicago society, nursing its conventionalities all the more tenderly since shafts were thrown at them by the advocates of probational marriage, and other isms that have for their purpose a revolution in marriage customs, received another staggering blow today when Mrs. William English Walling announced that to her friends she is still Anna Strunsky. She abhors the prefix 'Mrs.' and the name 'wife,' Mrs. Walling declares, because the appellation carries the sting of implied ownership. She refuses to be known as Mrs. Walling because she objects to surrendering her individuality in obedience to the command of what she calls "conventionality."

Moreover, the story went on, she registered at hotels as Anna Strunsky and received mail by that name. She found the term "husband," she said, as degrading as that of "wife." She expounded on the issue: "This taking of her husband's name by a woman when she marries is one of the symbols of the merging of her individuality into his. It is a convention against which I protest. In conventional circles I allow the calling of me by the name of Mrs. Walling to pass unchallenged. The people would not understand even if I explained to them. But in my work I desire the use of the name that means me."[4]

It is not difficult to imagine how the story reverberated in the branches of the Walling family (it was of course echoed in the Indianapolis papers) and in social Chicago, although these audiences may already have learned to discount radical statements by anyone associated with English. But in a country that professed to be shocked by Gorky's indiscretion, such a commonsensical assertion of independence—the kind of thing that Anna had been writing in her private letters all year—was bound to sound like outer-fringe radicalism. And the press, always the hypocritical guardian of propriety, made matters worse by associating Anna's not unmoral position with such practices as probationary marriage. Even so, faithful Rose, when she saw clippings of the stories weeks later, thought that when the reporter let Anna speak for herself she spoke with "sense & dignity."[5]

In this flurry, it may have been difficult to pay attention to their serious work. But on December 5, Anna and English made a joint appearance at Hull-House (she was billed as "Mrs. Anna Strunsky Walling") on behalf of a Russian socialist coalition, sharing the platform with the celebrated defense lawyer Clarence Darrow. English had two articles published that week: the second in his *Independent* series on the Russian peasants; and, for *Charities*, the trade magazine of social work and the settlements, "The Call to Young Russians," which drew an invidious contrast between the recreational and private goals of American collegians and the widespread teaching and agitation by Russian university students.[6]

Before the new year Anna and English returned to New York, first making the obligatory stop at Lexington, Indiana, to visit the formidable and faintly disreputable Uncle Will—Captain William English. Then they installed themselves in the A Club in New York.[7]

The A Club, a cooperative in existence a year or so, had become a haven for radical would-be writers and University Settlement alumni. It was more egalitarian in structure than in practice. Charlotte Teller Johnson, one of the founders, said that life there would not be "bohemian": "We have been driven to despair by the disadvantages of small flats with no room for the servants."[8]

Several friends from the old University Settlement crowd lived at the A Club: Ernest Poole, Walter Weyl (who was soon to marry Poole's sister Bertha), Leroy and Miriam Finn Scott, and Howard Brubaker, elected the co-op's first president. (It was Brubaker who named it by remarking, "Oh, just call it *a* club.") Also present were Hamilton Holt, editor of the *Independent*, and his wife, as well as the aspiring radical writer Mary Heaton and her husband pro tem, Bert Vorse. Early on, the club played host to a literary dinner in honor of Gorky and, after the deluge, when New York's hotels turned away Gorky and his companion, gave him shelter.[9]

Reminiscences of the A Club are blissful, almost Edenic. Poole recalled sitting on the stoop on warm spring evenings and sipping mint juleps from the Brevoort Café up the street. Mark Twain, then living around the corner, would "stroll over, in his white suit and great shock of snowy hair, sit down by the fireplace, light a cigar and drawl stories to our admiring group." The A Club played host to transient Russian revolutionaries, one of whom, according to Poole, stacked Poole's room full of crates of grenades to be smuggled into Russia.[10]

To the extent that Anna and English wanted a home, the A Club served for the moment. They settled there late in December 1906 for six weeks of what they hoped would be work. Early in 1907, though, English wrote to his parents that not all was work. They were going with two of Anna's cousins from Warsaw to see Nazimova in *Hedda Gabler*. On Christmas, there had been a masked ball ("deadly gay," English observed): "One Kentucky girl danced Chinese Japanese & Hawaiian dances in a manner quite bacchanalian."[11]

Still, English produced substantial writing. A story on the Russian famine appeared in *Charities*. He completed his series on the peasants for the *Independent* and wrote a sweeping call to action for the *Independent*'s competitor, the *Outlook*. In each of these efforts, he wrote with increasing authority and confidence, most strikingly in the article in the *Independent*, "The Village Against the Czar," which unveiled to American readers a theater of revolutionary activity that had gone largely unreported. After the articles appeared, a friendly critic, Anna's cousin Simeon Strunsky, who was an editor at the *New York Evening Post*, wrote to compare them to the work of the French historian Taine, and English was much encouraged.[12]

His most pointed and paradoxical observation occurred in the *Outlook* article. Referring at least in part to himself and his associates, he wrote: "So sensitive is the [Russian] Government to foreign opinion that, with one or two exceptions, every foreign writer or correspondent going into Russia has been treated with courtesy by the officials in spite of the fact that a large majority have been clearly and fearlessly hostile to the Government." The comment implied awareness of future risk.[13]

English and Anna intended to test the courtesy of the Russian government again, but not immediately. Their plan was to go first to Italy, in part to remedy English's chronic debility. In Chicago, his family, according to Anna, had told him "how badly he looks, and [he] got despondent and tired, and said he must leave America for southern Italy or he would die and we had altogether a depressing time of it." Whether the ailments were physical or, in the favored term of that time, neurasthenic (and they may have been both) the Amalfi peninsula was the prescription, as much for their marriage as for his convalescence. Even so, Anna maintained for Katia the pretense that writing came first: "I am hoping [for] much from this Italian visit because it will practically be the first chance for work—quiet undisturbed work—in over a year."[14]

On February 3, 1907, they boarded the *Deutschland* and, after pausing in Naples, greeted the spring on the outskirts of Sorrento, looking across a beach and the Bay of Naples toward Vesuvius. Much of what they did was ordinary tourism: a carriage trip across the peninsula to Amalfi, three visits to Pompeii, up Vesuvius, and out to the island of Capri to visit the exiled Gorky and his companion, Andreyev. Capri, Anna wrote to Rose, who was still in St. Petersburg, "reminded me a little of my visits to Piedmont."[15]

There were gestures toward serious work. English looked up a Russian immigrant medical student at the University of Naples, a scholar first mentioned to them by the student's aunt in New York, who had made dresses for Anna. Young Selig Perlman was invited out to Sorrento weekly on the pretext of giving Anna lessons in Russian; he preferred to talk about Marxian dialectics. Anna reported that he "leaves feeling like a millionaire, which makes us very happy," but that the price he paid was getting seasick on the boat back. A year later, Perlman reached America and English paid his way to the University of Wisconsin, where he remained more than fifty years as a labor historian, ever grateful to his benefactor.[16]

Perlman recalled that he had been vaguely embarrassed by the displays of affection between Anna and English, so much like new lovers that he even recalled mistakenly years later that they were not yet married. What he was seeing was a much belated honeymoon. One of Anna's daughters recalls that her mother told her they had received useful medical counsel, recommended by English's father, in America. Just what the difficulty was, and how it was remedied, is not clear from secondhand information ninety years later. But Anna no longer filled her notebook with essays on her unhappiness. More characteristic of this time was a note she left for him one morning: "Buon giorno, Carrissimo Camerrado mio! Forgive me for forgetting you last night, forgetting you in sleep. Anna."[17]

In her journal on March 22, 1907, in Sorrento, Anna wrote: "Twice in my life did I awaken to true love—once when Robert [Wilson] died—on King's Mt.—and again, to English in St. Petersburg. One love as full of sorrow as death, the other as full of joy as life, life which holds mastery over death." At last, she believed, she was starting to find the kind of life—free, fruitful, and loving—that they had projected for themselves in St. Petersburg.[18]

In April, Anna and English followed the spring north to Rome, where Rose joined them. They traveled to Florence, and Anna savored a reunion with her old Stanford professor, Melville Anderson. Rose left for Paris, and they went on to Venice. In a letter to his father-in-law, English quite unself-consciously made clear that the book on Russia that he and Anna had planned to write together (or so at least had been Anna's impression) had become his alone: "For the first time I can see all the chapters of my book in my mind's eye and am correspondingly elated. For the first time I am fully confident of its success. Of course I have always known that I could write a book that would be truthful, broad and sympathetic to the revolution, but now I'm also confident that I can write one that will be widely read."[19]

For her part, Anna reported tersely to Katia: "I am still writing the Pogrom." But she made it clear that she was not feeling well enough for sustained effort. Writing to Anderson from Lake Como, Anna said: "I have a rather bad headache myself to-night, or I would write you a little of Russia and the work which fills our hearts." From Venice early in June she wrote to Katia: "I am much distressed because I have been interrupted again and again by headaches and poor digestion. . . . And I am usually so strong!"[20]

The symptoms were to be expected; she was carrying a child, due early in 1908.

Before the end of June 1907, Anna and English left Italy, and climbed in the Tyrol. Anna later had reason to wonder whether she had been wise to go hiking and indeed whether she should have accompanied English on their frenetic travels. In Vienna, they heard that the Second Duma had been dissolved, and they assumed at once that Russian constitutionalism was dead and that revolution would again ride high. "Although I was ill," Anna wrote to Katia, "we did not dare lose time in entering Russia, for fear there would be a Railroad strike—such optimists as we are! . . . In Petersburg again discouraged talk on every hand about 'evolutionary revolutionism,' about the futility of any kind of action."[21]

Still in motion, they turned up in Stuttgart in August for the triennial meeting of the Second International, the organizational face of socialism's paper-thin universalism. They were joined by Rose and by Arthur Bullard. Among the nearly nine hundred delegates were the eminent and to-be-eminent, those destined to be antagonists or martyrs: Daniel DeLeon and Big Bill Haywood from the United States; Lenin and Trotsky from Russia; Rosa Luxemburg of Poland and Germany; Benito Mussolini of Italy. The major figures—Jean Jaurés of France, Karl Kautsky and August Bebel of Germany—wrestled over the issue of what action the working class must take in the event of war. The compromise resolution carried the hint that workers might prove in the end to be good soldiers.[22]

After Stuttgart, Anna and English traveled through southern Russia starting at Odessa on the Black Sea, site of the 1905 naval mutiny memorialized later in Eisenstein's classic film, *Battleship Potemkin,* and just as significantly the site of a slaughter of Jews during the Days of Liberty. From Odessa, English sent a manuscript to the *Independent* that appeared in the issue of September 26, 1907. "The Real Russian People" painted an almost idyllic picture of indigenous democracy and budding socialism, even communism, in Russia's hundred thousand villages. His final words carried a deliberate rebuke for American readers: "The Russians are likely soon to become the chief inspiration of other nations, a position recently lost after having been held for a century by the United States."[23]

Their travel lasted into October. Anna's pregnancy was now well past the queasy first trimester, and her improved spirits were apparent in a letter to her mother-in-law from Moscow: "Our trip among the peasants was most satisfactory, at times even inspiring, and we have met with unexpected good luck at every turn, meeting just the people we needed and making friends everywhere. . . . I have been writing all morning. I am still on my 'Pogrom'— the massacre of Hommel."

They intended to stop in St. Petersburg two weeks, she wrote, go slightly out of their way to visit Anna's village birthplace, and go on to Berlin and Paris. It was not to happen, or rather it was not to happen as they planned.[24]

22 *"Where Do You Hide Your Revolvers and Dynamite?"*

In the year, October 1906 to October 1907, that Anna and English were away from Russia, the old revolutionary news bureau in St. Petersburg maintained a skeletal and dwindling existence under its acting head, Rose Strunsky. Dealing as it did with every radical political faction, the bureau was a risky responsibility for a twenty-three-year-old who had previously lived away from home only as an undergraduate at Stanford.

Moreover, she was eventually left all but alone. Arthur Bullard was gone by the end of 1906, in pursuit of his career as a roving journalist. Kellogg Durland too was usually off on business of his own, and two University Settlement veterans, Leroy Scott and Miriam Finn Scott, arrived but did not linger. There were Russian friends who worked in, or with, the bureau, but associating with them became increasingly hazardous.[1]

Fundamentally, Rose relied on her American passport for protection; unlike Anna, she did not have the added safeguard of being married to an American. Thus she constantly faced the possibility that Russian officials might find out that she had falsified her place of birth on the passport.

Her letters to Anna and English, and other evidence, suggest that she pushed her precarious immunity to the limit. Although she described herself later as having merely attended the revolution, "sitting open-eyed with my head in both my hands watching," she was not entirely a bystander, let alone an innocent bystander. She had selected her friends in the revolutionary movement from the least cautious—in particular, from those she called in her letters "la jeunesse," the Maximalists, who were waging their war by assassinating czarist officials and expropriating czarist funds.[2]

Her reports were a mélange of bureau business, general news, and lightly coded references to revolutionary activity she had observed or abetted. "Life has been rather exciting here lately," she observed. She attended party meetings and observed the "fun" in the courtroom theatrics of a big political trial—the government's prosecution of labor deputies from the ill-fated First Duma. She advised Anna and English on transmitting money from America to the revolutionary parties. There was pathos interleaved with irony: "I made some new friends since you left. One of them has committed suicide. I can't get his face away. . . . He brought us candy once & asked for bromo. His nerves were a little unstrung he said—the blessed boy!" More typical was her disguised comment on a casualty: "Nick's leg was really an accident but if he had been playing with good boys it would not have happened."[3]

She urged her sister not to be concerned: "Now Anna, I know you—you are reading all kinds of things between the lines and are frighten[e]d. Here am I, honest and telling you everything that has happened since you left, and if you don't believe me, that I have had the greatest week of my life and more living & feeling than in my whole life. . . . If you don't believe I am doing the best I can I will not tell anything at all next time."[4]

A more candid version of her activities emerged later in Paris, when she no longer needed to skirt Russian censorship. Rose told her stories to a visiting California friend, Inez Haynes Gillmore, who transcribed them into her diary: "In St. Petersburg [she] shelters all kinds of students in her room. Some of them ravishingly beautiful; one an Irish type [,] violet eyes and jet-black hair. Talked once with a girl who was going the next day to shoot an official; girl very nervous, hated to die; only thing that upheld her was the feeling that such a man must not live. The wedding, hysterical with mirth, pelting down the station, Russian pseudo-groom saying his one word of English, 'Hello!'— two crysanthenums [sic]. The Maxamilists, Rose one of them, capture a lot of money. All goes for nothing; luxurious living, dynamite; police get part of it."[5]

Rose also talked of a "Big Fat Friend," a Finn who was providing shelter for Russian revolutionaries. Sensing herself to be vaguely in danger, Rose left St. Petersburg in November 1906 and moved into Big Fat Friend's house in Helsingfors, capital of Finland. Big Fat Friend—the name was not meant literally but as a nom de guerre—was Aino Malmberg, a teacher of literature and the operator of a kind of underground railroad. To Anna, Rose explained that "Aino" meant "the Only One" in Finnish, and that she, Rose, was tutoring the Only One's husband in English: "It is a shame to take the money, as Morris would say." She fantasized about all the revolutionaries, alive and dead, who had slept in the same spacious bedroom and iron bed that were now hers.[6]

In December, Rose moved to the Only One's country house and hideaway, in the wintry woods at Sammathe, fifty miles west of Helsingfors, where she listened to the crunch of snow underfoot and learned to stay upright on skis. She offered a coded communiqué:

> The "jeunesse" seem to be the only ones worth while though the S[ocial-ist]. R[evolutionarie]s are getting pretty busy too. If things don't fail something very beautiful ought to happen pretty soon because both these factions are vying . . . to do the same thing first. God knows, so many things have fallen through lately that you never can tell but I bet on my friends to get there first. . . . A lot of smelly stuff I told you about went off to the jeunesse when it really belonged to the older people. It

was extra fine imported. They might have got it back if I hadn't been such an innocent American who doesn't know anything about anything and now there is trouble.[7]

The nature of the "smelly stuff" was revealed in Inez Gillmore's diary: "In the mouse-trap in Finland, Rose had dynamite stored in her room for weeks—*only has to see that it's kept cool,* she says, as it explodes at too warm a temperature. Girls come in, bringing it concealed in their clothes—rubber pockets. As the stuff has an alkali smell, use musk. Smell of musk still makes Rose sick."[8]

Rose hinted at the depth of her involvement in a vignette she recounted to Anna:

> Oh God I am so happy,—maybe I will see Jesus.
>
> Also because Saturday a young man came back whom I sent off 6 weeks before never to see again. And he came back! Did I fall on his neck? The Darling! And he is going away again in a week! Oh he is the kind that ought to go! He is not fit for much else & the Revolution needs the martyrs. . . .

This was no doubt the same revolutionary whose death Rose recounted in a later sketch titled " 'Little Darling.' "[9]

In January 1907, Rose returned to St. Petersburg—so happy to be back that she "felt like kissing the spies in the Finland station." She wrote to Anna that she was going "to see the crazy people jump into the Neva"—the tradition of "walrusing," the Russian predecessor of the polar-bear clubs. "Did you ever have the cartilage in your nose freeze?" she asked. "It aches like fury." At the start of April, she briefly joined Anna and English in Rome and Venice, and went on to Paris to offer a helping hand to her nineteen-year-old brother, Morris, who had worked his passage stoking on a freighter (anticipating the day when, in his fifties, Morris shipped during World War II as an oiler on the perilous Murmansk run).[10]

About the time that Rose passed through Paris, Anna and English received word from Social Revolutionaries then touring America that Rose should not return to Russia—"that they are connecting her with the young people." Rose accepted the invitation of the Only One to live at the country place at Sammathe, where she could write history and add Swedish to the Russian that she already knew passably well. "Wonderful months coming to me!" she wrote of the invitation. "Is it because I am so good[?]"[11]

Despite the warnings, Rose came back to St. Petersburg at the end of the summer of 1907. She settled into an apartment, attended university courses. Meanwhile, by transatlantic mail she tried to make peace with her father, who was demanding to know what she was doing if she was not with Anna and English. He wrote a letter of forgiveness on the day of atonement, Yom Kippur, but Rose conceded to Anna that she was "*Homesick.* Two years is too much & in the language of the poet 'too much is enough.'"[12]

By the time Anna and English reached St. Petersburg from southern Russia on October 11, 1907, Rose had unwittingly laid the foundation of trouble for them all. A week after their return, Rose's friend Aino Malmberg and several associates turned up in St. Petersburg, planning to smuggle an escaped Siberian exile, an organizer of the Peasant Union, by train to Helsingfors. On the morning of October 20, Rose waited at the hotel with Malmberg for the escapee; he did not appear. Malmberg decided to take the train back to Finland alone and she and Rose went to the Finland station. Back at the Hôtel de France, Anna waited. Rose did not return.[13]

At midday, Anna met her husband's train from Moscow. English and Durland held a hasty conversation over lunch and English hurried off to search for Rose. At 4, Anna received a terse telephone message from English: "Your surmises were correct. Warn the others." At 6, he returned, tired and pale; he had been able to glimpse Rose and Aino Malmberg momentarily at the station, held incommunicado in a little interrogation room since 9 in the morning. Anna and English hurried to the American embassy.

The curiously hostile chargé d'affaires—a man named Schuyler—questioned them suspiciously about Rose: "She was arrested in the company of a dangerous woman." He asked: "Are you unaware of the fact that you are yourselves likely to be arrested?" He refused to say how he knew. They consulted a Russian lawyer: "He seemed to have no hope of saving my sister, and abandoned himself to grief." He advised Anna to petition, as soon as she was arrested, to be taken to the prison hospital to protect her unborn child.

At their hotel, English stopped at the front desk while Anna walked up to their rooms:

> When I opened the door of our apartment, I found a Chief of Police, ğendarme spies, the proprietor of the hotel, and servants. The contents of our trunks lay scattered on floor, chairs and bed. The desks were littered with books and manuscripts. . . . When I entered the room and saw the confusion of clothes and papers, my cheeks flamed with anger and horror. They were reading my letters, scrutinizing my photographs,— they were committing violence. "Where do you hide your revolvers and dynamite?" was the . . . first question. "Tell him," I said to the hotel proprietor, "that we are writers, and when we use weapons we use pen and ink and not arms."[14]

They were questioned for more than two hours and both were searched— Anna by two hotel maids—while the police pawed through their papers.

English surreptitiously transferred their address book from the unsearched to the searched pile. Finally, after being asked formally to identify their manuscripts—Anna commented later that "they were in English and mine were illegible, even to myself"—they were placed under arrest. Durland was also detained briefly, as were two friends, Harold Williams of the English *Manchester Guardian* and his wife, who was a Russian journalist.[15]

Thus dissolved the magic shield under which Anna and English, and Rose, had operated for nearly two years. Later, English dismissed the whole episode as a "mistake" on the part of the police, but other evidence carries darker presumptions. The family papers contain a rough translation of a story from the St. Petersburg newspaper *Tovarisch* with information that allegedly came from police sources. Its very inaccuracies—the kind of malicious misreporting one expects of intelligence agencies, such as the notion that Anna, being a Jew, was very wealthy and had given her fortune to English—paradoxically suggest its authenticity. If it is to be believed, this document indicates that English and Anna had been under surveillance by czarist agents during their months in America, that English was suspected of smuggling in large sums of money, and—accurately, of course—that he had published numerous articles supporting the revolution. What is not clear is whether at any time they faced a penalty worse than expulsion.[16]

At the police station, a search began to find the detainees space in the city's crowded prisons. English was taken away about midnight. Still later, a place was found for Anna; she and a police officer, who confessed himself ashamed to be escorting a pregnant American citizen, started to walk to the jail in the dead of night, but finally Anna agreed to pay for a cab. In a prison that was ostensibly for criminals, she found herself suddenly in a band of sisters: more than a dozen female political prisoners, jailed for such offenses as teaching laborers to read and write. When she entered, she recalled, "every face broke into a friendly smile." In another prison, Rose too found herself surrounded by women, two of whom she knew, one of whom she had thought dead.[17]

Word got back to America almost at once. Durland, released after a few hours, dispatched a cable to Captain William English, English's Uncle Will, urging pressure on the American embassy, but adding: "No cause for anxiety." Even so, there was anxiety aplenty in New York. Royal Freeman Nash, a friend from California, wrote afterward to Anna: "I wish you could have seen your mother that Monday morning." Nash and his companion, Fola La Follette, daughter of the senator from Wisconsin, wired Washington; Anna's mother told them to be sure to mention Rosie.[18]

It took only a day or so for the press, always enchanted with the adventures of millionaire socialists, to stir. The October 21 *Chicago American* had banner headlines: "Arrest of Wallings Forces U.S. Protest to the Czar"; the story identified Anna as "the famous Russian novelist." The *Boston Herald*, catching up three days later, headed its story: "Czar's Police Jail Harvard Men; Charge Revolution"—this although the Harvard connections of any of them were tenuous at best. The combination of family concern and press uproar led Secretary of State Elihu Root to cable the American embassy in St. Petersburg to stop dragging its feet.[19]

Early in the evening of October 21, less than twenty-four hours after the arrest, an officer summoned Anna: "A.W., American citizen, to dress and report at the Director's office." Her cell mates, fearing a trick, urged her not to respond. But Anna was anxious about the danger to Rose and wanted to accept any opportunity to leave. She went to the warder's office and, once she impatiently sat to hear vespers sung by the male prisoners, was free. Rose, she found, had already been released; English was last.

The matter could have been much more serious, especially for Rose, but evidently the secret police had little information on her activities beyond her having been found at the Finland Station with Big Fat Friend. Or perhaps the official protests deterred them from acting on their information. After their release, Anna confided to Katia, "The arrest worried me because of Rose. I was so happy when they arrested English and me, too, because I knew what protects him would protect her."[20]

Yet she insisted, as did English, that Rose had done nothing culpable. When Anna wrote to her father-in-law to thank him for his statements to the press, she admitted that it was possible that the police might have "succeeded in making a case against her [Rose]." She added: "It is all talk about Rose having been more implicated than we. She is absolutely clear, except, of course, for the enormous disadvantage of being of Russian and Jewish origin. On the strength of that they could have done anything to her if they chose, as they could not to me, who am the wife of an American. But, please, do not speak of this to others."[21]

In short order after their release, their notes, photographs, and manuscripts were returned and they were given exit visas. After their train crossed the Russian frontier into Germany, Anna and English sent a cable back to America: "Departure voluntary. Arrest partly due to inefficiency of charge d'affaire."[22]

English was more outspoken in a letter to his parents from Berlin. Both Anna and Rose, he complained, had had to deny their Russian and Jewish parentage to leave the country. He was particularly incensed at the embassy secretary: "Schuyler could not and does not know this [that Anna and Rose were Russian-born] but he suspects it and this gives him the whip-hand for his cowardly treatment of us and disloyalty to the U.S. and betrayal of his office." He added: "Schuyler undoubtedly got his information from the dissipated snobs, newspaper men and sharks seeking to share the booty of the Russian bureaucracy who constitute the so-called American colony." In her account, Rose wrote that a Russian official told her: "Your Ambassador here refuses to vouch for you. We are waiting for a telegram from Berlin"—where, of course, Anna and Rose had obtained their passports.[23]

Anna was uncharacteristically haughty and indignant about the arrest in her letter to her mother-in-law: "The idiots had no business arresting us in the first place, and they would have given a great deal later to have saved themselves from the ridicule which their stupid mistake brought on them. The whole Russian Press is now for us, and English has become a popular hero."[24]

They decided to remain in Berlin for a time before moving on to Paris. Anna's mother and her brother Max, the doctor, arrived on November 12, and the senior Anna declared her daughter to be in fine shape for childbearing. To her mother-in-law, Anna promised that she would be a mother and a writer:

> I have now about three months and a week before the little love-stranger comes and I am resolved to square my account with the world before the event by writing something beautiful.
>
> If they like my "Pogrom" in America then I shall have a book out simultaneous with the birth of our baby. It would make English so happy. My not writing has grieved him, has made him fear that something strong, positive, creative has stopped still in me. . . . He and the other dear ones who believe in me and the great life possible to me will yet see![25]

Before the end of 1907, Anna and English moved their headquarters from Berlin to Paris and eventually settled in the Hôtel de la Trémoille, "a fashionable, gilded, English speaking apartment house in the residential quarter where Americans live," commented Inez Gillmore in her diary after she visited them. The residential hotel, on the mildly expensive side even for that Americanized/Anglicized quarter, symbolized the change in Anna's status since her first visit to Paris four years before, when she stayed humbly in the Latin Quarter. English had a taste for the best, and he wanted nothing less for Anna's final weeks. For further insurance, they had Anna's physician brother Max to attend, in consultation with French doctors.[1]

Expectations now moved in parallel, with Anna's baby and the completion of English's book due at about the same time. As soon as they arrived in Paris, English wrote to George P. Brett of Macmillan to introduce himself and his book. He gave a number of conventional references, then added: "I hesitate to mention the name of my Wife, Anna Strunsky, for fear that you may think me in some way responsible for the discontinuance of her literary activities. However, I can assure you that they are being renewed and that you will hear from her very soon."[2]

English received a warm reply from Brett urging him to send the partly completed manuscript; another letter all but promised acceptance. In December 1907, English submitted thirty-five thousand words, a third of the book, and a third more in January. Anna wrote to her father-in-law: "I took off two days from my work to read his, and I wish I could tell you briefly how good I found it." English wrote to his parents, with a touch of not-very-light humor: "I shall telegraph you both when the child comes and my book is accepted. So dont be disappointed if you get a telegram announcing such a comparative trifle when you expect the other."[3]

As to her own work, Anna at last finished a draft of her report on the Homel massacre, sent a copy to the Wallings in Chicago, and asked them to forward it for her brother Hyman to translate into Yiddish. She told them: "English and Rose like it very much, and Mr. Brett may publish it by itself in a small book well illustrated. There is nothing in English besides Michael Davitt's book on the Kishineff massacre.[4] . . . If it is too short to publish by itself then it will appear with two other stories, one a chronicle of our two journeys among the peasants, another the Personalities of the Revolution. . . . I can have this published and my Pere Lachaise novel surely in the Fall if not sooner."[5]

She was in an equally expansive mood in anticipating, for her father-in-law, the arrival of their child: "If I don't bring you the little dark-eyed Rosalind your heart desires, you will forgive me, and accept William Hayden in place of her. Max has listened to the heart and says it beats fast, like a little girl's." She added: "And dear father, don't be afraid that I will neglect the darling baby for my work." She reported that they had hired a nurse, Sarah G. Plumb, an American of forty-plus with excellent recommendations, who had attended none other than Rudyard Kipling. Anna told her mother-in-law: "She is very matter of fact and practical."[6]

In the second week of January 1908, Anna received a cable from her brother Hyman that Macmillan had accepted her book on the basis of reading the Homel manuscript. But Brett's letter, when it was forwarded, proved to be something less than a commitment. The point was rather that Brett had declined to publish the Homel account alone and had agreed to read the other articles as a possible basis for a book. Everything hinged on Anna's completing the other articles.[7]

English pushed ahead with the remaining chapters of his book. He had already engaged in a postal debate with his father and Uncle Will over the content. He wrote to his father in response to their criticism: "In spite of your urgeing [sic] and Uncle Will's I must retain my concluding chapters. They are the one part of my book that contains anything like brilliant or important writing, the end for which I went to Russia and wrote the book. They will be the most read, the most criticized, and the most praised and so the most successful of all."[8]

Then achievement and adversity converged. On February 8, 1908, Anna gave birth to a daughter at the Hôtel de la Trémoille. She was named "Rosalind English," for English's mother. The news was cabled to America and cables of congratulation responded. On February 12, English, in the Remington company office in Paris, dictated the foreword of his book:

> Lincoln's Birthday Paris 1908
> To the men and women who in all walks of life are contending against the forces that are trying to introduce into America the despotism and class-rule of Eastern Europe; to all those who in the traditional revolutionary American spirit, are leading our country against all the reactionary tendencies prevailing in politics, morality, education, literature and science, to its great democratic and social destiny.

On February 13, English looked in: "When I found the baby & Anna both so well I even resumed work on my very important last chapter." By the afternoon, as English wrote later, "My book *was entirely finished.*"[9]

Late in the day, English was abruptly summoned by news that Anna was ill. He found her with the infant, blue and cold, lying upon her. Twenty-eight years later, she remembered the day, as she did every year, and wrote:

> When our First-born died and lay a little corpse on my breast, English not knowing she was still there and that nurse had not taken her away, flung himself full length on me, his arms around me, his tears falling full on my face and sobbed: "Let us not wash away our grief in tears! This is a grief for all our life: Let us not feel it all at once!"[10]

A day later, Anna wrote in her diary a harrowing account of the infant's death. The highly recommended Miss Plumb had become the villain, indifferent or even hostile to Anna's pleas and obdurate in her refusal at the end to summon the doctor in attendance or Max Strunsky. A few days later Anna wrote to her parents:

> We trusted our darling into the hands of a fiend. It seems as if the hand of God held us from snatching the child away from her, for none of us liked her, all of us now remember that she filled us with dread, that she was coarse and queer and eminently out of place amongst us, trusting and fond hearts that we are, and yet none of us drove her from the house. To be sure it was only five short days, and they were all so taken up with me, and English very little in the house being busy with the finishing of his book. In another day we would have driven her away, we are all convinced, because our feeling was rising against her, but that day was not to be.[11]

A week later, she wrote in a less vengeful tone to her in-laws: "It is twelve days since my baby died—the exquisite, beautiful, perfect little child that we were allowed to keep for only five days! . . . I called her 'my little International'—the beauty and loveliness of every country in Europe entered in the making of her."[12]

For decades, even after both Anna and English were gone, their family continued to retell tales of the nurse-fiend: that she had poisoned the baby, that she had exposed the child to the winter air because she was convinced that Anna was only a mistress not a wife because she did not use her husband's name (the same hint—a misleading one—of exotic sexuality that Jack London had found in Anna), that the nurse was attracted to English, that she was later executed for killing another child. English wrote to his parents that they intended to investigate the nurse and the agency that hired her, but, so Anna was told, she was beyond the reach of French law. Anna reported later: "Once English and I went to her house. I dragged him there. I felt I must ask some questions, look the murderess of my baby in the face, but she would not receive us. I will try to see her. I will ask her why she did not call the doctor, and then perhaps I will fly at her with my hands. Sometimes I have murder in my heart."[13]

But the confrontation apparently never took place, and whether Nurse Plumb was in fact culpable or guilty merely of harshness has never been established. Perhaps English secretly concluded that Nurse Plumb was not to blame. The child was buried in Père Lachaise, where Anna nearly five years before had been haunted by images of death. Far up the slope from the main gates, among modest stones commemorating thousands of Parisians, their child was laid in a grave eventually marked by a plain headstone:

ROSALIND ENGLISH WALLING

8 FEVRIER

13 FEVRIER

1908[14]

English took Anna on her first outing on March 8, a month after their baby's birth. Anna wrote to her mother-in-law: "I could not recognize Paris being so changed myself in my inner feelings, the whole world seemed changed." They had not visited the grave: "I wanted to go to-day because it is her birthday, but English said the [new] nurse thought I should wait till Monday. It must be such a little grave!"[15]

During Anna's long period of psychic convalescence she soon divided family and friends into two parties: those who were content to let her go on grieving and those who urged her to gather herself and continue her life. She resented the latter deeply, although they included her own family and her oldest friend. She was angered when her brother Hyman counseled her: "I must say that it pains me to see you melt in tears at the treatment of a cruel fate. I want you to feel the pain, but I want you to stand it better. Wash your face and dry your eyes, sweet sister, and embrace you[r] husband and think of Rosalind—think of her as something that you got, and not as something that you lost." In his next letter, he apologized for implying "an accusation of lack of strength."[16]

Nor was Hyman alone. Anna was irked at her mother, who had herself endured the loss of four babies, for suggesting that Anna's tragedy was not unique. Nor did she welcome a letter from Katia, who spoke both as friend and doctor, rebuking Anna for the deathly tone of her letters; the baby's claim on her, Katia said, should "not exceed all other human ties that bind you." As late as the fall of 1908, Kellogg Durland won an enmity that lasted to the end of his life when Anna heard that he had remarked to Rose: "What! Does Anna still speak of her baby?" Anna remarked: "I call this pretty shallow and heartless."[17]

She turned for comfort to her in-laws, and particularly to her mother-in-law, who seemed willing to underwrite her fixation on the loss indefinitely.

As if to reward them for their sympathy, she gave up the use of her own name, notifying Dr. Walling: "Father, dear heart, I shall never grieve you again by using my maiden-name, for I want my daughter's name for whatever I write and do."[18]

However reluctantly, she gradually responded to the demands of her old life. The death in exile of Gregory Gershuni, a founder of the Russian Social Revolutionary Party, brought her out of seclusion. Anna and English had seen him during their brief stay in New York in 1907 when, having been smuggled out of Russia via Siberia, he came to America to raise money. Now they were in the little group that met the body as it arrived from Switzerland. Two days later they walked behind the coffin, covered with a pall of red and surrounded by red flowers and red flags, on its way to burial in Montparnasse. The crowd of ten thousand heard eulogies in many tongues: "It was my part," Anna recalled, "to speak in English." She added: "We stood later than the police wished, and long after they had rushed at us with clubs and bayonets to disperse us."[19]

Late in March, Anna's old San Francisco friend Gelett Burgess came back to Paris, again accompanied by his sister. Anna's former role—the attractive younger woman friend—was now taken by the suffragist and budding writer Inez Gillmore, whose husband, Rufus, seemed to be along largely as a supernumerary. Inez Gillmore kept a detailed, irreverent diary of their weeks in Paris, and from her pages emerge snapshots of Anna, English, Rose Strunsky, and Arthur Bullard. On April 3, Inez Gillmore and Burgess went to call on Anna at the Hôtel de la Trémoille, but were turned away: "She unable to see us because of her recent maternity"—by this time, two months past.[20]

Two days later, Burgess went again to the hotel, whereupon Anna and English appeared at the Gillmore-Burgess quarters at 3, rue Soufflot in the Latin Quarter. Gillmore greeted them in some confusion and later recorded her first impression:

> She very charming, with the deep rich, warm voice, musically accented, that I expect; big brown eyes, a Russian face. Feeling around for conversation in my embarrassment, I stutter out that my two sisters met her last winter at G.B[urgess]'s party. She looks inquiring. I give their names; describe the party while she looks more and more crestfallen. I suffer agonies for her. "I'm trying to think," she says despairingly. "They teased my poor wife so," Mr. Walling interposes gently, "that she remembers nothing."[21]

A few days later, Gillmore had a chance to study Anna further at a restaurant table as she told the story of their arrest: "Anna is very beautiful I think; a creature of mahogany and jet—of red showing through the satin brown;

brown eyes, shining, clear and pure as pools with drowned stars in them—a most lucent gleamy agate. Her hands are lovely. Her voice is deep, rich with organ-notes in it. Her accent is charming. Her diction, as Frank [Burgess] always told me, exquisitely clear and elegant. I love her moist, rippling black hair. Her figure has thickened. She will be a haus-frau type in a few years. But always that soul will shine through that naive eloquence; always that temperamental fervor will prove an illuminating fire." Later, she observed: "Not terrific athleticism of feature; the result not a line in her face; clear-eyed and smooth-skinned; not a suggestion of that tangle that is on the brows of New England women."[22]

English, although he was frequently present, appeared more briefly in the diary. Three weeks or so after having met him, she wrote: "E.W. curiously impersonal; all that charming middle ground of gossip and little talk *intime* impossible with him. The moment the conversation turns to anything but theory, he walks away or reads a paper." She also made a shrewd forecast of relations between Anna and English: "E.W., a dynamo, bound to absorb her; pervading the room and making his personality felt by a series of explosions."[23]

The Burgess party saw a great deal of the Walling circle during its six weeks in Paris: dinners at Lapérouse on the Seine embankment or the Taverne du Panthéon in the Latin Quarter, evenings in cafés, an abortive call on Neith Boyce and her husband, Hutchins Hapgood, in the country (English had neglected to call to see whether the two writers were at home); visits to the studios of the "Independants" (Picasso reminded Rose of her old beau, Xavier Martinez) under the guidance of Gertrude Stein and her brother Leo; meetings with Russian and Finnish exiles living in Paris, and constant talk, talk, talk, about their time in Russia. Finally, a farewell dinner at Lapérouse— Anna reciting Browning's grisly "Porphyria's Lover"—and a night walk along the river toward Notre-Dame.[24]

Cheering as the Burgess party's visit may have been, as long as Anna remained in Paris, in the very hotel where the infant Rosalind was born and died, she could hardly emerge fully from the shadows. Early in the summer she and English left for a vacation in England and Ireland, and Anna began to recover her bearings. From North Wales, she wrote: "I must get my book out in the fall. If my baby had not died I would have fulfilled the promise my whole life has given, but my heart has been too heavy most of the time to even remember what my writing was about. . . . But now I am writing again and I am very, very happy."[25]

Later, in a letter to Rose from Cork, she declared, or renewed, her credo for her marriage and work, a modification of the perfectionism she had proclaimed from St. Petersburg: While she saw herself and English coming "together into an ideal mutuality," they would pursue their "partially separated ways." She added:

A mere mechanical arrangement of being together does certainly not lead to perfect union. I am going to work, make friends, travel, have children of him, and as far as he loves me he will be with me in all these things, and as far as his life permits—more and more with the years, I am certain.

He will be my best and most intimate friend and I his, besides our being lovers, and we will not be husband and wife at all, as despite our greatest efforts we at rare times have been.

I fell into a slipshod almost conventional habit of living through neglect of my work, but the new life is before me and it is already begun. Not even in St. Petersburg [in] those first great days was I happy as I am now, for indeed I feel as if light has been given me.[26]

English's Russian book appeared destined for the Macmillan Company of New York; his interests and connections made him a natural candidate for the Macmillan network, and George Brett seemed interested. But it went elsewhere; in March 1908 English received a cable from Doubleday, Page and Company accepting his book. Three publishers had seen it, Anna wrote to his parents, and "all maintained that it would be an honor to them to have it on their list." This sounds as if English shopped the book around, but it is also conceivable that Macmillan was put off by its size. In any case, the decision was made at a speed that would have seemed breathtaking later in the century; English had finished the manuscript only six weeks before, and in that time it was seen by three publishers, and taken by one.[1]

Doubleday, Page, an aggressive, relatively new presence on the publishing scene, was cofounded by Walter Hines Page, editor of *World's Work*, with Frank N. Doubleday. Four years before, English had written for Page's magazine, but he may have relied for entrée this time on Leroy Scott, who now wrote regularly for *World's Work*. English referred later to Scott as having done editing on the book.[2]

The book was not constructed of the same light stuff that the American public had been reading about Russia. The little circle of socialist-oriented American writers who had gone to Russia after Bloody Sunday had produced at least fifty articles for national magazines—most of them partisan and anecdotal. Ernest Poole specialized in a precursor of oral history, transcribing first-person stories of revolutionists; Arthur Bullard ("Albert Edwards") and Kellogg Durland wrote war stories emphasizing their own participation. There was little attention to the complicated politics of the revolution. Parties were stick-on labels; socialism got short shrift, even from these socialists.

The culminating phase of their reportage was books, or intended books. Ernest Poole, who had gone to Russia ten months before English, submitted a compendium of his articles to Macmillan before the end of 1905, only to be turned down by the great naysayer, George Rice Carpenter of Columbia University, who wrote: "Good journalism makes bad books." So Poole continued to feed the magazines.[3]

Durland was more successful. His book, brought out by the Century Company, beat English into the stores by nine months. *The Red Reign* (or "The

Red Rain," as it was inadvertently called in the *New York Times*) was framed as "The True Story of An Adventurous Year." It was writer-centered, largely a telling of Durland's bravado and narrow escapes; the tone was set in a photograph opposite the title page of Durland and his "brigand interpreter" in fur capes and hats and flowing scarves. Politics was smuggled in through such episodes as the chapter on Marie Spiradovna, assassin of a provincial official, later abused and violated in prison. Durland compared her to Charlotte Corday, and Scott later called her a Joan of Arc.[4]

The Red Reign was produced in a great hurry: Durland finished the manuscript in the summer of 1907, while he, English, and Anna were all still in Russia. Published in September, it contained references to material dated as late as July 23, and the index was only partly alphabetized. Inevitably, the circle around English viewed him as a competitor. Late in February 1908 Rose Strunsky wrote from London in a scandalized tone that the elderly anarchist, Peter Kropotkin, had spoken well of *The Red Reign*: "He sat at the table & praised Durland's book. 'Such boldness such temerity!' His daughter sat at the foot & said 'Oh I am just crazy about it.'" Indeed, English must have been vexed to have such a book emerge from the revolutionary news bureau, for it represented a buccaneering approach that was the diametrical opposite of his own self-imposed seriousness. However, he may have been able to take comfort in the fact that Durland's work was largely ignored by reviewers.[5]

Russia's Message: The True World Import of the Revolution was published in June 1908. Although it bore English's name alone, and mentioned Durland and Bullard/Edwards only on the last page, it was to an extent a joint venture of the revolutionary news bureau. Bullard wrote an outline and possibly a draft of the last chapter. Leroy Scott helped with final assembly. As for Anna, she was mentioned only in passing in a reference to "myself and wife." English claimed full credit and took sole responsibility.[6]

Russia's Message could scarcely have been more different from Poole's oral histories and Durland's derring-do. The first person was used only rarely and grudgingly; "I have not dwelt on personal experience," English announced grimly. He took pride in using live sources: "I owe little to writers of books and much to active leaders of the movement." Thirty-eight of the forty chapters offered the fruits of hundreds of interviews with officials and revolutionaries, peasants and workers, priests and politicians, among them Trotsky and Lenin; he called the latter "perhaps the most popular leader in Russia." He provided a detailed guide to the system of czarist repression, centering on persecution of Jews, and to the strategies of the entire range of political parties. The scope and detail of these chapters reveal an industriousness that a friend later recalled as "appalling."[7]

But the book was not designed simply to be a report on Russia. As implied in the title, it was intended to present revolution in Russia as the harbinger of a new world civilization. The theoretical basis for this claim was reserved for the last two chapters. It is small wonder that English's father and uncle urged him to drop these concluding sections; they no doubt found these discussions difficult, irrelevant, and far too radical. The sections constitute an attack on world capitalism for giving resources to the czar "to build prisons for hundreds of thousands of his people, to buy the rifles and machine guns of the Cossacks and to hire an army of thugs." The Russian people were winning the revolution, he concluded, until capitalism rescued the czar with a loan of a billion rubles.[8]

In the last chapter, he turned from the specifically Russian situation to a world context. The chapter is a tour de force, marching without pause through Rousseau, Montesquieu, Marx, and Tolstoy, and coming to rest at last on Maeterlinck's essay, "Our Social Duty": "In every social progress the great and only difficult work is the destruction of the past." Maeterlinck, and English, implicitly rejected scientific neutrality and evolutionary progress in favor of large revolutions, erasing society and starting over.[9]

Despite such conclusions, the book received wide, usually respectful attention. As early as August 1, 1908, English reported that he had seen thirty newspaper reviews, twenty-seven of them favorable; the three others he discounted as being biased in one way or another. Later, he received good reviews in the magazines. The *Independent*, his most dependable outlet, was of course favorable, if a bit terse. The *Outlook*, for which he had written on occasion, carried a long unsigned review taking exception only to his portrayal of the peasants as budding socialists. On the other hand, the *Nation*, usually more conservative, praised him for his treatment of the peasants and said that his book was the only one to rank with the work of the British scholar Bernard Pares. (Years later, John Reed quoted it in the introduction to his *Ten Days that Shook the World*.)[10]

By far the worst notice the book received came from within the family: a blistering letter from his uncle, Captain William English, because in the book English had criticized Uncle Will's friend and political associate, Albert J. Beveridge, the Progressive Republican senator from Indiana. By Uncle Will's account, English's brother, Willoughby, discovered the references while he was reading the book and had called them to the attention of the rest of the family. Whereupon Uncle Will was deputized to draft a note of regret to the senator on behalf of Willoughby and the senior Wallings. By the time Uncle Will wrote to English, Beveridge had already responded in a forgiving and slightly condescending manner. But Uncle Will was still determined to chastise his nephew:

To us it seemed so unwise and uncalled for to attack any Senator from Indiana and above all Beveridge who had come to your relief so promptly, willingly, and effectively on both occasions when you were in trouble [a reference to the arrests in St. Petersburg]. . . . It has placed me . . . at this time in a particularly unpleasant position as I have been nominated for the [state] Senate more largely by Beveridge's friends than any one else. . . . Unfortunately you not only took issue but made personal attack where is [sic] most sensative [sic]. . . . If there should be a further edition at any time [you will] remove this objectionable matter which in no way adds to your book. . . and puts you in an ungrateful and ungracious light. Throw your verbal bombs in some other direction than Indiana.

Uncle Will added that he did not care for the general approach of the book, either, and was "greatly disappointed to find that it is simply a socialistic pronouncement and argument. . . . [The book] will do one good thing certainly in any event and that is you can never go back to Russia. . . . For which all of us are thankful."[11]

The nub of the grievance was a critique of Beveridge's *The Russian Advance*, published five years before. English found "racial prejudice" in Beveridge's portrait of the Slavs as passive and fatalistic and wrongheadedness in Beveridge's conclusion that "the Russian masses are devoted to their czar and Church" and incapable of revolution. "The reader of Senator Beveridge's book," English concluded in a letter to his parents, "knows that this writer's judgment has been condemned out of his own mouth."[12]

English was caught off guard by the explosion, and seemed scarcely to remember the references to Beveridge. He wrote to his parents that he thought that he had cut all direct references to Beveridge and that perhaps Scott had reinserted the material. Although Anna found Beveridge's soft-spoken response "funny" and "discreet," English's blood was up, and he read the note as revealing Beveridge to be "conscience-stricken, afraid of me and heartily ashamed of his book." Not for the last time, he revealed himself in argument to be steely and unforgiving.[13]

Uncle Will proved to be right in one matter. English never returned to Russia.

PART FIVE

Springfield and After,

1908–1911

Anna and English and Rose returned to America together in the summer of 1908, laden with books, photographs, and files. They hung back until the customs inspectors were too weary to bother with imposing duties, and passed through free. This time they were not merely visiting America but, although they may not yet have admitted it to themselves, looking for a home. Russia, which had occupied their lives for nearly three years, had already begun to fade.[1]

It was characteristic of English that, once *Russia's Message* was finished and he had offered it to the world, he treated his hard-won knowledge of Russia as used up. It would not have occurred to him to become a lifelong specialist—a university teacher, for example. He, and to a lesser extent Anna, seemed always to be seeking the new crossroads, an intersection of public and personal destiny. Neither of them necessarily made any conscious decision to move on, and indeed they continued for a time to play the role of conscientious advocates of the Russian revolution; at the same time they sensed that the revolution was now only a glimmer in the public eye and they were shopping for new causes.

Their essentially journalistic instincts led them to the next stop. After their arrival in New York, they called on Anna's family and took the Twentieth Century Limited to Chicago to see the Wallings. They left Rose, "not quite well," behind on Graham and Rose Stokes's idyllic little island, Caritas (Charity), off Stamford, Connecticut.[2]

Within twenty-four hours of their arrival, the newspapers were carrying stories on a disturbance in the state capital, Springfield, known to the nation as the home of Abraham Lincoln. There a mob of several hundred whites, led at times by a swaggering "Joan of Arc," had rampaged through the little city, destroying businesses owned by blacks or thought sympathetic to blacks. The triggering incident, as in the tragic Atlanta upheaval nearly two years before, was an allegation that a black man had raped a white woman (a tale that a grand jury ultimately found to be fabricated). In the early hours of August 15, a black barber, defending his home, fired buckshot into the crowd; he was beaten unconscious, hanged from a dead tree (later torn apart for souvenirs), and his corpse stripped and mutilated.[3]

Anna sensed that this was an American version of the murderous hatred that she had seen at Homel. For his part, English knew the town well; his cousin Cora, Governor Tanner's widow, still lived there, as did other relatives. He consulted Graham Stokes, who was in Chicago; he encouraged them to go see for themselves, and they decided that they would take the night train to Springfield. They did not tell English's parents beforehand, possibly sensing that the senior Wallings might try to veto the trip. Instead, English scribbled a note on Chicago Athletic Association stationery:

> After talking it over at length with Graham Stokes and with one another we have just decided to spend tomorrow in Springfield. It was Anna's idea to begin with. She has been anxious for years to get an insight into one of these troubles and to write a broad, sympathetic and non-partizan [sic] account—as she did to the Homel massacre. She will send her story to her friend Norman Hapgood editor-in-chief of Collier's. I shall probably write for the Independent.

He added the rote assurances, so frequent in his letters from Russia: "It is needless to say that we shall seek out the best known people for interviewing, that we shall not go near any riotous parts—if the rioting should by any chance be renewed and that I will take good care of Anna."[4]

While they were on the overnight sleeper, the mob in Springfield, roaming the streets for a second night, attacked the home of an aged black shoemaker, slashed his throat, and strung a symbolic rope about his neck; he died next day in the hospital. By the time Anna and English arrived on Sunday morning, the state had sent in almost its entire militia, 3,700 in all, and the mob had broken up into small guerrilla units, easily dispersed. Two blacks had died, and four whites.[5]

Anna and English plunged into the fact-gathering and interviewing that had become second nature. They visited the mayor, the militia headquarters, the offices of the *Illinois State Journal* and the hospital—filled with mostly white casualties—and burned-out black neighborhoods.

They found Springfield a hard case: "We at once discovered, to our amazement, that Springfield had no shame," English wrote later. He and Anna were treated to "all the opinions that pervade the South—that the negro does not need much education, that his present education even has been a mistake, that whites cannot live in the same community with negroes except where the latter have been taught their inferiority, that lynching is the only way to teach them, etc." They even interviewed Joan of Arc, one Kate Howard, who proudly said that she drew her inspiration from the South and showed off the buckshot wounds in her arms.[6]

By Sunday, respectability, speaking through the town's three daily newspapers, had come around to deploring the actions of the scruffy mob, but insisted, as had General Orlov at Homel, that the blame lay with the victims: "It was not the fact of the whites' hatred toward the negroes," the *Journal* wrote, "but of the negroes' own misconduct, general inferiority or unfitness for free institutions that were at fault." The vernacular version, repeated to Anna and English a dozen times, was: "Why, the niggers came to think they were as good as we are!" A movement calling itself the Political League—reminiscent in its way of Russia's Black Hundreds—was setting about to drive the entire African-American community of nearly three thousand from Springfield permanently.[7]

Anna and English, accustomed to violence and destruction, did not flinch at what they saw. But English's family connections in Springfield must have made the couple feel as if they were strange creatures indeed. A hint of the gap between cultures emerges in Anna's recollection of a remark by a cousin: "Cousin Anna, I just heard Cousin English call himself a Socialist. I can't understand it. I always thought that people were *called* Socialists. I never knew that anyone called *himself* one."[8]

Anna and English stayed in Springfield long enough to gather what they needed. As they made their way back, first to Chicago, then on to New York, English wrote his article for the *Independent.* That weekly had been the outlet for most of his Russian articles, but there was a second reason for the choice; the *Independent,* dating from 1848, was the surviving voice of the abolitionist heritage. Hamilton Holt, the managing editor, was linked to the abolitionists not only through tradition but by descent from the Tappan family of New York. Within days of the Springfield incident, Holt rushed into print an editorial condemning the affair as worse than the Atlanta riot. Given not only Holt's sympathies but his policy of letting contributors say what they wanted, English knew that he could speak out.[9]

His experience in Russia—and perhaps the tiff over *Russia's Message*—had now liberated him from deferring to family opinion. The youth who, ten years before in Cambridge, had reported punctiliously to his parents that he had refused to sit at table with "niggers," was superseded or overshadowed by a man with a hair-trigger sense of injustice. If maturity had not freed him from personal bias, it had at least fixed his public stance: that, having seen so much of oppression, he could recognize it instantly. He put the manuscript in Holt's hands before the end of August, and it appeared in the issue of September 3, with one editorial emendation—a note that Kate Howard, Joan of Arc, indicted by a grand jury, had committed suicide.

The article in the *Independent* was dramatic in the extreme, from the heading—"The Race War in the North"—to the prediction that the issue of racial justice could eventually jeopardize American democracy. It was an instance when English was able to rise beyond cold factual analysis to strong argument—that is, to march from details of what he saw in Springfield to questions of national destiny.

The tone of the article was startlingly unequivocal for that era. English charged that the whites of Springfield and environs, in imitation of the South, had "initiated a permanent warfare with the negro race." He wrote:

> If the new Political League succeeds in permanently driving every negro from office; if the white laborers get the negro laborers' jobs; if masters of negro servants are able to keep them under the discipline of terror as I saw them doing in Springfield; if white shopkeepers and saloon keepers get their colored rivals' trade; if the farmers of neighboring towns establish permanently their right to drive poor people out of their community, instead of offering them reasonable alms; if white miners can force their negro fellow-workers out and get their positions by closing the mines, then every community indulging in an outburst of race hatred will be assured of a great and certain financial reward, and all the lies, ignorance and brutality on which race hatred is based will spread over the land.[10]

At the end, he uttered a grim, extreme, and not unprophetic warning:

> Either the spirit of the abolitionists, of Lincoln and of Lovejoy must be revived and we must come to treat the negro on a plane of absolute political and social equality, or Vardaman and Tillman [two of the South's leading spokesmen on race] will soon have transferred the race war to the North. . . .
>
> The day these methods become general in the North every hope of political democracy will be dead, other weaker races and classes will be persecuted in the North as in the South, public education will undergo an eclipse, and American civilization will await either a rapid degeneration or another profounder and more revolutionary civil war, which shall obliterate not only the remains of slavery but all other obstacles to a free democratic evolution that have grown up in its wake.
>
> Yet who realizes the seriousness of the situation, and what large and powerful body of citizens is ready to come to their aid?[11]

Anna, who had supplied the initial impetus to go to Springfield, again fell victim to hesitation. She did not finish her Springfield story and it fell into the hopper to compete with other unfinished projects. Once more, she and English had started out as partners and she had been left, or had left herself, behind.

For a time after the publication of "The Race War in the North," it appeared that Anna and English might regard the riot in Springfield as merely an isolated episode, an adventurous interlude. In September 1908, back from Illinois, they set about becoming New Yorkers, leaving their temporary rooms at the Brevoort to rent a three-room apartment at 21 West Thirty-Eighth Street—the address as well of the Hearst editor Arthur Brisbane, whom English had known since Hearst's 1904 presidential campaign. They also rented a weekend place from Brisbane, in the then-rural town of Hempstead, Long Island, and parked Rose there when she complained that New York's noise got on her nerves.[1]

They resumed old business. At the start of September, from Atlantic City, where he and Anna were spending an untroubled Labor Day weekend, English listed their schedule for his parents: On Monday they were giving a lunch for the celebrated advocate Clarence Darrow and Brisbane; three days later they were to speak at a Tolstoy observance; two days after that they were to address a meeting at Cooper Union on socialism in Europe.[2]

Anna still had not escaped her conviction that she needed long stretches of isolation to write, but with English managing their lives there were bound to be continual interruptions. They had joint lectures in New York in September, and early in October were to go to Washington, where English, seeking to block the extradition of a Latvian revolutionist, had an appointment with President Roosevelt. Later in the fall, they were to be peripherally involved in Eugene Debs's Socialist presidential campaign, speaking at a Gaylord Wilshire fundraiser featuring the "Wilshire girls and the Red Special boys," the latter named for Debs's famed campaign train.[3]

Anna concentrated as best she could on trying to finish her "little work on the Russian Revolutionary Lives," seeking to pursue what she called "Balzac's method" of burying herself in her work. She told her mother-in-law that she would bring her the completed draft of her book as a Christmas present. But this proved to be simply another in the sequence of unfulfilled predictions; the strategy of making promises to friends and family failed again. December arrived and "Revolutionary Lives" was not finished.[4]

But a new agenda emerged. If any single event marked its start it was their joint appearance on September 12 at Cooper Union in New York, the site nearly fifty years before of Lincoln's landmark speech against the spread of slavery. Their scheduled lecture on European socialism abruptly turned into a discussion of comparative oppressions, and Anna found her old, passionate voice when she branched out from what she had seen in Homel to an eyewitness account of Springfield. For his part, English asserted boldly that American racial violence was worse than Russian pogroms. Afterward, they were approached by Mary White Ovington, a white settlement worker who lived in and studied Manhattan's black community and, according to family recollection, adjourned with her to the apartment of Rose and Graham Stokes on Grove Street for a night of intense discussion.[5]

In a subsequent letter, Ovington urged English to take the lead in organizing the "large and powerful body of citizens" that he had demanded in his article. English put her off until the new year, but it was clear that a fire had been lighted. In November, English responded to an invitation to speak to a black audience, and Anna reported to his parents that English had found a new passion: "English made a great speech lasting two hours in a negro church. None of us who were there will ever forget that meeting. . . . All my family were there and they all insist it was so far his best speech." She did not report its content, although clearly it sprang from his discovery of racial oppression.[6]

During December, they cleared away obligations. They appeared in Philadelphia, in New York at the University Settlement, at the University of Chicago, and in Indianapolis. The stay in Indianapolis turned out to be, surprisingly, "delightful." English patched things up with the Indiana relatives, especially with Uncle Will: "I am sure he wont misunderstand us as he has in the past, both as to our arrest and as to the poor reception he expected for the book." Will's wife, Aunt Nellie, came to hear Anna speak at the city's Cosmopolitan Club where, English reported, she "made a tremendous hit." "[W]e have quite erased the impression of the slighting remarks of the [Indianapolis] News at the time or our arrest," English wrote. "We dont need apologies from anybody." He added, referring to Anna: "She is really much better than last time and stood the traveling well." Anna was again pregnant.[7]

The framework in which English had set his account of the Springfield riot was naive, the mark of a man just learning the complexities of racial politics in America. For authority he appealed to the principles of long-dead white northern abolitionists—Lovejoy, Garrison, Wendell Phillips—and laid on the South the entire blame for spreading the infection of racial hatred. He may have been following a rhetorical strategy, but more likely he and Anna, as newcomers, were little acquainted with contemporary figures and positions.

In this dismal era, the South, encouraged by the Supreme Court's decision in *Plessy v. Ferguson*, had added a regime of official segregation to the older forms of oppression. As for the North, English's call for "absolute political and social equality" went far beyond what even enlightened opinion was ready to support. Only months before, a dinner sponsored by New York's Cosmopolitan Club had raised a furor by seating together blacks and whites of both sexes. The affair attracted not only predictably violent abuse from the South but innuendo in the New York press: The stuffily respectable *Times* (owned by a family that was as Southern as it was Jewish) complained that the dinner provoked "public disgust and indignation."[8]

Charles Edward Russell, the socialist newspaperman and muckraker, recalled the vehemence of the South and the indifference of the North: "Wittingly or unwittingly, the entire South was virtually a unit in support of hatred and the ethics of the jungle. The Civil War raged there still, with hardly abated passions. The North was utterly indifferent where it was not covertly or sneakingly applausive of helotry. . . . The whole of the society from which Walling emerged was crystallized against [the black man]; to view the darker tinted American as a human being was not good form; to insist upon his rights was insufferable gaucherie."[9]

English had yet to be schooled in the deep divisions over black aspirations—symbolized on the one hand by the celebrated Booker T. Washington, whose Tuskegee Institute in Georgia was the capital of accommodation, the doctrine that blacks must earn their way to equality by first accepting economic and social subordination; on the other by the scholarly W. E. B. Du Bois, leader of the short-lived Niagara Movement, which had declared that rights are, and ought to be, inalienable and enforceable. The outspoken neo-abolitionism of the Springfield article fell into the Du Bois camp, and Mary Ovington, to whom Du Bois was a friend and mentor, drew English into that faction.[10]

Early in 1909, English responded to Ovington's call for action by convening a tiny meeting in the apartment on West Thirty-Eighth Street. Ovington remembered the meeting as comprising three persons: herself, English, and English's old traveling companion, Henry Moskowitz of the Ethical Culture Society; Charles Edward Russell was invited but could not come to the initial session. Ovington later recalled: "[W]e liked to remember that of the three people present, one [herself] was the descendant of an old-time abolitionist, the second a Jew . . . and the third a southerner." She found English a pleasing type: "It always seemed to me that English Walling looked like a Kentuckian, tall, slender; and though he might be talking the most radical socialism, he talked it with the air of an aristocrat." She did not note that no black was present at this meeting. Nor did she mention Anna, who was probably ill in the first trimester of her pregnancy.[11]

The numbers gradually grew. Ovington brought in two black clergymen: Bishop Alexander Walters and the Reverend William Henry Brooks, both

Methodists. Russell came to the later meetings, and English tapped Lillian Wald and Florence Kelley from the settlement community. English also enlisted his old magazine rival Ray Stannard Baker, whose book, *Following the Color Line*, explored the consequences of segregation in Atlanta. Baker was still more of a centrist than English, and closer to Booker T. Washington than to Du Bois, but he could not be left out.[12]

Nor could they omit one other figure of significance. English recalled that "in view of the influence and uncompromising attitude of the *New York Evening Post* we made a special point at the outset of laying the whole project before Mr. Oswald Garrison Villard and of securing his active cooperation." Villard, a few years senior to English, entered the discussions with a proprietary air. Grandson of the abolitionist William Lloyd Garrison and son of the wealthy journalist–railroad magnate Henry Villard, he was, thanks to his father's wealth, editor both of the *Post* and of the weekly *Nation*, whose outspokenness on civil rights was rivaled only by the *Independent*; on other matters English considered both the editor and his publications to be very conservative.[13]

By the time Villard joined, the group was focusing on a call to be issued February 12 for a conference to be held later in 1909. To this point, Villard had been close to Booker T. Washington and had proposed to Washington after the Springfield riot the creation of a "Committee for the Advancement of the Negro Race." Having received little response, he joined the Ovington-Walling group and, he recalled, "drafted for them the call for the Lincoln's birthday conference."[14]

In fact, the production of the conference call was the focus of a disagreement that foreshadowed later divisions. English wrote a first draft before the end of January and showed it to the editor who had printed "The Race War in the North," Hamilton Holt of the *Independent*. Holt, perhaps still wary after southern attacks for his role in the Cosmopolitan Club's interracial dinner, tried to tone down the rhetoric about the South. "I don't believe," he wrote to English, " 'a literal reign of terror has become more firmly rooted than ever.' " "It is not true," he continued, "that 'the most respectable elements of the present ruling class in the South are inflaming the worst passions in the human heart.' " Holt concluded: "The whole paper is extravagant and is ignorant of the forces for good."[15]

Four days later, English wrote Holt to say that Villard had not liked the draft, either, but he maintained his position:

> In view of his importance to us and the position he took, I asked him if he would be good enough to re-cast it altogether. . . . However, I do not believe that Mr. Villard or any of those interested in the movement share in any way your extreme optimism. It may be that lynchings are decreas-

ing, just as executions are decreasing in Russia—that is, that "order is being restored"; in other words, that the negro is thoroughly terrorized and everywhere in the South in constant fear of murder. Indeed such a moderate portrayal of the situation as that of Ray Stannard Baker thoroughly bears me out in this position.

After further rebuttal, he concluded with personal testimony: "Of course you know I am Southern born myself and know a little not only of the position of public men but of the average private respectable citizen."[16]

Villard's draft was completed in time to be issued on Lincoln's birthday, and names were added to the list of signers, who ultimately numbered sixty. The list encompassed a broad array of reformers, journalists, educators, and literati, such as the muckraker Lincoln Steffens, the novelist William Dean Howells, the educator-philosopher John Dewey. Most imposing was the name of William Lloyd Garrison Jr., son of the founder of the *Liberator.* Among the black signers, two names stand out in retrospect: those of Du Bois and of Ida Wells Barnett, known for her fearless newspaper campaign against lynching. Villard had hoped for a spectrum wide enough to unite the contending wings of black activism, but the roster, while not thoroughly radical, offered no comfort to Washington.[17]

For Anna and English, the events in February 1909 strangely echoed those of the year before. On Lincoln's birthday, 1908, English had written the final words of his book on Russia, a day before the death of the infant, Rosalind. In 1909, the call for the National Negro Conference, in which English had invested so much energy, went out on February 12. Four days before, Anna miscarried at three and a half months, on the first anniversary of Rosalind's birth.[18]

There had been an ordeal beforehand. English's cousin Cora Tanner and her daughter had come from Illinois to visit. Rather than send the relatives out to a hotel from the apartment each night, English, with Dr. Max Strunsky's consent, transferred Anna and her nurse to the nearby Hotel Navarre. There she remained for seven weeks, as if in a hospital, while (as she complained) the nurse starved her. English came to see her and did his reading and studying there, but inevitably was gone long periods.[19]

There was also a hint of discord: a suggestion that English distrusted Max's expertise. Anna wrote later to her in-laws: "English has a wholly unfounded prejudice against him on the ground that he is not, or does not seem to be, as good a Socialist as himself." English may have laid on Max part of the blame for what happened in Paris. In any case, English called in a Dr. Edgar, who gave Anna a "new serum" for her nausea, this after Max had dosed her with bromides for a purported ulcer.[20]

Later, Anna blamed the medication, but at the time she saw herself victimized by a relentless fate. She wrote to the Wallings: "I do not feel that I can survive this horror that has come to me. And if ever I prayed at all I would pray that the peace which passes understanding, the peace which comes only with death wrap me round for ever." In the aftermath, she made another symbolic retreat from the notion of equality in marriage, much as she had decided to use her married name after Rosalind's death. She wrote to her mother-in-law that she had bought "a little wedding ring, so there may not be so much misunderstanding about us when we go among strangers. I have had engraved inside—English—June 28, 1906."[21]

1. Anna Strunsky about 1892, when the *New York Herald* praised "Miss Annie" as an outstanding scholar. (*Anna Walling Hamburger*)

2. The Strunsky
family in San
Francisco, 1895.
Back: Albert, Anna,
Elias (father). *Middle:*
Hyman, Mary
(Hyman's wife, who
died in 1903), Anna
(mother). *Front:* Rose,
Morris. (*Courtesy
English Strunsky*).

3. Anna Strunsky at 20, the "girl socialist" lecturing on the
ethics of socialism, as depicted in the *San Francisco
Examiner*, October 3, 1897.

4. Anna and her sister, Rose, about the time that Rose was a Stanford undergraduate. (*Yale University Library*)

5. Anna Strunsky, a San Francisco portrait, about the time of her involvement with Jack London. (*Anna Walling Hamburger*)

6. Jack London, a photograph he inscribed for Anna, about 1901. (*Bancroft Library, University of California, Berkeley*)

7. William English Walling, about the time he was studying at the University of Chicago. (*Anna Walling Hamburger*)

8. Studio portrait of Anna Strunsky made in Homel, Russia, while she was reporting the pogrom there in February 1906. (*Anna Walling Hamburger*)

9. Victims of the Homel massacre, February 1906, a photograph found in Anna Strunsky Walling's papers. (*Henry E. Huntington Library and Art Gallery*)

10. Anna on the balcony of the Hotel Slaviansky Bazar in Moscow, spring 1906, photographed by her fiancé. (*Anna Walling Hamburger*)

11. William English Walling, a portrait in his late twenties, about the time that he married Anna Strunsky. (*Anna Walling Hamburger*)

12. Anna Strunsky, a photograph taken in Chicago after her marriage to William English Walling in June 1906, during the period in which she was declining to use his last name. (*Anna Walling Hamburger*)

13. Anna in a carriage with a translator and a driver during the newly-weds' trip down the Volga, in the late summer and fall of 1906, a photograph taken by her husband. (*Yale University Library*)

14. Anna (*second from right in rear*) with a Russian peasant family, 1906. (*Anna Walling Hamburger*)

15. Anna's sister, Rose, perhaps about the time that she was left in charge of the revolutionary news bureau in St. Petersburg, 1907. (*Henry E. Huntington Library and Art Gallery*)

16. The press treated the arrest of Anna, English, and Rose in St. Petersburg as major news—for example, in the *New York Evening Journal*, October 22, 1907.

The Race War in the North

BY WILLIAM ENGLISH WALLING

"LINCOLN freed you, we'll show you where you belong," was one of the cries with which the Springfield mob set about to drive the negroes from town. The mob was composed of several thousand of Springfield's white citizens, while other thousands, including many women and children, and even prosperous business men in automobiles, calmly looked on, and the rioters proceeded hour after hour and on two days in succession to make deadly assaults on every negro they could lay their hands on, to sack and plunder their houses and stores, and to burn and murder on favorable occasion.

innocent negroes should be driven by the fear of their lives from a town where some of them have lived honorably for half a hundred years. We have been assured by more cautious and indirect defenders of Springfield's populace that there *was* an exceptionally criminal element among the negroes encouraged by

LINCOLN'S HOME
He is very unpopular in Springfield just now and the house was attacked.

The American people have been fairly well informed by their newspapers of the action of that mob; they have also been told of certain alleged political and criminal conditions in Springfield and of the two crimes in particular which are offered by the mob itself as sufficient explanation why six thousand peaceful and

the bosses of both political parties. And now, after a few days of discussion, we are satisfied with these explanations, and demand only the punishment of those who took the most active part in the destruction of life and property. Assuming that there were exceptionally provocative causes for complaint against the negroes, we have closed our eyes to the whole awful and menacing truth—that a large part of the white population of Lincoln's home, supported largely by the farmers and miners of the neighboring towns, have initiated a permanent warfare with the negro race.

We do not need to be informed at

589

17. Opening page of the article on the race riot in Springfield, Illinois, that led to the founding of the NAACP—from *The Independent*, September 3, 1908.

18. Anna testifies near the end of the breach-of-promise trial—sketches from *The World*, March 4, 1911.

19. Sketch of English Walling made during the trial of Anna Berthe Grunspan's breach-of-promise suit, from the *New York World*, February 21, 1911.

20. The growing family: the Wallings' daughters Rosamond, Anna, and Georgia, with Lee Warrel, nursemaid, 1915, probably on Nantucket. (*Yale University Library*)

21. Anna Strunsky Walling and son, Hayden, born 1916, probably at the summer rental in New London, Connecticut, summer of 1917. (*Yale University Library*)

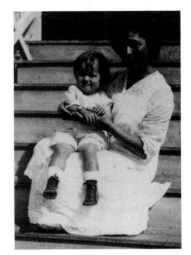

22. English Walling in full cry during the Great War—a portrait that appeared with his attack on American socialists as disloyal in *The Independent*, November 10, 1917.

23. Anna Strunsky in her forties. (*Anna Walling Hamburger*)

24. Socialism long behind him, English Walling ran unsuccessfully in 1924 for the congressional seat in southwest Connecticut. (*William English Walling Papers, State Historical Society of Wisconsin*)

In the six months after the Springfield riot, English was thrust to the fore-
front among white proponents of black rights. The coalition of "new abolitionists" made room for him and looked to him for leadership. As for English,
it was his first association as an equal with some of the notable figures of
American reform. Certainly, as a man who had encountered the most formidable personages in the Russian hierarchy, he was not intimidated, but he
often struggled with the nuances of American racial politics and found himself temperamentally ill at ease in conventional parliamentary settings.[1]

After the call for a National Negro Conference at the end of May, the
enterprise took on bulk and formality. Because of its growing size (and possibly in deference to Anna, recuperating from her miscarriage), the committee
moved its meetings from the Wallings' apartment to the new quarters of the
Liberal Club, at 103 East Nineteenth Street. English alternated in the chair
with Charles Edward Russell. In its sequence of meetings, the group developed a list of one hundred fifty sponsors and authorized a thousand invita-
tions. Oswald Garrison Villard, who grumbled to a relative that he had to
give more time to the effort because "[t]he people who have it in charge are
well-meaning but they are inexperienced and impractical," made a last-
minute gesture of inviting Booker T. Washington to the meeting but in a
manner that let him decline. Washington did not come.[2]

On May 31, 1909, three hundred representatives of the black and white
elites (many more, of course, of the latter than the former) gathered in the
assembly hall of the United Charities Building, on Fourth Avenue not far
from Gramercy Park in Manhattan. They were drawn not only from the aged
abolitionists and their descendants, but from the settlement houses, and
from among black church leaders, academics, and journalists. They were
interlaced with socialists and many more who sympathized with socialism.
A major number were women.[3]

English called the National Negro Conference to order and turned over the
chair to William Hayes Ward of the *Independent*, seventy-four years old,
the son of abolitionists, and the country's most caustic commentator on
the follies of racism. There followed two long presentations, by an anthro-
pologist and a zoologist, comparing human brain sizes with those of other
mammals. These disquisitions were designed to refute scientific theories of

black inferiority, but the comparisons with primates must have made hearers squirm.[4]

The speech by English later in the afternoon was possibly the most radical that the gathering heard. He saw the oppression of blacks gradually spreading to white workers, especially immigrants, and warned of an antilabor, antiblack alliance between southern aristocrats and northern corporations. In terms that echoed his Springfield article, he said: "The class that stands for persecution of the Negro once given a share in our national government will stand for any and every other form of attack on free and democratic institutions, every form of reaction known to eastern Europe. The Negro's only hope is at the same time the sole safeguard of the nation." Although they approached the problem from different directions, it was clear that he and Du Bois, who had spoken earlier in the day, were destined to be allies against those who saw the mutual goal as simple reform rather than social realignment.[5]

On the next day, June 1, the mood of the conference grew turbulent. Speaker after speaker referred to two recent grievances: the strike by white railroad firemen in Georgia to oust black firemen from their jobs, and the abandonment by President Taft, in a speech at Howard University, of the Republican party's historic advocacy of blacks' rights. But as the hour approached for determining what the meeting would say and do, there was a surge as, in Du Bois's words, the "black mass moved forward and stretched out their hands to take charge." The conference became a tense struggle for dominance, expressed through interminable resolutions and amendments from the floor.[6]

Reporting for the committee on organization, Villard, the advocate of order, sketched an association shaped along the lines of other reforms: "Is not to-day every great crusade, whether on behalf of child labor, the conservation of our national resources, or the warfare on tuberculosis, conducted on precisely these lines suggested—with a publicity bureau and a national committee?" But the restive body was not ready to be shaped in the mold of being just another white reform cause.[7]

English, initially presiding over the resolutions committee, stumbled both as a mediator and as a drafter. (Villard remarked afterward that "Walling, though an 'able' fellow, was no writer.") At one point, so tumultuous did the discussion become that English and Villard considered abandoning the whole concept of a new national organization. In the end, English yielded to Villard, who had the seniority and will to force the gathering to reach conclusions before it adjourned, but the task took nearly until midnight. The resolutions ultimately adopted were narrow, urging strict enforcement of constitutional rights, equal education, and "incorporation of a national committee to be known as a Committee for the Advancement of the Negro Race" (the term "Advancement" being a personal favorite of Villard's).[8]

The last act of the conference was the reading by Du Bois of the membership of an organizing committee of forty, with English designated as chair, to prepare the way for a permanent governing committee. The committee was quickly approved and Russell gaveled the meeting to adjournment. But there was outrage on the floor; the list excluded blacks who had made trouble in the proceedings, notably William Monroe Trotter of the *Boston Guardian* and Ida Wells Barnett, the anti-lynching campaigner, who had been suspicious from the start that Villard would try to "tie us to the chariot wheels of the industrial education program" of Booker T. Washington. Wells Barnett angrily refused reinstatement and swept out of the building.[9]

Though handled roughly by Villard, English did not seem to be bruised. Anna wrote to the senior Wallings on the day after the meeting: "The conference on the Negro situation is over, and English rightly gratified at the result. He has worked very hard and we are both relieved now it's over. The press comment has been excellent."[10]

The conference left a great deal of unfinished business. The next week, English wrote somewhat disjointedly to Du Bois, with whom he was still so slightly acquainted that he initially sent a telegram to the wrong university. With Villard pulling the strings, black membership on the organizing committee had been further reduced. English told Du Bois: "It is impossible that twelve colored members could thoroughly represent all the ideas, sentiments, standpoints and organizations which ought to receive a constant hearing inside our committee." English now proposed expansion to fifty members, to include not only Wells Barnett but enough names to increase the black membership to twenty. As ultimately published, the list contained only thirty-eight names, with more than a dozen blacks but fewer than twenty.[11]

Two weeks after the conference, the *Independent* published English's long article, "Science and Human Brotherhood," a sweeping assault on the scientific racialism dominant in America, England, and western Europe. The text of the article did not mention the conference, and it was probably prepared weeks before. In his rambling discussion, English spared neither Jack London's old favorite poet, Kipling, nor fellow socialists. But he won for himself an adversary by criticizing Booker T. Washington in print. The Wizard of Tuskegee responded through the *Age,* the New York newspaper he controlled, charging that English had confused civil rights and social privileges. Nor did he forget.[12]

With the future of the new organization in momentary suspension, English and Anna left New York. All spring, Anna had been on the sidelines, even after she was declared physically recovered from her miscarriage. Still trying to place her story on the Springfield riot, Anna had been advised by Hamilton Holt of the *Independent* to send it to an agent he knew in London. But now there was to be no more work, for English wished to recuperate from his strenuous efforts for the National Negro Conference. A week or so before they sailed for Europe, Anna found that she was pregnant again, only three months after the miscarriage. Despite her qualms, she decided to brave the voyage.[13]

It proved to be a beneficent choice. Late in June, English wrote to his parents from Paris, reporting a resumption of the familiar old traveling life: "We are living economically. Our room—with toilet attached—*and breakfasts* cost us altogether 7.50 fr ($1.50) a day. . . . Every week we are going to spend a day or two in the country and about the end of July will leave for Switzerland." Anna basked in the change of scene after the "terrible winter" and in the all but unique experience of being alone with English. The only question for her was whether she would be able to see this third drama of motherhood to a successful conclusion.[14]

Early in July 1909, Anna wrote to the senior Wallings from Paris: "We visited Pere Lachaise. We found a beautiful yellow flower growing over the little grave." They were seeing old friends among the Russian exiles, she reported, and English had also looked up the novelist David Graham Phillips and his sister and introduced them to Anna. She was won over at once, because Phillips told her of meeting an old man at Karlsbad who had all but memorized *The Kempton-Wace Letters.*[1]

The placidity of their summer was disrupted when newspapers in America announced that Berthe Grunspan, English's sometime companion of the months before he met Anna, was filing suit in New York for breach of promise, using his letters as evidence. The *San Francisco Examiner*, still considering Anna a local celebrity, gave her top billing: "Balm for Her Heart Sought From Anna Strunsky's Husband." The *Chicago Record-Herald*, fed by Dr. Walling, put a defensive twist on the story:

SOCIOLOGY, NOT LOVE,

IN WALLING LETTERS

'Exhibit A' in Anna Berthe

Grunspan's Heart Balm

Suit Proves Cold.

ATTRIBUTED TO SYMPATHY

Interest Shown by Writer in

Young Russian Jewess Is

Called Philanthropic[2]

The suit had not come as an utter surprise; a Chicago lawyer who had been asked to represent Grunspan had telephoned English's brother, Willoughby, who had sent a warning. Lawyers were already at work on English's behalf in New York; he had hired Emil Fuchs, whom he had known since University Settlement days. Dr. Walling's statement in the newspaper was scoffing: "Nine cases out of ten of this sort are blackmail . . . and I haven't much doubt about the character of this one. . . . English is the last man in the world to become involved in such a matter. He has the scholar's temperament and most of his life has been passed among books and the study of political problems. . . . No one who knows English will be inclined to believe that he allowed himself to play fast and loose with a young girl."[3]

From Switzerland, early in August, Anna wrote a Panglossian letter to the senior Wallings: "I wish English could have told you beforehand, by word of mouth, the true story of this annoying business, for looked at closely, nothing does him more credit nor more sets off the beauty and the goodness of his character than his attitude and conduct towards this woman. He told me all about it when we first fell in love with each other, and we were of one opinion concerning her, that she was an unworthy person. . . . I have known for three years that this would have to come up, because of this person's tenaciousness, and I have not been worried about the outcome. . . but only for fear that it would annoy English too much. But he takes it very calmly."[4]

For his own part, English commented to his parents: "There is only one aspect of the matter that bothers me—the irregular way in which the case seems to disappear and then bobs up again. This makes it look as if Miss G. is likely to be pretty persistant [sic]. . . . She seems to have given up her crazy idea of a grievance against me three or four times, only to take it up again on seeing us on the street (twice in Paris, once in N.Y.)"[5]

English read the matter accurately. Berthe Grunspan's suit did not evaporate; gradually it became clear that the case would go to trial, and he and Anna soon had a foretaste of what was in store. Rosalind Walling wrote: "The newspapers have had some very mean articles about you both. . . . [A California newspaper] said [Anna] was the co-respondent in Jack London's divorce and the tables were turned on her now and she was hav[ing] the same trouble Mrs. London had suffered from on her account—other articles said Anna's refusing to use her husband's name was on account of his relations with this woman."[6]

For the time being, they had a more important matter on their minds—trying to assure that Anna had a successful pregnancy. They spent much of the rest of their time in Europe seeking the counsel of a certain Dr. Mende, who was based in Zurich but was frustratingly elusive. Anna recalled that during their visit to Tolstoy in 1906 Tolstoy's daughter had told her of having five stillbirths and of being treated in Zurich; Anna had been "slightly bored" at this distraction. But now she was seeking out the same doctor, who broke two appointments and eventually turned up just as they were about to catch a train. He wrote some advice and disappeared again. Then at last he reappeared and diagnosed them both: Anna as suffering from colitis and gaunt English as afflicted with "a catarrh of the lower intestine" that kept him from absorbing food properly and thus lowered the supply of blood to his brain, creating excitability. Dr. Mende was an advocate of repose.[7]

They had a rough voyage back to New York, and Anna had to lie in her berth most of the way. She wrote: "We were both horribly bored and we sang songs, talked, chattered, to pass the time away and then burst into real moaning for very boredom."[8]

Home again, Anna and English tried to observe Dr. Mende's prescription of the quiet life. Anna's brother Albert had already moved their furniture from the summer place in Hempstead to Caritas, the Stokeses' chic little island. Socialist and settlement friends shuttled on and off Caritas, some lingering to live there. Anna and English had received an invitation from Graham Stokes as early as 1907; but English, then in Sevastopol, had responded that while they were "proud and grateful" for the invitation they were not likely to settle down.[9]

Two years later, however, Anna was willing enough to stay in a little house on Caritas while she waited out her third pregnancy. Around Thanksgiving, she wrote a rambling letter to her in-laws about island life: "We have a good colored cook, a typical mammy. . . . I have gotten a good start on the last part of my book. I have some sound hopes of completing it before the blessed baby arrives. . . . I have always been emotional, and it is my emotions that distract me so ruinously from my work. I have not lost confidence in my future, but I have certainly lost time."[10]

Their lives—English's life, at least—did not remain calm for long. Early in November 1909, the much-disputed Committee of Forty set up by the National Negro Conference met at the Liberal Club in New York, with English presiding. He promptly announced that ill health would keep him from continuing in the chair, although he planned to attend all meetings. Historians have explained this surprising step variously as a result of friction arising from his efforts to expand the black membership of the committee or as an effort to spare the new organization possible embarrassment from the Grunspan suit, which had already inspired scathing comment in Booker T. Washington's *New York Age*. Oswald Garrison Villard willingly took over for English, complaining in subsequent family letters about English's temperament.[11]

The complaint of ill health may not have been entirely a cover; on previous occasions, the far from robust English had been laid low by what were then called neurasthenic complaints. Moreover, his pattern of activity during the latter part of 1909 suggests a freneticism bordering on instability. The Grunspan suit may have placed him under the extreme stress of trying to maintain a good public character while newspaper publicity continued to undermine it.

The same feverishness was evident in his abrupt intervention in Socialist Party affairs. Although socialism had supplied the perspective of his writings, he had had only sporadic contact with socialist organizations and was not a member of the Socialist Party of America. A change in his attitude was forecast in a panoramic letter on November 18, 1909, to the brahmin of English socialism, H. M. Hyndman: "I favor not only the ordinary Socialist opposition to all wars, but the taking of the most desperate means to prevent them." He saw British imperialism as no better than German and discerned American imperial aspirations as well in Latin America and China. He opposed a congress of English-speaking Socialists because it would present "a pronunciamento . . . against the inferior races." On the American scene, he observed, the greatest obstacle to socialism was the convergence of interests between the skilled workers of the American Federation of Labor and the capitalists.[12]

It was this last issue, it turned out, that had caught and fixed his attention and ultimately led him to precipitate an historic and fruitless intraparty dispute. Months before, he had published in the Chicago-based *International Socialist Review* an article opposing the creation of a British-style labor party in America because he feared that such a movement might absorb the Socialist Party. On November 19, 1909, Algie Simons, an old friend from Chicago days and now editor of the *Chicago Daily Socialist*, wrote to English an incautious letter discussing a realignment of the socialist movement so as to incorporate the strength of the labor movement; in other words, to make common cause with sympathetic elements in the AFL.[13]

The response from English was symptomatic of disorder. Ignoring past friendship, his own past ties with the AFL, and his tenuous, almost nonexistent connection with the Socialist Party of America, English sent off Simons's personal letter to be read—that is, to be exposed—to the party. Moreover, he added a letter of his own interpreting Simons's letter as evidence of a conspiracy among the members of the National Executive Committee majority (of which Simons was a member) to maintain themselves in office while dissolving the socialist movement. When Simons's letter was read aloud to a New York local committee, a "near-riot" took place. Simons was aghast; he wrote to English a few days later: "The thing that shocked and pained as nothing I have had happen to me during my work in the Socialist movement, is the terrible revelation of the character of one in whom I have always had the most complete confidence."[14]

English instantly became the issue. He had selected as adversaries not only Simons but all the moderates on the National Executive Committee, including Robert Hunter, who had recruited him to come to the University Settlement; Morris Hillquit of the Lower East Side, one of the party's most popular political figures; Victor Berger of Milwaukee; and the muckraker John Spargo, author of *The Bitter Cry of the Children*. His heedless treatment of old friends and his fixation on conspiracy lend support to the diagnosis by Spargo in a letter to Graham Stokes: "Mentally unbalanced, erratic in his movements, Mr. Walling is one of the most pathetic figures I have ever encountered." Hunter wrote to Simons offering his regrets that he had not warned him of English's "present mental and moral irresponsibility."[15]

Yet Spargo and Hunter overstated the matter, or stated it too crudely. However destructive his actions, the substantive position English took was not irrational, given his alignment with the socialist left wing, the "impossibilists" who opposed any measures that would merely moderate the capitalist system. He retained at least one important ally, his Caritas neighbor and host, Graham Stokes. Although more philanthropist than journalist, Stokes bore the title of Sunday editor of the socialist *New York Call*, and was able to place in the Sunday *Call* material favorable to English.[16]

Moreover, English defended himself ably in a long letter to the party's senior figure, Eugene V. Debs. Knowing that he was being attacked as an outsider, a nonmember, he claimed that he had been a loyal socialist outside the Party—that he had recruited his brother and that Anna had been a member for fifteen years (that is, from the time when she joined the old Socialist Labor party as an adolescent). But his own position as an author, he insisted, forbade him to join: "I have been working for years on a book, not on Socialism but on the Socialist movement. If this book is to be read by a non-Socialist public, which is exclusively the one to which I am addressing myself, it would have to be written either by a famous Socialist like yourself, or else by one who could claim to be strictly non-partisan in his attitude. . . . I feel that I have a moral right to complete the work and put it before the public as non-partisan, and that I can best serve the Socialist cause in this way." Debs replied sympathetically.[17]

Out of this turmoil came little but ill feeling, a deepening division between party factions. The elections for the National Executive Committee in February 1910 returned all of English's opponents to office save one, the unfortunate Simons. English complained to Debs that the result showed that "a large part of the rank and file of the party are fools," for Simons had been the least discreditable of the lot: "I am as bitterly and absolutely opposed to the 'Socialism' of Victor Berger and Robert Hunter as I am to the trade unionism of Gompers or the politics of Hearst. In fact, as bourgeois reformers, if that is to be the game, I find the latter far superior."[18]

In February 1910, English at last joined the party that he had so thoroughly roiled. In doing so, he defied the advice of friends. One, a card-carrying member, warned him that he would find the meetings intolerable. Another letter-writer advised: "If I had your talent, time, and opportunities, I would direct myself to the movement and not to the party. The two are not identical." His father wrote an angry letter after the fact. He was coming to visit, but he would not discuss two matters on which they disagreed deeply: the "negro question" and English's party membership—"the most grievous thing that has come into my life lately." He observed, with accuracy: "You are not fit for *party* connection."[19]

On January 29, 1910, Anna completed her long journey to motherhood. English sent a telegram to Chicago from New York: "Your grand daughter much resembling Anna arrived this morning both well." Rosamond English Walling was watched with extreme anxiety through her first days, with Anna's hand rarely leaving the edge of the bassinet. Despite one or two conventional, brief illnesses, Rosamond thrived. At an age, thirty-three, when many women were completing their childbearing, Anna was starting hers.[1]

Even as he was thrashing about in the sectarian struggles of the Socialist Party, English continued to work with the National Negro Conference. There his conduct strongly resembled his behavior among the socialists: reckless and extreme argumentation combined with not inarguable positions. After the March 1910 meeting of the organizing committee, Frances Blascoer, a former University Settlement worker brought onto the staff by Oswald Garrison Villard, wrote candidly to a woman—somebody close to the new organization—whom she addressed as "Dear Lady." The letter was partisan, to be sure, because Blascoer was reflexively hostile to anybody who crossed Villard. At the same time her description of English's tactics in the meetings is consistent with other reports in this period: "Everyone seemed possessed of a very devil of don't care, and Walling acted like a six-months' old infant, angering Mr. Villard so that he nearly got off the Committee. I think Mr. Villard is a pretty fine fellow, even if he hasn't Walling's damnably acute intelligence. I am having my hands full to keep them both working on the committee, I can tell you. I don't know what makes Walling do the things he does unless it is a devil of perversity."[2]

Her remarks on Anna were even more revealing, if more complex. A recent Du Bois biographer hints that Blascoer regarded Anna (whom the biographer calls the "very Russian Mrs. Walling") as a termagant who had plunged Blascoer into a "blue funk." In fact, Blascoer's letter, while suggesting that Anna's efforts to help had led to her being considered an annoyance, nonetheless defended her in a backhanded way: "I have seen a good deal of Mrs. Walling, and I think you and the others really do her an injustice in many ways. Granted she is sentimental and a bit tiresome, I find a lot of good in her too, and if I had to live with Walling, granted that I loved him as she undoubtedly does, I am quite sure that I should be a lot worse than she is. Her baby is darling, and I think she is a dandy mother—and she has the nurse my cousin had, so I hear all about it. I think Walling's friends treat her abominably."[3]

These words were a measure of how far the public Anna had fallen in relation to her husband. Blascoer depicted a woman who had become half-bore, half-victim, who had intruded herself where, apparently, neither Blascoer nor English nor English's friends wanted her. From being at the center of an arena they once shared, she had been driven to the fringes. Nor was this merely the consequence of motherhood; their lives were entering an enduring pattern in which English was the public figure and Anna's public activities were considered less than serious.

The committee organizing the second annual meeting of the National Negro Conference scheduled it for April 1910, in Washington, then found that it could not obtain unsegregated facilities and reset the conference for May, in New York. The theme, officially, was disfranchisement, but the real agenda was the creation of a permanent national organization. Before the meeting, English wrote his parents claiming the lion's share: "The whole thing[,] policy, resolutions[,] plan of organization is all mine—though I've give[n] comparatively little time to it this year." On May 14, 1910, he emerged from the conference with a new position, chairman of the executive committee (this despite his earlier abrupt resignation as the chair of the Committee of Forty); Villard had the title only of assistant treasurer, but in fact he held the purse strings and a great deal of untitled authority. Not incidentally, the meeting named the new organization the National Association for the Advancement of Colored People, as Villard had wanted.[4]

English set his sights on obtaining for the new organization the services of W. E. B. Du Bois. In his pride and implacability Du Bois was a kind of a spiritual counterpart of English. But he far exceeded English in self-discipline and achievement. He was one of the two major black contributors to American magazines, and while he could scarcely outdo Booker T. Washington's writing factory he was a worthy competitor. To come to New York to work in the NAACP represented not only an opportunity to move on from his academic career but the promise of a magazine of his own, to be entirely devoted to advancing the race.[5]

The one major drawback for Du Bois was that he would have to work with Villard. Between the two meetings of the National Negro Conference a feud had sprung up between the two. Both had been working on biographies of the abolitionist John Brown; Villard had even asked Du Bois for assistance. But when Du Bois's *John Brown* was published, Villard took it upon himself to review it ungenerously in the *Nation.* Du Bois submitted a rebuttal, which was rejected for publication in a letter that lectured Du Bois on historiography. Villard eventually wrote a conciliatory letter, but the ill feeling remained.[6]

It was left to English to be the facilitator. By June 1910 relations between Villard and Du Bois had returned to a civility sufficient to permit English to write Du Bois a recruiting letter. English described the financial shakiness of the new association—wealthy donors had all left the cities for the summer, he explained—but he hoped that money could be raised within the committee. English promised a definite offer by the end of the month. "If I were an old and intimate friend of yours," English wrote, "I should certainly urge you to take the risk. If I am not mistaken, the moment is a critical one for your work and public activities; but such moments come in the lives of all, and there are certain risks which ought to be taken." Du Bois responded in five days that he was "willing to accept any reasonable risk for the privilege of engaging in a work which, I agree with you, is of paramount and critical importance."[7]

One last obstacle lay in the way. Frances Blascoer, possibly thinking herself to be acting as a proxy for Villard, bitterly opposed the idea of placing Du Bois at the head of a research and publicity department when basic organizational work was yet to be done. Du Bois took her opposition as a personal reluctance to work with him. After the committee sought to reassure Blascoer it formally approved the offer to Du Bois, with Villard's acquiescence. Mary Dunlop Maclean of the committee, an African-American and a writer for the *New York Times,* sent Du Bois an enthusiastic telegram: "miss B was all right, large office for you in Vesey Street, Wallings arrangement[.] I approve and am happy." A few days later, Du Bois resigned from Atlanta University and became director of publicity and research for the NAACP. English had scored a coup, for Du Bois proved to be the key to the organization's vitality.[8]

English made one other historic contribution more casually. As Mary Ovington told it later, a small group was sitting about in the new offices in the *Post* (that is, Villard's) building in downtown Manhattan, speculating on what to call the magazine that Du Bois wanted to create as the voice of the new organization. Ovington began to talk about James Russell Lowell's "The Present Crisis" ("Once to every man and nation . . .") and English seized upon the word; the magazine became *The Crisis.*[9]

Du Bois, having moved to New York, was among the visitors to the Wallings' house at Caritas that summer. In a letter written fifty-two years later, Anna hesitantly unveiled a residue of racial contradiction in English. After recounting how English had changed from the time that he objected to eating with blacks at Harvard, she added:

But now I am impelled to tell all of the truth—he did not change viscerally. When Dr. Dubois, the great man, did us the honor of spending two or three week-ends with us on Caritas Island, Wallock's Point, Stamford, Conn., and he went in swimming with English and me, English confessed to me that he felt he was "swimming with a monkey."

I did not reproach him. I was silent. He could not help it—this was [two words illegible] part-of-him—visceral. This is what happened to him in early childhood. How sad!10

But the revelation itself is puzzling. It is a recollection concealed for half a century, testifying to its vividness in Anna's mind but also raising doubts about its accuracy. Still, she could hardly have fabricated it utterly, and it was the kind of thing English was capable of saying. Yet, finally, there is the question of why he should have addressed such a remark to Anna, whom he knew it would offend, rather than remaining silent.

The incident becomes even less understandable when compared with testimony in a letter from a black businessman that English received about that time. B. F. Lee Jr. asked whether English recalled talking with him during a meeting of the Negro Business League in New York. Lee added: "I wish to say that your discussion was so fair, broad and just, that, in spite of your color, I took it for granted that you were in some way connected with my race."11

Such a response could scarcely arise from attitudes that were put on merely to please or flatter. Certainly injustice, as always, spoke clearly to English's reasoning mind, but as a social being—despite his call in the Springfield article for political *and* social equality—he remained not so much a southerner as a man of his time, to whom intimate association with blacks remained strange and unsettling. Given Du Bois's temperament and pride, if he had noticed a slight he would not have let it pass. But the correspondence between him and English that summer remained cordial, if a little impatient because English, engrossed in vacationing, did not always respond promptly. And Du Bois could not have failed to note that while English and Anna entertained him socially, he never received an invitation from Villard.12

Du Bois was eager to move ahead with the inaugural issue of *The Crisis* by October 1 and was unhappy that the executive committee, chaired by English, was not scheduled to meet until later in that month. Ultimately a special meeting gave approval to the enterprise and the first issue of *The Crisis*, which was to continue under Du Bois's editorship for twenty-four years, appeared in November.13

In the fall of 1910, English and Anna set off on an organizing trip for the NAACP. Still unwilling to trust the eight-month-old Rosamond to a nurse, Anna took the infant along. They spoke in Chicago and moved on to Cleveland, where they were intensely scrutinized by Booker T. Washington's operatives, who reported back to Tuskegee. George A. Myers, a black Republican political boss and barber, provided an account of the Wallings' effort to set up a local NAACP branch. Their chief contact was the lawyer-novelist Charles Waddell Chesnutt. Chesnutt petitioned Myers to help him set up a meeting for the Wallings, and Myers offered to provide a session with the Cleveland Association of Colored Men. But Anna and English insisted on "a mixed meeting," so as "to get in touch with the white people of the community who were friendly to the brother." In the end, Chesnutt held the meeting in his own home. Myers was confident that the anti-Washington movement would go no farther: "As the small boy said to the one begging—'There aint going to be no core.' There will be no more meetings."[14]

Anna and little Rosamond returned home by the end of October. In a diary she had started to record Rosamond's progress, she reflected on her own new role:

> But the question arises always how much a mother who truly takes care of her child can do for art or work outside, how much is left after the broken, sleepless night[s], the seven half hours a day of breast feeding, the baths, changings, supervising of the nurse-girl that the carriage be properly placed outside of the sun and wind, that the netting really does protect her from flies and gnats and yet does not exclude too much air, after the inevitable quarter hours and half hours of holding the child, after the twenty or thirty times of going upstairs for her for one thing or another.
>
> This is the mere physical side of the case, to which must be added the loss of health, the overfatigue, the backaches, the occasional side-aches, the weakness when she has nursed too long when the milk wasn't abundant, the giddiness on first jumping out of bed from a heavy sleep in the middle of the night. What is all this besides the psychical disqualification for work? The interruptions make consecutive thought almost impossible, the preoccupation with the child is an even more serious handicap.

She confessed as well that the shade of the lost "Little International," Rosalind, still hovered around Rosamond.[15]

The Grunspan trial loomed early in 1911. Initially, English intended to park Anna and little Rosamond far away for the duration. In January 1911, the three of them went to a resort in Georgia. But as soon as he went back to New York Anna chafed: "Sweetheart, this is the first and last time I leave myself behind!" She offered fretsome advice; distrusting or disliking the defense lawyer, she urged English to seek out the celebrated Clarence Darrow. She also urged him not to appear in court: "The thing is wholly out of the question, from any human or revolutionary standpoint. I don't care if the whole world thinks otherwise."[1]

The experience turned out to be as public and as humiliating as anything they might have imagined. Members of New York's socialist community turned up in great numbers and the proceedings, in a state court in lower Manhattan, automatically qualified—being compounded of wealth and sex, nicely framed in a morality tale—for detailed attention in the New York popular press. For Anna and English, to whom in the past newspapers had been attentive and generous, this new casting must have been unsettling. Hearst's *Evening Journal* tipped its hand early. Besides offering a full-length, page-one photo of Berthe Grunspan, the *Journal* told the reader what to think of her story: "It is a remarkable tale, romantic and pathetic, and as the bewitching teacher of Russian [Grunspan] told it between convulsive sobs, the women in the courtroom wept in sympathy." The *World* was more reserved during the initial sessions, but let Grunspan's story of seduction and betrayal dominate.[2]

Anna could not tolerate being hundreds of miles away. On February 23, Berthe Grunspan capped the day's dramatics by reading a letter she had sent to English in 1906 threatening suicide. But the *World's* reporter was diverted by the abrupt appearance of Anna and sister Rose, who made no secret of their presence:

> For the first time since the trial began, Mrs. Walling—Anna Strunsky, authoress and revolutionist—was present in court. With her seventeen-year-old sister [Rose was twenty-six] she sat at Walling's side. Several hundred "comrades," men and women, packed the big courtroom. At the recesses they formed excited groups and discussed the trial in many languages.

During the morning the trial was halted dramatically. Mrs. Walling had apparently found great amusement in the heart-broken letters of love which Miss Grunspan had written to her husband. She laughed, smiled, nudged her husband and shrugged her shoulders contemptuously.

Suddenly Miss Grunspan broke down and wept bitterly.

"Oh, that man, that man," she cried, pointing a wavering figure at Walling, who was smiling complacently. "I just can't stand the way he's looking at me. His look goes right through me, and it's the nastiest kind of a look. It just gives me the horrors. And then, too, the way he and that woman, his wife, chuckle and laugh together."

The judge directed the Walling table to behave itself. The next day, a sketch of Anna and Rose appeared in the *World*. Anna, it was clear, had made her choice—that she was going to be an active participant, even at the cost to her dignity.[3]

The next day, Emil Fuchs, representing English, went about requisite business of trying to soil Berthe Grunspan's reputation. Deterred by the judge's warning, those seated at the Walling table avoided staring at her. The reporter noted that Anna seemed amused by only one portion of the testimony, when Berthe Grunspan described how freely English spent money on her. After airing vague allegations about men seen in Grunspan's company, Fuchs concentrated for hours on destroying the notion that English might have been seriously interested in a woman as young and unlearned as she. He inquired about her reading, her education, her sexual behavior.[4]

The trial adjourned for a weekend, but the newspapers persisted. A reporter called on Berthe Grunspan at her quarters: "Her dark hair fell in two soft braids on either side of her piquant, clear-skinned face. Her eyes shone lustrously." Love, she confessed, had come to her like a "blinding light," but it had passed and she now wished she were a swordswoman, so as to torment her former lover. She added: "And his wife—how she laughed in the courtroom! Nothing hurts any one so much as ridicule, especially a woman in my position."[5]

To this point, it must have seemed—to newspaper readers, at least—that Berthe Grunspan was a sure thing. She had fended off cross-examination spiritedly, and the press seemed all but ready to hand her all she demanded. But as it resumed on the last day of February, the trial had a new element: the intervention of the all-male jury, which under the state's rules could ask witnesses questions. In particular, Juror No. 5, eventually identified in the *World* as one Charlie (or Bill) Hirsch, began to take an active role, and indeed developed a formidable courtroom manner, as he badgered witnesses in his "rasping insistent voice." Not that Juror No. 5 posed questions that sounded helpful to the defense. He asked witnesses produced by Fuchs bluntly whether they had actually *seen* Berthe Grunspan behave improperly, and each had to concede that he, or she, had not.[6]

On March 1, English took the stand to tell his long-prepared version of the affair, which agreed in its essential chronology with Berthe Grunspan's account, but in which he continually implied that she had been sexually knowledgeable and available. On the next day, he faced "a merciless volley" of questions from Juror No. 5, who concentrated on the episode in which English obtained a false passport for Berthe Grunspan from the American embassy in Paris:

> "Did you have to take your oath to the statement on the passport that Miss Grunspan was your wife?" he demanded.
>
> "I think I did," Walling replied.
>
> "Oh, so you admit, do you, that you swore falsely?"
>
> "Yes."
>
> "Well, did you have a sleeper going to Berlin with Miss Grunspan?" the juror asked, taking another tack.
>
> "No. You see, I thought that by giving the guard a dollar or two we could have the compartment to ourselves. You know you don't pay $10 when you can get out of it for one. But the train was crowded and we found that another man had been put in the compartment with us in spite of the tip."
>
> "Did you have a sleeper going to Geneva?" No. 5 wanted to know.
>
> "Yes."
>
> "So you thought that this trip was worth more to you than the other?"
>
> "No. It wasn't that, but you see I had learned the lesson of the other unfortunate experience.[7]

Finally, the foreman, who had fidgeted through this string of queries, exploded: "Oh, for heaven's sake, Bill!" But Hirsch was not deterred and led English through embarrassment after embarrassment: he had left a trunk of papers with Grunspan; he had given her a picture of his young nephew; he had abandoned Anna in Paris to take a cab ride with Grunspan. English flushed as he insisted that it was difficult to escape her grip.[8]

At this point, Grunspan's counsel took up the chase and read passages from postcards and letters English had sent to her. English insisted: "I wanted to be just as friendly as possible without expressing love." So it continued far into the day, to the accompaniment of hisses and guffaws from the jammed courtroom.[9]

One interested reader of the newspaper accounts was Booker T. Washington. A month before, already on the scent of the Wallings, he had written to a New York ally, the editor T. T. Fortune: "It seems rather strange . . . that persons like Walling, who[se wife?] is a Russian, and some white woman, whose name I cannot recall [Frances Blascoer] . . . should come in at this late date to take charge of our race."[10]

After English's embarrassing day on the stand, Washington wrote to Charles William Anderson, his chief lieutenant in the North:

> I believe you are keeping up with the case of Mr. Wm. English Walling. He is a great fellow to become the leader of the colored race, to advise them along moral lines. You know he is the chairman of the executive committee of the new "movement."
>
> I wonder if you cannot get Moore to "burn Walling up" in an editorial in his paper.[11]

Fred R. Moore, proprietor on behalf of Washington of the *New York Age*, obliged with an editorial: "We hope that no colored man or woman will in the future disgrace our race by inviting Mr. Walling in their home or ask him to speak at any public meeting." (This moralistic position was dented a few days later when Booker T. Washington himself was assaulted while on an unexplained visit to a Manhattan neighborhood known for prostitution.)[12]

In the courtroom, the increasingly impatient judge pushed the breach-of-promise trial to its conclusion, but not before permitting one unscheduled witness. At noon on the last day of testimony, March 3, Anna found that her husband's lawyer was resting his case without calling her. She petitioned the judge to let her take the stand: "I know Mr. Fuchs has agreed not to call any more witnesses . . . but this isn't a point of law with me. Twenty years from now I may be dead, but this accusation from that woman—that my husband besmirched my name—may be thrown in my daughter's face, with the added slur that I never denied the charge. I want my statement to go on the records." The slur to which she referred was Berthe Grunspan's assertion that English had told her: "She [Anna] has been living with a man for six or seven years. I couldn't love her." The judge acceded to Anna's request.[13]

That news brought an even heavier crush to a courtroom already filled. A mob pushed toward the doors, and a dozen police officers were brought over from City Hall to keep the corridors clear. When she was called, Anna gave her version of the encounter of June 16, 1906, when she and English and Rose had seen Berthe Grunspan in the Place de l'Opéra in Paris. She spiritedly defended English's good faith and claimed as well that he had shown her all of the correspondence between him and Grunspan. Juror No. 5 questioned her, not too sharply. But just as she was reaching the point of defending her own good name, her husband's lawyer, Fuchs, cut her off and she had to step down.[14]

It is not clear whether, beyond the solidarity it evinced, Anna's testimony was important. As it turned out, the notorious Juror No. 5 may already have done in Berthe Grunspan that morning. When Grunspan was recalled, Juror

No. 5 questioned her repeatedly as to why her letters to English never referred directly to an engagement or to plans for marriage. Her replies were fluttering, even evasive. Late in the day, there was an adjournment for supper, and a night session. Grunspan's lawyer, in summation, averred that had he been her brother he would have committed murder. Fuchs, anticipating defeat, asked the judge to specify that only out-of-pocket losses could be compensated. But the judge was much more to the point in charging the jury: "It must be established . . . that there was, without reasonable doubt, a promise to marry. If you decide that there was, you must grant the damages allowed by the law of the country in which that promise was made." That country was France. At 10:45 on a Friday evening the jury was sent out.[15]

It returned eleven hours later. The *World* reporter found that there had been a majority against Grunspan from the start of deliberations, that one of her supporters had held out until 7 A.M., the other until 9:55 A.M. The verdict was announced, Berthe Grunspan's eyes filled with tears, and her head dropped on the table. Her lawyer moved to set aside the verdict and to have a new trial, but both were immediately denied. Anna commented, for the *World*: "I never had any doubts of the outcome, because, Socialist writer though they call me, I think I know American jury systems and I believe I could read that jury very easily." English was not quoted as saying anything.[16]

At the end, Anna finally won equal billing with Berthe Grunspan and the Monday *World* carried parallel interviews. Grunspan reported that she had received numerous marriage proposals by mail and even a vaudeville offer. But she pictured for herself a solitary life of playing the piano, singing, reading. On her side of the page, Anna took advantage of the opportunity to discuss her theories of love and marriage. Seated in a parlor at the Brevoort, she told the *World*'s reporter that she believed in romantic love and monogamy, and "absolute freedom of divorce" when a relationship failed.[17]

From St. Augustine, Florida, where the elder Wallings were spending the winter, English and Anna received his mother's unvarnished evaluation of the proceedings:

> We saw the testimony & press comments and with our long experience of life could form a pretty accurate opinion—She was a nasty liar and from an unprejudiced point of view proved herself unworthy of credence before the case was given to the jury—English acquitted himself well on the stand & I was greatly alarmed for fear of something in the cross-examination making trouble. . . . I think Anna's corroboration of her husband's testimony was good, & she said just what she ought to have said, and just enough. . . .
>
> [Grunspan's] own conduct must have hurt her to sensible unprejudiced people. . . . Juror No 5 seemed to be her friend, or he likes to be at

front & show off by being contrary & opinionated. He might have hung the jury tho', and two of them were a long time—It was the "Millionaire socialist" & the poor girl that made the prejudice. . . .

I dont blame English for his interest in the girl, but he wrote too many *fool letters,* tho' he didn't do half as badly as many other men under like circumstances. . . . The papers have given me a lot of trouble over English for a long time. . . . I think you both carried yourselves with a quiet dignity during the trial that was effective & in striking contrast to the frissy hysterical plaintiff with her airs & poses.[18]

The trial had an unanticipated consequence. During the proceedings Anna blossomed again as a public presence, while English, for the moment, diminished. When the NAACP executive committee met on March 7, he was not there. He attended a special meeting later in the month, but did not come in April; it was clear that he had been damaged and that he would never altogether recover his influence in the NAACP, although he remained on the board for years to come.[19]

PART SIX

At the Apex of Socialism,

1911–1914

The same winter that brought the ordeal of the breach-of-promise trial paradoxically led to a kind of renaissance for Anna and English. Both of them had been fallow. After finishing *Russia's Message,* English had written important articles, starting with "The Race War in the North," that related to racial justice or to socialist politics, but he had found the road to a second book long and hard. Anna still worked episodically on her old projects—the article about the Springfield riot, the account of the Homel pogrom, the old manuscript of the novel set in Père Lachaise—but she had had nothing published since their marriage nearly five years before.

Oddly, Anna gathered strength against the background of the trial. Perhaps she felt more capable because she was, for a time, neither pregnant nor recovering from a past pregnancy. But in addition the trial subtly shifted the balance of power between them for a time, and she may have begun to see herself as the stronger; she gained and flourished as the trial cast English for once as vulnerable rather than dominating.

She may also have been stimulated by her membership in what amounted to a family writing workshop. Her siblings Rose and Hyman were energetically freelancing, and the three of them wrote back and forth continually about their efforts. Rose insisted that she was going to write her way to independence at a thousand words a day: "The house may burn around me & I *write.*"[1]

She had little choice but to earn her own way, for the whole Strunsky family had struggled since the earthquake. Only the physician, Max, enjoyed a steady income and the family depended on his generosity. As Rose wrote: "Albert comes and borrows from Max, little Rosie comes & takes [more] from Max, which she surreptitiously shares with Morris. That is the picture." Although these confidences never carried an overtone of complaint, it could not have escaped Anna that while Rose was scrimping she, Anna, was luxuriating. Yet when Anna tried to send help—she mailed a necklace for Rose to pawn—Rose always rebuffed her.[2]

Early in 1911 Rose earned two checks. The first was for a story-sketch-memoir in the January 1911 *Forum* (her second appearance in that prestigious monthly) called " 'Little Darling',," a recollection of the revolutionary who returned to St. Petersburg from Finland and was hanged. She also wrote an article commemorating Tolstoy, who died late in 1910, and sent it to the *Atlantic*, which accepted it at once. Rose basked in the praise of their friend, the novelist David Graham Phillips: "He said I write like Tolstoy & all the great Russians & have style for which he craves so & fails (I am still giddy with the compliment)."³

As it happened, Phillips—or, rather, his untoward fate—was responsible for pushing Anna back into print. Anna, English, and Rose all knew Phillips and his sister, Caroline Frevort. Phillips, unmarried, admired little Rosamond, who was almost a year old, and Rose reported that he wanted better prints of two pictures Anna had sent him: "He is showing them to everybody, but they are fading & he is heart-broken." Rose had seen him on January 22, 1911. On January 23, a paranoid who had been stalking him for months because of a fantasized grievance—that his sister had been libeled in a Phillips novel—waited with a revolver near the Princeton Club, on Gramercy Park in Manhattan. He shot Phillips five times, and killed himself with his last bullet. Phillips, forty-three years old, died the next day.⁴

A week later, Anna, still at the resort in Georgia, wrote to the senior Wallings: "English and I shed bitter tears over his death for he was a dear friend and we loved and honored him for one of the finest, most highminded spirits that ever lived. . . . Phillips believed so generously in people, expected so much of them that we was [*sic*] inspired while in his presence."⁵

Without her usual hesitation, she sent an article about Phillips, who had been a socialist without calling himself one, to the socialist *New York Call.* In it, she expressed her doubt that Phillips would have been killed had he not been a radical: "Did it ever occur to Phillips that he was taking his life in his hands by pillor[y]ing the plutocratic American woman?"⁶

Later, she responded to a request from Phillips's sister and wrote a more elaborate eulogy for the *Saturday Evening Post.* In the article, she recalled that the last time he saw her he warned her against excessive use of the automobile, because riding in cars separated one from the people on the sidewalk. Anna's evaluation of Phillips was favorable, perhaps a little overblown: "He succeeded in expressing the falseness and inanity of our society, I thought, by virtue of a great talent, guided by an intense, intelligent and wellbalanced radicalism. I delighted in his analysis of modern life, in the strength of his belief in progress, in his hatred of war and the idea of caste, in his mockery of anarchy." The conservative *Post,* perhaps not wishing to rush into print with observations about "the falseness and inanity of our society," held the article seven months before publishing it.⁷

The Phillips articles for a time broke Anna's fatal old habit of holding back her writing until its currency had passed. In March, she finished another article, this one appraising the work of the yellow press during the Grunspan trial. She shipped it off to the weekly *Collier's,* which paid her $100 and published it in April under the heading, "A Tribute to the Yellow Press, Its Virtues and Vices as Estimated by a Victim."[8]

The introduction, asserting that Anna had been "except for certain actresses—perhaps the greatest Sunday supplement feature among American women," was hyperbolic. The article itself offered a reasonably sophisticated view of the press. More than a mere complaint against inaccuracies, it perceptively traced Berthe Grunspan's gradual decline from sainthood until the newspapers "dropped their heroine gently, but certainly." Anna concluded:

> Despite the temporary unpleasantness of being reviled and hounded, despite the utter misrepresentation and the lies, there is something basically true and democratic both in the process and in the effect of yellow journalism. For the lies are so framed that they overreach themselves, so that, after all, the facts of the case become finally established.
>
> The popular press stands for the things of life itself, for the concrete phases of existence. It is precisely because of this that it is emotional. Where there is not yellow journalism there is a people which does not read. Yellow journalism, in concerning itself with the soul and not the externals of life, goes beyond journalism into literature.

Anna sent a copy of her article to L. A. Giegerich, the judge who had presided at the trial, and he responded that he thought that she had been too charitable.[9]

Late in the afternoon of Saturday, March 25, Hyman Strunsky burst into the Wallings' apartment to tell Anna that an enormous factory fire was in progress. Anna, sighting the column of smoke, made her way downtown to Washington Square and in the dusk joined the enormous throng behind the police lines shielding the chaotic, tragic shards, a block away, of the Triangle Shirtwaist Company fire, in which 140 women workers died.[10]

On Monday, Anna delivered an article about the fire to *Collier's*, which rejected it a day later. She turned to *Success* magazine, where one of English's old University Settlement associates, Howard Brubaker, was working. Brubaker reported that the piece would be placed in the first issue of an affiliated new biweekly, the *National Post*: "They are going to work it over themselves and save you the trouble." Anna was pleased when she received a check for $150, but appalled when she saw what the editors meant in saying that they would "work it over." She complained to her mother-in-law that she considered the article to be "completely ruined." She added: "I shall never have any dealings with these people again." She did not need to have any more contact with the *National Post*; it collapsed before the end of the year.[11]

The serious literary business of their lives was transacted with Anna's old mentor, George P. Brett of the Macmillan Company. In the spring of 1911, both Anna and English were ready to besiege Brett with manuscripts. English submitted the manuscript of his book on socialism first, in March. Macmillan had already issued works on socialism by John Spargo and English's former friend Robert Hunter, as well as an armload of professorial surveys. Nonetheless, Brett signaled that he was interested, and urged the Wallings, who were momentarily in Washington, to come to New York for consultation. Anna responded that English could go any time, but that she still maintained her anxious policy of not leaving Rosamond: "I could not easily take such a trip myself as that would be fatiguing to my baby whom I could not leave for a whole day and night."[12]

Rather than wait for a visit, Brett offered a full critique of English's book by mail. First and primarily, he said, at 250,000 words it was too long. He quoted from adverse reports by unidentified readers: "The writer is sometimes wrong and inconsistent even from his own point of view, and unfortunately neither the author's style nor method is as good as his thought." On the day he received this letter, English responded in three pages single-spaced. He insisted: "Of course I do not believe that my book is at any point inconsistent." He discussed possible titles, warning Brett away from "Revolutionary Socialism" as repellent to some readers. Brett responded that he preferred "Organized Socialism" as a title.[13]

Pushing hard, English completed a revision in just under two months, packed it off to the typist, corrected it, and sent it to Brett on June 29 from Lake Placid, New York, where they had moved for the summer. His cover letter had an undertone of anxiety. He had reduced the work to a modest size, he wrote, only forty-six chapters. The rest had been set aside for a second book. Although he did not expect an advance, he hoped that Macmillan would make a commitment on money: "There have been several heavy expenses connected with the writing of the book, to say nothing of the time; moreover my financial condition is not in the least what it is sometimes supposed to be."[14]

When he heard nothing in three weeks, he peremptorily demanded an opinion on the book by return mail. Brett obliged by returning the manuscript, saying (in his courtly way, as always) that Macmillan could not publish the work as it stood, hinting broadly that English might try another publisher, and advising him that he was perhaps "attempting to hasten the work on this book too much." Hair-trigger fashion, English wrote back at once: "Please inform your readers that I am not thin skinned. Rest assured that no criticism will fall on barren soil." A few days later, he wrote another letter defending his work and promising: "*I shall certainly rewrite the whole book.*" English gritted his teeth and returned to work.[15]

During the spring, Anna had been giving herself "neuritis" in her arm from writing so persistently on the Père Lachaise manuscript. She had the reborn version completed and typed before the end of April, but then her old hesitation, the critic within, held her back. She kept it until near the end of June, then (by happenstance, on the same day that English submitted his revised manuscript) sent it, tremulously, to Brett:

> The mss. [*sic*] I am now mailing to you has been finished over two months. I did not send it then because I wanted so much to bring it to you in person and tell you something of its history and purpose, and how, if it appealed to you at all, I might expand and improve it. But I am not well these months and do not want to wait any longer. . . . The friends who have read it as well as my conscience urge me to submit it, as it is, and so I do![16]

She explained further to her father-in-law: "I should have brought it in in person, but had not stepped inside the office since before I was married, and I hated to go feeling ill and nauseated. I finished it just as my 'sickness' began as luck would have it." Anna's sabbatical from pregnancy—nearly fifteen months—had ended not long after the trial and she was now expecting a child near the end of the year. As always, the first months were hellish for her, and any thought that she would be able to keep up her pace as a writer-journalist had to be set aside. Pregnancy was proving to be either her husband's means of setting her limits or her means of accepting them.[17]

Macmillan's response to Père Lachaise came in four weeks. In rejecting the novel, Brett was the soul of courtesy, blaming the coarseness of the audience rather than the deficiencies of the author: "The manuscript is charming, artistic and beautifully poetic in thought and conception, and the work itself is very well done, but I am sorry to say that I cannot believe that there would be any considerable demand for a work of this character at the present time when the public seems to demand books which amuse or which interest it from the sensational standpoint."[18]

Anna put up a brave front in her acknowledgment: "I regret now that I had not waited before submitting it until I had really finished it, for I knew that the biography of a socialist nature and temperament can have a popular appeal if the work is done with sufficient vividness and dramatic force. Your criticism is going to prove most helpful to me in rewriting the little book."[19]

Both of them, Brett and Anna, wrote around what must have been the core of their disappointments: he, that she had not produced the powerful socialist novel he had so long expected of her; she, that the dream of becoming a productive writer now seemed farther away than ever. Moreover, the balance of power that had tilted in her favor now returned to the status quo ante. English might exhort her to keep writing, but the family's work, it was increasingly clear, was his work.

Anna and English and eighteen-month-old Rosamond stayed through the summer of 1911, and beyond, at Lake Placid. English immersed himself in revising his still unwieldy work on socialism, and Anna contemplated another version of Père Lachaise.

Rose was in England, on an invitation from the Reginald W. Kauffmans. Kauffman was a minor celebrity, author of *The House of Bondage,* a best-selling, implicitly socialist novel about prostitution written at the crest of the "white slavery" furor. Kauffman passed on to her an assignment from a British publisher, Methuen, to write a book on Lincoln. She arranged to do her research at a drafty table in the British Museum and settled with her old Finnish revolutionary friend Aino Malmberg in a skittish household of exiles. She did not return for ten months, and then aboard the *New Amsterdam,* which sailed only a few days after the loss of the *Titanic.* Anna was apprehensive, but Rose ultimately returned safely.[1]

Anna and English heard, too, of their old associates in the revolutionary news bureau. Arthur Bullard—now a journalistic wanderer whom they glimpsed only every year or two—visited them at Lake Placid for a week, having finished a book on Panama, and was off to Morocco. He had finished a novel, to be published by Macmillan, called *A Man's World,* frank for its day in its approach to sex and destined to be esteemed as one of the best socialist novels of its era. He still signed his work by his old nom de guerre, Albert Edwards.[2]

Kellogg Durland was also a rover, abandoning his interest in revolutions for articles about European royalty; he wrote a book called *Royal Romances of To-day* (1911). In November 1911, Anna and English heard that he had committed suicide several months before. Anna, who had never concealed her dislike of Durland, was disturbed nonetheless: "I can only hope that his old mother whose only child he was and to whom he was always devoted is dead before him. I can't get the miserable sadness of it all out of my mind."[3]

Now well beyond her first trimester, Anna felt strong and fit as fall arrived in the Adirondacks: "Last night I slept out (English staid [*sic*] in his room) and at about three in the morning my bed covered with frost." They planned to stay until mid-October and then find a new home. With a second child to fit in, Anna, "after a propaganda on my part of several months," had obtained

English's agreement to move to the suburbs. "We shall thus be relieved of living in a city apartment with its necessary lack of space, air and light," she declared, "and the inevitable exodus as soon as warm weather comes."[4]

They found an ample house near the south shore of Long Island, in then-remote Cedarhurst, for a hundred dollars a month. It had two attic servants' rooms and a tennis court, and lay near the great wetlands of Jamaica Bay. There was as yet no telephone. Anna commented to her mother-in-law, "At last, after five years of experimenting, we are living in a civilized manner." No regret was voiced over the reversal since the time she had boldly proclaimed that they would roam the world, "never have a home."[5]

Six weeks after they moved to Cedarhurst, with the new year two hours away, Anna was seized with labor pains. English dashed out to the nearest telephone to call Max Strunsky and the local back-up doctor, leaving Anna with Lee, Rosamond's nursemaid, who, while hardly a specialist, managed competently. By the time English returned, birth was imminent, and their new daughter greeted the world as 1911 changed to 1912: "Our hearts that a little while before were oppressed with sorrow and terror were lifted up in joy. So we heard the New Year's bells, and we listened wordless." The local doctor appeared, then Max, hampered by the holiday train schedule. All was well, but Dr. Walling warned his son: "Your experience as an accoucheur . . . is being gathered at too much of a risk. Of course the chances are in favor of a normal labor, but had Anna, in either of her last two experiences, had an abnormal one, or a complicated one, she might simply have lost her life."[6]

The infant was named Anna Strunsky Walling. A cable went to Rose in London, and a letter to Jack and Charmian London. But the letter missed them, they were en route to New York. Anna wrote again, to their hotel:

> At last I learned the fate of my letter to you written in child-bed, with trembling fingers and tear-filled eyes announcing the advent of my third daughter, an altogether new little Anna Strunsky. I thought it a beautiful omen for her that you were about to appear again in the life of the old one, and my happiness and inspiration in the fact was boundless.
>
> This is a wonderful New Year that brings me my daughter and my friend again—my daughter so strangely like my lost first-born. In all the world there is not a more elated heart than mine—I dare say it before all the jealous gods![7]

She signed the letter "Anna Strunsky."

Jack and Charmian paid their call, but only after they had been in New York for a difficult month. After their arrival, Jack had parked Charmian in a hotel uptown at Morningside Heights while he kept company with a reporter from the *Evening World* who looked a great deal like Anna. Incautiously, he threw over George Brett and Macmillan for another publisher, Century.

Charmian, still recovering from the needless death of an infant daughter the year before (an experience strikingly parallel to Anna's losses) seemed momentarily ready to jettison the marriage.[8]

Yet all had been resolved when Jack and Charmian came out to Cedarhurst. Anna's recollection was of easily renewed intimacy: "He came and it was as if he had never been away. We stood laughing [in] low, hushed voices, in joy at meeting after so much peril escaped." Anna described the visit to her mother-in-law: "We had a beautiful visit from the Londons. To me he seems to have improved in every way, to have grown in stature as it were. He is very happy in his marriage, but they had the sorrow of losing their baby who lived only thirty-six hours. She doubts whether she can successfully have another, as she must be quite forty years old, if not older."[9]

After the Londons left for Baltimore, Anna's mood darkened. She recognized that depression followed naturally on birth—the "melancholia of lactation," she called it—but she inevitably felt more alone and powerless to resume her working life, and she may unconsciously have been comparing herself and her fallow career with Jack's. She wrote to Rose:

> I am so wholly cut off from my work, and from any kind of activity other than the maternal. Somehow, it is difficult to resign oneself to it, much as I joy and glory in the children. I sit all alone with the little baby. Rosamond is out with Lee, English is in N.Y., you are in London—I sit all alone and think fearful thoughts, how life glides by, how dreamlike and swift it is, how it betrays and mocks the yearning heart. . . . I think I love English more romantically than even that first spring in Moscow, and to have such love is to live. But I want time, I want space, and being a mother I live in a world where neither time nor space exist. I want to live a passionate, personal life and my whole personality is submerged, hangs on a thread. If I were more careless, or more efficient!

Rose reproved her: "Don't you think it is something very temporary? Poor little Anna is such a very few days old!"[10]

In January 1912, English received a troubling letter from Macmillan on what he had hoped would be the final revision of his book. His friend Graham Stokes had liked the manuscript, but Brett's readers remained unfriendly: "Too many of the chapters . . . read like editorials in daily or weekly newspapers. They apply to the news of the hour and may be made obsolete by a turn of events before the book is off the press." Another: "The writer has tried to journalize and the result is an incomplete statement of a situation that is transitory." These commentators had identified a chronic weakness: English's tendency to be influenced—carried away—by the latest, the nugget that would place him at the hub of currency. In his hands, timeliness became a liability.[11]

Brett added his own complaint that the book still stood at more than two hundred thousand words, "too great a bulk for a book of this kind intended for the general reading public." Despite all these negatives, Brett relented and on January 30 English dashed off a note to his parents: "Have just signed my contract with McMillan [sic]." He said that he hoped to sell as many as five thousand copies, which might earn him as much as thirteen hundred dollars.[12]

The book, *Socialism As It Is*, was published on schedule in April 1912. It was the product of an effort so draining that English said for a time that he might never write another book. In fact, it constituted his bid for a place in the sun: the establishment of his voice in the national debate over the nature of the state, of democracy, and of society, in which the landmark works by nonsocialists were Herbert Croly's *The Promise of American Life*, published in 1909, and Walter Weyl's *The New Democracy*, just published.[13]

But the austerity and impersonality of *Socialism As It Is* denied it the general readership won by Croly and Weyl. English's style was stiff rather than fluent; he built his case mostly by rebuttal rather than straightforward argument; and he could not resist patching in new data right up to the deadline. There were references (for example, to the great textile strike in Lawrence, Massachusetts) dated only a few days before he signed his contract. The result, for readers, was a rocky, frustrating trail.[14]

Yet his argument could be found in the interstices. The book carried on the quarrel he had picked two years before with the moderates of the Socialist Party. Socialist support of reform was not socialism at all, he contended, so long as it took place within a capitalist society, and he condemned reform socialists as socialists in name only. In particular, he was outraged at the declaration of his antagonist John Spargo that reforms would constitute the revolution.[15]

Beyond the party perspective, he condemned what was later to be called "creeping socialism"—government policies, such as old-age pensions, designed to soften the impact of capitalism on workers—as calculated merely to reinforce the system. In the same vein, he refused to accept as authentic what was widely called "state socialism," government participation in the economy and government ownership of major components; he saw it rather as an advanced, transitory stage of capitalism.

No society, he maintained, could be considered socialist until it reached "equality of opportunity," which by his definition meant a society that was neither ruled by capitalism nor geared to the capitalist system of distributing rewards. He focused particularly on educational opportunity, observing:

"The most anti-social aspects of capitalism, in its individualist or collectivist form, are the grossly unequal educational and occupational privileges it gives the young."[16]

English presented his first copy to his parents, who were visiting in Cedarhurst, and sent out other copies with a form letter. His book received, selectively, a strong response; Anna told her mother-in-law that "the letters that English has received from prominent persons are of a most striking nature—far from being just perfunctory praise, and showing that the book stirs them and moves them, an intellectual event in their lives." But his diffidence was striking, according to Anna: "This is the way it goes[:] 'I received a very warm letter from Max Eastman, Anna dear.' 'Let me see what he said.' 'Oh, I tore it up,' he answers, 'but it was a stirring letter.' "[17]

This seeming indifference to his own reputation, in such dramatic contrast with his intense argumentativeness, may have been linked to the role he now saw for himself—that of a publicist. A publicist was then defined not as a publicity agent but as a practitioner of a higher calling, an illuminator of issues, an adviser to the society at large. The critic Francis Hackett defined the term well when he wrote (describing Walter Weyl) that a publicist was one "who gives to political and social thinking the form in which it can be assimilated by educated people." English may implicitly have described his own step upward in his book when he referred to his calling as being "the publicist as opposed to the mere journalist." After his death, Anna asserted that he spurned personal reputation: "He was interested in reaching those specialists in sociology, economics, politics, philosophy who had the public ear. He would have been perfectly willing to allow others to sign his books and articles if in this way his writings might have exerted a larger influence."[18]

One barrier to exerting such influence was the growing throng of publicists, and particularly of those discussing socialism. Even the advertisements tucked in the spare pages at the end of *Socialism As It Is* offered eighteen other works related to socialism on Macmillan's list alone. English received favorable, even glowing, reviews, but these by no means created a best-seller; no more than three hundred fifty copies were sold in the first week and fewer in the weeks thereafter, but at least there was enough continuous interest for Macmillan to keep the book in print.[19]

And there was enough theoretical muscle in *Socialism As It Is* to save it from the historical obscurity that has enfolded most of the other works on the Macmillan list. Later scholars, acknowledging its faults, have treated it with respect: most notably Christopher Lasch, who fixed on the book's effort to distinguish left-wing socialism not only from the reformers on the right but from syndicalism, the revolutionary movement rising from unionism and evincing itself increasingly in general strikes—for example, in the quasi-syndicalist "revolutionary strike" at the Lawrence mills.[20]

The clearest indications that English was establishing himself as a publicist came from within his own circle. Weyl, once a fellow resident at the University Settlement, had supplied in *The New Democracy* a prescription for American society that situated itself between the left wing of progressivism and mild socialism. Weyl was at work on a successor book, to be called "The Class War." His wife, Bertha (sister of another settlement resident, Ernest Poole), wrote to Anna that her husband was reading *Socialism As It Is*: "Walter is getting great help from it. But our socialist friends of the reformer bent, I suppose, are at sixes and sevens. However they *cannot* disregard the book. It is a piece of work to be proud of." In his own diary, Weyl wrote that he was "working through Walling's book and getting lots of good through . . . opposition to it." Weyl never finished "The Class War," probably less from inability to refute *Socialism As It Is* than from reasons of temperament.[21]

English too was already plunging ahead with a successor volume, to be created from parts he had deleted from the first book. He wrote to his father: "All the economic and political features were dealt with before. Now I am concerned solely with what might be called the larger aspects of Socialism. This will be [of] much more interest to young people, to women and to the educated public generally. Its practical interest and immediate importance will, of course, be somewhat less—though it may get some attention from preachers, literary men, and so forth, not much interested in my late volume." In the phrase "the larger aspects of socialism" he had hit upon his next title.[22]

The first years of the second decade of the century were the heyday of an amorphous, multidoctrinal American socialism, which not only proposed a new society but drew on the widespread literature of exposure to display the flaws of the old. It was as if all that the muckrakers had said about the shortcomings of capitalism had at last sunk in, and there was now an audience for alternative systems embodying, as Walter Lippmann put it, "a will to beauty, order, neighborliness, not infrequently a will to health." Not that the general run of Americans were interested in becoming socialists, but at least socialism was for the time being presented to them as a benevolent option, not a foreign infection. By 1912 and 1913, not only was there a plethora of books and magazine articles discussing socialism itself, but magazines were permeated with treatment of issues that socialists had adopted as their own: poverty, the status of women and children, the hazards of employment and unemployment.[1]

Much of this exposure was the work of the nucleus of socialist and crypto-socialist editors and writers that permeated publishing companies and the general magazines. One writer observed, without braggadocio: "Socialism is the answer, but it is not my own little pet answer. I know personally above two score of our best writers who would give the same answer and would like to write that answer if they could find a market for what they write. I know at least a dozen editors who admit the essential truth of Socialism. In short, our whole daily and monthly publishing business is honeycombed with Socialists."[2]

Those few who wanted to read about the theories rather than applications of socialism could turn to specialized periodicals. Until 1913, the dominant publication of left-wing socialism was the *International Socialist Review*, issued from Chicago by the veteran publisher Charles H. Kerr. But *ISR* had tried to popularize itself and had become cluttered and a little shabby, incorporating not only socialist theory and the struggles of the working class but such trivia as patent-medicine ads written with a socialist slant.[3]

Both English and Rose Strunsky had written for *ISR*, but English was immediately attracted when a plan emerged for a left-wing journal based in New York. The *New Review* was designed to provide more astringently intellectual discussion than *ISR* in a neater package. English was one of thirty original stockholders when the *New Review* began weekly publication from Nassau Street in Manhattan in January 1913.[4]

Although English was neither editor nor publisher, his temperament and tone were reflected in the *New Review*—straightforward, usually humorless, strewn with nuggets of original thought—to such an extent that at times it seemed almost to be his personal vehicle. Occasionally the publication even looked like a family preserve: in one issue, Rose had the cover story, an article by English immediately followed hers, and farther back Anna contributed a book review.[5]

English wrote furiously for the first issues. After his four-year struggle to produce a single book on socialism, he now provided a veritable torrent of writing to keep the new magazine stocked. In the first issue, he wrote a long critique of the Socialist Party's agricultural policy or lack of it. In the following weeks he offered articles on "revolutionary unionism," inspired by the Lawrence textile strike; then a series contemplating the new president, Woodrow Wilson. His pace eased when the magazine shifted to monthly publication in May 1913.[6]

During this same spring of 1913, English's second book appeared. *The Larger Aspects of Socialism* constituted in great part an attempt to hook socialism to the engine of pragmatism, as designed by John Dewey. English no doubt knew Dewey, a professor of philosophy at Columbia, from Dewey's involvement with the Friends of Russian Freedom and the founding of the NAACP. Dewey was neither a socialist nor a Marxist; indeed, his pragmatism could be viewed as the kind of reformism that English had attacked in *Socialism As It Is*. No matter; Dewey was made to serve as a vehicle, as were, to a lesser degree, Marx and Engels, Herbert Spencer, William James, and the fashionable Nietzsche.[7]

All of these became adjuncts to English's positions on socialist religion, education, sex, and families. Not unexpectedly, he had no kind words for organized religion, concluding, with Marx, that it served largely "for maintaining the masses in ignorance and for furnishing some makeshift that will serve in [the ruling class's] minds as a defence of the iniquities of class rule." He expressed a justified doubt that public, classless schooling would ever receive sufficient support, for the ruling classes would "never voluntarily pay to give the children of the masses an equal educational opportunity and an equal chance to compete with their own children."[8]

The last chapter, titled "Man, Woman, and Socialism," came closest to home, in a literal sense. English relied primarily on Ellen Key, a Swedish writer recently introduced to American readers, who propounded a theory of women's development through maternity. Secondarily and somewhat contrarily, he cited the work of a senior American feminist, Charlotte Perkins Gilman, advocate of communal homes and state-run child care.[9]

In keeping with his rigidly impersonal approach, he made no direct reference in this chapter to himself, to his marriage, to Anna, or to their two children. Even so, the personal could be glimpsed between the lines. In the discussion of Key he offered an assertion that must have contained an autobiographical element, a heavily veiled reference to the Grunspan matter: "The art of love, then, is not only offered as desirable for all, but it is especially necessary to the woman who has only had a single love, for it is only when she is an artist in love that such a woman may humanize the man who has loved in a mistaken and incomplete way before."[10]

Similarly, he could scarcely have avoided thinking of his own home when he observed that "the problem of rearing children without a monstrous cost to the mother has not yet been solved." But he discussed the domestic obligations of men only in the briefest and vaguest terms, suggesting that as men and women came to share work and home life "sports, heavy drinking, cynical talking and vile stories will no longer appeal to men." He did not add that these recreations had never much appealed to him in any case.[11]

The book received favorable reviews in both general and scholarly publications, so it must have been disconcerting to English to have the book's least respectful notice appear in the New Review. In the July 1913 issue, Larger Aspects was subjected to a whimsical going-over by an old antagonist, Robert Rives La Monte. La Monte employed an extended nautical metaphor in expressing his doubt that pragmatism was a marvelous instrument "by which the most clumsy landlubber may nonchalantly navigate the seven seas of modern thought." He concluded that English had fallen victim to conceptual mal de mer.[12]

English replied mildly enough in the next issue, but later found a more determined advocate in a new friend, Walter Lippmann. The decorous Lippmann, not yet twenty-four years old, already was gaining a formidable reputation as the author of A Preface to Politics, published almost at the same time as Larger Aspects. Lippmann did not rise to English's defense because he agreed with English—Lippmann was already abandoning socialism—but because of manners: "An extremely significant book has been smeared with inanity in what might claim to be the most serious magazine in the American movement."[13]

English had come to know Lippmann not only because they both contributed to the New Review, but because both attended the newly celebrated salon of Mabel Dodge at her apartment on Fifth Avenue, directly across from the Brevoort and just up the street from the site of the old A Club. Mabel Dodge, the quintessential out-of-towner, had moved to New York from Buffalo to remake herself and ultimately to shed a husband. She took up with Lippmann and with Lippmann's Harvard classmate (but hardly soulmate) John

Reed and eventually she and they and a few other literary friends concocted regular weekly Evenings.[14]

English was a principal at one of the most memorable of these —a discussion-debate featuring Big Bill Haywood of the Western Federation of Miners and the IWW, Emma Goldman, and English—speaking respectively for revolutionary unionism, anarchism, and socialism. Dodge recalled that Haywood, eloquent before crowds, became shambling and uncertain before people in evening dress; Goldman she thought excessively didactical; and she awarded English—suave and reasonable—such laurels as were to be had.[15]

Anna did not become a figure in Greenwich Village society. Cedarhurst was close enough to Manhattan for English but too far for Anna; she was still reluctant to be away from her children but she may not have been asked to come along in any case. She who had thrived on San Francisco's seacoast of Bohemia scarcely glimpsed the shores of this one.[16]

For a time, though, she was able to help in re-creating the *Masses*. Initially, the magazine, founded in 1911, was a stodgy journal promoting the consumer-cooperative movement. (The early *Masses* is remembered primarily for Art Young's drawing of two slum children looking at the heavens and observing that "the stars are as thick as bedbugs.") It sputtered to a stop at the end of the summer of 1912. A crew of resuscitators, led by Art Young, decided to bring it back to life and named Max Eastman, a twenty-nine-year-old socialist, editor without pay.[17]

The magazine resumed near the end of 1912. The revived *Masses* was initially published at 105 Nassau Street, from the same address as the *New Review*, and there was considerable overlap of personnel. Both English and Anna sat in the editorial meetings of the *Masses* staff, but only English was listed in the roster of editors. English and Anna did not remark on the circumstance, but at the *Masses* they found themselves no longer the youngest in a gathering. Their mindset, of being forever a part of *la jeunesse*, was reflected in a letter Rose wrote to them from Paris about a joint meeting of French and German socialists: "I am not used to having the socialist platform occupied by grey-haired pot-bellied deliberative old men." While, at thirty-five, they were hardly pot-bellied and rarely deliberative, they must have felt like elderly Victorians when confronted with the highly individual, flamboyant new Greenwich Village radicals.[18]

Still, English and Anna were welcomed warmly enough, and participated in the meetings that produced a magazine in which the high standard set by the artists was never quite matched by the writers. English wrote in his standard style, quite out of key with the more personal and literary approach favored by such writers as Mary Heaton Vorse, John Reed, and his old settlement compatriots Leroy Scott and Howard Brubaker. He was relegated to the thankless assignment of writing a department of items about doings in worldwide socialism, a drab final page in a magazine that was otherwise starting to glow.[19]

Doing her bit, Anna tried hard to recruit Jack London: "Max Eastman mailed you yesterday the three copies of The Masses that have so far appeared. We are all quite mad about this publication, and we want something from you, if it be only a paragraph. Eugene Debs wrote a letter—do the same, if you are not inclined to write anything more at the present moment, but a word from you at this critical juncture in the infant life of the magazine we must have."[20]

Jack did not respond. When she next wrote to him, three months later, her most recent leave from pregnancy had ended, and with it any role at the Masses: "I have been frightfully, dangerously ill for six weeks, and then last week, I suddenly recovered. It is a new baby to be born in October, and the first months of pregnancy are always for me months of unendurable torture. This baby is to be my last—this, owing to my recent sufferings has been decided by a great family conclave. Someday I shall emerge from the nursery, in about two years' time."[21]

English, writing to his parents that spring, reported obliviously that all was well with Anna's pregnancy, and he was buoyant about his public activities, boasting that he had bested a Republican politician in a debate at Cooper Union and was basking in good reviews for The Larger Aspects. There was an undertone of discouragement as well. He saw himself as a victim, telling his father that he was utterly worn out and could not come to Chicago to visit his mother after she had surgery. Moreover, he complained, in managing the household there was "only one person deeply interested in it—myself." This theme—of Anna's purported indifference or incompetence—was to persist.[22]

In May 1913, English rented a place in East Hampton, near the eastern end of Long Island. In response to an inquiry from his parents, he wrote: "Dont think of Anna and babies as isolated at Easthampton. It is 2 hours and 20 minutes from New York, has three excellent though not large hotels and every imaginable convenience." But there was later a further note of exasperation: "Of course I have to superintend *everything* from the old house to the new, Anna's hats to the babies' shoes."[23]

Late in the summer, English left his family at East Hampton and made a deferred visit to his parents, who were at a resort hotel in Atlantic City. He and Anna exchanged letters frequently. His often took a hectoring tone, with profuse underlining. He urged her to get out of the house: "This hermit existence must stop." He reported that he was learning the turkey trot.[24]

For her part, Anna struggled to take up, once again, the Père Lachaise manuscript: "It's this way about my writing—I can't get into the swing of the second part of Pere Lachaise, and to begin something else would be to do what David Graham Phillips called 'letting your mind make a fool of you.' So, I must stick it out, fight it out." He replied: "*Do* keep your promise to yourself of writing something for me. To break a promise to another is nothing. To continually break promises to oneself is *an extremely serious matter.*"[25]

After she sent a batch of writing, his didacticism and impatience overflowed:

> Tolstoi is right. One can and should write only of one's own life and experience. This Pere Lachaise is perfect. But so were the others. Each was profoundly interesting and important because it was a document of you. Each should have been published. Or rather no year should pass without some complete record. The story might change or the publication be delayed. The thing is to record yourself—then to *leave the record intact, sacred.* It is just as impious to attack one's past self, because of greater experience, as it is to attack any other younger person for the same reasons. . . .
>
> I regret deeply the destruction or disfigurement of your past Pere Lachaises (Nos. I, II, III, IV, etc). But I feel far more deeply the importance of putting into your present writing your present state of mind, which I believe you have done perfectly in the chapters you have sent.

He urged her to finish the draft "and then *leave it alone forever.*"[26]

He was right. Instead of finishing and releasing her work, she had let it lie about for years—not only Père Lachaise, but the Homel pogrom, the Russian chronicle "Revolutionary Lives," and her story of the Springfield riot, all far past any timeliness. There were excusing circumstances always: pregnancies, children, travel. English always completed his own work and he always seemed supportive of hers, and yet, even with servants and nurses, she did not have, even figuratively, what Virginia Woolf was to call a room of one's own.

Even had she carved out such a space, she seemed always to lack the writer's effrontery, the conclusion that a given piece of work was as good as readers were going to get. She struggled to meet the expectations of friends and family, but hesitated to believe that what she wrote would ever be good enough. Eventually, she was to finish Père Lachaise, and Homel, and "Revolutionary Lives," but in a way that left each one all but stillborn.

On October 13, 1913, English wrote to his parents, assuring them that he was "with Anna every minute" as they waited through the final days of her fifth pregnancy. The next day, she gave birth to a fourth daughter, the third to live. English wrote to Chicago: "Her name is Georgia"—the feminine adaptation of a name used in the Walling family as far back as English's great-grandfather—"and she is by far the strongest and healthiest we have had. Anna looks as well as when you saw her. Five hours labor, half hour of severe pains."[1]

When he wrote a month later, he devoted a single sentence to family: "Anna is well, so are the babies, especially the new ones." And then he turned to business: his new book, the third in three years, another book he was editing, the fortunes of the *Masses* and the *New Review*, his coming lecture tour in New England, and his plan to visit his parents in Florida come January.[2]

After the new year he went to vacation at the Alcazar, a resort hotel in St. Augustine, with his parents. Anna remained in Cedarhurst with the three children (the eldest, Rosamond, nearly four) and Lee, the nursemaid. At first the correspondence between Anna and English was routine. English: "Send me one of knitted undershirts and drawers." Anna: "Georgia is three months old to-day."[3]

But immediately after writing her routine letter on January 13, Anna wrote a "Letter II": "I took Pere Lachaise to a Publisher and they offered me $2000 outright, so I accepted and followed you South with the Three and Lee, first stopping to-day at Giddings for myself where I invested $150 in beautiful clothes, and at Best's for the children where I spent $50." Then, she wrote, she arrived in St. Augustine at noon and embraced him, and he wept for joy. "Such vengeance," she concluded, "the imagination of a hedonist takes in the situations of reality! I have never seen why we must accept everything—even my dreams are that of a revolutionist." Then she abandoned capricious fantasy and returned to reality: "I was sick yesterday—vomiting and great pains in the stomach."[4]

Fortuitously, Jack London reappeared, traveling on his own this time. This was a much-battered Jack, just past his thirty-eighth birthday, no longer the fierce warrior of Anna's youth. He still wrote copiously but he was in a physical decline. He and Charmian had suffered through a miscarriage, and then the magnificent Wolf House he was building in the hills above San Francisco burned. They were left so short of cash that he had to make the trip alone to restore his relations with Macmillan and to confront other business matters that had gone awry. Within days, his activities were creating a stir in the press, and Anna's first greeting to him was "Another Scandal, Jack?"[5]

When Anna and Rose called on Jack at his hotel, he read for two hours to them from a work called, she said, "The Straight-Jacket," which Anna declared the best thing ever written on capital punishment. But she was downcast: "After the reading I spent an hour walking alone, depressed that I was not writing, feeling that had I written, were I writing, I would have done more than he, as much as he and the others whose writing is even greater—conceit or conviction? It does not matter. It is what I feel to be true."[6]

The next evening, January 28, a taxi Jack was taking downtown from a club in Harlem overturned and left him bruised and cut across the face and arms. On January 29, Anna celebrated Rosamond's fourth birthday by taking her and young Anna to the city, calling on Jack, then going on to more birthdaylike diversions. If his injuries from the accident were visible, she was too kind to mention them in her letter to English.[7]

Next day she and Rose and her old radical San Francisco friend Jane Roulston met Jack for lunch at the Hotel Astor; it turned into a memorable occasion, which she recounted in detail to English. Miss Roulston, although she now led the rough-and-tumble life of an IWW organizer, recited sonnets she had written and brought a tear to Jack's eye. Then Robert Erskine Ely, an academic who had been involved in the Friends of Russian Freedom, joined them unbidden and began to argue in favor of corporal punishment of children. Anna exclaimed: "We ate him up alive. He tried to get around me by flattery. 'Mrs. Strunsky Walling, something has made you what you are, and it must have been an early discipline of some sort like that which I have in mind.[']" Her response was deeply revealing: "I assured him that I have no recollection of ever having obeyed anybody in my life; I did not add that I have distinct recollections of loving people and of desiring deeply to please them, and of being impressed by their example and of desiring to emulate them."[8]

She went on to appraise Jack:

> I found this visit with my old friend very stimulating. He is not a philosopher as you are, but his mind is agile, and his nature generous and practical. I appreciate him much more than I did years ago, and I think you would feel as I do about him. It is easy to criticize him, of course, because his faults are large and obvious, but it is more profitable to get on the inside of him and sympathize with his outlook upon life. He is an

ardent I.W.W. man. He insists that nothing in the world matters but love, therefore a woman (and a man, too) ought not to care about anything but love. (Dane Kempton gone mad!) He isn't going to educate his daughters very much for fear it will incapacitate them for their [word illegible] functions!"

She noted his reversal since the days, a decade before, when he insisted that she must become a great writer: "[H]e is not interested in my career because he is afraid it would interfere with my love for you and the babies. 'When you are working you are not loving(!)' " She did not report this comment in an aggrieved way, but rather, it seemed, as still another aspect of his unpredictability.[9]

The response she received from English was utterly free of jealousy but candid nonetheless: "You are mistaken if you think I do not fully appreciate Jack, or if you forget how strongly he attracts me. The only thing that arouses me against him is the way he so often wastes himself—and that only comes from the high value I place on him. He is one of those—like Nietzsche & Tolstoi—that are better than their work. He is constantly on a false road, dressed in the wrong uniform, and saying the wrong thing—but even then his personality appears. And you see him always young, fresh, sensitive and sympathetic, with a zest for everything. Only often you cant follow him and are no less than grieved to part company—even for a time."[10]

Within months, English had just such an occasion to part company with Jack. During the spring of 1914, the Wilson administration, dabbling in Mexican revolutionary politics on behalf of American oil interests, inflated a minor incident into a pretext to occupy the port of Veracruz, and Mexico and the United States stood briefly on the brink of war. *Collier's* asked Jack to cover the hostilities, if any, and he agreed, so long as he could bring both Charmian and a servant. While John Reed, ten years younger, was off covering the real Mexican Revolution for *Metropolitan* magazine, Jack and Charmian hung out with the crowd of reporters and officers' wives in Veracruz.[11]

The articles Jack produced invited criticism. English was not alone in condemning them, but he was the most stern, accusing Jack of "preparing the ground for a race war." "He seems," wrote English, "to have remembered nothing of his Socialism" and abandoned his former support of revolution to lead the cheers for American dominion: "Neither the masses of the Mexican people nor the American working class are to be consulted—unless the latter can be misled by London's tawdry jingoism."[12]

It is doubtful that Jack read these words; by the time they were printed he was shut up in a New Orleans hotel, ill with dysentery. Nor, in any case, did English, oblivious as always to the personal impact of criticism, regard his words as disrupting their acquaintance. A few months later, he wrote to Jack from the offices of the *New Review* seeking financial support for the magazine. English, it appeared, was simply demonstrating again that fair was fair: friends should be criticized as severely as strangers, perhaps even more so.[13]

English returned from Florida in February 1914 after having been away more than a month. He was to repeat this winter jaunt with his parents, never until later years with Anna or the children. It apparently became the subject of an understanding between them: that for him it was a working vacation, good for his health and perhaps for hers, too. They intended to go away for the summer (this too an almost unchanging pattern) to Spring Lake, on the New Jersey shore south of Asbury Park, a spot recommended by his parents and not far from Belmar, the site of a resort hotel owned by the Strunsky family.[14]

Before summer, Anna cast off one of her writing burdens, although not in the way she had once hoped. She started at last to circulate her seven-year-old manuscript on the Homel pogrom. The *Century Magazine,* for which Rose had written often, responded that the story was "very powerful—almost too powerful." The editor also questioned its currency: "However critical the Jewish situation is in Russia, it does not appear so to us in America at this time; our eyes seem to be all elsewhere." Later, the *Atlantic* also demurred: "The very extremity of the suffering you describe . . . involves, as it seems to us, the propriety of giving names and dates. And just here the fact that these events took place long ago presents an argument adverse to acceptance." Ultimately, she delivered her account before the New York Section of the Council of Jewish Women, which issued it as a humble pamphlet.[15]

English completed another book on socialism, his third, in the spring. *Progressivism—and After* returned to the themes of *Socialism As It Is* and reshaped them. Progressivism, which English preferred to call by the alternative name "state capitalism," would give way, he predicted, to "state socialism." But where state socialism was anathema in his earlier books, he now saw it as part of an evolution that would lead to his classless, equal-opportunity socialist democracy, within, say, twenty-five years.

The centerpiece among the many reviews was that of Walter Lippmann, who had defended the seriousness of *The Larger Aspects of Socialism.* But now he challenged English on two grounds. First, he charged that English was wrong in insisting that having equal shares of society's wealth was more important than installing what was later to be called a "safety net"—minimum standards of living below which none would be allowed to fall. Such minimums, Lippmann hinted, could be achieved without socialism. Second, he viewed English's approach as fundamentally deterministic, describing a process in which mere political activity could play only a minimal role, hence obviating the need for a socialist party, or any other party.[16]

When he replied a month later, English suggested mildly that a socialist party would always be needed "to prepare gradually" for the future. But he exploded at Lippmann's other contention: that extenuating comforts, rather than equality, would suffice for the poor. He further accused Lippmann of "the most colossal and extraordinary blunder I have ever met in economic criticism"—his suggestion that socialist progress had to take place at the expense of economic growth: "My whole book—every page of it—is devoted to showing that not only the capitalistic development of production, but also its political expression—progressivism—leads to Socialism. . . . Lippmann is the only critic, and, as far as I know, the only reader, who has failed to find out what my book is about."[17]

Neither apparently being content with the first exchange, they had a second round five months later, this one considerably more personal on Lippmann's side. Lippmann called the philosophy of *Progressivism—and After* "impossibilist to the last degree, and like most impossibilism it's a hobby that requires a fixed income before you can indulge in it." He added: "Walling never draws conclusions upon which people can act. He has become that distressing person—the observer with a key to destiny." English did not respond to the personal innuendo, but insisted that Lippmann had made at least a dozen "gross misstatements" in his original review. With this the former allies separated as tacit adversaries.[18]

By early June 1914, the Walling family was settled at Spring Lake. English reported to his father that Anna had decided to let an agency arrange a few lectures for her at not less than seventy-five dollars net each. She had to have a circular prepared. "Of course," he wrote in exasperation, "this fell on me and I came to town yesterday to fix it up."[19]

The irritation was not all on one side. On July 30, Anna wrote to Rose in a torrent of feeling:

> I will be all right as soon as I write and speak and make money—and the thing to do is to bear everything until I achieve that goal—absolutely everything. I have to surrender principles, ideals, tendencies—all personal codes and standards for . . . loving life together; must forget them, even, and just go ahead, work ahead. It is my only safeguard against destruction.
>
> Yesterday after one of English's outbursts about the soap not being in the right place I found myself talking aloud to myself in my room and I could not stop!
>
> It's querrulous [*sic*] insanity on his part, brain-storms, and I ought to regard it all from that standpoint and not care so much.
>
> I slept in your bed with Anna and Rosamond who both wanted me at the same time.[20]

Like most outbursts, the letter proved soon to be less than it appeared. Still, English's criticisms of her ineffectiveness cut deeply, for she remembered some of them nearly fifty years later when she sent his papers to the University of Wisconsin. But rather than truly declaring independence, she was still mourning the freedom that she first realized she was losing when they floated down the Volga seven years before. She was restive, but she would remain dependent.[21]

PART SEVEN

The Great War at Home,

1914–1920

In the exchange between English and Walter Lippmann in June and July 1914, both mentioned, for rhetorical purposes, the possibility of a war—a hypothetical, far-fetched war, with Japan, for example. They were oblivious to the approach of a real war. At the start of the summer of 1914, neither of these men, both so intent on the fate of humanity, evinced any sense of darkening crisis, any foreboding that by the second week of August millions of men would be struggling and killing across Europe, in a conflict that was immediately called the Great War. They shared this obliviousness with most other Americans.[1]

In Europe, interlocking agreements and reckless ultimatums mobilized the armies, and the surging crowds in the streets of the capitals—cheering, singing, waving hats—whooped the war into being and shivered with joy as the troops marched past to their trains. Within a space of a few days in August 1914, Russia and Serbia were engaged in the east against Germany and Austro-Hungary, while in the west Germany invaded Belgium to get at France, and British forces straggled across the Channel to join what was to be known as the western front.[2]

The American literary left was bewildered. The Wallings' friend Hutchins Hapgood, hanging out with the Greenwich Village crowd on Cape Cod, recalled the turmoil—activists wanting to do something and having no means to do anything: "The War in our souls broke out. We were the Cause of the War: the violence and inconsistency of our emotions, the impotence of our ideas." They drank heavily and tried to send telegrams to the leaders of the belligerents calling for peace.[3]

Before the war was many weeks old, it began to rearrange the lives of the Wallings' old circle. Two of the University Settlement group, Ernest Poole and Arthur Bullard, came back together from Europe just before hostilities started. Bullard was hired by the *Outlook* magazine to compile a weekly summary of war news, an indoor task that bored the old war correspondent. In a letter to a confidant, he debated what he should do next: continue to write novels or respond to the distant sounds of battle. "The issue seems to boil down to the proposition: Do I want to be a novelist or a publicist. . . . I get more fun out of writing novels than from any other work. My dearest friends are all more interested in 'Literature' than in 'Journalism.' . . . On the other hand this European turmoil interests and fascinates—as well as horrifies—me." Fascination won out. At the end of his six-month commitment to the *Outlook*, he hurried to Paris, then almost within the range of German guns, and resumed his old trade.[4]

Poole had just finished a book, a strike novel called *The Harbor*, more openly radical than anything he had written before. When the war started, he retreated to his house in the White Mountains and extensively revised the galleys. In longhand, he incorporated a voice of the masses trumpeting the peace doctrine of international socialism: "For we shall stop this war of yours and we shall take your governments—and in our minds we shall put away all hatred of our brother men. For us they will be workers all. With them we shall rise—and the world will be free." As he wrote, socialism's most tenacious advocate of peace, France's Jean Jaurès, was gunned down, and international socialist solidarity began to crumble. Having written the new ending to his novel, Poole like Bullard responded to the call of war. Leaving his wife and two children, Poole sailed for Europe in November 1914, and made his way into Germany as an accredited correspondent for the *Saturday Evening Post*.[5]

In the immediate family, Rose Strunsky's responses were the most instantaneous. She was just back in August 1914 from the upstate Woodstock arts-and-crafts colony, where she had reluctantly eaten "dry salad & rice" and contemplated artists of both sexes dressed in harem skirts. Like many other Americans, she utterly disregarded President Wilson's exhortation on August 19 to be "impartial in thought as well as action." Their father, she wrote to Anna, detested the Russian czarists above all, but she was more contemptuous of Germans. "Why didn't somebody blow up the Kaiser[?]" she demanded. "I feel as if a hundred years have dropped from us & Napoleon is rampaging about." Nonetheless, as a socialist she favored peace and accepted an invitation by Oswald Garrison Villard's wife to participate in a demonstration: "I have promised to march but I wont if it is too hot." In her own way Rose was soon caught up too. She stayed on in New York for a few months, but eventually she, like Bullard and Poole, heard opportunity in the call of war.[6]

For his part, English expressed no desire to rush overseas, but he immediately adopted the war as his own. Again, he showed the publicist's temperament: the irresistible impulse to provide immediate answers to big questions. He remained, in Lippmann's taunting phrase, "the observer with a key to destiny."

Because his studies had familiarized him with the politics of the major European nations, English was at least aware of the forces that had been pressing toward conflict. In *Progressivism—and After*, he had seen both state capitalism and state socialism as providing the foundations for war through their encouragement of nationalism. He had noted with dismay the support labor and socialist parties in Britain and Germany gave to imperial expansion, and was most critical of German socialists for voting in favor of the kaiser's military appropriation in 1913. Eventually he saw this one action as the crucial break in international socialism. He never forgave, but he too soon showed that he had little resistance to the appeal of flag and nation.[7]

Even in his first pronouncements, there were intimations that war would tear English loose from his moorings. Years before, he had declared himself as supporting "not only the ordinary Socialist opposition to all wars, but the taking of the most desperate means to prevent them." But he conceded, in an article written for the *Independent* only days after the German invasion of Belgium, that "the Socialist parties of the countries involved have done nothing whatever to stop the war." Moreover, he scorned as hypocritical the call of the Socialist Party of America for peace in the name of the fraternity of all working people, "irrespective of *color*, creed, *race*, or nationality." (He added the italics.) What kind of fraternity could it be, he asked, when the party favored immigration restrictions based on race?[8]

But he was hardly downcast by the failure of international solidarity; he had already persuaded himself that enormous good could come of the war. In the *Independent* article, he all but predicted that the German army would shoot its own officers and lead a revolution against the kaiser. In the *New Review*, he quoted with approval the forecast by the English writer H. G. Wells (whom in the previous issue he had attacked as an "advocate of plutocracy") that Germany would be defeated and that czarism and kaiserism would fall. English concluded that if the war were to lead to the overthrow of Europe's ruling aristocracies and plutocracies, then "within a few years it will have amply repaid its cost in blood and treasure, no matter how staggering this cost may be." Of course it was still August 1914, and neither English nor anybody else could imagine that cost.[9]

As the fall of 1914 passed, his enthusiasm redoubled, for the war was putting him back in the center of the arena. He was now writing not only for the sectarian audience of the *New Review* but for the general magazines of opinion—the *Independent, Harper's Weekly,* and the *Outlook* (which was primarily identified with the bellicose views of Theodore Roosevelt)—as a certified American authority on European socialism. From the Fall River Line, on his way to a lecture tour in New England, he wrote to his parents that newspapers had been praising him; "The Advertiser, the most conservative[,] has recently referred to me as 'the ablest thinker among American Socialists.' " He saw himself as an arbiter of opinion: "The Outlook is apparently going to have an article of mine, 'Are the German People Unanimous?' Of course I say, no. This is important because Bullard has taken the other stand." This first rift with Bullard was prophetic.[10]

Early in 1915, he wrote buoyantly to Jack London: "Personally I am an ultra-optimist about the war. I think it is altogether going to eclipse the French Revolution and have an infinitely greater result for good in all directions—*before we are through with it.* . . . the everlasting smash of German civilization and all it stands for is worth almost any price.[11]

Anna alone seemed to take little note of the war. At first, she seemed more preoccupied with home life than with the fate of nations. The family was moving—leaving Long Island for a rental house selected for them, or at least approved, by the senior Wallings. The new address was on Field Point Road in Greenwich, Connecticut, twenty-eight miles by commuter rail from New York. The larger house meant not only more space for the family but for Anna as well. As her friend and typist Winifred Heath exclaimed: "Dearest— I'm so glad to think you are going to have a room to work in."[12]

Anna, now a year past her last parturition, began to reemerge in public during the fall of 1914. She responded to an invitation to speak in Manhattan on the IWW, an address that she prefaced with a confession: "Despite the fact that I have often, again and again in my life, been inspired and moved and energized by listening to a brilliant and sincere and revolutionary speaker, I have a deep-seated feeling against all kinds of public speaking." Still, she performed well enough that Elizabeth Gurley Flynn of the IWW asked her back to speak to a meeting of women members.[13]

In February 1915, English again traveled south to stay with his parents at the Alcazar in St. Augustine. But this year Anna seemed prepared for the long absence. English reported regularly on his work: a short book on Horace Traubel, socialist friend of Walt Whitman; a compilation of documents about socialists and the war; a long article for *The Survey*; more dancing lessons.[14]

As for Anna, she wrote back with startling ebullience. She wrote that she had "been buried so long, and been so physically incapacitated for so many years, that I feel so wonderfully young, wonderfully, strong, and terribly hungry for people, for the opportunities intellectual, aesthetic, psychical that New York offers just for the asking." To "Dearest in the World," she wrote, as she returned home from a Purim gathering at her parents' home to celebrate her mother's birthday, and her own: "I am so happy these days, dearest in my life! I am working, and I seem to be getting my bearings in every way."[15]

English must have gritted his teeth, however, when she reported that she had spoken to "the Jane Addams group." The founder of Hull-House was the leading figure in a broad alliance of peace committees that was calling for a meeting of women at The Hague that spring, and the Greenwich branch of the peace movement was named for her. The whole effort was representative of what English was already condemning in print as "bourgeois pacifism," which he loathed as worse than useless.[16]

Nor could he have been pleased at Anna's recounting of their eldest daughter's advice before her talk: "When I told Rosamond where I was going and why, that I would say that people ought not to fight one another, she said: 'Go, mamma, and stay as long as you like. I want you to go and say that, and my Daddy will be glad, too.'" A week later, as she prepared a talk to a feminist group in New York, Rosamond had further counsel: "Rosamond made up this speech for me to-night, as I was undressing her: that war is bad and that all people are good, and that everybody must be kind to children. (Is there anything more worth saying?) I hugged her."[17]

Suddenly she was very busy. After the New York speech—which went well, although she afterward suffered her usual "artistic misery"—she attended a party for *Mother Earth*, the magazine of anarchism founded by her old friend Emma Goldman, and was asked to speak at the *Mother Earth* anniversary celebration in April. In the meantime, a New York lecture bureau prevailed on her to go to Grand Rapids, Michigan, to speak on "The Women of Russia." She also shipped some of her work to the just-founded *New Republic* magazine, and for her pains got back a fastidious rebuke from Lippmann, in his new role as one of its editors: "I admire [these articles] beyond words and don't agree with them at all. I am afraid I was brought up in the tradition in which the word 'better' is used more frequently than the word 'best.'"[18]

Through this period, she was moving at last toward ridding herself of her oldest burden, the Père Lachaise manuscript. Two years before, she had been so close to resubmitting it that she had written a foreword, only to hold back. Now it went out again, to the Frederick A. Stokes Company.[19]

On April 27, 1915, she wrote, in a tone of reserved triumph, to Jack and Charmian London: "They did take 'Pere Lachaise' and the unanimous report of Mr. Stokes, Mr. Morrow, and the readers is that it is a great book. It is coming out in September. It will be called, 'Violette of Pere Lachaise.' . . . Although I call it a subjective biography, it is a euphemism for abstract and makes a demand for thought on the part of the reader, which is as much as saying that there is the slightest chance in the world that it will be widely read." On the day she signed the contract, she wrote to the senior Wallings: "I feel just as mother [Rosalind Walling] said I would feel—freed from within. The thing tied me; I could not get away from it nor could I finish it."[20]

She enclosed with the letter to her in-laws a copy of a new foreword that recounted how she had started writing the novel on Kings Mountain in 1905, had carried it about Europe, and then had ignored it for long periods. Passing over the rejection of the earlier version by Macmillan, she said that she resumed when she was pregnant with Georgia and again lapsed: "The book waited till now when the world is at war with itself, and death and devastation are upon us. It is now when tragedy stalks abroad that I am moved to assert the unconquerable strength of the individual, the eternal spell of beauty, the innate goodness and reasonableness of people."[21]

Her doubts that the book would be widely read were confirmed when Ellery Sedgwick of the *Atlantic,* calling *Violette* a "story of an inner life, which is really a series of meditations," decided that it was a poor choice for serialization. To the Wallings, Anna wrote that she agreed with this assessment but remained optimistic. As to title, she leaned toward plain *Violette,* because she was weary of *Père Lachaise* and people would not know how to pronounce it, anyway. She rattled off, giddily, the great novels that carried women's names: *Anna Karenina, Madame Bovary, Marie Claire, Trilby.*[22]

When the slender book appeared in September 1915, it did not include the foreword; in its place was a brief dedication to Rosalind English Walling, the dead infant. The dust jacket, in purple, announced: "A delicate and original idealization of the biography of a girl. A subjective biography, the author calls it. But, though it is the spiritual development of a specially gifted individual, it is also the development of every individual, the adjustment of everyone to life and death. . . . In this way, Mrs. Walling, herself a prominent figure in the social revolution, embodies her conception of the modern philosophy of love and revolution idealism and democracy. Violette is a forerunner of the future." The price was a dollar.[23]

Violette was hardly a novel in the conventional sense, although it was, to be sure, a chronicle of a fictional girl who grew up with her grandfather in a floral shop near Père Lachaise. But the work had little of the specificity, realistic detail, or verisimilitude associated with the twentieth-century novel. Instead, it was an interior portrait, some of it fabricated, some of it drawn, evidently, from Anna's own life—the brilliant student days, an older friend very much like the Robert Wilson who committed suicide in 1905, the socialist faith. But it had none of the radical fire of Poole's *The Harbor* nor of the great proletarian novel George Brett had expected of her. Closer in spirit to the ornateness and elegance of *The Kempton-Wace Letters,* it was, as Sedgwick said, a very late Victorian "series of meditations."

The book did not create a stir, even in socialist circles. Anna had a polite note from Brett, who had rejected *Violette* in 1911, to the effect that the volume was "an excellent specimen of book making," which he had not yet read. There was a short notice in the *Herald.* Max Eastman said a few kindly words in the *Masses,* and Rose Pastor Stokes did the same in the *Intercollegiate Socialist.* At Christmas time, Anna cheered herself by inquiring after the book at Brentano's, Wanamaker's, and Gimbel's and obtaining upbeat reports from the clerks. But sales were not substantial, and, essentially, that was the end of *Violette,* of Anna as a novelist, and of the path on which Jack London had set her years before.[24]

By the time *Violette* was published in September 1915, it must have become apparent to Anna the war would overwhelm all else, for her as well as English. Her ability to preserve her conscience and her marriage, or either, was increasingly threatened.

❋

As she entered her thirties, Rose Strunsky remained adventurous. In 1912, she had crossed the Atlantic just after the *Titanic* sank. In 1915, she elected to sail from New York only days after the torpedoing of the British passenger ship *Lusitania* on May 7. At least she was on a presumably safe American liner, which arrived in Liverpool, she reported, "with the stars & stripes flying, & at night poles stuck out from the boat on either side with electric reflectors which shone on an enormous S.S. PHILADELPHIA."[1]

She reported the trip's complications to Anna. The sex scholar Havelock Ellis and his wife were fellow passengers and Rose complained: "We had a wretched time with Mrs. Ellis. Poor dear little Havelock!—Such a woman! We had to take turns in sleeping with her & holding her hand." One evening Rose and Mrs. Ellis and Rose's traveling companion Aino Malmberg sat tippling the cherry brandy Rose's father had given her. Aino flew into a rage and denounced England's alliance with czarist Russia. Rose concluded that Aino had been overheard because English customs detained her on landing. A Finnish friend at the Russian consulate ultimately resolved the matter.[2]

The unpleasantness at sea was nothing compared with what Rose encountered when she reported for the job that had drawn her to London, as a scout for the Sunday *New York Tribune*. She found the *Tribune* bureau chief "a bit jealous" of her assignment of signing up celebrities for articles, and heard grumbling from other members of the staff. She smoothed matters over, only to run into a worse obstacle, the prices that British men of letters wanted for producing minor articles for the *Tribune:* Arnold Bennett asked for a thousand dollars, Bernard Shaw for three thousand.[3]

A few weeks later she went to Paris to write articles of her own, among them an account of a Zeppelin raid soon after her arrival. She sent Anna the manuscripts, with elaborate marketing instructions. She added, ruefully: "I am treating you very much as the Tribune treated me. Do this, do this, do this, and not a penny coming in." There were bright spots. Her brief flame Arthur Bullard was leaving her his apartment and a twenty-dollar commission for paying his bills while he returned to America. She was a little jealous when she found his article, "Zeppelins over Paris," in the *Outlook*, for she had had no luck placing her own "July 14."[4]

During the summer Rose encountered Edith Wharton. The American novelist was living in France for the duration and supporting war relief. To Rose, a quarter-century younger, she looked jaded: "Mrs. Wharton has a hard American face with a layer of 'gentle aristocracy' borrowed from the continent. Her lips are rouged & she wears matched pearls & diamonds in the morning. However, I think this is very 'comme il faut' & there is no mistake in her being a grand lady, but it struck me as unbecoming for an American to be anything but a delightful plebeian. I think she is a genius & I think she understands her characters very well, which she gets out of her own hard heart. . . . I even detected a little scorn for the 'indulgent complacent selfish lives the American leads.' I am getting tired of this continual scorn of Americans."[5]

At the end of September Arthur Bullard returned to Paris. Rose moved out to a noisy hotel and then to a quiet furnished room. In October, she went back to America.[6]

In contrast with Rose, who was still free to roam, Anna and English could hardly dash to the action. But the war engaged them deeply nonetheless. Even in St. Petersburg in 1906, English had not felt a need to hear gunfire, but then as now he had an urgent desire to take possession of the issues of the war, to demonstrate that by sheer intensity he could bend readers to think of the war as he did and to favor the outcomes that he wanted. He may not have noticed that the war was bending him, that he was no longer entirely a socialist commenting on the war—although the press still liked to cast him in that role—but also a nationalist eager for American participation.

By 1915, the strenuous pace of his writing was stepped up yet another notch. In addition to the stream of articles he wrote for the *New Review* and other magazines, he assembled a book of exactly five hundred pages called *The Socialists and the War.* The book was not a true successor to his three earlier books on socialism; it had a different publisher, Henry Holt, and was less a book of theoretical argument than a compilation of documents, prepared at the request of the Intercollegiate Socialist Society, which was serving at that time almost as an alternative party for those out of tune with the peace-oriented Socialist Party of America.[7]

Yet the book was more than an assemblage of reprints; English wrote thousands of words of summary and analysis binding the disparate documents. Nor could a writer of his temperament always remain neutral in presenting such material. He picked away at opponents, particularly Morris Hillquit, the New York leader who spoke for the Socialist Party of America, figuratively interrupting Hillquit in mid-document to imply that the party's neutrality in the war masked sympathy for Germany. The book appeared at about the time of the *Lusitania* sinking, and he commented to his parents: "If Germany repeats her insanity—which she will, it will mean war—and the close of the European struggle by the end of the year [1915]."[8]

English inevitably brought his increasingly aggressive views into the parlor. Whenever guests came to Greenwich, conversation was about the war, and English wrung agreement from most in their circle—but not from Anna. She wrote to Charmian London in April 1915: "We talk of war day and night. We [are?] having quite a large house party to-day and I have fought all my guests on the subject of militarism in the good old San Francisco way."[9]

Emma Goldman, realizing that she could write confidentially, commented to Anna: "I hope you and the children are well and that English is not quite as rabid on the war question as in the past. It is absolutely inexplicable to me how revolutionists will become so blinded by the very thing they have been fighting for years."[10]

The most definitive statement English made in the first year of the war was in a lead essay in the *New Review* for June 1, 1915, under the heading, "The Great Illusions." The greatest illusion, he wrote, was not belief in the efficacy of war, as bourgeois pacifists contended, but belief that peacemaking mechanisms could be effective. War could be abolished only gradually, he said, through economic forces that were leading gradually to modern, democratic, internationalist societies. He returned to the theme three months later, in "The Futility of Bourg[e]ois Pacifism," dismissing as futile all the peace panaceas offered by the peace movement.[11]

More fully than in his formal writings, his rampant state of his mind was reflected in such correspondence as a letter to his father during the summer of 1915:

> A Washington friend on the inside told me to-day he expected that Germany would declare war on us after we had taken certain hostile commercial action. I expect this too—within a few weeks.
>
> I desire it—because of pro-Germans, wild Irish, Catholics, anti-Japanese, peace fanatics, treasonable Socialists and the armament trust in *this* country. Only *that* will silence them all.[12]

English wrote with the consciousness, of course, that his home harbored an irrefragable ally of the bourgeois pacifists. Anna, like Rose, had become involved with the Woman's Peace Party not long after its founding in the fall of 1914. Many of its most prominent participants came from the core of settlement workers, reformers, and philanthropists who had supported Theodore Roosevelt's Progressive campaign in 1912. The former president himself was now of course on the other side, blowing the bugle for military preparedness. Antiwar socialists were welcomed into the peace coalition and Anna, freed now of staying home to work on *Violette,* came to meetings, spoke, wrote letters to the newspapers and was listed on the letterhead of the Woman's Peace Party of New York, the most radical branch, as an honorary vice-chairman.[13]

Although Anna and English argued, they held back from irreparable conflict. When English went on a trip (as he did in June 1915 to visit his father, who had been knocked down by a horse) their correspondence was cordial and largely devoted to family business. From their summer rental in Nantucket Anna wrote that she was doing a long review of a Nietzsche biography, and commented that "the latest Press opinion now is that Socialism leads to suicide—also to vegetarianism." For his part, English wrote back a curious comment—considering his outspokenness on racism—about seeing D. W. Griffith's film about the Ku Klux Klan, The Birth of a Nation: "The show was not as anti-Negro as I had expected."[14]

As to their disagreements about the war, Anna offered terms for a continuing truce: "I am not excited, dearest, by anything, and don't distress yourself if we look upon this matter [an incident involving the peace activities of Hamilton Holt of the Independent] and a few others, in connection with this war, from different angles. At bottom we are nearer than any other two people in the world. And I know that you think more scientifically than I do—only I feel that I think strongly, as strongly as you do."[15]

Although their differences were no secret to friends, there was no outward rift in family solidarity. They were hosts early in the fall of 1915 to the senior Wallings. (Anna was rewarded with a thank-you note from Rosalind Walling that reprimanded her for serving coffee too strong for her son's health.) English was master of ceremonies at the golden wedding celebration for Anna's parents on November 27, 1915.[16]

In February 1916 Anna took her longest leave of absence from the children since the birth of Rosamond six years before. The lecture bureau had arranged a speaking tour in Illinois and Indiana; she was gone thirteen days and spoke ten times. At the end, inevitably, she was punished for her independence. When she arrived home she found Rose, who had volunteered to be chief sitter, looking bedraggled and all three girls sick.[17]

English soon departed for his annual visit with his parents in Florida. While he was gone, Anna's old friend Emma Goldman, now the editor of Mother Earth magazine, invited Anna to speak at a birth-control meeting at Carnegie Hall. Anna was reluctant but Goldman insisted: "I'd much rather have the assistance of my comrades and friends than the capitalistic class of the 'Prominent Ladies,' and you are my friend and comrade are you not?" At the meeting, Anna became flustered and lost her way during her speech. Goldman consoled her in a letter afterward: "It is alright dear about your speech on Wednesday. I realized while you spoke that something must have disturbed you or caught into your thread of thought, because you were so much at sea and found it so difficult to finish."[18]

It was certainly out of the ordinary for Anna to lose her train of thought; she was an experienced speaker. But in this instance she may have been distracted by the ambiguity of her own position. She was after all addressing a meeting on birth control and yet she may have been pregnant again, despite the firm family decision after Georgia's birth to have no more children. Neither she nor English said much about this pregnancy, even to their families. Emma Goldman, not knowing, continued to urge her to turn out for meetings. Finally, after the family had gone to Nantucket for the summer, Goldman found out, and wrote to Anna: "What a strange girl you are to have so many kiddies, especially when you go through such a terrible ordeal during pregnancy."[19]

Strange indeed, that she was again pregnant at the age of thirty-nine. She certainly must have known birth-control methods, but must not have used them. The circumstances suggest that there was more involved than carelessness: a determination on English's part to have a son and a desire by Anna to please him or, worse, an impulse on English's part to control his wife through a pregnancy when he could not control her mind. These were not matters discussed in writing, even in the most intimate family letters.

For a time in 1916, during Anna's sixth pregnancy, English reined in his explosiveness. His stream of opinions in magazines and newspapers diminished, and he devoted attention to finishing two unpolemical book projects. One was, for him, oddly avocational: The little volume *Whitman and Traubel* grew out of his addresses to the annual dinners of the Whitman Society in New York, and explored the quasi-socialist aspects of the lives of Walt Whitman and Horace Traubel, the surviving biographer-friend of Whitman. The other book was also light work, a compilation of documents from several countries to be called *The Socialism of To-Day;* he shared the editing with his old friend Graham Stokes and other members of the Intercollegiate Socialist Society. Late in the winter, as usual, he left his family behind and vacationed with his parents in Florida.[1]

His and Anna's correspondence while he was gone was placid. Anna reported progress on her "new" book, the old "Revolutionary Lives" sketches of their Russian experiences. She thanked him for his criticism of a book review ("I certainly need, in my writing, data or reality or substance, the facts in life which affect me so strongly and yet seem to elude me") and for the oranges he sent. She reported: "Rose received a most interesting letter from Arthur [Bullard] on what he calls the sex question—an intelligent, suggestive letter of about twenty pages. He says the thing we must all do is to answer the question 'What love might be.' He will write a book on it."[2]

Bullard, now much caught up in heavy questions of war policy as an adviser to the powerful, never wrote his book on sex. If he intended the letter as a covert overture to Rose, it was very belated. He was on the verge of becoming engaged to Ethel Bagg, from a well-connected Washington family. And Rose had long since committed her heart to Louis Levine, a reserved scholar-journalist she met at the Liberal Club four years before. Levine had never married, but he was the father of a son, Valentine (Val), from a brief relationship of a decade before. Levine had gone on to earn a doctorate in economics at Columbia, and was now at Wellesley College on a short-term appointment. The progress of their courtship was Sisyphean.[3]

In May 1916, Rose crossed the Atlantic again, going this time to Stockholm to work with the "Fords," as the Swedes called the Neutral Conference for Continuous Mediation, an outgrowth of Henry Ford's much-ridiculed Peace Ship. Both English and Louis Levine opposed the venture as perilous but, writing to Levine, Rose scoffed: "Why don't you think I ought to go now? On account of the submarine controversy? English thinks so too. But he loves to see trouble with Germany."[4]

Safely in Stockholm, Rose wrote lightly to Anna: "I dance and go motor-boating . . . & swim in bath houses as elaborate as Caligula's. I have fallen in love with the blond type—I have never lived with as much pure nakedness as I have this summer. . . . If one goes boating it is a feast. . . . They don't look half as nice in clothes as without especially the ladies." She eventually got a job at the conference typing out spot translations with her new little Corona on her lap, but the work lasted only until the end of the summer.[5]

Meanwhile Anna, pregnant and still a bit nauseated, traveled with English and the children to Nantucket for the summer, a site even more isolated than East Hampton. Anna wrote to assure her sister that she had not yielded to English's position on the war:

> Of course, I feel and think just as you do, and it is a relief and a positive help in living our daily life to come in personal contact with anyone that one can agree with as I do (nowadays) only when a word reaches me from you, dearest only sister. . . .
>
> I long to escape to the emancipated, the civilized, but for effectiveness it is really better to live constantly, face to face with the Opposition. It stirs me up more. . . . Prof. [Melville] Anderson popped up from Italy to harrow me with a request to help in a propaganda against "les bosches," etc., etc. (and dear English, of course is always the same.)[6]

In August, Anna and English entertained the eminent feminist Charlotte Perkins Gilman—English wrote his parents that she was "regarded as the brainiest woman in the country"—and her husband, George Houghton Gilman. She and English had overlapping interests: they were both socialists and had both been founders of the Intercollegiate Socialist Society; they were both publicists, she primarily through the *Forerunner*, a personal journal of opinion. Now, it appeared, she and English might be converging as well on the war question, despite her earlier peace activity.[7]

For Anna, the Gilmans were part of a summer of too many visitors, but she was pleased that English liked them. "I, too, am deriving a great deal of pleasure from their visit," she wrote to her in-laws, "only her view of life strikes me as being rather mechanical and theoretical—especially when she gets on the subject of children. But I have been most discreet and polite, and have avoided discussions!" Later, Anna had another, slightly envious, thought about their guest, which she confided in a letter to her sister: "Mrs. Gilman writes so easily and finishes everything she begins!! I am determined to learn the trick. I am sure I can if I try hard enough. So far I have done nothing this summer but as ever hope springs perrenial [*sic*], and I think I shall accomplish wonders before my important vital New Years Day"—that is, before the predicted arrival of their child.[8]

By the start of September, Anna had had enough of the summer. Aggrieved by English's cutting remarks about how little time she spent with the children, she started a secret grievance diary—much like the one she had kept on their Volga trip—documenting that her days were spent entirely, except for an hour or two, with the three children. Soon she added reflections that depicted her belief that she had become a victim of her marriage:

> While dressing in the bath-house G.T. [Gertrude Traubel, Horace Traubel's daughter, a house-guest] said to me: It makes me angry how English talks about the babies as if only Lee brings them up [and] you have nothing to do with them!
>
> "He knows better" I said.
>
> "Well," she continued, "but he says such things right before company!"
>
> I laughed as best I could . . . but walking home from my invigorating swim I had to fight down the depression caused by her remark.
>
> Remarks of E's so lacking in justice and in sense oppress my spirits. If he were not so violent I could set him right and forget the offense immediately after it—as it is I find relief in writing things down.[9]

Three days later she wrote:

> The last remark English made last night in bed was "Who ever got any service out of you??"
>
> "What about my serving the babies day and night?" I remonstrated and I might have added had I not followed my new plan of avoiding as much as possible personal conversation, even when it begins most pleasantly because he always makes it end speedily in disaster—I might have added "I have served all my life unstintingly—when I taught English to foreigners for nothing all through my girlhood, when I sat up nights correcting other people's articles and stories, when I helped workingmen friends prepare for Regents exams, when [I] nursed momma[,] suffered because I was not allowed to do more for my motherless nieces; when in the Socialist Party, I did endless drudgery like being secretary of the Central Committee for 2½ years, and on other committees to which I gave my precious time—time for which my soul and my young fiery senses had other uses altogether. I have given, given, given and now in my babies I give a thousandfold more than ever." . . .
>
> So this morning he refers to his leaving himself free to go or not to go to Boston. "I never tie myself up, if I can help it."

"That's splendid," I say to him[.] "I always tie myself up. I love freedom, but I have so many duties always."

"Well," he says deprecatingly, "You are like my father." I remonstrate. "I am anything but rigid in my plans; I have always broken my own appointments with myself, in order to keep the last least appointment with everybody. I lose my freedom through being so social, father through being so set on his own ways he ties himself up. I let others tie me up."

"You," says English, "are neither social nor individual. The one who possesses you gets nothing out of you, for you are tied up to the first person that comes along.["]

This is what I call a thought to cheer me on the way, to start the day upon.[10]

They had perhaps arrived at another truce when English left Nantucket on September 20, for Anna went with him as far as Martha's Vineyard, where they had part of a day alone. English went on to attend an Intercollegiate Socialist Society conference in Maryland, where he delivered an address on "Defensive Warfare," predicting that socialists would become patriots if the United States entered the war. Then he came back to Greenwich to search for a house to buy, under the stern and mistrustful guidance of his father. He warned Anna against returning with the children because of an outbreak of what was then called infantile paralysis. His letters tended to the managerial: *"Please send my laundry by parcel post."*[11]

The tense presidential contest that fall between Charles Evans Hughes, former governor of New York, and President Wilson caught their attention. Both Anna and English were sympathetic to Wilson's candidacy—Anna because, as the Democratic slogan proclaimed, he had kept America out of the war, English because Wilson was the alternative to supporting the Socialist Party, from which he was increasingly alienated. Anna confided to her older daughter that she favored Allan Benson, the Socialist, but that she would give her (hypothetical) "second vote" to Wilson. English was originally scheduled to sign a statement in the *New Republic* supporting Benson, but he declined at the last moment. He wrote to his father that he might support Wilson, although his reasoning sounded paranoid:

> I agree that Hughes is completely surrounded by as dangerous a crew of men as ever surrounded any president or candidate for president.
>
> I believe now that Wilson has some chance of being elected—though the combination of Wall Street, the Kaiser, Roosevelt and the Catholic Church is terrificly [sic] strong. . . .
>
> I shall act regardless of the personal attacks that will certainly follow, including attacks on me as an author, social reformer, etc.[12]

In a statement in the *New York World*, English came still closer to supporting Wilson, saying in effect that many Socialists, if they could vote on a
preferential ballot, would cast protest votes for Benson and "effective votes"
for Wilson. But Wilson still tried his patience; English wrote to his father that
he hoped that a German submarine-supply ship might be found in American
waters, thus forcing Wilson toward war. His father replied, tartly and sensi-
bly, that "if Wilson should before the election, estrange the peace element
and the woman voters (which are ¾ for him) by any war move he would be an
arrant fool."[13]

The negotiations for the new house in Greenwich, on Brookside Drive,
were completed late in October 1916 with a contribution of twenty-five
thousand dollars from the elder Wallings. Anna dashed off a note: "The last
time I owned a house was when I was six years old, the house in Russia in
which my mother, her mother, and all of us children were born. It's a far cry
from Babinotz to Greenwich!" A few days later she wrote that English had
made himself ill in his enthusiasm: "He overdid in New York, speaking on
two successive days and coming home on late trains and then he worked over
the garden too long, measuring out the tennis court by moon-light." A house
of their own—it was the completion of the transition from world rovers to at
least superficially conventional suburbanites.[14]

Late in October or early in November, Dr. Walling suffered a stroke and had
to be carried to the polling place to vote for Wilson. (English's mother, casting
the first presidential vote of her life under the new Illinois suffrage law, also
voted for the president.) Later in November, Rosalind Walling urged English
and Anna to come to Chicago, but they followed Dr. Walling's earlier instruc-
tion that Anna should not come before she gave birth; she remained in
Greenwich while English went to his father's bedside. He sent back a note
saying his father was weaker; he also gave her detailed instructions on paying
the household bills and added: "Read this over a second time and you wont
fail to get it right."[15]

The note reached Anna at a moment of grief. On November 22, 1916, Jack
London died at his California ranch, forty years old, a victim of too many
impositions on his wracked body. She wrote condolence letters to Charmian
London but, given the vehemence of her reactions to death it seems extraordinary that there should have been so little about Jack in her other letters
until weeks later. English's letters from Chicago offered no word of sympathy, and her replies made no references to Jack, perhaps in deference to her
father-in-law's final crisis.[16]

When she received word that Dr. Walling had died, she referred only indirectly to her own suffering: "I cannot say much to comfort you, my darling,

being so comfortless myself. I can only beg you to spare yourself all you can. You belong even more to me, to me and to our tiny ones, born and unborn, than to yourself. . . . With love that can only die when I die, Anna."[17]

En route to Indianapolis for the burial service, English, far from responding in kind, sent an imperious batch of instructions headed "*House Notes Important,*" starting with an order to get rubber lifts put on his shoes. Later he wrote that he was stopping over in Englishton, the family seat in Indiana, returning to Chicago with his mother, thence home on December 11.[18]

He returned to Greenwich before the birth, on December 22, of their son, William Hayden English Walling, but somehow he was again absent from the house for the event itself, as the widowed Rosalind Walling heard from Anna. Rosalind wrote back: "I wish I had been with you. I know what that terror is & English was away when you wrote too—I do hope he came soon after— Well, it is all happily over and a son is born unto you."[19]

In January 1917, when Hayden was three weeks old, Anna wrote to Charmian London saying that she intended to write a memorial to Jack. Three months later, she wrote to Charmian again to say that Max Eastman of the *Masses* had asked her for such an article; she wrote it in time for publication in the July 1917 issue. In this tribute she unveiled for the first time an assortment of the dozens of letters Jack had written to her years before. Although the memoir was gracefully elegiac, recalling Jack as an "indescribably virile and beautiful boy," it contained no overt expression of personal grief.[20]

Yet Anna was quietly staking her claim to being a custodian of Jack's memory in tacit competition with Charmian. Near the end of 1917, Charmian complained because Anna had lent Rose Wilder Lane, for use in her article in *Sunset* magazine, an intimate letter from Jack that Anna had not used in her own *Masses* article—the one of December 1900 defining "a white beautiful friendship" between them. Anna responded by telegram: "Shall not publish anything against your desire[.] letter however is to Jacks credit and refutes definitely and absolutely popular slander[.] the question is not of me but of him[,] what he was and what he was able to bring to a friendship like ours[.] many will see jack in new light because of beauty and idealism of this letter[.]" This was but the first of a series of such muted encounters, always framed, Anna-like, in avowals of friendship and love.[21]

Early in 1917, with English grieving for his father and Anna in a postpartum disposition, the household on Brookside Drive, Greenwich, was unquiet. There was an incident. On January 27, Anna wrote a letter to English, unusual in that she addressed her grievance directly to him instead of locking it up in a diary:

> It was Miss Dixon [the nurse] who told me that you had thrown the box with the crackers. Something struck me hard and painfully on the instep and a red bruise which she saw when she gave me the alcohol rubs remained for two days.
>
> I did not see myself what you threw. I did not even see crackers. I was ashamed to look. I remember vaguely that Miss Dixon stooped and shoved something angrily away. I sat with my eyes fixed on the infant-boy nursing my breast, and I had that sinking sensation that [I] had complained [of] to you about a few days before Hayden English was born.
>
> I did not tell Dr. Parker anything about the "throwing" and I would not have spoken of it to Miss Dixon had she not been in the room when it happened. I excused you to her.
>
> She told me that you would behave better to me if I did not show my love for you so much, and Max said the same thing when one day recently I cried and told him I was suffering—that is perhaps why I attempted to be firm and to resist evil with evil this morning. I wont try to do that way again—It is not my way, and I know that it is not the best way.
>
> It is true that sometimes I do not grasp your meaning. When you cut off your love from me you cut off all access to me.
>
> Anna[1]

Although ultimately trivial, English's act betrayed a strain of recklessness in his always barely harnessed temper. Whether his disagreement with Anna was personal or political is not clear, although his loss of control suggests that it was political. She wrote other letters to him in a few days, in a more conventional although not affectionate tone, discussing the household, the children.

After Germany announced unrestricted submarine warfare and Wilson broke diplomatic relations on February 3, 1917, Anna resumed a conversational manner: "Will we have a war with Germany? To me President Wilson is a great soul—a spirit of extraordinary moral courage. I expect Germany will retract at the last moment." At the end of the same letter she wrote: "Tuesday. It looks like war certainly."[2]

In fact, Wilson was still nowhere near belligerent enough for English. He wrote to his mother complaining that Wilson had not taken action after the sinking of the *Lusitania*, nearly two years before; if he had, English contended, "the war would now be over and millions of lives would have been saved." His assessment of the president he had supported for reelection had turned cold: "He has intelligence but no vision or inspiration. He is no Washington or Lincoln."[3]

In mid-February, English entered Polyclinic Hospital in Manhattan for repair of a hernia. From his bed, he kept an eye on developing crises. There was the upheaval in Russia that led, on March 14, to the abdication of Czar Nicholas, and the establishment of what was later known as the Kerensky government. There was increased tension between Germany and the United States with the release of the Zimmerman telegram, in which the German foreign minister instructed his ambassador to promise American territory to Mexico. After spending his convalescence at the City Club in New York, finishing work on a much-trimmed edition of *Russia's Message* for the new publisher Alfred A. Knopf, English took his customary trip south to St. Augustine to stay with his mother.[4]

It was during this trip, apparently, that English wrote a notorious letter to Anna that has been quoted several times by historians in the years since it became available in his papers as epitomizing the harshness of his feelings on the war. In fact, although the letter bears a St. Augustine letterhead, it bears no date and the precise context that triggered it is not stated explicitly.

The subject Anna raised in her first letter to him in Florida was her joy over the revolution in Russia: "Darling, it is enough to have lived to see this day, and we shall see greater and more [?] historic days yet!" Although he was already beginning to worry that Russia might withdraw from the war, English could hardly have been angered at her exultation over the fall of the czar. More likely, he was touched off by her association with the Emergency Peace Federation, formed in February 1917 by the most determined segments of the pacifist coalition to agitate for a war referendum. Late in March, the organization filled Madison Square Garden with a last-gasp rally for peace. Anna, still confined to home, was hardly one of the federation's leaders, but she supported it and was listed in its literature.[5]

English started his letter with a brief discussion of routine family business, then switched abruptly:

Of course I think your proposal to attack in the back those who are giveing [sic] up their lives for democracy, peace, and anti-militarism is criminal to the last degree. But the world is moving in spite of all you do to help the militarists and reactionaries. You are their accomplice and neither I nor mankind, nor the genuine idealists and revolutionaries of the world will ever forget or forgive what your kind has said and done in this great hour. If I fight it will be against the traitors to internationalism—I trust you will not be among them.

Thus culminated English's deep anger at the resistance he had found at home, informed by his absolute conviction that the American peace movement was nothing more than an arm of German subversion.[6]

A letter that Anna wrote on March 21 may or may not be the direct response; at least it constituted a defense.

Not being a Junker you cannot turn me into one by saying so. It is as just to call my opposition to war Junkerism as it would be for me to say that because you do not always oppose war that you are cruel and bloodthirsty and proud to avail yourself of [two words illegible] by torturing and slaying people known to mankind!

You are not a militarist, and I am not a Junker.

A Revolutionist believes in the People and opposes the established order—my faith in the people and opposition to establishment law and order are deep and integral with my whole being. I am not a Junker because I not only give my consent to the rioters of the streets of Petrograd for what they did, but had I not you and our children I would not have hesitated, even at this distance to join them and fall by their side for a regenerated Russia. As it is, rich and wonderful as my life is with you and my children I do not at all feel that I belong wholly to myself and the time may come when I, the most passionate lover of life ever born, may go out to meet death for my Cause—as gallantly as any soldier ever did— but I will make sure that it is my Cause and not the Cause of my enemy.

Some day you will understand and understand me as well as I understand you and then we will laugh together at our past sufferings. That is my day and night dream. It lies in your power to make it come true.

I have had a happy birthday. . .[7]

The exchange was theoretical, of course. Anna was not to die for her cause, nor was English to fight in the war in any literal sense.

Nor was the break between them truly climactic, for a week later Anna offered a surrender of sorts. For the sake of the new Russian revolution, she said, she would change:

I have capitulated to your point of view about this War. What else can we do with the enemy at the door of the Russian Revolution but give him battle and rout him? Until the German people revolt we have to repel their advance upon freedom and democracy with the edge of the sword. . . .

I am forced to descend from my height "Above the Battle" freely to adopt new processes of thought and feeling altogether from those that have guided me for two and a half years. But you cannot dream how it tortures me to have been weak and sick all day to consent to war! I do finally "vote the money and the men" but I do not expect to survive it. In a sense I have already failed to survive it—so much has fallen together in me and died since this morning when my new conception was borne in upon me.

Ever since Rosalind English was born I have seen everybody as a little baby shining on a pillow or on a mother's breast; I have had a mother's tenderness towards the world of men and women; I could always see everybody as they were born to be, not as they were. I feel as if this, my motherhood, were slain this morning when I read the papers and read of the German danger to Russia and when I vicariously flew to arms. . . . You are more fortunately constituted than I am. You are never divided against yourself. Whatever you think is right and best you have strength for.[8]

Whether this letter restored a peace between them, or whether English even acknowledged it, is unknown. What is known is that by March 1917 English was probably paying less attention to what was happening at home, being utterly preoccupied with America's rush toward war. He was vigorously attacking the peace movement and the antiwar positions of the Socialist Party of America. He was lionized in the *New York Evening Post* for his patriotism:

THESE SOCIALISTS AMERICANS FIRST
Stokes, Walling, Russell and
Others Proclaim Their
Loyalty to This Country.[9]

In the first week of April, Wilson asked Congress to declare war.

In May 1917, Randolph Bourne, the unreconciled soul whom John Dos Passos memorialized as a "tiny twisted unscared ghost in a black cape," contemplated America's declaration of war in an essay that he once would have written for the *New Republic.* That weekly was no longer hospitable to dissent, and Bourne appeared in the June issue of the struggling *Seven Arts* magazine to charge that intellectuals had led "an apathetic nation into an irresponsible war."[1] He reserved his special scorn for the prowar socialists:

> For they called to us in terms that might have emanated from any bour-
> geois journal to defend democracy and civilization, just as if it was not
> exactly against those very bourgeois democracies and capitalist civiliza-
> tions that socialists had been fighting for decades. But so subtle is the
> spiritual chemistry of the "inside" that all this intellectual cohesion—
> herd-instinct become herd-intellect—which seemed abroad so hysteri-
> cal and so servile, comes to us here in highly rational terms.[2]

In a few weeks of war, Bourne had seen the little circle of American (that is, nonimmigrant) socialist intellectuals declare themselves patriots, sever their ties with their party, and scurry toward the "inside," the centers of action and esteem. Not least among them was the old group from the University Settle-ment. By May 1917, Ernest Poole and Arthur Bullard were in Washington at the new central propaganda office, the Committee on Public Information, working on a pamphlet-sized book justifying American entrance into the war. Graham Stokes organized a movement for secession from the still-pacifist Socialist Party of America, and Leroy Scott and Howard Brubaker came along quietly. Only Walter Weyl, now an editor at the *New Republic,* held back; he disappeared from the masthead for a time and worked on a book about peacemaking that was later condemned as subversive.[3]

English too heard the call to the "inside." Late in April, President Wilson decided to organize a mission to meet with the new Kerensky government in Petrograd (the old St. Petersburg), partly to encourage Russia to stay in the war. To head the mission he named Elihu Root, an elderly Wall Street lawyer, head of the Carnegie Endowment for International Peace, and secretary of state under Theodore Roosevelt. Either to balance the commission or to sup-ply a member who could talk intelligibly with the socialists in the Kerensky government, a search began for an American socialist member. English, Stokes, Charles Edward Russell, Upton Sinclair, and William Ghent had already sent a telegram to Kerensky warning against a separate peace, and all thus became candidates.[4]

Support soon coalesced for English. On April 30, the *New York Globe & Commercial Advertiser* published an editorial urging the appointment of English, as "our leading authority on all questions relating to the Russian revolution." On the same day, William B. Wilson, secretary of labor, sent to the president a warm recommendation: "I know of no Socialist in this country who has been more in touch with the Socialistic group of Russia or understands them better than Mr. Walling." Perhaps the secretary had seen English's name in the papers, but more likely it had been passed to him by Samuel Gompers of the AFL.[5]

Even before English could know of this endorsement, he took the initiative himself. On May 1, he sent off to the secretary of labor his article from the *Globe* of that morning headed "The Pro-Hyphen New York Socialist," which opposed considering Morris Hillquit for the mission; Hillquit was a leader of the Socialist Party of America and thus, in English's view, pro-German. On the next day, English followed up with a letter to the secretary attacking not only the foreign-born leaders of the party but "the relatively small ultra-pacifist, American-born group, composed of such men as Debs and Benson." (Debs must certainly have known of English's attitude, and it is a mark of his saintliness that the next month he supplied to the publisher a flattering comment on English's *Whitman and Traubel*.) English further urged that no representative of the Socialist Party be issued a passport to join a conference of socialist parties in Stockholm, which he regarded as having been "engineered in Berlin."[6]

In a day or two English's article reached the president's desk. One Charles Ranslett Flint of New York, an arms dealer, had visited Elihu Root and had left the clipping with him. Root wrote to Robert Lansing, the secretary of state, suggesting that English might fill the slot on the commission. Lansing sent the clipping and a note on to the president: "Judging from this article I should say Walling was very possibly the man who should be selected as the Socialist on the Commission." The president at once sent a letter asking English whether he would be available.[7]

To this point, it must have looked as if English had run an adroit campaign for the appointment, playing to the questions of loyalty that the Wilson administration would want to raise about any socialist before it sent one abroad. But it turned out that English was not really interested in going to Russia. The hindrance could have been family, although in general family had never constrained his travel. He told the children at the time that he was afraid that he might be in danger in Russia, that a bolshevik "geranium pot" might fall on his head. More apparently he was less interested in a subordinate role in a mission, even a mission to Russia, than in pursuing freelance his new role as the scourge of dissent.[8]

Somewhat related business took English to Washington before he had received the president's letter. He had already helped Stokes draft a plan for a new quasi-socialist organization separate from the Socialist Party of America, which was clinging to its antiwar position. Now he, Poole, Russell, and other American socialists convened to denounce the Stockholm conference. Learning that he was being considered for the commission, English dropped in at the State Department and disqualified himself. Days later, Russell, who knew little more about Russia than about the surface of the moon, got the appointment.[9]

When English returned to Greenwich, he found the president's letter offering the appointment and wrote back: "I hope to be of real service to the cause of internationalism which, like yourself, I place above all else, and also to the American government, by remaining in this country." He got a thank-you from the president acknowledging his "unselfish and patriotic attitude."[10]

English did not rest. On May 16, he sent a peremptory telegram to the State Department: "Immediate renunciation of no annexations no indemnities program by President may save Russia Nothing else will." During the previous hectic month, English had turned out an article for the *Independent* condemning the newly floated peace formula of "no annexations, no indemnities" as a concoction of German socialists, although it had been offered in a different form in Wilson's "peace without victory" speech in January. Now, it appeared, Germany intended to offer the new Russian government peace based on Wilson's formulation, and English was urging the president to abandon the whole idea of a negotiated peace.[11]

On May 18, English was back in Washington, where he and Gompers were sandwiched into the president's afternoon schedule. Now encouraged to believe that he was truly on the inside, he wrote from Greenwich three days later enclosing a memorandum in French he had received on the position of the French socialists. In his letter, he attacked the position of Jean Longuet, who eleven years before had been a witness at his marriage to Anna.[12]

The *New York Times* continued to serve almost as a personal outlet. On May 24, the *Times* carried an interview with English applauding the administration's decision to deny passports to American socialists. Two days later, it published a letter from him attacking Hillquit. At the start of June, the newspaper printed his statement that he would resign from the Socialist Party of America unless the party repudiated its resolutions opposing the draft. (It did not, of course.) It is unclear whether English ever sent in his resignation, but already the formal step, if he did take it, was superfluous.[13]

In June, Emma Goldman's *Mother Earth* magazine published an issue with a drawing on the cover of a gravestone inscribed "In Memoriam—American Democracy." Where Bourne's essay, published that same month, had named few names, Goldman struck home:

> The black scourge of war in its devastating effect upon the human mind has never been better illustrated than in the ravings of the American Socialists, Messrs. Russell, Stokes, Sinclair, Walling, et al. . . . As to English Walling, he was the reddest of the red. Though muddled mentally he was always at white heat emotionally as syndicalist, revolutionist, dissenter, etc.
>
> With Charles Edward Russell as the conferee of Root, English Walling [is] the colleague of the New York *Times,* and Stokes, Simons, Sinclair, Poole, etc. [are] still waiting for the reward from Washington. . . .
>
> One might overlook the renegacy of a Charles Edward Russell. Nothing else need ever be expected from a journalist. But for men like Stokes and Walling to thus become the lackeys of Wall Street and Washington, is really too cheap and disgusting.[14]

What response this sally from Anna's old friend received in the Wallings' household is not known, but Anna saved the clipping. English's response might be guessed from a story their friend Hutchins Hapgood told in his memoir: Hapgood wrote to ask English how he could advocate the punishment and imprisonment of his former comrades; Anna later told Hapgood that when English received the letter, he said nothing but put it on her desk and walked out of the room.[15]

Days after the June issue of *Mother Earth* appeared, the magazine was banned from the mails. On June 15, Goldman and her companion, Alexander Berkman, were arrested at the offices of the No Conscription League in New York for violating the Draft Act passed by Congress less than a month before—specifically, for violating the provision forbidding conspiracies discouraging registration. Ten days later, they were placed on trial and by July 10 were convicted and on their way to their respective prisons. No comment on these events appears in either Anna's or English's correspondence, yet they both must have known that English was feeding the fire of repression.[16]

English remained hyperactive through the first months after the declaration of war. He made further appearances in the *New York Times,* dashed back and forth to Washington, saw the president again, helped Samuel Gompers draft a message to the Russian Workmen's Council, and joined Gompers in organizing the American Alliance for Labor and Democracy, a conglomeration of unionists and prowar socialists—the kind of alliance that he once would have considered anathema. Posing as an independent prowar organization, the AALD was actually a propaganda outlet secretly underwritten by the government's Committee on Public Information, one of a spectrum of such enterprises spawned by CPI to develop uniformity of opinion—or, as English put it, "to fight treason in the labor unions and the Socialist Party." A later historian saw the AALD as comparable to the union-sanctioned organizations subsidized in the 1960s by the Central Intelligence Agency.[1]

Early in the summer of 1917, English deposited the family at a summer site, this time on the mainland, perhaps out of fear of submarines, at New London, Connecticut. When Anna wrote to English (he was in Indianapolis to visit his mother and his uncle) she delicately avoided commenting on the war. She was in a hopeful mood, for she had finished a revision of the "Revolutionary Lives" manuscript, under a new title, "They Who Freed Russia," and had packed it off to a publisher, hoping that the fall of the czar would give it relevance. William Morrow, of the Frederick A. Stokes Company, wrote to her of a favorable first reader's report, and a letter from Rose, in New York, confirmed that the publisher was "kind of crazy about it."[2]

Rose had gone to see Morrow because she wanted to travel overseas, for the third time since the war started—this time to revolutionary Russia. Morrow promised her three hundred dollars and she hoped that English would cosign a bank note for her covering the rest of what she needed. At the same time, she sought magazine commissions (easy) and a passport (difficult, no doubt because of her peace connections). At last, late in August 1917, she settled down to await her ship's departure. But the boat was held at the pier, and English, while he had lent a hundred dollars outright, had not endorsed the note. Rose fretted: "I am afraid Mrs. Walling [his mother] will discourage him, because she once said she doesn't think I ought to go in such troublesome times. He might take that as an excuse to back out." Just which of the obstacles—the boat, the note, or the passport—blocked her is not clear, but she did not go.[3]

Anna meanwhile suffered an equal disappointment. After the first favorable report on her Russian manuscript, it was sent on to one Cooper. Morrow chose Rose to carry the message, and she wrote to Anna: "[Cooper] is opposed to the whole business—You should choose [as] your 'revolutionary' not the 'red handed assassin' but the nice kind gentle one—Besides perhaps the Revolution of 1906 had nothing to do with the one of 1917!!!! It just makes me furious, the wil[l]ful, obstinate perversion of the truth. It is criminal lies they want us all to push down the throats of the people. . . . They are all a pack of cowards. They were afraid to take on the Tolstoi translation [by Rose] . . . [but go] for a book on mesmerism or rugs!"[4]

Anna soon had the limp text of the critique itself: "It is rather a pity that these sketches did not see the light a few months ago, when the whole of America was on the pinnacle of emotion for everything connected with Russia. It is partly, I think, because our senses are dulled by the tales of horror which have been assailing us in every despatch from the scenes of war, and partly because there is a certain impatience at the length of time it seems to be taking Russia to find herself, that these descriptions of scenes and people seem curiously far away and relatively unimportant." The reader conceded that "the work is of undoubted interest" and that the sketches of revolutionaries "are drawn with an intensity of emotion that keeps us on a high key." Morrow wrote to ease Anna's disappointment, explaining that the reader had "seized upon certain political views he had lately heard expressed as a possible explanation of why a manuscript by so skillful and delightful a writer should fail to satisfy him." Although Anna gamely continued to revise and hope, the blow was fatal to publication of the book.[5]

During the summer English joined the family in New London and haggled and quibbled by mail with Graham Stokes over the arrangements for the Social Democratic League—the new prowar quasi-socialist entity. He did not like the proposed plan to create an alliance with the Prohibition and Progressive parties. Even more, he disliked the choice for president, John Spargo, a bitter adversary before the war, and he particularly disagreed with Spargo's tolerant position on wartime dissent.[6]

Stokes did his best to mediate; he obtained Spargo's approval for English to sit on the new organization's board, only to be rewarded with a thorny and quarrelsome letter from English. Stokes responded: "You sometimes make it terribly hard for your friends to work with you." English chose not to attend the founding meeting of the new organization in Minneapolis early in September, and threatened to boycott the organization until Spargo removed himself. "I regret more deeply than I can tell you," Stokes wrote, "that you should have hard feelings toward me. . . . It will be a terrific grief to me if you force a break between us." There was no final break, but it was clear that the madness of controversy was again upon English.[7]

English turned to strengthening his ties with Samuel Gompers and with George Creel's Committee on Public Information. He signed on with still another propaganda concoction, this one called the League for National Unity. It was created by Ralph M. Easley of the National Civic Federation, whose views on the congruent interests of labor and capital English would once have considered intolerable. English also signed up to write for a syndicate called the Vigilantes. He was quietly active, he said, in opposing Morris Hillquit's Socialist candidacy for mayor of New York. (Hillquit ultimately received a surprising 20 percent of the vote.) In November 1917, he quit the Intercollegiate Socialist Society's executive committee over its speaking invitation to Hillquit.[8]

During this period he produced a strange article—which was accompanied by a grim, hollow-eyed photograph of the author—for the *Independent*. Titled "Socialists: The Kaiser-Party," it depicted the Socialist Party of America as being in command of "several million German-drilled voters," all eager consumers of treasonous propaganda. He called for the extirpation of dissent: "We must isolate it, brand it and set the rest of the nation against it. . . . we can be certain of nothing unless we take the offensive against these Allies of the Kaiser—and take it NOW." In essence, the article was a call for a country already in the grip of war fever to become hysterical.[9]

The October Revolution in Russia further invigorated English. Early in November (late October, Old Style) the Bolsheviks ousted the Kerensky government and installed a regime bent on making a separate peace with Germany. (The story handed down in the family is that when English heard of Kerensky's fall he exclaimed to Anna: "Now look what you've done!")[10] Indeed, there were efforts to prove that the whole upheaval had been a German-sponsored conspiracy. For English, the revolution supported his contention that any talk of peace was subversive. He was most suspicious of those who, in calmer times, might have been his allies.

He aimed a broadside in an article for the *New York Globe* headlined, "High-Brow Hearstism: The Peace Agitation of The New Republic." The invocation of Hearst was poisonous in itself, for the Hearst press had been correctly accused of taking German subsidies in return for its neutrality. But the article was primarily a charge of treason involving, as was so often the case, a former ally, this time Walter Lippmann, one of the magazine's editors. English declared the *New Republic* guilty of "intrigue to secure peace now—a peace favorable to German militarism."[11]

The real purpose of the article, beyond further flexing his techniques as a polemicist, was evidently to make himself once more visible to the administration. In any case, English sent a clipping to Creel, who forwarded it to the president. Wilson replied to Creel: "Walling seems to me to have a great deal of sense." An odd response, since another Wilson aide, Colonel House, had recently engaged Lippmann to participate in a secret committee called The Inquiry, charged with drafting a peace plan for the president. The draft formed the basis of the famous Fourteen Points, announced in Wilson's speech of January 8, 1918. Thus the eternal ambivalence of the presidency: Wilson seemed to agree with English's attack on the *New Republic,* but drew on that magazine's positions for his own peace formulation.[12]

English's search for subversion soon led him to destroy yet another friendship. He was touched off by a story in the *New York World* on January 11, 1918, three days after the promulgation of the Fourteen Points and two months into the Bolshevik regime. The Bolsheviks had already met with the Germans at Brest Litovsk in Russian Poland, had signed a provisional armistice, and had started peace negotiations. The story, signed by Herbert Bayard Swope, suggested that the Wilson administration might be willing to work with, and even recognize, the Bolshevik government, meanwhile removing the American ambassador, David Francis, who had been an obstacle to cooperation.[13]

Even a whisper of recognition was bound to inflame English. He immediately wrote a response to the Swope story for the *Times.* It was a curiously complex document. After noting efforts to make the Fourteen Points appear to be an endorsement of the Bolshevik peace negotiations, English offered a rebuttal that was framed as if it were coming from the mind of the president: The president is aware, the president knows. In his *Russia Leaves the War,* George F. Kennan attributes to the letter "a strangely authoritative tone" but is unable to conclude that it was authorized or even encouraged by the administration. If there was authorization, Kennan concludes, "his article would stand as perhaps the most revealing and important single reflection about the feelings of the President with respect to the new regime in Russia during the early months of its power."[14]

Yet such authorization seems doubtful; the promptness of the response to Swope's article shows that there was almost no time to clear a text with the White House, and the article, read between the lines, reflects English's own interests and prejudices more than the administration's. After Arthur Bullard and Ernest Poole went to Russia in June 1917, Bullard stayed on to become second in command of the Russian operation of the CPI. Swope included an aside in his story that could easily have been seen as identifying Bullard: "The representatives of the Committee on Public Information sent to Russia . . . helped to remove the misunderstanding" of the new regime. English concluded that Bullard was agitating for recognition.[15]

And Bullard, when he saw what English had written, knew that that was what English thought. The clipping of English's article that Bullard saved had three passages marked:

> The real source of the pro-Bolshevist and anti-Francis agitation is, it seems, in some emissary or emissaries of the Committee on Public Information.

> Here is an amazing statement. An official representative of the United States Government assures us that there is nothing anarchistic about the frequently and fully published doctrines of Trotzky and Lenine!

> It is highly improbable that the Committee on Public Information has any idea of the fearful misrepresentation of Russian conditions made by its agent or agents—misrepresentations which can be explained only on the supposition that one or more of these agents is himself involved with the anarchists or Bolsheviki.[16]

Here again was English's willingness to treat even old friends as enemies in the heat of controversy. Bullard had been English's first associate in the old revolutionary news bureau, the longtime friend of his sister-in-law, Rose, and, while differing in perspective, generally on English's side since the start of the war. Yet English did not hesitate to believe him capable of betrayal.

There was one grain of truth in the accusations. Bullard had been a member of a circle seeking to remove Ambassador Francis. But any accusation that Bullard was sympathetic to the Bolsheviks was far off the track. Kennan quotes a letter that Bullard wrote that same month: "I find it desperately hard to work with the Bolsheviki. They are undemocratic, in our Western sense, as the former Tsar. They are as cold blooded in their disregard for truth as any thugs I ever knew. And they have no more idea of tolerance toward a difference of opinion than Torquemada." The closest he came to a pro-Bolshevik position was to sign a draft statement urging a modus vivendi that would permit American propaganda operations in Russia to continue. But for the time being, Bullard had to let English's insinuations stand; he had to remain silent during the war.[17]

English was not done. He made clear that he had Bullard in mind when he followed his article in the *Times* with a letter to Franklin K. Lane, secretary of the interior, attacking not only Bullard but Creel:

> The pro-Bolshevik attitude of the Chairman of the Committee on Public Information is more marked and dangerous than I knew. . . . Mr. Creel has issued orders against all further criticisms of the Bolsheviki on the part of his numerous writers—most of them, including the labor men, are strongly anti-Bolshevik. . . .

I regard the President's diplomacy towards Russia as wise and correct. The policy of Mr. Creel however is suicidal. Not only Bullard, but several other of the New York correspondents are Socialists and I believe this is the source of Mr. Creel's error.[18]

Astoundingly, almost as if he did not realize the implication of what he was saying, English made the basis of his accusation against Bullard the fact that Bullard was what English himself was or had been—a socialist. Or, if he was conscious of its implication, he was announcing that he no longer defined himself as a socialist but as an anti-Bolshevik—a role in which he believed that he could set aside all civility. As for Bullard, English neither made amends nor tried to resume their friendship.

His new role as the foe of bolshevism led English to condemn not only American socialists but the entire range of socialist and labor movements in the Allied countries. A memorandum that he prepared for Gompers on the significance of European revolutionary movements could be viewed as deeply cynical; it treated the working classes of Europe merely as fodder in the ultimate objective of crushing Germany. English warned that the success of bolshevism in Russia was encouraging "pacifist strikes" in Germany and Austria, and saw such strikes as a belated expression of international working-class solidarity. Such agitation, he warned, might bring the war to an end too soon—before American resources could be brought into full play to devastate the enemy. He was willing to let not only soldiers but workers die for the kind of victory he preferred.[19]

The memorandum made its way to the White House, and went on to the State Department, with the president's comment that it seemed to him "to speak an unusual amount of truth and to furnish a very proper basis of the utmost caution in the conduct of the many troublesome affairs that we are from time to time discussing." Under the wool-wrapped language, the president was again playing a double game: in the Fourteen Points he had proclaimed to the world a basis for peace; in endorsing English's memorandum, even backhandedly, he was supporting a somewhat contrary position that the war must last indefinitely, until both Germany and bolshevism were controlled.[20]

The memorandum apparently represented the apex of English's influence in the administration. If there was estrangement, it was to a degree initiated by English; neither the president nor any other functioning politician could long meet English's standards. Even after his memorandum on revolutionary movements gained such respectful attention, he wrote to his mother that he had met with Wilson's aide Colonel House and was unimpressed with Wilsonian diplomacy. Of course, because diplomacy might bring the war to an end prematurely, English found it antipathetic. Even a president who had taken

English into his confidence, who was himself accused of a similar remoteness from human considerations, could not measure up to English's standards.[21]

During the winter of 1917–18, Anna again became pregnant, for the seventh time in eleven years, and for the second time since the decision that the family would grow no larger. It was an ill-starred pregnancy. Anna was of course nauseated; late in January she had a "fright" and was put to bed and given small doses of morphine. English was with his mother in Florida at the time, just after his attack on Bullard and his controversy with Creel. When he got back to Greenwich, he reported that Anna's condition was stabilized, but his mother, perhaps responding to his complacent tone, warned: "Of course there is danger of Anna's losing her child, but there is also danger of something much more terrible." In his reply, English reported briefly on Anna's condition and at greater length about his activities in the arena with the *Times* and with Gompers.[22]

He wrote on March 18 that Anna was stronger and would be out of danger in a week. Four days later, he wrote that she had miscarried: "Anna's attitude both before and after was perfect and all went well." When she miscarried in 1909, a year after the death of their infant, it had seemed the end of her life; now she no longer had the passion to spend on a lost child. She had turned forty-one that day.[23]

In the summer of 1918, Rose Strunsky resumed her quest to go to Russia. This time, she hoped to be appointed as a translator with yet another commission. She wrote to Anna enclosing a recommendation form for English to fill out. Knowing that English might think of her as a subversive, she added a caution: "Don't give him the letter, if you think he thinks he had better denounce me than endorse me."[1]

Soon back in New York from Washington, Rose wrote: "Don't bother English about endorsing me for the Commission. There will be no Commission worth mentioning & the whole thing is a fake. Washington took on its true colors when intervention set in." Allied troops, including Americans, had landed at Vladivostok and Archangel a few days before, and eventually joined in the effort to topple the Bolshevik government. Commissions became moot.[2]

Something else happened that summer that spurred Rose to utter a valedictory for the whole of their prewar life. The Committee on Public Information had ordered Arthur Bullard out of hostile Bolshevik territory in western Russia and he had paused in Washington on his way to reassignment in the Russian Far East. Rose wrote to Anna:

> Arthur married Ethel Bagg (those rich Baggs he knew in Paris & thought too bourgeois!) at the home of the [Herbert] Hoovers in the country 2 weeks ago. They stayed in Hoovers town house & are now on their way to Harbin. He always knew he was an aristocrat & the Bolshevik revolution decided it. He is [in] the diplomatic world, & rich & high.
>
> He used to shock me with all this in him ten years ago, but he fought against it. I suppose my behaviour had something to do in turning him. It is sad to see them go—one by one—topple right over like nine-pins and yet the exquisite surprises one gets. Such a shifting and shaking down.[3]

Although she had never come close to marrying Bullard, she found it difficult to adjust to his marriage to someone else. She also had to face the probability that she would not reach Russia. What, then, was her life to be? She had two formidable advisers. The first was Levine, to whom she clung after six frustrating years: "Monday I had dinner with Levine, strong, cruel, real & with good brains—why literature? Your name will be against you. What will your future work be? Stupidity. History is your field—Modern European history. The War is making that the most important faculty in the universities & you will succeed in it."[4]

Rose went up to Columbia University and arranged for a master's course, but then she saw her other adviser, her father, on Rosh Hashanah, and he pointed another way: He promised her an allowance of ten dollars a week for a year to write. She gave up the degree, and felt immensely relieved: "I am young & strong again. I laughed all day. The crying I did for Arthur was nothing over the giving up of my joy [in] life." She set out on her "Vita Nuova" with the announcement: "I bobbed my hair to-day!"[5]

By the middle of 1918, the war's "shifting and shaking down" had settled English into his role as a socialist who was the worst enemy of socialists. For the sake of labeling, the press still called him a socialist, and he accepted the label, for it won him the attention of a prodigal. Formally speaking, his remaining socialist affiliation was the tiny Social Democratic League (ninety-nine dues payers). Setting aside his earlier quarrel with Graham Stokes, he let himself be named secretary of the SDL early in 1918. To the extent that the SDL supported notions of "industrial democracy," it offered a tepid socialism, but its soul lay, like English's, in fighting bolshevism and dissent.[6]

Meanwhile English was embraced by socialism's longtime enemies. William Howard Taft, the Republican former president, tapped English to speak at a "Win-the-War-for-Permanent-Peace" convention organized by the League to Enforce Peace, which Taft headed. Such former radicals as English, Taft hinted, could control subversive movements. English was invited to a "training camp" of still another puppet organization of the Committee on Public Information, the National Conference of American Lecturers, where he discussed the shortcomings of European socialists. Eventually, he even contributed material to the militarist National Security League, supported by DuPont, Morgan, Rockefeller, and Frick wealth. The league was not only stridently antiradical but also antilabor. For English, for the time being, any vehicle seemed to serve.[7]

During the summer of 1918 English engaged in another dispute with John Spargo. Such a disagreement was not in itself surprising, but the grounds of this controversy revealed anew the lengths to which English would go, in his wartime state of mind, in crushing disagreement. The matter developed when the Social Democratic League sent a small delegation overseas, led by Spargo, to talk to socialist and labor leaders in England, France, and Italy. English, who remained in America, soon found himself riding two horses: he was not only monitoring the SDL mission but was advising a parallel and incompatible labor mission led by Gompers. While Spargo worked to enlist Allied socialist leaders under Wilson's banner, Gompers treated them as the enemy.[8]

English started hearing rumbles of trouble even before Gompers sailed for Europe. Spargo observed to the press that he had found minimal antiwar agitation in the British labor movement. Such a comment threatened the whole scenario English had constructed: that the socialist and labor parties of the Allied countries were linked in a conspiracy with the kaiser and, secondarily, the Bolsheviks. English was also irked at Spargo's defense of socialist moderates—Arthur Henderson in Britain and Jean Longuet in France. English finally sent a cable to the SDL mission demanding: "Recall Spargo immediately."[9]

Spargo defended himself vigorously, calling English's demand "monstrous." English, he asserted, was "wroth at the simple reporting of facts" that contradicted English's insistence that "practically all of the men in the Socialist movement of the different countries are, to his mind, pro-Germans and pacifists, peace-at-any-price men." But Spargo left the mission as directed and, later in the fall, abandoned the presidency of the Social Democratic League as well, leaving the organization to English.[10]

The leading historian of this episode interprets it in cosmic terms, contending that the actions by English reflected not only Gompers's views but a new, rigid policy of the Wilson administration designed to exclude the left from the peacemaking process. Indeed, English may have been moving in parallel with the administration for a time, yet—beyond control as he surely was—he could hardly be perceived as a reliable tool of policy. Moreover, curiously, it was not English to whom the administration listened in the long run but Spargo, who after the war advised Wilson on his policy toward the Bolsheviks.[11]

English seemed scarcely to notice as the end of the war approached. Only two weeks before the armistice, as Germany parlayed for a cease-fire before Allied troops reached its borders, he assembled a Social Democratic League conference that declared Germany was not yet sufficiently beaten. When the war nonetheless stopped on November 11, 1918, English did not express any gratification; he saw an undefeated enemy in bolshevism.[12]

As English traveled and declaimed through the last months of the war, Anna seemed to be in a kind of internment, having made a peace of her own. She wrote subdued letters to him from their summer place in New London. They contained none of Rose's fury and indignation; Anna may have decided by this time that contention was futile, and perhaps destructive. Her basic views had not changed, as Rose attested: "How have you kept yourself so straight & clean. I wonder at your strength. I so easily see rationalistic arguments which make me compromise & compromise. I have a deep and profound respect for you."[13]

Further evidence that Anna was perceived as independent of her husband could be seen in a confiding letter written to her during the summer by Rose Pastor Stokes, who had just been sentenced to ten years in prison under the federal Espionage Act for a speech she had made to the Woman's Dining Club of Kansas City. Anna had written to her after her conviction (which was ultimately reversed on appeal), and Rose Stokes replied by recounting an old dream in which she had believed herself a cliff "against which the sea hurled itself in vain."[14]

A week before the armistice Anna wrote to Charmian London, perhaps more in hope than in belief: "The War is practically over, will be over I think by the time you get this letter. The World is entering upon its new day—Liberty for the Common Man. Yours for the Revolution—more than ever before."[15]

On December 4, 1918, less than a month after the Armistice, President Wilson and his entourage departed for Europe. While Wilson made his triumphal tour of the Continent's capitals, ships laden with other delegations intent on affecting the peace settlement left New York. In January, English boarded a Cunard liner in a small party dispatched by the Social Democratic League, accompanying a labor delegation headed by Samuel Gompers.[1]

He had last been in Europe nearly ten years before. Bidding him farewell, Anna wrote: "If there were such a thing as the logic of the emotions then I should have desired to be there at your side and making for Russia and Germany, and that is exactly what happened. Well, it's only the First Year of the New World, and the hour is young and so are we. Far more, I feel, is all life before us than it was in that wonderful time, a decade ago." Her buoyancy evinced a deep sense of relief; the war that had made her husband a combatant in their own home was behind them.[2]

English seemed to share the new mood when he wrote back from shipboard. Within earshot of the applause from a salon where a concert was in progress, he wrote to praise his heterogeneous shipmates: "[Gompers's] delegation are splendid intelligent and sympathetic men. [Charles Edward] Russell is also a charming travelling companion. Mrs. Vincent is aboard with a large YWCA delegation, also the Japanese Mission, several Poles, including a sporty Jewish millionaire judge their patron (a friend of mine)[,] Brandeis secretary and several Zionists."[3]

He debarked in Liverpool, paused in London, and went on to Paris, where, he found, war damage had been miraculously cleaned up. From the Hôtel Continental, he wrote of an endless whirl: "My time has been exceptionally absorbed for these reasons: I have had probably hundreds of conferences on my own initiative. . . . The results have been that I have been too tired either to write letters or even to amuse myself."[4]

Although he wrote several times that he was about to return, he was still in Paris in March 1919. He wrote to Anna, almost in the self-praising tone he used with his parents: "The opportunity came a few days ago, without any possibility of my having been able to foresee it for my [sic] to take the lead alone in an extremely important international matter which I can only describe latter [sic]. So far my leadership has been brilliantly successful and this success will continue. . . . I have had unexpected success in every one of my undertakings here. But the one of the next two weeks will eclipse all the others put together." He said that he would sail with the Gompers delegation on the *Lusitania*. (A telling slip; he meant the *Aquitania*.)[5]

Just what he did, and just what its significance might have been to the peace negotiations, he never made clear; he was but one of hundreds in Paris, most of whom thought their roles were crucial. One fragment of his activity was recorded by the editor William Allen White, who had been asked by Wilson to attend a meeting with the Bolsheviks on the Turkish island of Prinkipo, in company with the American expatriate radical George D. Herron: "One day Herron and I in our missionary endeavors invited Gompers and William English Walling, his friend and ideological interpreter, to lunch at the Vouillemont. I never saw Herron perform more brilliantly. He had Gompers, who was a first-rate talker and a man of conviction, on the mourners' bench ready to concede that a meeting with the Bolsheviks at Prinkipo might be a good thing. I could understand as I watched Herron coopering Gompers and Walling, how Herron did so much." Even so, Gompers and English did not stay coopered; they remained committed to noncooperation with bolshevism.[6]

During English's absence, Anna found herself under pressure from Charmian London to help with the massive compilation that eventually was published in two volumes as *The Book of Jack London*. Sensing herself again engaged in the tacit contest over Jack's legacy, she temporized, but eventually sent off a dictated memoir and a few of her treasured letters from Jack, with elaborate excuses for the delay.[7]

Midway in her recollections, she heard of the fate of Rosa Luxemburg and Karl Liebknecht, the dissident German socialists whom English had spurned during the war, now assassinated by a military gang in the aftermath of the left-wing Spartacist uprising in Berlin. She combined her memories of Jack with a memorial for Luxemburg and Liebknecht that carried her back to the hyperbolic rhetoric of two decades before:

> A bitterness courses in all my veins—I have felt so much for Jack London because I saw in him potential martyrs and heroes like Luxemburg and Liebknecht. He was symbolic of the movement and its struggle and future, and in his beauty was the pristine beauty and greatness of the race. So I said when I first beheld him, so I say now, after his death, and I say it in this hour of tragedy when one is impelled to withdraw every word of praise ever uttered for anybody who in any way accepted the old order, now, when we are bereaved and tortured with the bayonets of the whole world pointing at our breasts.

This meditation was eventually published in the socialist *New York Call*, restored after having been smashed up by a mob of soldiers, sailors, and civilians on May Day 1918.[8]

Anna was still trying to stir interest in her unpublished book, "Revolutionary Lives." She went to see the patient George Brett at Macmillan, whom she had so often disappointed. Brett received her courteously and extracted from her a promise to complete a new chapter on Katherine Breshkovsky, whom Anna had interviewed, within a month. It is not clear whether Macmillan ever saw the revisions. In any case, neither Macmillan nor any other publisher accepted the book.[9]

No doubt the timing was wrong; she had let essentially journalistic notes molder for nearly a decade, until the failed revolution she covered had been superseded by the next. Rose had been furious that the Stokes company could not see the continuity between 1905 and 1917, but a publisher could hardly be blamed for avoiding work that its reader found "curiously far away and relatively unimportant."[10]

Even so, when the requirement of timeliness is set aside, the book was Anna Strunsky's most fully realized, most mature writing. It was a vivid, engaged prototype of journalism as romantic literature, combining deft touches of memoir with sketches of places she and English visited and revolutionists they knew. The centerpieces were profiles of Gregory Gershuni, at whose funeral in Paris she spoke; Breshkovsky, grandmother of the revolution; Vera Figner, imprisoned for seeking to educate the peasants; Vera Zassulich, terrorist and failed assassin; Mark Lieber, of the Jewish resistance; Sonya Ratkoff, deranged after imprisonment, torture, and rape; Medved, The Bear, a Maximalist executed for a daring currency theft—all of them largely forgotten by the world but given life in Anna's vivid, intimate accounts. None of this ever got beyond manuscript and was ultimately consigned to the archives.[11]

Anna, hoping that English's self-perceived successes in Paris might have washed away his wartime ferocity, found him genial enough on his return. Rose was at her parents' place in New York when he walked in unannounced, just off the boat, and split a bottle of champagne with them. But his politics remained unrelenting. He urged the most drastic measures to bring down the Bolshevik regime, including the withholding of food relief, because "there are some matters that take precedence even to the prevention of starvation of innocent millions."[12]

To his brother, English confided that he believed the Wilson administration to be infected with bolshevism:

> I can assure you that I find *every day* evidence of some new influential supporter of Mr. Wilson who is more or less pro-Bolshevik. . . . The evidence from public expressions of influential friends of Mr. Wilson is

sufficient enough to make a book to prove the pro-Bolshevist tendencies of our government. . . . I really believe that every revolutionary movement in Europe from the mild and revolutionary Socialism of [Arthur] Henderson to Bolshevism has been largely sustained by the Wilson appointees with the full knowledge of Mr. Wilson himself.[13]

English made a second, unplanned trip to Europe in July 1919, arranged at the last moment by Gompers. Gompers was now almost seventy years old, and in his fourth decade at the head of the American Federation of Labor. He and English might have seemed mismatched, both temperamentally and politically. Although they had been acquainted as long ago as 1903, when English helped at the founding of the Women's Trade Union League, in his most radical days English expressed his abhorrence of Gompers's apolitical unionism.

But Gompers had never considered English a true adversary, and their similar views on the war brought them back together. Gompers had recommended English for the mission to Russia, had worked with English on founding the American Alliance for Labor and Democracy, had solicited English's advice and opinions, and had relied on him for information and interpretation at the Paris peace conference. Now most of all they shared an antipathy to revolutionary socialism in general and bolshevism in particular. More than that, they evidently reached across differences in age and culture to become genuine friends.[14]

On July 17, 1919, English wrote excitedly to his mother that Gompers had telegraphed him the night before and that he would sail the next day, with reservations, passports, everything arranged. He and Gompers planned to participate in an international trade-union meeting in Amsterdam, then go to Lucerne to observe (probably with hauteur) an international socialist meeting. He wrote to Anna from Europe: "I sit next to Gompers as special assistant international secretary or something of the kind & he often advises with me."[15]

Anna wrote faithfully, usually confining herself to family news. They were again in New London in the summer of 1919, and later transferred to the vast old Ocean House, in Watch Hill, Rhode Island, a few miles to the east. She reported that she had taken driving lessons, but would not drive his new Marmon, a car as temperamental as English himself. She noted that Chicago had had a race riot, with "a negro burned." But the incident did not touch her as Springfield had; she mentioned it only in passing. On August 5, she wrote to praise the book of "our friend" Charles Edward Russell on bolshevism, which she read also as a lesson in the futility of war. "But why," she asked, "do I bother you with my ideas?"[16]

After traveling with Gompers to Paris and Lucerne, English rejoined his family in Watch Hill early in September. If Anna had hoped that he would become more equable, she was soon disappointed. He produced five articles about the threat of radicalism in European labor, and was eager to resume his task of exposing domestic bolshevism. He wrote to his mother: "My next job may be the most important I have undertaken. A write-up of the pro-Bolshevists in America. I shall begin in a day or two and finish before leaving [Watch Hill]. . . . The pro-Bolshevik agitation grows daily. Fortunately the Administration is at last right—but it is as usual 'too late.' Wilson deserves impeachment."[17]

By the time English returned from his second postwar trip to Europe, America was slipping into what became known as the Red Scare. One of its early symptoms was the narrowing of the arena for publicists and intellectuals— an enforcement of orthodoxy, official and unofficial. Walter Lippmann, returning from the Versailles conference, said he had found at home "the blackest reaction our generation has known" and Ray Stannard Baker, who had served as an aide to Wilson, complained, "If [a liberal] try to see honestly what is happening he is promptly tagged . . . as a pro-German, or a bolshevist, or an agitator." Officials of the Wilson administration whose views were suspect were subject to congressional censure or were driven from office altogether.[1]

What gave the Red Scare its weight, however, was not the work of such freelance enforcers as English but the intervention of the federal government, still armed with wartime legislation and investigative powers. A few days after English wrote to his mother of the dangers of "pro-Bolshevik agitation," Wilson collapsed during his strenuous speaking tour seeking support for American membership in the League of Nations. With the president enfeebled, his attorney general, A. Mitchell Palmer, became the avenging sword of repression.

The left now offered Palmer a particularly inviting target; it had been atomized by the war and by bolshevism and was all but helpless to resist effectively. During the summer of 1919, the Socialist Party of America fragmented, and in Chicago late in August two new pro-Bolshevik Communist parties, composed to a great degree of immigrant membership, split off from the SPA.[2]

Meanwhile, the little Social Democratic League of America, led by English and by Graham Stokes (whose nonconformist wife, Rose, went to Chicago to help found the Communist Party of America), aligned itself with the government, oblivious to the truism that such campaigns, once unleashed, are ultimately undiscriminating in their sweep.[3]

The government moved in the final months of 1919. In November, the Department of Justice raided the offices of more than seventy radical organizations and arrested nearly a thousand people. Not long before, Anna had received a notice from Emma Goldman and Alexander Berkman that they had been freed from federal prison. By December 21, Berkman and Goldman were aboard the *Buford*, the "Soviet Ark," bound for Russia with 247 other political deportees. At the end of the year, five thousand more aliens were arrested in raids in thirty-three cities.[4]

Early in 1920 came a turning point, with the dawn at last of a sense of the ridiculous. The previous year, the federal House of Representatives had refused to seat Victor L. Berger, a conservative Socialist from Milwaukee, and later barred him permanently. On January 5, 1920, the New York Assembly did the same to five Socialist members elected from New York City. Many of the same newspapers that had been applauding the Palmer raids now found a principle at stake, and turned against the Assembly, and against the anti-Bolshevik campaign in general.[5]

Here English had an opportunity to define the limits of his anti-bolshevism, to back off from the extreme positions he had staked out. But it was unlike him to take an easy or accommodating position. He insisted in a letter to the *New York Tribune:* "The seating or unseating of the Socialists at Albany, important as this question is, must be regarded as utterly subordinate to the main issue. Is the so-called American Socialist Party a Socialist or a Bolshevist organization?" He equivocated a little in writing to his mother about the same time: "My aid has been repeatedly sought for in the Albany Socialist case—in which there is some justice on both sides."[6]

His public position was too much for the prickly John Spargo, his sometime associate in the Social Democratic League, who had himself written his share of anti-Bolshevik tracts. Spargo wrote to the *Tribune* to dissociate himself from English, asking how anybody who considered himself a democrat and a socialist could support such an "outrageous assault on parliamentary government." Spargo turned in his resignation from the SDL and another member, Upton Sinclair, wrote to admonish English that his "present attitude works against all Socialists . . . and for the blackest reaction." But Sinclair went further, to charge with some accuracy that English's writings before the war had helped to lay the foundation for the left-wing positions that he now attacked.[7]

English no doubt greeted these criticisms with the same sad shake of the head that he always gave contrary opinions. But he ultimately backed down to the extent of grudgingly supporting the principle of seating properly elected legislators, in this case to permit these "camouflaged Communists" to remain on public view instead of working covertly. Spargo wrote to Sinclair interpreting English's new position: "In the case of any one else I should have said it was not quite honest. His statement seems to me to be verbally correct but essentially false, nevertheless."[8]

By April 1920, when the New York Assembly voted to make permanent its expulsion of the Socialist members, even the Republican candidate for president, Warren G. Harding, and Attorney General Palmer himself had criticized the action. But English was unfazed; he wrote to his mother in a mood of buoyant, even manic, optimism about the Social Democratic League, about the latest anti-Bolshevik articles in the magazines, about the help he was giving his friend Ralph Easley of the National Civic Federation. He felt so well, he confided to her, that he hardly knew himself in the mirror.[9]

The gulf that separated him and Anna was symbolized in the infamous Lusk Report, a compendium by a New York State Senate committee linking the American peace movement during the war with bolshevism. Anna was listed as a supporter of the Emergency Peace Federation, the last-ditch effort to keep the United States out of the war; English was credited as providing the Lusk committee with material for its work. (Rose Strunsky had the special cachet of being listed in a chapter headed "Anarchist Communism" with, for example, Helen Keller.)[10]

During the spring of 1920, after the true fervor of the Red Scare had passed, English finished his book attacking bolshevism. Like all of his books since *Progressivism—and After* six years before, this one was a compilation, a scrapbook. It was called *Sovietism: the A B C of Russian Bolshevism—according to the Bolshevists*, and contained excerpts designed to show how the rulers of Russia gave themselves away with their own words. But characteristically he found the greatest threat to be domestic, in "parlor Bolshevism," which he called "a serious, persistent and world-wide attack on the foundations of democratic civilization—more insidious, more flexible and more dangerous than Bolshevism itself."[11]

Not unexpectedly, the work created turbulence in his own home, as Rose observed: "English's book against the 'Dirty Bolsheviks' is out & he is horrid & cock-sure. Or was. Saturday, he behaved like a raging Turk & when I arrived yesterday, the clouds of the Tempest still hung over the house. My coming saved the Day, for he clings to me as an outsider to dispel the atmosphere. So I am doing a little good."[12]

Given the changed climate, the book's reception was mixed or worse. The weekly *Outlook* and the *American Journal of Sociology* ("an antiseptic against the bolshevist poison") were almost alone in praising it. Other journals raked English over for tendentiousness, misquotation, and "characteristic anti-bolshevist hysteria."[13]

This reception mattered less than the fact that Gompers liked the book so much that he asked English to repeat the performance—to produce a book covering roughly the same ground, but with Gompers's name attached. Essentially, *Out of Their Own Mouths* was a ghostwritten book, with Gompers courteously permitting English to share the credit. Although the book was received with indifference by the reviewers as a warmed-over dish, in its joint byline was forecast much of the course of the remainder of English's life.[14]

One of the last writings of Walter Weyl, long-ago colleague of English at the University Settlement, before he died of cancer in November 1919 was an essay titled "Tired Radicals." While most of it is built on the conventional observation that radicalism diminishes with age, the opening paragraphs are a slashing portrait of a man rampant with righteous hate. The *New Republic*, where Weyl had worked since the magazine's founding in 1914, turned down the piece because a fellow editor, Walter Lippmann, believed that Weyl had written it about him, but it is difficult to see how the chilly, moderate Lippmann could have seen himself in it. Ultimately, the essay did not appear in print until 1921, two years after Weyl's death, in a collection of previously unpublished papers.[15]

To readers who knew the small circle of prowar socialists, the lineaments must have seemed unmistakable:

> I once knew a revolutionist who thought that he loved Humanity but for whom Humanity was merely a club with which to break the shins of the people he hated. He hated all who were comfortable and all who conformed. He hated the people he opposed and he hated those who opposed his opponents in a manner different from his. Zeal for the cause was his excuse for hating, but really he was in love with hate and not with any cause.
>
> The war came, and this vibrant, humorless man, this neurotic idealist who was almost a genius, found a wider vent for his emotion. His hatred, without changing its character, changed its incidence. He learned to hate Germans, Bolshevists, and radicals. He completed the full circle and soon was consorting most incongruously with those whom he had formerly attacked. Today nothing is left of his radicalism or his always leaky consistency; nothing is left but his hatred. At times he hates himself. He would always hate himself could he find no one else to hate. He is becoming half-reactionary, half-cynical. He will end—But who knows how anyone will end?[16]

Obviously, the portrait most closely fitted Weyl's one-time friend, English. It is difficult to imagine (although the essay was written before English joined in the Red Scare) that it could have been anybody else. Even given the distant possibility that Weyl constructed this characterization around a more obscure figure or as a composite persona, the verdict, harsh as it is, is just. English's mode of dispute was always merciless, disregarding friendship and civility in the effort to be eternally in the right, to teach the world a lesson.

But whether Weyl was correct in attributing hatred to his exemplar could not be known; English's onslaughts—even those directed at a specific individual—were almost always cloaked in one principle or another, and always cast in the manner of a gentleman rather than a gutter fighter. But the attacks were inevitably punishing, leaving deep injuries—deepest among those closest to him.

PART EIGHT

Divergence, 1920–1964

When the war and its aftershocks had passed, Anna and English were left to live with their own terms of peace. The war had visited other households much like theirs. Fifteen years before, two other American-born University Settlement workers had married Russian-born Jews. In all three instances, the man supported the war and the woman eventually opposed it. Afterward, when the men had jettisoned their prewar incarnations, the women to various degrees held to the old faith of socialism and socialist pacifism. The political parallels of the three marriages are too strong to be coincidental, but they resist reductive explanations; they were not exactly alike.

Leroy Scott and Miriam Finn, who followed Anna and English to Russia in the wake of the 1905 revolution, did not become the subject of the kind of gossip that circulated about Anna and English. Scott, a sometime editor at the *Masses*, exclaimed after the declaration of war that he was "sick of the Socialist Party," but was quiet about his belated support of the prowar socialists. Rather than rushing into controversy, he concentrated on writing, mostly hack novels. For her part, Miriam Finn—who became a widely published authority on childrearing—boasted years later: "I fought for *Peace!*" But they did not separate.[1]

The celebrated American-dream marriage between wealthy Graham Stokes and Rose Pastor, the one-time immigrant cigarmaker, was ruptured by the war. Graham Stokes took the lead in organizing the prowar socialists. Rose Pastor initially followed him out of the Socialist Party, but soon regretted her decision and then metamorphosed after the authorities blunderingly indicted her under the Sedition Act for a mildly critical speech on war profiteers. She ultimately became a pioneer in the budding American Communist Party. The political division between them, and its personal accompaniments (she wrote to Anna that Graham's "puritanism . . . made what came inevitable") set them irrevocably on the road to divorce, which took place in 1925.[2]

What happened between English and Anna was closer to the course of the Stokeses than of the Scotts. But Anna lacked Rose Stokes's nihilist temperament and never undertook a full-scale revolt against her spouse. After the frenetic wartime spring of 1917, she took cover from her husband's ferocity, perhaps sensing that he was not only unpersuadable but uncontrollable. She had more at stake than the childless Stokeses, for she required the resources to rear four children. And, still clinging to the romantic figment of St. Petersburg, she continued to assert unquenchable love for English, even when she was most embittered.

As is the case with most marriages that stay out of court, the private compact that kept Anna and English together was never fully revealed to the outside world. Anna herself ultimately looked back and wondered why she clung to a marriage that she eventually understood to be abusive in spirit.

In 1920, Anna found herself in another long-distance skirmish with Charmian London. Charmian had worked hard to make herself custodian of all that pertained to Jack, but Anna believed that she too had a claim, at least to the niches in Jack's life that were peculiarly hers. It was increasingly apparent that she clung to this franchise not solely out of loyalty to his memory but because she realized that Jack was to be the most enduring source of her minor celebrity.

This particular discord arose when one Walter McGinn proposed a film based on *The Kempton-Wace Letters*. Charmian opposed the McGinn proposal, made it clear that she considered *Kempton-Wace* her property, and insisted that *she* would decide who was to make any films. Anna burst out indignantly: "The McGinn offer is one of those exceptional opportunities that fall from the sky. It might have meant for me what Jack has enjoyed in life but never I—fame and success. . . . You made the mistake (and almost everybody does it) of not reversing the roles and seeing yourself in my place. . . . I don't want you to even appear like a business woman. If I am a socialist because I think that economic individualism is exploitation and the cause of human suffering I am perhaps even more a socialist because it creates the business type so characteristic of our civilization and morally so repellant [sic]."[3]

Anna was further exasperated by the appearance of Charmian's book on Jack in 1921. She was unhappy about misquotations in the letters she had lent to Charmian, and she may have been displeased as well, on the return of the letters, to read Charmian's longhand comments on them, such as an annotation of Jack's "white beautiful friendship" letter as "booful." The book, moreover, skirted any hint that Jack had been seriously involved with Anna. The experience again persuaded her that she must write her own memoir of Jack.[4]

Early in the summer of 1920, Anna's sister, Rose, wrote from the Strunsky Atlantic Hotel in Belmar, New Jersey, an enterprise of Anna's older brothers. Rose was at a low point in contemplating Louis Levine: "All his desire seems to have petered out. . . . As for my side of it—if I could have aroused any tenderness in him—the thing between us would have happened 7 years ago." She fled and joined Anna and English at Watch Hill.[5]

At this point the ice broke at last. By mail, Levine proposed, or at least suggested, marriage and in September he and Rose were married. She moved with him to Wisconsin, where he had a new teaching job at Beloit College. At last Rose, thirty-seven years old, was no longer the third party in a family not her own.[6]

Rose and her husband spent less than a year at Beloit; he accepted an offer from the *Chicago Daily News* to be a correspondent in the Soviet Union. When they left America, Rose was pregnant and remained behind in Paris when her husband went on to Moscow. Her old Finnish revolutionary friend Aino Malmberg arrived to keep her company. Later, Anna was with her when she gave birth to a son, Boris, in a German clinic in October 1921. For her part, Anna was able to write a pair of articles for *McClure's* about the clinic's techniques for safe, gentle births.[7]

Late in the next year, 1922, Anna went to Paris, the fulfillment of a long-standing promise from English. The four children came with her, and they lived in a house in the Passy district. In December, Rose and her family joined the household, under circumstances that puzzled Louis Levine: "We were treated as guests, and we made no contribution to what must have been a heavy expense of carrying that house. I can not now understand why no one—not even Rose—mentioned money or suggested that we pay our share, however small." Later, Louis and Rose, who was ill, left the infant, Boris, and his nurse with Anna while they took Rose to a clinic in Berlin. Most distressingly, Elias Strunsky, Anna's and Rose's father, died in January 1923 and neither could attend his service. What with children and guests and guilt, Anna no doubt found it a sorry sabbatical.[8]

Her least-deserved burden was Charmian London, with whom she still felt compelled to maintain a friendship. Charmian came early in the spring of 1923 and stayed and stayed. English wrote from America to tell her indignantly what she already knew: "[I] would not at all think you had made a mistake to sacrifice a day, or four days to her. But 4 weeks! How preposterous! Neither you nor the children by any chance can have one single normal day while she is there. How could you do it? . . . I never want to see her again as long as I live." Probably coincidentally, Charmian's visit definitively stopped the work that Anna was doing on her memoir of Jack.[9]

Through the early 1920s, English remained devoted to his new avocation, sniffing out bolshevism. Levine recalled a visit in London: "As usual, English was a trying guest since he was vehement about the Bolsheviks and could not take my calm way of talking about them." Back in America, English charged that the stodgy *Book Review Digest* was insinuating Red propaganda into libraries.[10]

In 1924, he presented himself as a Democratic candidate for Congress in the southwestern Connecticut district, endorsed by the AFL and by the Progressive Party, which was running Robert La Follette for president. English listed in his campaign literature the very socialists he had attacked during the war: Jean Longuet, Karl Liebknecht, Rosa Luxemburg. But he made clear that he was no longer a socialist himself. Samuel Gompers, in the last weeks of his life, sent a personal letter of endorsement to all union locals in the district, and other major AFL figures campaigned for him. But the district in that era was of no mind to embrace a Progressive, Democrat, laborite, or reformed radical; newspapers in fact attacked him as a "soldier of fortune," who never stuck to any set of beliefs very long. On election day, the incumbent won by roughly a three-to-one margin.[11]

English did not again become a candidate. Instead, he devoted himself ever more closely to assignments from the AFL, even after the death of Gompers late in 1924. He wrote *American Labor and American Democracy*, a book that presented the AFL as a world paradigm for organized labor. A reviewer in the *Nation* commented perspicaciously: "while prosperity lasts, there is nothing to prevent [the AFL's leaders] from sitting tight and applauding the energies of Mr. Walling in exhibiting them to the world as monuments of American idealism."[12]

Early in 1926, there was a reunion of the A Club—that is, of the cluster of members married about the same time in 1905 and 1906—at the Scotts' Greenwich Village home. Whatever Anna's private thoughts may have been about the bittersweetness of the occasion, she wrote blandly to her mother-in-law about seeing the Scotts and the Brubakers, and missing the late, great couple, the now-divorced Graham and Rose Pastor Stokes: "Graham Stokes was asked and he wrote back declining with great regret that he had an imperative engagement—was getting married that day on the same block."[13]

Late in 1925, Anna wrote in her diary: "Despair! Despair! It cannot go on. . . . Despite [what] is in my heart, I am at the end, the very end." The context suggests that the difficulties were not merely marital, for the entry was followed by notes concerning her chief personal treasure: "J.L. wrote me a hundred letters."[1]

What she had in mind became clear a few weeks later when she offered the letters to the Huntington Library in San Marino, California (chosen perhaps because Charmian London was sending Jack's other papers there). "I stand in a singular relation to Jack London," she wrote, "in that I am the only one who has ever been his collaborator." Having received a positive response, she wrote: "If you could place upon these letters the maximum worth which they have for you it would help me to decide whether such a sum meets the need which has made me think of parting with them." The library wrote back that the letters might be worth three hundred to five hundred dollars. Anna was appalled: "I had three or five thousand dollars in mind when I wrote you. I would not part from the material for less." She did not, and her plan collapsed.[2]

In fact, well before the Great Depression, the Walling household in Greenwich was running short. English had never believed that he was obligated to build on his inherited money nor did he believe himself fit for salaried work. Despite a degree of management exercised by his brother, Willoughby, now a public-spirited bank president in Chicago, English and Anna were continually nibbling at their resources. Yet their routines rarely varied: English always took his trip to Florida to stay with his mother; there was always a summer place—Watch Hill, Westport, Woodstock—and always more money poured into his writing projects than came out. In 1926, despite help from his mother, there was a crisis and Willoughby wrote in exasperation: "I am simply aghast at the amounts of your capital which have disappeared since Mother's great generosity in stripping herself."[3]

In an unusually frank letter to Rosalind Walling a few weeks after her brother-in-law's warning, Anna appraised their financial history:

> If I had the twenty years to live over again I would from the first, insist that English follow a career of some definite remunerative character

rather than depend wholly on his inherited income. As long as the world is organized as it is—on a competitive basis—happiness and self confidence are to be had only on condition that one's work is recognized as marketable. . . .

We did perhaps keep open house too long but this has stopped. If we are short it is because English's career not only does not bring him anything in a material way but is a very costly one, as when he ran for Congress or went to Paris for Gompers or to Mexico or made frequent trips to Washington for the American Federation of Labor or gave away many hundreds of his books on the publication of each, with the typists bills, etc. that it implies. . . .

I am not primarily the practical type but neither am I improvident. Both in my girlhood at home and in college I practiced rigid economies. And my tastes, if anything, are rather too simple from English's standpoint. . . .

So to my mind whatever difficulty exists arises mainly from the fact that English, who is a genius, was not a bread winner and was never intended to be one.[4]

Previously, Anna had tried unsuccessfully to play Lady Bountiful to her sister, but in 1928 she finally turned reluctantly to Rose for help. She proposed that Rose, her son, and her two-year-old daughter, Rosalind (named for Anna's firstborn), come live in Greenwich, with Louis remaining with his job in Washington at what was then known as the Brookings Institute. (When he accepted the position, Louis, out of deference to the mores of the time, changed his last name to Lorwin, maintaining an original family name, Levitzki, in the middle.) Louis recalled sadly: "So, the arrangement was made. I paid Anna three hundred dollars a month, which was a fair sum in those days. . . . But I can not say that I liked the arrangement. Aside from the separation from Rose and the children, I found it hard to visit them in Greenwich, which I did about every two or three weeks, because of English's personality. Sitting around the table with him at dinner was painful—he was so tense and ready to fight about any issue. The sight of Anna trying to keep his temper under the lid and to create a spirit of harmony was not pleasant either." The arrangement ended after a few months.[5]

English seemed oblivious to the household financial crisis. Not long after Willoughby's warning, he went to Mexico for two months and in 1927 published another money-losing book, on United States–Mexican relations. Early in 1928, he traveled in Cuba, and later he became involved, through his old Lower East Side associate Henry Moskowitz, in Governor Al Smith's campaign for the presidency. (Moskowitz's wife, Belle, was a key Smith operative.) In August, while he was rusticating at a lodge in the Adirondacks, English reported to his brother that he had helped with Smith's acceptance speech, but could not refrain from his customary touch of scorn: "certainly Smith is no intellectual at all. He reads *nothing."* After Smith's defeat, he worked the next year in Fiorello La Guardia's initial and unsuccessful campaign for mayor of New York, and spoke at a Madison Square Garden rally, attacking "self-appointed high-brows who offer themselves as the mentors of New York liberalism," not dreaming that the reference could be to his past self.[6]

The great revolutionary romance of 1906, strained by financial shortfalls and subjected to impatience on the one side and self-pity on the other, was crumbling by 1929. Anna's diaries and letters broke out in inchoate bursts of lamentation and hope. On the twenty-first anniversary of their firstborn's death, she wrote to English: "To assuage the fever of pain and suffering which rages in me to-day, which throbs in my caked and swollen breasts almost as violently as it did that week when grief nearly laid us low I call upon love to help and sustain us. . . . Let us rededicate our lives to all we ever held dear and sacred—that our First-born shall not have perished in vain!" That summer, she told her diary: "So we start out in a new life, my English and I, and as ever I am full of hope and enthusiasm—but I am quite a little afraid too." Two months later, the summer truce had been broken and she was writing into the night about a new "constructive plan." Whatever the upswings, the trend was inevitably down.[7]

By 1932, even the shreds of comfortable family life vanished. After the stock-market collapse, English's brother imposed new financial restrictions that treated English, so English complained, "as a minor or defective." His mother died in 1930, but he had already used his share of the inheritance, and was no better off. The children left home one by one: Rosamond became a graduate student in Europe and married a handsome Albanian diplomat, Rifat Tirana. Their second daughter, Anna, abruptly eloped with the novelist Norman Matson. Georgia and Hayden went away to college and school. English drifted off as well, to engage in an affair. Anna agreed to a separation, but English wrote that "all was over" and in the fall of 1932 obtained a Mexican divorce, which Anna scorned as a "stunt." But their marriage, tenuous for so long, lay devastated. Rather than stay alone in the house in Greenwich, she moved to a studio apartment on Washington Square South in New York owned by her brothers.[8]

Even so, Anna wrote with a degree of equanimity to her son-in-law Rifat Tirana: "English promised me he would come back when he left me. Eventually he will keep that promise. . . . He has made mistakes and so have I, and for the most part each was the cause of the other's mistakes. . . . Now we have come to an impasse, because I look upon my life with English as a collaboration. He cannot ask me to write the wrong ending to the book we have been writing all these years. All he can do is suspend publication—which is exactly what has happened."[9]

But a few months later, on the twenty-fifth anniversary of the death of their firstborn—February 13, 1933—she wrote less confidently: "Now our love has entered the stage of coma. After the long struggle for life, death wins." Two days before, her mother had died.[10]

A few months later, writing in her diary, she at last turned against English:

I was wrong when I fell in love with him and began my life with him.

I was never safe in his hands. He worked against me in the dark with my children, his mother, so passionately dear to me, my friends and family. He did worse—he worked against me in the dark with himself, in his own heart, for he never gave me a chance to explain, to defend myself.[11]

Thus steeled, she entered a truce, but not a reconciliation. They saw each other: "We walk across the Square in the beautiful, cold, clear night. He comes upstairs with me, sits opposite me at my desk, writing to Hayden while I write Valentines for Georgia and Anna for him to mail. Then he says: 'Well, you're all right,' as he turns to go. And I say quickly, impulsively: 'Who says I am all right?' I can't bear to see him go! Stupid business—and I feel spurned as a woman. . . . I think simply his taste is bad, kind of cheap—and I feel a real coldness to him. I would like to hurt him a little, tell him that I am in love, that I am loved—but it passes. Thank God! It passes."[12]

She had an opportunity to be loved. Her old friend, Leonard Abbott, offered himself passionately. She loved him, she told herself, but she did not admit him to the status of lover. She remained always radical in public, Victorian and bourgeois in private.[13]

Late in 1935, English accepted a position as executive director of the Labor Chest, organized to aid refugee unionists in Europe. He gave speeches around the country and organized a rally in Madison Square Garden, New York. On June 6, 1936, he sailed for Europe. Anna, alone in Watch Hill, wrote, despite all, in her diary: "O if I were sailing with you."[14]

Even at the age of fifty-nine, English Walling never resigned himself to spectatorship or to mulling over the past. After he landed in Europe in June 1936, he spent two weeks in Geneva working with the International Labor Organization to form a committee for refugee workers, then went on to London and Paris, where he organized similar committees. He scheduled himself to be in Amsterdam on September 4 to meet with underground opponents of Hitler, smuggled out of Germany. He felt increasingly troubled by arthritis and after he finished his work in Paris he went to Cagnes-sur-Mer, on the French Riviera, to recuperate. On August 29 he drove back to Paris.[1]

In fact, his health was no better, but he insisted on going to Amsterdam. Once there he could not keep his appointment; instead, he was confined to the American Hotel in Amsterdam, delirious and weakening. He forbade Edo Fimmen, the Dutch unionist who had invited him to the Netherlands, to notify Anna. He was still in the hotel room on September 9, when the *Aquitania,* on which he had booked passage, sailed from Le Havre. Fimmen was the only friend at his bedside on Saturday, September 12, when he died of pneumonia. On the bedside table, Anna was told, was a new edition of Montaigne, with a passage marked: "Do not be afraid to die away from home, do not abandon travel when ill or old."[2]

Before midnight of September 12, Anna was aboard the *Europa* in New York harbor, bound for Europe.

There was a service in Amsterdam, with the coffin incongruously draped with a red flag, but the American memorial meeting took place on October 21, 1936, in St. George's Memorial House, at St. George's Episcopal Church on Stuyvesant Square in Manhattan. The country was in the midst of a clamorous presidential campaign and, overseas, proxy armies of fascism and communism fought in Spain, but this assembly fixed firmly on an earlier era. Simeon Strunsky, Anna's cousin, led his hearers back:

> It is a commonplace to speak of the dead world which we only faintly discern through the mists of our later sad wisdom. Oddly enough, this aspiring and questing world of twenty-five years ago . . . insists on retaining validity despite the grim realities that have refuted it on the actual

pages of history. . . . Somehow, as one meets it all again in Walling's pages the effect is that this better world which people were building remains the real world. The actual, ugly, bitter things of the next twenty years are the dream, the ugly nightmare which will sooner or later pass away.[3]

The words could have been conventional, merely suggesting that his generation was no longer young. But Simeon Strunsky had gone beyond convention to propose a paradox: a "world"—a common ground—that was at the same time obliterated and real. Was there really a path left from there to here, from then to now?

Simeon Strunsky held out to them the hope that something, some quintessence of what they had been and done, had survived. But he did not state just what it was. Nor did he suggest any key that might unlock the man whom he was eulogizing, the impenetrable man who had declined to invite his family to his deathbed.

With, for her, unusual promptness, Anna assembled a memorial volume for English from the eulogies and other articles she solicited. Although even some of those with whom English had quarreled agreed to contribute, there were a few absences, most notably that of her sister, Rose, usually so strong in meeting deadlines, who was unable to complete a tribute of the epic sweep that she wanted. Anna herself offered the premier essay in the collection, a seamless reminiscence of an all but flawless man, informative in its way but utterly ignoring—as she no doubt believed befitted the occasion—the storm and conflict that had marked their lives together.[1]

Another writer who was unrepresented was Upton Sinclair, who declined. He wrote: "I have often had the feeling that you did not agree with his later ideas." Sinclair urged her to resume writing on her own, particularly her story of Jack London.[2]

But five years passed before she again took up her memoir of Jack. In the summer of 1942, while on Cape Cod, she started over and produced a manuscript that dwelt, as always, on the first fresh days of their friendship. In 1943, she was Charmian London's guest in her first visit to San Francisco in thirty-seven years. She just missed the launching of a Liberty Ship named for Jack. The vessel was embellished with words he had written to her forty-three years before: "The ship, new-launched, rushes to the sea." But even a visit to the old Jack London ranch did not produce more writing. She never gave up the idea of writing about Jack, but in 1953 she at last relinquished one hundred fifty-five of Jack's letters to the Huntington for fifteen hundred dollars.[3]

Instead, she became more and more a historical resource herself. Scholars sought her out for information about Jack, Gelett Burgess, Gaylord Wilshire, English, and the others in her past—but rarely about herself. She scattered the papers she owned to depositories across the country: the Jack London letters, English's papers, and portions of her own letters and writings. She even sent off a batch of material to a Jack London scholar, Vil Bykov, in Russia.[4]

When she sent English's papers to the State Historical Society of Wisconsin in 1961, she wrote a long letter reflecting with some bitterness, still, on her life with him. But she concluded with the sweetness and slight extravagance that was always part of her character. She was being visited on Cape

Cod, she said, by the four children who had taken the place, she once believed, of a writing career: "The most devoted and lovely children . . . all of them working for humanity, all of them beautiful beyond compare. Poor, dear English to have left the Party so soon."[5]

As any survivor must, she witnessed many deaths. Her son-in-law Rifat Tirana died in 1952; her friend Leonard Abbott, in 1953; and the last of her three older brothers, Max, four years later. In March 1963 her "alter self," Rose, died. On February 25, 1964, less than a month before her eighty-seventh birthday, her daughter Anna found her in her apartment, lying among papers that she was still struggling to put in order.[6]

Four years after English Walling died, Hutchins Hapgood, who had comforted the Wallings in Paris after the loss of their firstborn, contemplated him in his memoir: "He was a pure flame. But, like so many of our radicals and revolutionists, he had no inevitable basis, as deepseated as the unconscious, which kept him irresistibly in the same general direction."[1]

Hapgood understood well the temperament that barred English from permanent commitment to any cause or calling. There was more than a casual truth in English's remark to Anna, "I never tie myself up, if I can help it." His industriousness, when he was in the heat of a project, was (as Howard Brubaker remarked) "appalling"; he spared neither time nor energy. But he was always ready to move off to the next thing, a pattern that began with his youthful economic yearbook project and was repeated as he warmed and cooled toward Russian revolution, racial equality, and socialism itself. Inevitably, his contributions were episodic and, ultimately, likely to be forgotten.[2]

His long-term association after the war with the AFL constituted perhaps more of a refuge than a new commitment; by that time he was an outcast among radicals but not truly welcome in mainstream politics. He was annoyed from time to time in later life to be identified still as a socialist, but he must have known that his old identities would trail him through his life. To his credit, he never tried to compensate for the past by becoming, as did his contemporaries Robert Hunter and John Spargo, vehemently backward-looking. Somehow his intemperate antibolshevism coexisted with a degree of progressivism, and at the end he was as opposed to the Nazis as he had been to the Bolsheviks.[3]

Anna too fell under Hutchins Hapgood's gaze. While kindly in tone, his comment on her was in its way equally damning. He chose to recall that Anna had once been grist for a talented caricaturist named Christine, who ran the restaurant above the Provincetown Players in Greenwich Village: "Christine called the attention of the observer to Anna's intense seriousness, unrelieved by any sense of humor. Her deep weeping voice, her lachrymose tones in pronouncing the name of 'English,' her husband, the profound emotional way in which she pronounced the word 'revolution' or 'socialism' (indeed, probably nobody in the world ever said "socialism" with so much intensity, overflowing like a huge wave the infinite beach of life)." Hapgood paid conventional tribute to Anna's sincerity and constancy, but he implied her ineffectuality as well, with the inevitable insinuation that she had been much diminished by her marriage.[4]

It was true that she had fallen far short of her aspirations. Although she never renounced her faith in a vaguely cooperative, utopian socialism, doctrine hardly played a greater role in her later life than, say, theology among suburban Christians. Once she had made her true lifetime commitment, to marriage, she retained her freedom of opinion but gave up freedom in her economic environment. She lacked the will and the urgent circumstances of the women she portrayed in her account of the revolution to make her own life truly revolutionary.

English and Anna's inconstancy, their lack of Hapgood's "inevitable basis," led to their virtual disappearance from the public arena from the time, in their thirties, when they were celebrities of American radicalism, to their fifties, when he still struggled for relevance and she nursed nostalgia and regrets.

Yet this long passage, however determined by their individual personalities, was hardly unique. To a degree, it was representative of a generation of middle-class radicals—the one that found itself cast adrift, like Hapgood, as Victorians in a modern world. The roles in which English and Anna originally cast themselves were essentially Victorian: He was a gentleman controversialist, choosing to speak for principle rather than pay; she was a genteel novelist, shunning realism for belles-lettres. Even their work as didactic journalists derived from an outdated conception of magazine and book writing, as a marketplace of opinion rather than profit. Yet they struggled to remain abreast of their times, to remain on the crest of the new.

Many in their community underwent parallel experiences, sharing for a time a common belief that their prescriptions—socialist, reformist, or something between—might change the world for the better and lay the basis for new democratic societies. But by the end of the Great War they found themselves in a nation that had little patience with such nostrums. Their old world vanished, as Simeon Strunsky implied in his memorial, so thoroughly and abruptly that even those who wrote autobiographies could hardly reconstruct it convincingly; they remembered dates and places, of course, but often could not or did not retrieve much that once really mattered: who they once were, what they believed, why and how they acted. They shared a sense of the opacity of their common past. As Leonard Abbott wrote to Anna in 1926: "My impulses are the same as they were when I first knew you (how sweet those days were!), but the War and Bolshevism have smashed that old world, & I find myself now in a world in which I cannot function."[5]

Later, when historians came to deal with Anna and English, they found bits and pieces, some of them important enough to be retrieved; what they did not find was the skein of achievement, career, or power from which historical reputations are made. English appears in the histories of the founding of the NAACP and, to a lesser degree, of the Women's Trade Union League; most recently, however, scholars have found his three prewar books on socialism his most memorable achievement. They see in these works the essence of prewar American socialism, its unwieldiness and its hetereogeneity, its tendency to gravitate toward bourgeois values.[6]

Anna has inevitably remained known primarily as Jack London's one collaborator, a role she ultimately accepted for herself. And she has enjoyed posthumous success. In the years since her death, she has been contemplated more seriously: both as a serious influence on Jack London's work and as a model in varying degrees for characters in his fiction.[7]

English and Anna's careers have thus been reduced to patches of three or four years—a fraction of their lives as lived. Yet their lives as a whole are worth contemplating as an illustration of loss—not merely the conventional failure to succeed but the failure to maintain themselves in the evanescent American public sphere. The arena was open for a time to such publicists as English and Anna, yet even before the Great War it was being closed under pressure of commercial restraints and conventional opinion. The war sealed it tight. English managed to maintain access through the war by turning prodigal— that is, by ferociously voicing the new dominant opinion. But in the long term they both found themselves on the outside as surely as if they were refugees from a devastated land, speaking in another language.

Anna dimly grasped their condition—that they lived on in a lost country— when she stumbled on an old notebook:

> How long was long ago?
> I see the penciled words "Jack London["] in the back of this book—25 yrs. ago—but the words are plain—and I have not changed. I look through the book. It was very long ago that I wrote these pencilled notes. I have not changed! Life and my world have changed, but I remain as I then was—true to all my dreams—a dreamer still. ["]Wake up, my soul!"
> Dreams assail me! . . .
> Love and work now grapple with my soul.
> The slave of dreams, day is like night to me and night like day.[8]

Acknowledgments

This enterprise has depended on the kindness of strangers and friends. Invaluable help came first from members of the Walling-Strunsky family who, neither knowing me nor necessarily eager to have a stranger picking through the family's past, nonetheless responded with unfailing generosity and historical detachment to my project.

My Columbia journalism student of long ago, now rediscovered as a friend, Turhan Walling Tirana, a grandson of Anna Strunsky and William English Walling, first opened the family's doors for me and subsequently encouraged and read my work. Anna Walling Hamburger, daughter and namesake of Anna Strunsky, put at my disposal not only her full trust but the inner family history of which she is the repository. Although she professed to be learning about her parents from my research, I came to realize how hollow my archival work would have been without her interpretations and interpolations. Moreover, she was a temperate and acute critic of the work in draft form. With her sister, Rosamond Walling Tirana, she provided help that is only partly reflected in their frequent appearances in my footnotes. I received welcome assistance as well from Boris Lorwin, son of Anna Strunsky's sister, Rose, who made available his mother's correspondence with the man she married, Louis Lorwin, as well as his father's memoir. In addition, he generously read and commented on the draft manuscript. I am also grateful for the assistance, in varied ways, of Denise Marcil, Bardyl Tirana, Peter Matson, and Christopher Walling. (It was through Christopher Walling's efforts that the largest collection of Anna Strunsky's papers came to be deposited at Yale University.)

I am indebted to the staffs of the four libraries to which the Strunsky and Walling papers were scattered for their assistance and for granting permission to quote from their holdings: the Department of Archives and Manuscripts at Yale University and its curator, Judith Schiff; the Huntington Library in San Marino, California, and its curator of literary manuscripts, Sara S. Hodson; the State Historical Society of Wisconsin and Harold L. Miller, reference archivist; and the Bancroft Library, University of California, Berkeley, and Anthony S. Bliss, curator of rare books and literary manuscripts.

Similarly, I am grateful for staff assistance and permission to quote from the James Graham Phelps Stokes Papers at the Rare Book and Manuscript

Library, Columbia University; the Macmillan Company Records at the Rare Book and Manuscript Division, New York Public Library; the Arthur Bullard Papers at the Seeley G. Mudd Manuscript Library, Princeton University, Ben Primer, archivist; the Arthur J. Kennedy Papers at the Social Welfare History Archives, University of Minnesota, David Klaassen, director; and the Hamilton Holt Papers at Rollins College, Winter Park, Florida. At my old home, I benefited from the support and holdings of the W.E.B. Du Bois Library, University of Massachusetts, Amherst.

Stanford University Press, publishers of *The Letters of Jack London,* edited by Earle Labor, Robert C. Leitz III, and I. Milo Shepard, granted permission to quote from this invaluable work. I thank Mr. Shepard as well for granting access to the Jack London collections at The Huntington and at Utah State University, and for permission to quote from these materials.

I am particularly grateful to those who read the manuscript or portions thereof: Clarice Stasz of Sonoma State University, for an invaluable critique of the entire manuscript and substantial research help; Mari Jo Buhle of Brown University, whose appraisal was equally valuable; Earle Labor, Wilson Professor of American Literature at Centenary College, for reading the sections involving Jack London; Spencer Klaw, who provided an incisive critique of an early draft; Rob Miraldi of the State University of New York College at New Paltz; and Ron Marmarelli of Central Michigan University. I am also indebted for advice and goodwill to Jack Meyer Stuart, who wrote a valuable 1968 dissertation on William English Walling (cited herein). I also acknowledge a long-term debt to William E. Leuchtenburg, who taught me how to mess about in archives.

At the University of Massachusetts, Amherst, I received guidance from many colleagues, but especially from Jules Chametzky, Judith Fryer, Gerald McFarland, Norman Sims, and Howard M. Ziff. The task of finding and copying century-old documents fell to a tireless aide, Rick Seto, who went beyond mechanical requirements to provide valuable summary and commentary. I am grateful, finally, for the welcome given my manuscript by Bruce Wilcox, director of the University of Massachusetts Press, and its conscientious handling by the managing editor, Pamela E. Wilkinson, and the copy editor, Betty S. Waterhouse, as well as the rest of the staff. I thank Phyllis Shapiro for her astute proofreading.

Betsy Wade supplied the counsel that only a superb editor can offer while giving the moral support that can come only from a spouse. She appraised my efforts generously but never hesitated to remind me that the result of my research must be writing, not merely transcribed notes.

Notes

Abbreviations, Works Frequently Cited

AS, ASW   Anna Strunsky, Anna Strunsky Walling.

ASWH   Anna Strunsky Walling Papers, The Huntington Library, San Marino, California.

ASWY   Anna Strunsky Walling Papers, Yale University.

AWH   Anna Walling Hamburger.

Gillmore diary   Manuscript diary, March–May 1908, of Inez Haynes Gillmore (Irwin), transcript lent by AWH, original in Inez Haynes Irwin Papers, Arthur and Elizabeth Schlesinger Library, Harvard University.

JL   Jack London.

JLH   Jack London Collection, The Huntington Library.

Katia   Dr. Katherine E. Maryson, ASW's friend.

LJL   *The Letters of Jack London,* ed. Earle Labor, Robert C. Leitz III, and I. Milo Shepard, 3 vols. (1988).

London MSS   Manuscript writings by ASW titled "Jack London," folders 392 and 393, ASWY.

MACM   Macmillan Company Records, New York Public Library.

NYT   *New York Times.*

RS, RSL   Rose Strunsky, Rose Strunsky Levine/Lorwin.

"Revolutionary Lives"   ASW, "Revolutionary Lives: Russia—1906," unpublished book manuscript (1917), microfilm copy C-H 95, Bancroft Library, University of California, Berkeley.

Stuart, "William English Walling"   Jack Meyer Stuart, "William English Walling: A Study in Political Ideas" (Ph.D. diss., Columbia University, 1968).

SWB   Strunsky-Walling Collection, The Bancroft Library, University of California, Berkeley.

Walling Symposium   Anna Strunsky Walling et al., *William English Walling: A Symposium* (1938).

WEW   William English Walling.

WEWP   William English Walling Papers, State Historical Society of Wisconsin.

Introduction

1   "Millionaire Socialists": The term was apparently coined, in a not unfriendly manner, by the socialist Gustavus Myers, in "Our Millionaire Socialists," *Cosmopolitan,* October 1906, cover and 605. Stokes and Pastor: Arthur Zipser and Pearl Zipser, *Fire and Grace: The Life of Rose Pastor Stokes* (1989).

2 Victorians: Hutchins Hapgood, *A Victorian in the Modern World* (1940).

3 "Aspiring and questing world": Simeon Strunsky, in *Walling Symposium*, 54.

4 AS, "On the Principle of Loyalty in Biography," *Impressions Quarterly* 3 (March 1902): 1–2. The Bancroft Library, University of California, Berkeley, has a file of *Impressions*.

Part One

CHAPTER I

1 "The City That Was": originally, the headline on Will Irwin's story in the *New York Sun*, 21 April 1906. San Francisco's pre-earthquake culture is acutely characterized in Kevin Starr, *Americans and the California Dream, 1850–1915* (1973), 253–65.

2 "The Crowd": ASW autobiographical writings, folder 393, ASWY; Oscar Lewis, *Bay Window Bohemia: An Account of the Brilliant Artistic World of Gaslit San Francisco* (1956); and Elsie Whitaker Martinez, *San Francisco Bay Area Writers and Artists*, oral history interview by Franklin D. Walker and Willa Klug Baum, Regional Oral History Office, The Bancroft Library, University of California, Berkeley, 1969.

3 Burgess: Lewis, *Bay Window Bohemia*, 82–86; see also the compendium, with commentary by Joseph Backus, of Burgess's journalism, *Behind the Scenes: Glimpses of Fin de Siècle San Francisco* (1968). Arnold Genthe: memoirs, *As I Remember* (1936). Martinez: George W. Neubert, *Xavier Martinez (1869–1943)*, catalog, exhibition at The Oakland Museum of Art Special Gallery, 12 February through 7 April 1974. Coppa's: Agnes Foster Buchanan, "The Story of a Famous Fraternity of Writers and Artists," *Pacific Monthly* 17 (August 1907): 73–83, clipping, folder 435, ASWY.

4 "Anna Strunsky!": Rose Wilder Lane, "Life and Jack London," *Sunset* magazine, November 1917, 27–30, tearsheets annotated by ASW, box 3, WEWP.

5 "Girl Socialist": John Hamilton Gilmour, "Girl Socialist of San Francisco," *San Francisco Examiner*, 3 October 1897, clipping lent by AWH. "Exceptionally good copy": JL to AS, 1 April 1902, *LJL*, 1:287.

6 "The only recollection . . .": ASW, "Revolutionary Lives," 8.

7 Family history is derived primarily from the memoir of Anna (Horowitz) Strunsky, "Chronicle" (1928–1929), manuscript translated from Yiddish; copy lent by AWH. Valuable additional information was supplied by two of Anna Strunsky's daughters, Rosamond Walling Tirana and Anna Walling Hamburger, in interviews on 19 September 1991, 15 June 1992, and 20 August 1993.

8 Birth date: AS listed 21 March 1877, as her birth date in Stanford University records; see transcript, copy obtained by Turhan Tirana.

9 Transatlantic crossing: The *Egypt* left Liverpool on 8 September 1886 and arrived in New York on 19 September; *NYT*, 20 September 1886.

10 "Peopled wholly with Hebrews": Jacob A. Riis, *How the Other Half Lives: Studies among the Tenements of New York* (1890), 42.

11 "Miss Annie": *New York Herald* [1892], clipping lent by AWH.

12 "My best school": ASW, "The Golden Wedding," manuscript [1915], box 1, SWB.

13 Socialist Labor Party: Paul Buhle, entries on Daniel DeLeon and the Socialist

Labor Party in *Encyclopedia of the American Left*, ed. Mari Jo Buhle, Paul Buhle, and Dan Georgakas (1990); Daniel Bell, "The Background and Development of Marxian Socialism in the United States," in *Socialism and American Life*, ed. Donald Drew Egbert and Stow Persons, 2 vols. (1952), 1:215–405. Women's activities: Mari Jo Buhle, *Women and American Socialism, 1870–1920* (1983), 75–78, 119–20.

14 "Hardly more than a child": ASW, "The Golden Wedding."

15 "Proposed calling": AS, Stanford transcript.

16 Stanford, Jordan, and Ross: Edith R. Mirrielees, *Stanford: The Story of a University* (1959); Orrin Leslie Elliott, *Stanford University: The First Twenty-Five Years* (1937); and Julius Weinberg, *Edward Alsworth Ross and the Sociology of Progressivism* (1972). Ross recollection of AS: Ross to WEW, 28 April 1917, box 4, ASWH.

17 William James: ASW to Hilda Abel, 16 June 1958, box 5, ASWH. "Bathed in ether": James quoted in Starr, *California Dream*, 309.

18 Melville B. Anderson: AS correspondence with Anderson is in boxes 1 and 5, ASWH. "Crude little laggard": AS to Katia, 13 December 1903, folder 112, ASWY. "Madonna Marie": AS to Mary Sheldon Barnes, 26 October 1897, folder 146, ASWY. Memorial: AS diary, summer 1901, folder 300, ASWY.

19 AS academic record: Stanford transcript. Patricia White, archives specialist, The Stanford University Libraries, supplied additional information; White to author, 26 July 1993. "Condition" in history: ASW, London MSS.

20 "Tortured me": AS to Katia, 13 December 1903. "Intellectual machine": JL to AS, 15 January 1900, *LJL*, 1:143.

21 "Male visitor": Emma Goldman, *Living my Life* (originally published in 1931; one-volume edition, 1934), 227. The 1934 edition contains an erratum slip reading: "The author wishes to state that the passage on page 227 relating to Anna Strunsky and Leland Stanford University is unfounded. The mistake in the text was due to a misunderstanding." "Good morals and decency": Elliott, *Stanford University*, 410.

22 Debate and party activity: "A New Californian Writer," newspaper article [summer 1903], clipping lent by AWH. Telegram from family: 5 December 1897, folder 153, ASWY. "Endless drudgery": ASW diary, 12 September [1916], folder 303, ASWY.

23 "Specialization of Vocation": manuscript, 24 August 1897, box 1, SWB.

24 Living at Stanford: JL asked for her Stanford address in January 1900; JL to AS, 21 January 1900, *LJL*, 1:144. "Tost out of here": AS notebook, 10 December 1903, box 1, SWB. Berkeley: A directory of all students who ever attended the University of California lists Anna Strunsky as "x04," but no record exists of courses completed; William M. Roberts, university archivist, to author, 2 September 1993.

25 "Death, love, work": AS diary, 19 February 1901, folder 300, ASWY. "Death called me 'Love' ": AS, "Edward Howard Griggs [ethics professor at Stanford] Ex Profundis," manuscript copy, 22 January 1901, lent by AWH.

CHAPTER 2

1 Turk Street Temple scene and account of meeting JL: ASW, London MSS. ASW's unfinished manuscripts entitled "Jack London" are in folders 392 and 393, ASWY. One is dated September 1942; other fragments appear to be older. The most substantial is about a hundred typed pages long.

2 "Do you want to meet him?": ASW memoir, 17 January 1919, folder 81, ASWY; published in part in Charmian London, *The Book of Jack London*, 2 vols. (1921), 1:319–22. "He was proud": ASW, London MSS.

3 "Younger and older": ASW, London MSS. "Lassalle, Karl Marx, or Byron": ASW, in Charmian London, *Book of Jack London*, 1:320.

4 "My dear Miss Strunsky": JL to AS, 19 December 1899, *LJL*, 1:133.

5 "Aimless, helpless, hopeless": AS, quoted in JL to AS, 21 December 1899, *LJL*, 1:135. Only JL's side of the correspondence has survived; AS's letters must be inferred from portions quoted or paraphrased in JL's letters to her. Shortly after JL's death, ASW asked his widow not to destroy any pre-1906 letters from her that she might find. Apparently, none were found. ASW to Charmian K. London, 14 January 1917, folder 81, ASWY.

6 "Stray guest": JL to AS, 21 December 1899, *LJL*, 1:135.

7 "The light played": ASW, London MSS. Missing a tooth: AS, in Charmian London, *Book of Jack London*, 1:320. Kipling: ASW, London MSS.

8 "We read Swinburne": ASW, London MSS.

9 "Boy Socialist": headline in *San Francisco Examiner*, 25 December 1895, quoted in Clarice Stasz, *American Dreamers: Charmian and Jack London* (1988), 56.

10 "Haggle and bargain": AS, quoted in JL to AS, 29 December 1899, *LJL*, 1:137. "O Pshaw!": JL to AS, 21 January 1900, *LJL*, 1:144; AS change of salutation: JL to AS, 20 February 1900, *LJL*, 1:161.

11 Daily letters: ASW, London MSS. Hiking: autobiographical fragment, box 1, SWB.

12 "Stand over you with a whip": JL to AS, 13 February 1900, *LJL*, 1, 156. "Beggar exposing his sores" and "gulfs of difference": ASW, London MSS.

13 "Had wooed her:" ASW, London MSS.

14 "[I] had his letter": ASW, London MSS. "It was rather sudden": JL to AS, 6 April 1900, *LJL*, 1:179.

15 "Casual way": ASW, London MSS. Bessie Maddern: Joan London, *Jack London and His Times: An Unconventional Biography* (1939).

16 "Fire in the grate": ASW, London MSS.

17 "Don't disappoint me": JL to AS, May 1900, *LJL*, 1:187.

18 "Comrades!": JL to AS, 31 July 1900, *LJL*, 1:198.

CHAPTER 3

1 "He was speaking of eugenics": ASW, London MSS.

2 First Dane Kempton letter: JL to AS, 15 September 1900, *LJL*, 1:205. "Overpraised": ASW notation on undated JL letter, box 5, ASWH; text of letter is in *LJL*, 1:261.

3 "Didn't I explain": JL to Cloudesley Johns, 17 October 1900, *LJL*, 1:214.

4 "Well worth meeting": JL to Elwyn Hoffman, 6 January 1901, *LJL*, 1:234.

5 "Russian Jewess": Jonathan Auerbach discusses the significance of AS's Jewishness in relation to *The Kempton-Wace Letters* in *Male Call: Becoming Jack London* (1996), 148–77.

6 "Creature of a lower evolution": AS, quoted in JL to AS, 15 November 1900, *LJL*, 1:219.

7 *Jude the Obscure*: JL to AS, 27 November [1900]; "white beautiful friendship": JL to AS, 26–28 December 1900, *LJL*, 1:221, 229.

8 Birthday invitation: JL to AS, 6 January 1901, *LJL*, 1:235.

9   AS, "Book of Ideas": folder 300, ASWY.

10 "Windlestraws": Joseph Wright, ed., *The English Dialect Dictionary* (1905), 6:506–7; *The Oxford English Dictionary* (1933 ed.), 12:105; William Grand and David D. Murison, eds., *The Scottish National Dictionary* (1976), 10:194–95; and C. T. Onions, ed., *The Oxford Dictionary of English Etymology* (1966), 1008.

11 "Epigraph": William Ernest Henley, *Poems* (1898), 256.

12 Redo everything: JL to AS [March 1901], *LJL*, 1:242. "It puts us on our mettle": JL to AS, 9 May 1901, *LJL*, 1:248.

13 "Suggestions for Jack": AS, "Book of Ideas," folder 300, ASWY.

14 "Studies in Suicide": AS, "Book of Ideas," folder 300, ASWY.

15 "I did not play with this man's soul": AS quoted in JL to AS [1901], *LJL*, 1:261–64.

CHAPTER 4

1   Typewriter: JL to AS [January 1902], box 3A, ASWH. "Exercise your dire & shaking fist": JL to AS, 22 January 1902, *LJL*, 1:274.

2   Support of Henley speech: JL to AS, 18 and [?] January 1902, *LJL*, 1:273, 275. Not to flatter: AS, "On the Principle of Loyalty in Biography," *Impressions Quarterly* 3 (March 1902): 1–2. JL praise: JL to AS, 27 February 1902, box 3A, ASWH.

3   "Dear You": JL to AS, 5 January 1902, *LJL*, 1:269; 16 January 1902, *LJL*, 1:271; [February 1902], *LJL*, 1:284. "As I sit here": JL to AS, 16 January 1902, *LJL*, 1:273.

4   Going to San Quentin: JL to AS, 22 January 1902. "Stuttered & failed": JL to AS, 5 February 1902, *LJL*, 1:276. Long, aggressive letter: JL to AS, 11 February 1902, *LJL*, 1:278–81. See also JL to Cloudesley Johns, 23 February 1902, *LJL*, 1:282, reporting that he had witnessed a hanging the day before.

5   "I went astray": JL to AS, 11 February 1902; longhand: manuscript letter, box 3A, ASWH. "Dear Anna" letter: JL to AS, 18 February 1902, *LJL*, 1:281. "Dear, dear you" resumed: JL to AS, 14 March 1902, *LJL*, 1:284.

6   To San Rafael: JL to AS, 27 February 1902, box 3A, ASWH. "Day by day I look out," JL to AS, 22 March 1902, *LJL*, 1:285.

7   "*Go! Go! Go!*": JL to AS, [March 1902], *LJL*, 1:287. Come live with them: JL to AS, 24 April 1902, *LJL*, 1:289.

8   "Alone together": ASW, London MSS.

9   Mother's advice: Hal Waters, "Anna Strunsky and Jack London," *American Book Collector* 17 (November 1966): 28–30. "Within two weeks": ASW, London MSS.

10 "During the first few days": AS, quoted in *San Francisco Chronicle*, 30 June 1904, repr. in John Perry, *Jack London: An American Myth* (1981), 177.

11 Sitting on Jack's lap: mentioned, for example, in Stasz, *American Dreamers*, 120; Perry, *Jack London*, 175; and Joseph Noel, *Footloose in Arcadia: A Personal Record of Jack London, George Sterling, Ambrose Bierce* (1940), 147. "At the unusually early hour" and other details: quoted from divorce complaint, June 1904, in Alameda county records, transcribed in Franklin Dickerson Walker, "Notes re: Jack London's divorce from Besse [*sic*] (Maddern) London," folder HM45261, Franklin Dickerson Walker Collection, The Huntington Library.

12 "Sahib" letters: JL to AS, 6 June 1902, *LJL*, 1:297; JL to AS, 6 June 1902, *LJL*, 1:297. Waters, "Anna Strunsky and Jack London," states that she signed her letters to him "Protean," perhaps after his reference to her "Protean moods" in his "Comrades!" letter of 31 July 1900, *LJL*, 1:198.

13 "Very, very much better": JL to AS, 18 July 1902, *LJL*, 1:301.

14 "Some writing of the London slums": JL to John Spargo, 28 July 1902, *LJL*, 1:302. "Ink-beteared": JL to AS, 29 July 1902, *LJL*, 1:303. From *RMS Majestic*: JL to AS, *LJL*, 31 July 1902, 1:303. Letters from England: JL to AS, 16 and 21 August 1902, *LJL*, 1:305.

15 "Plunged into the other": JL to AS, 25 August 1902, *LJL*, 1:306.

16 "She had tried to write indifferently": ASW, London MSS. "It does not help me": AS, "Book of Ideas," folder 300, ASWY.

17 "Your letter was cold enough": quotations from AS's letter in JL to AS, 28 August 1902, *LJL*, 1:306–9. London scholars have differed on the exact nature of AS's complaint. Stasz hypothesizes that Bessie London herself told AS about her sex life (*American Dreamers*, 104). Auerbach, in *Male Call*, states that AS was informed of Bessie London's pregnancy by JL's mother, Flora London, and that AS wrote to JL as soon as she found out (271n).

18 "Sending me the 'news' ": JL to AS, 9 September 1902, *LJL*, 1:311.

19 Draft of sixty-three thousand words: JL to AS, 28 September 1902, *LJL*, 1:312.

20 "Realize her cruelty": ASW, London MSS.

CHAPTER 5

1 "Prevalence of epistolary fiction": *Atlantic* to JL, 1 August 1902, box 1, ASWH.

2 "I am astonished": Carpenter to Brett, 6 September 1902, box 86, MACM.

3 Letters relating to collaboration: JL to Brett, 9 November 1902, *LJL*, 1: 315; JL to AS, 9 November 1902, *LJL*, 1: 316; letter of introduction for AS, JL to Brett, 9 November 1902, JL folder, box 86, MACM.

4 Commitment to publish: Brett to JL, 16 September 1902, Brett letterbooks, MACM. "One of the largest": JL to AS, 28 September 1902, *LJL*, 1: 312. "Make a hit": JL to Brett, 29 September 1902, *LJL*, 1: 314.

5 Letter from Rome: JL to AS, 15 October 1902, box 3A, ASWH.

6 Royalties: Brett to Bessie London, 11 November 1902, Brett letterbooks, MACM. "Unlucky mischance": JL to AS, 25 November 1902, *LJL*, 1:323.

7 "You will find her charming": JL to Brett, 9 November 1902. *LJL*, 1:315. "Do not be disheartened": JL to AS, 9 November 1902, *LJL*, 1:316.

8 *Wilshire's*: Howard Quint in *The American Radical Press 1880–1960*, ed. Joseph R. Conlin, 2 vols. (1974), 1:72–81. Manhattan Avenue: AS to Brett, 21 December 1902, box 16, MACM. Whittier Hall: AS to Katia, 7 April 1903, folder 112, ASWY.

9 Titles: ASW noted that a French edition of *The Kempton-Wace Letters*, published thirty-seven years later, was called *L'Amour et la jeunesse*; ASW to Hilda Abel, 16 June 1958, box 5, ASWH. Joe Juron found a copy of a 1983 French edition under the title of *Rien d'autre que l'amour*, after the Dante inscription at the opening of the novel; Juron, "Jack London and Anna Strunsky," *Jack London Newsletter* 17 (September–December 1984):95.

10 "The third great side": undated, unsigned memorandum in AS's hand, box 16, MACM. "Letters on love": JL to AS, 6 December 1902, *LJL*, 1:323–24. "Fifteen thousand words": JL to Brett, 11 December 1902, *LJL*, 1:324–25

11 "Had a good time": AS to Brett, 21 December 1902, box 16, MACM. The "Prologue" manuscript is in folder JL1705H, JLH.

12 "I am very doubtful": in handwriting identified as Brett's in ASW's notes with the "Prologue" manuscript, folder JL1705H, JLH. Letter rejecting prologue: JL to AS [mid-January 1903], *LJL*, 1:336. Relieved: ASW, notes with "Prologue" manuscript.

13　JL's agreement with Macmillan: correspondence with Brett, especially Brett's initial proposal, Brett to JL, 3 December 1902, Brett letterbooks, MACM. For background on JL's rise to commercial success and his relations with publishers, see Christopher P. Wilson, "The Brain Worker: Jack London," in his *The Labor of Words: Literary Professionalism in the Progressive Era* (1985), 92–112. Revision of letters: JL to AS, 7 January 1903, *LJL*, 1:335. Anonymous publication: JL to AS, 20 December 1902, *LJL*, 1:328–30. Royalties: JL to Brett, 21 November 1902, *LJL*, 1:317.

14　Age: In fact, JL was almost twenty-seven and she, almost twenty-six. "Neither in joy nor sorrow": JL to AS, 20 December 1902, *LJL*, 1:329–30.

15　"I love this book": AS dedication transcribed in David Mike Hamilton, *"The Tools of My Trade": The Annotated Books in Jack London's Library* (1986), 153.

16　Slips of paper: JL to AS, 20 January 1903, *LJL*, 1:339. "Flattering news": JL to AS, 3 February 1903, *LJL*, 1:341. Ever write again: JL to AS, 13 March 1903, *LJL*, 1:352.

17　"Girl away from home": AS, "Book of Ideas," 15 December 1902, folder 300, ASWY. Reaction to Mary Strunsky's death: AS notebook, box 1, SWB. Influenza: AS to Brett, 17 February 1903, and Brett to AS, 18 February 1903, box 16, MACM.

18　Lost quotations and proofreading: Brett to AS, 2 and 10 April 1903, Brett letterbooks, MACM; JL to AS, 6 April 1903, *LJL*, 1:359; AS to Katia, 7, 9, and 15 April 1903, folder 112, ASWY.

19　Wilshire luncheon: ASW, autobiographical fragment, folder 363, ASWY. "All kinds of rot": JL to AS, 29 May 1903, *LJL*, 1:364. Cheered by notices: JL to Brett, 19 June 1903, *LJL*, 1:368.

20　Brett on sales: Brett to JL, 27 May, 26 June, and 15 July 1903, Brett letterbooks, MACM.

21　"Spiritual misprint": Sterling quoted in Noel, *Footloose in Arcadia,* 185.

22　"Courage, devotion": Noel, *Footloose in Arcadia,* 186.

23　"You must know it of me": This wording of the conclusion in AS's handwriting was substituted for a longer version on the galley proofs (folder JL1705H, JLH) and appears in the book as published; anonymous edition, *The Kempton-Wace Letters* (1903), 256.

CHAPTER 6

1　Fate of manuscript: ASW to Hilda Abel, 16 June 1958, box 5, ASWH.

2　Advance on royalties: Brett to AS, 3 June 1903, Brett letterbooks, MACM. "Enables me to take a long looked-for trip": AS to Brett, 3 June 1903, box 16, MACM.

3　"Second novel": Brett to AS, 4 June 1903, Brett letterbooks, MACM. Brett's character as a publisher: Wilson, *Labor of Words,* 76–77.

4　"We are beside ourselves": AS to Katia, 9 July 1903, folder 112, ASWY.

5　Sightseeing: AS diary, folder 300, ASWY, and AS notebook, box 1, SWB. "Who should turn up in Oxford": Louise Imogen Guiney to Bruce Porter, 12 August 1903, in *Letters of Louise Imogen Guiney.* ed. Grace Guiney, 2 vols. (1926), 2:87. "Lupe": purportedly Samoan for "lark," a nickname given to Burgess when he edited *The Lark.* (Guiney, *Letters,* 2:17).

6　"The love of life" and "this I saw": AS notebook, 2 August 1903, box 1, SWB.

7　South of France: AS notebook, 11 August 1903, box 1, SWB. Le Baux: AS diary, 28 January 1905, folder 301, ASWY. "Our compartment was dark": AS notebook, 14 August 1903, box 1, SWB.

8 "The warmth of his hand": AS notebook, 23 and 25 September 1903, box 1, SWB.

9 "He would not have interfered": AS notebook, 25 September 1903, box 1, SWB.

10 Brevoort: ASW to Hilda Abel, 16 June 1958, box 5, ASWH. "Friends, real friends" and "I will dedicate my book": AS notebook, box 1, SWB.

11 "Sad homecoming": AS to Katia, 26 October 1903, folder 112, ASWY. "Standing over Mary's grave": AS notebook, 1 November 1903, box 1, SWB. "Written definitions": AS to Katia, 5 November 1903, folder 112, ASWY.

12 "How you must be enjoying yourself!": JL to AS, 5 September 1903, LJL, 1:386.

13 "The Divine Anna": magazine article [1903], clipping lent by AWH.

14 "Love family": Charmian London, The Book of Jack London, 1:319. Publicity on separation: "Jack London Writes the End of His Own Love Story," magazine section, New York World, 16 August 1903. "As the reporters could not ascertain": JL to Brett, 2 September 1903, LJL, 1:383.

15 "Cameron sent me a newspaper clipping": AS, quoted in JL to Charmian Kittredge, 29 September 1903, LJL, 1:391. Affair between JL and Charmian Kittredge: Stasz, American Dreamers, 109–25.

16 New address: AS to Brett, 26 October 1903, on Max Strunsky's letterhead, with "901 Golden Gate Avenue" crossed out and "974 Sutter Street" written in, box 16, MACM. Work on "Windlestraws": AS to Katia, 5 November 1903, folder 112, ASWY. "My nieces and my manuscript": AS to Brett, 26 October 1903.

17 Visiting Stanford: AS to Katia, 13 December 1903, folder 112, ASWY. "There is a book for you": AS notebook, 10 December 1903, box 1, SWB.

18 "Shot or maimed": AS to Katia, 7 January 1904, folder 112, ASWY.

19 "If war is declared": AS to Katia, 3 January [misdated 3 December] 1904, folder 112, ASWY. "The Siberia for Japan": AS notebook, box 1, SWB.

20 "War is not declared": AS to Katia, 7 January 1904, folder 112, ASWY.

21 "Tyrants": AS to Katia, 3 January 1904, folder 112, ASWY.

22 "How my life spirals!" AS to Katia, 26 February 1904, folder 112, ASWY.

23 "Sometime in life": AS notebook, 29 February 1904, box 1, SWB.

24 Thirteenth chapter: page dated 15 March 1904, longhand draft of "Windlestraws," lent by AWH, now in ASWY; other notes and fragments are in folder 403, ASWY. Leaving "Eden": AS to Katia [March 1904], folder 112, ASWY.

25 "My father could not understand": ASW, autobiographical fragment, box 1, SWB.

26 "One should learn to work": AS to Katia [May 1904], folder 112, ASWY. "I have done nothing": AS to Katia, 4 June 1904, folder 112, ASWY.

CHAPTER 7

1 Divorce petition: documents from the Alameda County courthouse, summarized in Walker, "Notes re: Jack London's divorce," folder HM45261, Walker Collection.

2 "Tissue of lies": JL to AS, 25 August 1902, LJL, 1:306.

3 "Little intellectuals": Noel, Footloose in Arcadia, 147.

4 Siberia rumor: New York World, 28 June 1904. Anna as transgressor: San Francisco Chronicle, 29 June 1904, repr. in Waters, "Anna Strunsky and Jack London." Gonorrhea: Walker, "Notes re: Jack London's divorce," folder HM45261, Walker Collection.

5 "Bizarrely furnished apartment": "Absurd and Vulgar, Says Miss Strunsky," San Francisco Chronicle, 30 June 1904, repr. in Perry, Jack London, 177. "Outside

of the time": *San Francisco Chronicle*, 28 June 1904, quoted in Perry, *Jack London*, 175.

6 Pawn in divorce: interview with AS, in Joan London, "The London Divorce," *American Book Collector* 17 (November 1966): 31. JL's analysis: JL to Charmian Kittredge, 6 July 1904, *LJL*, 1:431; JL to Caroline Sterling, 15 September 1905, *LJL*, 1:520–26.

7 "I do most earnestly hope": JL to AS, 23 July 1904, *LJL*, 1:436.

8 "If it's typed": JL to AS, 28 July 1905, *LJL*, 1:438.

9 "Jack has his divorce": AS to Katia, 2 September 1904, folder 112, ASWY.

10 "I chose a mountain": "On King's Mountain," undated manuscript, folder 375, ASWY.

11 "I thought I realized" and "I would make some changes": AS diary, 20 and 21 January 1905, folder 301, ASWY.

12 "The Road": Several versions, dated from 1905 to 1915, are in folder 385, ASWY.

13 "Revolution in Russia!" AS diary, 25 January 1905, folder 301, ASWY.

14 "I walked about a mile": AS diary, 26 January 1905, folder 301, ASWY.

Part Two

CHAPTER 8

1 "Why I Am a Socialist": for example, Charles Edward Russell, *Why I Am a Socialist* (1910).

2 Private channels: interviews with AWH, 19 September 1991 and 3 May 1996.

3 Willoughby Walling, WEW's father: *National Cyclopedia of American Biography*, 18:209.

4 William Hayden English: F. Gerald Handfield Jr., "William H. English and the Election of 1880," in *Gentlemen from Indiana: National Party Candidates, 1836–1940*, ed. Ralph D. Gray (1977), 85–116; *National Cyclopedia of American Biography*, 9:376–77. On English's racial views and role in the admission of Kansas, see Allan Nevins, *The Emergence of Lincoln*, 2 vols. (1950), 1:292–301, 402.

5 English's postwar career: Handfield, "William H. English," 91–97.

6 Edinburgh: WEW to "Pa," 25 September 1887, box 1, WEWP. Mary Jackson Walling (1 July 1884–25 January 1887): Walling family genealogy, box 3, WEWP.

7 WEW's childhood: ASW in *Walling Symposium*, 7–9.

8 "English acquits himself": E. L. McClelland, headmaster, Trinity Hall, to Dr. Willoughby Walling, 22 February 1890, box 1, WEWP.

9 "500 is perfect": WEW to "Mama," 5 February 1890, folder 263, ASWY. Demerits: WEW to parents, 16 February 1890, folder 263, ASWY. Hyde Park High School: ASW in *Walling Symposium*, 8; report card, 21 December 1891, folder 482, ASWY.

10 Admission inquiry: WEW to Frank F. Abbott, University of Chicago, 22 March 1892, box 1, WEWP. "Harper's Bazaar": Richard J. Storr, *Harper's University: The Beginnings, A History of the University of Chicago* (1966), 164.

11 Fraternities: WEW to parents, 16 September 1895, folder 263, ASWY; WEW to parents, 11 and 22 October [1897], box 1, WEWP; Storr, *Harper's University*, 166–70.

12 Academic record: WEW, Official Academic Record, Office of the University Registrar, University of Chicago, transcript copy dated 16 August 1994. Bardyl R. Tirana assisted in obtaining this record. Declined to wear key: Ernest Poole in *Walling Symposium*, 22.

13　Inheritance: AS to Elias Strunsky, 19 March 1906, box 5, ASWH. Father's retirement: Willoughby Walling (brother) to WEW, 9 May 1934, box 1, WEWP. Agate Springs: WEW to parents, undated fragment [1897] from Hotel Cecil, London, box 1, WEWP; 25 August 1897, folder 263, ASWY; 28 August 1899, box 1, WEWP; 24 September 1902, box 6, ASWH; and 30 July 1904, folder 265, ASWY.

14　"Aunt Bessie and Albion" and "Dekes": WEW to parents, 22 October [1897]; "Cousin Hannah" and Miss Middleton: WEW to parents, Friday evening [fall 1897]; Miss Cutts: WEW to parents, 8 November 1897; Sandow system: WEW to parents, 13 December 1897 —all in box 1, WEWP; see David L. Chapman, *Sandow the Magnificent: Eugen Sandow and the Beginnings of Bodybuilding* (1994).

15　"Three niggers": WEW to parents, 22 October [1897]. "Terribly cold & stiff": WEW to Willoughby Walling, 29 October [1897], folder 278, ASWY.

16　"No time or leisure": WEW to parents, 8 November 1897; "I had to take issue": WEW to parents, 10 December 1897, box 1, WEWP. James Barr Ames: *The Centennial History of the Harvard Law School, 1817–1917* (1918), 175–89.

17　"A rational view of the work": WEW to parents [February 1898], box 1, WEWP. "Law and business": longhand document [early 1898], folder 482, ASWY.

18　Beveridge's election: Claude G. Bowers, *Beveridge and the Progressive Era* (1932), 66–93. "You are fine types": Beveridge to WEW, 23 January 1899, box 1, ASWH.

19　Sociology: Robert M. Crunden, *Ministers of Reform: The Progressives' Achievement in American Civilization, 1889–1920* (1982), 79–89. *American Journal of Sociology*: Frank Luther Mott, *A History of American Magazines*, vol. 4, *1885–1905* (1957), 191–92.

20　Veblen: See, among many studies, Joseph Dorfman, *Thorstein Veblen and His America* (1934) and Rick Tilman, *Thorstein Veblen and His Critics, 1891–1963: Conservative, Liberal, and Radical Perspectives* (1993). Veblen-WEW connection: N. I. Stone in *Walling Symposium*, 60–61; Brian Lloyd, *Left Out: Pragmatism, Exceptionalism, and the Poverty of American Marxism, 1890–1922* (1997), 136–56.

21　Grades: WEW, Official Academic Record, University of Chicago.

22　Tenement: "Russian Prison for Young Chicagoan?" article in Chicago newspaper [19 January 1906], clipping, box 2, WEWP.

23　Tanner: ASW in *Walling Symposium*, 7. Identification card: folder 483, ASWY. Fig Newtons: AWH, interview with author, 3 May 1996.

24　Kelley as chief inspector: Josephine Goldmark, *Impatient Crusader: Florence Kelley's Life Story* (1953), 36–41. Arrington's complaint: *Fifth Annual Report of the Factory Inspectors, Illinois, for the Year Ending December 15, 1897* (1898). Convention paper: WEW, "The Dangerous Trades," proceedings of the Fourteenth Annual Convention of the International Association of Factory Inspectors of America, Indianapolis, 2–5 October 1900, 35–42. Child labor essay: *Eighth Annual Report of the Factory Inspectors, Illinois, for the Year Ending December 15, 1900* (1901).

25　"This young lady": JL to Willoughby G. Walling, 31 July 1900, box 3A, ASWH.

26　Travel plans: WEW to parents, 9 and 15 March [1901]; "alligator hunt": WEW to parents, 25 March 1901, folder 263, ASWY.

27　Industrial Commission: described in William D. P. Bliss, ed., *The New Encyclopedia of Social Reform* (1908), 616; see also Martin J. Sklar, *The Corporate Reconstruction of American Capitalism, 1890–1916* (1988), 56–60.

28　Commons's career: *Myself: The Autobiography of John R. Commons* (1963), 50–78.

29 "The two brothers": Stone in *Walling Symposium*, 62.

30 Accountants and Book-keepers: certificate, 14 February 1902, box 3, WEWP. Stone account: *Walling Symposium*, 63–64.

31 "I envy you": quoted by Stone in *Walling Symposium*, 64. "Something radical": Willoughby Walling to father [March 1901], folder 278, ASWY.

32 "Shaking up": WEW to parents, 11 April 1902, folder 264, ASWY.

CHAPTER 9

1 "Come to the Settlement": Hunter to WEW, 1 April 1902, box 17, University Settlement Papers, State Historical Society of Wisconsin.

2 Toynbee Hall: Asa Briggs and Anne Macartney, *Toynbee Hall: The First Hundred Years* (1984). American settlement movement: Allen F. Davis, *Spearheads for Reform: The Social Settlements and the Progressive Movement, 1890–1914* (1967); Albert J. Kennedy, "The Settlement Method," typescript in box 1, supplement, Albert J. Kennedy Papers, Social Welfare History Archives, University of Minnesota; and Mina Carson, *Settlement Folk: Social Thought and the American Settlement Movement, 1885–1930* (1990). "Dear and distinguished": fiftieth-anniversary telegram, Toynbee Hall to University Settlement, 7 January 1937, box 3, Kennedy Papers.

3 Reynolds: John J. Carey article in *Biographical Dictionary of Social Welfare in America*, ed. Walter I. Trattner (1986). Reynolds and Citizens Union: Gerald W. McFarland, *Mugwumps, Morals and Politics, 1884–1920* (1975), 107–123. Hunter: transcript of article from *Co-Operation*, 22 March 1902, box 8, University Settlement Papers; story on appointment, *Charities*, 8 (28 March 1902): 289; Davis, *Spearheads for Reform*, 129.

4 Reynolds's continuation: *New York Tribune*, 23 June 1903.

5 "I wish you were to be in New York": Hunter to WEW, 19 June 1902; editorship: Hunter to Milo R. Maltbie, 5 September 1902, box 17, University Settlement Papers. "Perfect rest and freedom": WEW to parents, 24 September 1902, box 6, ASWH.

6 University Settlement building: James Graham Phelps Stokes to Albert J. Kennedy, 15 May 1931, box 4, James Graham Phelps Stokes Papers, Columbia University. "Too large a scale": *Seventeenth Annual Report of the University Settlement Society of New York . . . Report for 1903*, 28. Women's Auxiliary: Albert J. Kennedy notes, box 18, University Settlement Papers. Fireplace: Stokes to Walter Leo Solomon, 18 August 1926, box 4, Stokes Papers.

7 Architects: Stokes to Kennedy, 15 May 1931, box 4, Stokes Papers; *New York Herald*, 5 June 1898, clipping, box 4, Stokes Papers; Deborah S. Gardner, "Practical Philanthropy: The Phelps-Stokes Fund and Housing," *Prospects* 15 (1990): 359–411. "Most fashionable charity": WEW to parents, fragment [November 1902], folder 265, ASWY.

8 Stokes family: Gardner, "Practical Philanthropy." Boards and committees: Stokes to Kennedy, 15 May 1931, box 4, Stokes Papers. "Trained monkey": "The New York Sickness," *Springfield Republican*, 30 November 1902, clipping, box 4, Stokes Papers.

9 "Exquisites": Robert A. Woods, quoted in Robert C. Reinders, "Toynbee Hall and the American Settlement Movement," *Social Service Review* 56 (March 1982): 39–54 (45). "Solicitude of 'settlements' ": Thorstein Veblen, *The Theory of the*

Leisure Class: An Economic Study in the Evolution of Institutions (1899), chap.
13, "Survivals of the Non-Invidious Interest."

10 "Noble work" and "uplifter": Brubaker in *Walling Symposium*, 36. "Life among
the lowly": Poole in *Walling Symposium*, 24.

11 "High-strung": Poole in *Walling Symposium*, 21. "Opened its rooms": Brubaker
in *Walling Symposium*, 37.

12 Settlement activities: *University Settlement Bulletin*, December 1902; *Sixteenth
Annual Report of the University Settlement Society of New York: Report for
1902.* Exercise class: Poole in *Walter Weyl: An Appreciation*, ed. Bertha Poole
Weyl (1922), 47. "Labor and Social Movements": Leroy Scott to Stokes, 12 No-
vember 1902, box 4, Stokes Papers. "What was expected": Brubaker in *Walling
Symposium*, 36. "That will be plenty": Poole in *Walling Symposium*, 23.

13 Contacts with Sullivan: Poole in *Walling Symposium*, 26; "Reform Grasps
'Tims'," *New York Tribune*, 18 June 1903; "Merry War in 'De Ate'," *New York
Tribune*, 23 June 1903. See Dan Czitrom, "Underworlds and Underdogs: Big Tim
Sullivan and Metropolitan Politics in New York," *Journal of American History* 78
(September 1991): 536–58.

14 City Club: Hunter to Trustees of the City Club, 10 December 1902, box 17,
University Settlement Papers; McFarland, *Mugwumps, Morals and Politics*, 93.
"Walling's immense program": Hunter, quoted in Albert J. Kennedy notes, box 8,
University Settlement Papers. Poole's rise: Ernest Poole, *The Bridge: My Own
Story* (1940).

CHAPTER 10

1 Page and *World's Work*: Christopher P. Wilson, "The Rhetoric of Consumption,"
in *The Culture of Consumption: Critical Essays in American History, 1880–
1980*, ed. Richard Wightman Fox and T. J. Jackson Lears (1983), 39–64; Burton J.
Hendrick, *The Training of an American: The Earlier Life and Letters of Walter H.
Page, 1855–1913* (1928). Capital of the New South: Isaac Marcosson, quoted in
Frank Luther Mott, "The World's Work," in *History of American Magazines*,
4:773–88 (780).

2 "Long talk": WEW to father, 22 November [1902]; "delayed invitation": WEW to
parents, 19 December [1902]; "series of articles": WEW to father, 22 January 1903,
folder 264, ASWY.

3 Article on Hearst: "The Mission of Mr. Hearst," *Wilshire's Magazine* 5 (April
1903): 28–32.

4 Mardi Gras: WEW to father, 17 January 1903, folder 264, ASWY. Willoughby and
California: WEW to parents, 7 March 1903; "April fool": WEW to parents, 4 April
1903, folder 264, ASWY.

5 Hunter's engagement: *New York Tribune*, 17 April 1903; *NYT*, 18 April 1903.
Stokes resignation: Stokes to William M. Sloane, chairman of council, 20 April
1903, box 4, University Settlement Papers. Hunter resignation: *New York Tribune*, 29 April and 21 June 1903.

6 Hunter-Stokes wedding: *NYT*, 24 May 1903; *New York World*, 24 May 1903. Celtic: *NYT*, 30 May 1903.

7 Settlement plan: *New York Tribune*, 13 July 1903. Stokes-Pastor interview: Rose
Harriet Pastor, "The Views of a Settlement Worker," *Jewish Daily News*, undated

clipping, folder 2, Rose Pastor Stokes Papers, Yale University. Xenophobia: review of Robert Hunter, *Poverty* (1904), *Independent* 58 (12 January 1905): 97–99.

8   Hamilton: *New York Tribune*, 16 September 1903; *Charities* 11 (19 September 1903): 235.

9   Lost on Mt. Marcy: Raymond Ingersoll in *Walling Symposium*, 96. *World's Work* article: WEW, "Building Trades and the Unions," 6 (August 1903): 3790–94. "I entirely agree": WEW to parents, 24 August [1903], box 1, WEWP.

10 "I have decided": WEW to parents, 24 August [1903], box 1, WEWP.

11 Weyl: Charles Forcey, *The Crossroads of Liberalism: Croly, Weyl, Lippmann, and the Progressive Era 1900–1925* (1961). Arguments: Ernest Poole in *Walter Weyl: An Appreciation*, 36.

12 Trip to Boston: WEW to parents, 9 October 1903, folder 264, ASWY; Poole in *Walling Symposium*, 22–23; Forcey, *Crossroads of Liberalism*, 69. Women in unions: Nancy Schrom Dye, *As Equals and Sisters: Feminism, Unionism, and the Women's Trade Union League of New York* (1980), 14–17.

13 Creation of WTUL: Dye, *As Equals and Sisters*, 38–44; Philip S. Foner, *History of the Labor Movement in the United States*, vol. 3, *The Policies and Practices of the American Federation of Labor, 1900–1909* (1964), 228–31; Rose Schneiderman in *Walling Symposium*, 82–83.

14 New York activity: Dye, *As Equals and Sisters*, 38; Mari Jo Buhle, *Women and American Socialism, 1870–1920* (1983), 188–90. Historical recognition: WEW to Elizabeth Christman, secretary-treasurer, WTUL, 11 May 1929, box 1, WEWP.

15 "Popular front": T. D. Seymour Bassett, "The Secular Utopian Socialists," in *Socialism and American Life*, ed. Donald Drew Egbert and Stow Persons, 2 vols. (1952), 1:176. Friend of settlement: Hunter to Brisbane, 28 May 1903, Series 4, University Settlement Papers.

16 "Brilliantly points a moral": WEW, "The Mission of Mr. Hearst," 32. "Strong impression": WEW to parents [early 1904], box 1, WEWP. "Everything is going beautifully": WEW to father, 29 January [1904], folder 265, ASWY.

17 Hearst's campaign for president: W. A. Swanberg, *Citizen Hearst: A Biography of William Randolph Hearst* (1961), 208–29. "Hearst Campaign": WEW to father, 3 February 1904, folder 265, ASWY.

18 Stokes and Hearst: C. J. Mar, Hearst Syndicate, to Stokes, 15 January, 3 and 13 February 1904, box 19, Stokes Papers. "Brilliant record": *New York Evening Journal*, 28 February 1904, clipping, box 19, Stokes Papers. "Little dinner party": Stokes to mother, 28 February 1904, box 85, Stokes Papers.

CHAPTER 11

1   *The Independent*: Frank Luther Mott, *A History of American Magazines*, vol. 2, *1850–1865* (1938), 367–79; articles in the sixtieth anniversary issue, 65 (10 December 1908). Holt: Warren F. Kuehl, *Hamilton Holt: Journalist, Internationalist, Educator* (1960). *The World To-Day*: Mott, *History of American Magazines*, 4: 455, 499–500.

2   Construction trades: WEW, "The Labor Truce in New York," *World To-Day* 6 (March 1904): 346–52.

3   Bahamas: WEW to father, 11 March 1904; "World's Work article": WEW to father, 29 March [1904], folder 265, ASWY.

4   Baker as a journalist: John E. Semonche, *Ray Stannard Baker: A Quest for Democracy in Modern America, 1870–1918* (1969).

5   *McClure's*: Harold S. Wilson, *McClure's Magazine and the Muckrakers* (1970), 129–47. Weyl and anthracite strike: Weyl, "Award of Anthracite Coal Strike Commission," *Review of Reviews* 27 (April 1903):460–64; Commons, *Myself*, 92.

6   Baker at University Settlement: Poole, *The Bridge*, 72–73. "This time I was very careful": WEW to father, 3 February 1904, folder 265, ASWY.

7   Baker articles: "The Trust's New Tool—The Labor Boss," *McClure's* 22 (November 1903): 30–43; "The Lone Fighter," *McClure's* 22 (December 1903): 194–97.

8   Cripple Creek strike: Foner, *History of the Labor Movement*, 3:395–400; Benjamin McKie Rastall, *The Labor History of the Cripple Creek District: A Study in Industrial Evolution*, Bulletin of the University of Wisconsin, Economics and Political Science Series, 3 (February 1908); J. Anthony Lukas, *Big Trouble: A Murder in a Small Western Town Sets Off a Struggle for the Soul of America* (1997).

9   WEW articles: "The Great Cripple Creek Strike," *Independent* 56 (10 March 1904): 539–48; "The Labor 'Rebellion' in Colorado," *Independent* 57 (18 August 1904): 376–82. Baker article: "The Reign of Lawlessness," *McClure's* 23 (May 1904): 43–57.

10 "The Open Shop Means the Destruction of Unions": *Independent* 56 (12 May 1904): 1069–72. "Right and just": WEW to father, 18 May [1904], box 1, WEWP.

11 Baker on open shop: "Organized Capital Challenges Organized Labor," *McClure's* 23 (July 1904): 279–92. Lower East Side: Baker, "The Rise of the Tailors," *McClure's* 24 (December 1904): 279–82. Pressure at *McClure's*: Semonche, *Ray Stannard Baker*, 120–25.

12 Poole in Chicago: Poole, *The Bridge*, 92–97. Shooting elk: WEW to parents, 22 August 1904; "twice as long": WEW to parents, 30 July 1904, folder 265, ASWY. Essay: "The New Unionism—the Problem of the Unskilled Worker," *Annals of the American Academy of Political and Social Sciences* 24 (September 1904), 296–315.

13 "Plans for next year": Hamilton to WEW, 24 August 1904, box 17, University Settlement Papers.

14 Scott resignation and Miriam Finn: Kennedy notes, box 18, and questionnaire, box 27, University Settlement Papers. Durland: Hamilton to James Speyer, 25 May 1904; "with all his faults": Hamilton to Speyer, 28 May 1904, box 17, University Settlement Papers.

15 Bullard: *University Settlement Studies*, including *Eighteenth Annual Report of the University Settlement Society* (March 1905); longhand biographical summary in folder 2, Arthur Bullard Papers, Seeley G. Mudd Manuscript Library, Princeton University.

16 Election analysis: WEW, "The Labor Vote," *Independent* 57 (24 November 1904), 1188–90. AFL convention: WEW to parents, 18 November 1904, folder 265, ASWY. Reports on AFL: "The Convention of the American Federation of Labor," *World To-day* 8 (January 1905): 89–91; "The Defeats of Labor," *Independent* 58 (28 February 1905): 418–22.

CHAPTER 12

1   Bloody Sunday: Walter Sablinsky, *The Road to Bloody Sunday: Father Gapon and the St. Petersburg Massacre of 1905* (1976). American reaction to Bloody Sunday: Arthur W. Thompson and Robert A. Hart, *The Uncertain Crusade: America and*

the Russian Revolution of 1905 (1970); and Arthur W. Thompson, "The Reception of Russian Revolutionary Leaders in America, 1904–1906," *American Quarterly* 18 (Fall 1966): 452–76. *NYT* headline: 23 January 1905. See also the *New York World* and *New York Evening Journal* for 23 January 1905 and days following. Reaction of ambassadors: Thompson and Hart, *Uncertain Crusade*, 30.

2 Bullard's report: "Massacre at St. Petersburg and the Russian East Side," *Independent* 58 (2 February 1905): 252–56.

3 Friends of Russian Freedom and links with settlement workers: Thompson, "Reception," 453–61. Breshkovsky visit: Alice Stone Blackwell, ed., *The Little Grandmother of the Russian Revolution: Reminiscences and Letters of Catherine Breshkovsky* (1917), 110–30. Poole article: "Katharine Bereshkovsky [*sic*]: A Russian Revolutionist," *Outlook* 79 (7 January 1905): 78–88. See also Catherine Breschkovsky [*sic*], "The Internal Condition of Russia," *Independent* 58 (5 January 1905): 12–16.

4 Poole and *Outlook*: Ernest Poole, "Maxim Gorki in New York," *Slavonic and East European Review* 22 (1944): 77–83; Truman Frederick Keefer, "The Literary Career and Literary Productions of Ernest Poole, American Novelist" (Ph.D. diss., Duke University, 1961), 83–85.

5 WEW assistance: Poole, *The Bridge*, 113; Poole in *Walling Symposium*, 27–28.

6 Disguised story: Poole, " 'St. Petersburg Is Quiet,' " *Outlook* 79 (18 March 1905): 681–90.

7 Leaving Women's Trade Union League: National WTUL minutes, 25 March 1905, cited in Stuart, "William English Walling," 26–27. Intercollegiate Socialist Society: WEW signed a proposal dated June 1905, box 25, Stokes Papers. Ely assignment: Ely to WEW, 27 April 1905; WEW to Ely, 2 May 1905, box 31, Richard T. Ely Papers, State Historical Society of Wisconsin. "An American Socialism": *International Socialist Review* 5 (April 1905): 577–84; La Monte reply: "Veblen the Revolutionist," *International Socialist Review* 5 (June 1905): 726–39.

8 Good-by to parents: WEW to mother, 17 April 1905; WEW to father, 19 April 1905, folder 265, ASWY. Anecdotal journalism: for example, Poole's interview, "The Night that Made Me a Revolutionist," *Everybody's Magazine* 13 (November 1905): 635–40. "Glamorous writing adventure": Poole, *The Bridge*, 166.

9 Poole and WEW in London: Keefer, "Literary Career of Ernest Poole," 97–100; Poole in *Walling Symposium*, 28. Stokes-Pastor engagement: "J.G. Phelps Stokes to Wed Young Jewess," *NYT*, 6 April 1905.

10 "Little hotel" WEW to parents, 12 June 1905, folder 265, ASWY.

11 Longuet: Longuet in *Walling Symposium*, 30. Phillips: WEW to parents, 12 June 1905, folder 265, ASWY.

12 "Several American friends": WEW to parents, 12 June 1905. "Better and better": WEW to parents, 30 June [1905], box 1, WEWP.

13 Meeting Grunspan: testimony of Anna Berthe Grunspan, reported in *New York World*, 21 February 1911. WEW did not challenge Grunspan's account of these circumstances.

14 Grunspan account of liaison: *New York World*, 21 February 1911; WEW account: *New York World*, 2 March 1911.

15 "I hate goodbyes": Poole in *Walling Symposium*, 28–29.

16 Trip to Poland: Grunspan account, *New York Evening Journal*, 21 February 1911; WEW account, *New York World*, 2 March 1911. "Offer of company": WEW to parents, 23 July [1905], box 1, WEWP.

17 Lodz situation: WEW to parents, 23 July [1905], box 1, WEWP. "Armed with confidential letters": WEW, "Revolution in Poland," *Independent* 59 (2 November 1905): 1040–42.

18 Berlin incident: Grunspan testimony, *New York World*, 25 February 1911; WEW testimony, *New York World*, 2 March 1911.

19 Border incident: Grunspan testimony, *New York World*, 21 February 1911; WEW testimony, *New York World*, 2 March 1911.

20 "The trip prolonged itself": WEW to parents, 23 July [1905], box 1, WEWP.

21 "Over-work": WEW to parents [August 1905], box 1, WEWP. WEW articles: "Revolution in Poland"; "The Siege of Warsaw," *World To-Day* 9 (December 1905): 1304–6.

22 "Change partners": WEW to parents, 23 July [1905], box 1, WEWP. Henry Moskowitz: Elisabeth Israels Perry, *Belle Moskowitz: Feminine Politics and the Exercise of Power in the Age of Alfred E. Smith* (1987), 99–101; Robert A. Woods and Albert J. Kennedy, *The Settlement Horizon: A National Estimate* (1922), 196.

23 "A Roumanian Jew": WEW to parents, 23 July [1905], box 1, WEWP.

24 "Residents who can regularly be relied on": Hamilton to WEW, 16 August 1905, box 9, University Settlement Papers.

25 "I therefore take her to Geneva": WEW, notes on breach of promise suit, box 2, WEWP. Train to Paris: WEW testimony, *New York World*, 2 March 1911. Pitman school: *New York World*, 24 February, 2 and 3 March 1911.

26 Masaryks: WEW to parents [September 1905]; WEW to parents, 4 October [1905], folder 265, ASWY. Shipments to Ely: WEW to Ely, 4 October [1905], box 32, Ely Papers. "Improved French & German": WEW to parents, 10 October [1905], folder 265, ASWY.

27 "*Ethical* for *esthetic*": WEW to parents [4 October 1905], folder 265, ASWY. "It is a hot one": Walling to parents, 16 October [1905]; "we 'jewed' the Turks down": WEW to mother, 23 October [1905], box 1, WEWP.

28 "God help him": WEW to parents, fragment [September 1905], folder 265, ASWY.

Part Three

CHAPTER 13

1 "Russian Review": AS to Katia, 9 February 1905, folder 113, ASWY.

2 "Long live the Revolution": AS to Katia, 9 February 1905, folder 113, ASWY.

3 Stanford visit: AS diary, 12 February 1905, folder 301, ASWY. Wilson: newspaper article quoted in AS diary, 18 February 1905, folder 301, ASWY; AS to Katia, 19 February and 4 March 1905, folder 113, ASWY. Memorial service: AS diary, 24 and 25 March 1905, folder 301, ASWY.

4 "I refused myself": AS diary, 19 February 1905, folder 301, ASWY.

5 "Awaken to true love": AS diary, 22 March 1907, folder 301, ASWY. "But the heart is gone out of me": AS to Katia, 4 March 1905, folder 113, ASWY.

6 "I have finished": AS to Katia, 19 February 1905, folder 113, ASWY. Letter waiting: AS to Katia, 4 March 1905, folder 113, ASWY. "The Cause": Brett to AS, 7 February 1905; short story: Brett (acknowledging AS's letter) to AS, 6 March 1905; novel finished: Brett to AS, 16 May 1905, Brett letterbooks, MACM. "In Mr. Brett's hands": AS to Katia, 6 May 1905, folder 113, ASWY.

7 Friends of Russian Freedom: AS to Katia, 8 April 1905, folder 113, ASWY. Committee roster: pamphlet [April 1905], folder 370, ASWY.

8 "I almost shouted with delight": WEW to AS [April 1905], folder 210, ASWY. *War of the Classes*: negative evaluations by George Rice Carpenter (Carpenter to Brett, 19 September 1903) and "H.W.M.," box 86, MACM.

9 Ruskin Club dinner: JL to AS, 6 April 1903, *LJL*, 1:359. Thanksgiving picnic: ASW diary, Thanksgiving [29 November] 1934, folder 310, ASWY; Gillmore diary, 19 April 1908.

10 Postcard portfolio: WEW to AS [August 1905], folder 210, ASWY.

11 "They have butchered it": AS to Katia, 28 August 1905, folder 113, ASWY. *San Francisco Bulletin* article: 27 August 1905, clipping, box 2, SWB. Austin Lewis and JL reactions: JL to AS, 4 September 1905, *LJL*, 1:517.

12 "I am working day and night": AS to Katia, 1 November 1905, folder 113, ASWY.

13 Notes and dates: AS diary, October–November 1905, folder 301, ASWY. Round-robin: AS to Frederick I. Bamford, 6 November 1905, reprinted in Georgia Loring Bamford, *The Mystery of Jack London, Some of His Friends, also a Few Letters: A Reminiscence* (1931), 206; "nihilistic work": 201. "It takes strength and time": AS to RS, 13 November 1905, folder 86, ASWY.

14 "I reach for your hand": AS to Charmian Kittredge, 6 October 1905, folder 19857, JLH.

15 "The awful part of it": Elsie Whitaker Martinez, *San Francisco Bay Area Writers and Artists*, oral history interview by Franklin D. Walker and Willa Klug Baum, Regional Oral History Office, The Bancroft Library, University of California, Berkeley (1969), 128.

16 "Geneva is your fate": WEW to AS [November 1905], folder 210, ASWY.

17 "A little bomb": Agnes Foster Buchanan, "The Story of a Famous Fraternity of Writers and Artists," *Pacific Monthly* 17 (August 1907):74.

18 "Went directly from my couch," RS to Louis Levine, 13 December 1913, Louis Levine/Lorwin Papers, held by his son, Boris Lorwin. "Throbbing great-souled thing": RS to AS [November 1905], folder 86, ASWY.

19 Portrait: AS to Katia, 28 August 1905, folder 113, ASWY. Martinez was painting portraits of both sisters. The portrait of RS is now in the possession of her son, Boris Lorwin, who also has the portfolio of illustrated daily letters from Martinez to RS.

20 "I have caught the Geneva fever": RS to AS [November 1905], folder 86, ASWY.

21 Ruskin Club dinner: "Farewell Dinner Tendered to Miss Strunsky," newspaper article [November 1905], clipping lent by AWH.

22 "Bohemian friends": magazine page [December 1905], with photograph of AS, lent by AWH.

23 "His art was more important": Cameron King to AS, 20 January 1906, folder 73, ASWY.

24 "Heroically immolating": "Revolution Will Not Claim Miss Strunsky," *San Francisco Bulletin* [November 1905], clipping lent by AWH.

25 "She was always so sure": ASW, "The Golden Wedding," manuscript [1915], box 1, SWB.

CHAPTER 14

1 "I shall not run the slightest risk": WEW to mother, 28 November 1905, box 1, WEWP.

2 "There is no use going further": WEW to parents, 3 December 1905, folder 265,

ASWY. *American Federationist* was published by the American Federation of Labor.

3   "I have two friends": WEW to parents, 8 December 1905, box 6, ASWH. All dates are according to the Gregorian, or conventional, calendar rather than the Julian calendar used at that time in Russia, which then lagged thirteen days behind the Gregorian. For example, the Russian Christmas in 1905 fell on 6 January 1906, Gregorian.

4   "A young dude's romance": John Dos Passos, "A Hoosier Quixote," in *U.S.A.* (3 vols. in 1, 1937), vol. 2, *Nineteen-Nineteen,* 180.

5   "I am the only English speaking person": WEW to parents, 6 December 1905, box 6, ASWH.

6   "We are on the verge": WEW to father, 16 December 1905, box 1, WEWP.

7   "Moscow has been heard from": WEW to parents, 25 December 1905, box 1, WEWP. "'Tis passing dangerous here": WEW to Grunspan [December 1905], printed in *New York World,* 24 February 1911.

8   "Days of Liberty": This summary and subsequent references to developments in the revolution draw primarily on Abraham Ascher, *The Revolution of 1905,* 2 vols. (1988, 1992), 1:211–303.

9   Moscow uprising: Ascher, *Revolution of 1905,* 1:304–336. "I shall not visit the scene": WEW to parents, 25 December 1905, box 1, WEWP.

10 Articles by WEW: "'The Revolutionary Way'," *Independent* 60 (18 January 1906): 143–45; "The Social Revolution in Russia," *Independent* 60 (25 January 1906): 192–95; and "Moscow," *Independent* 60 (15 March 1906): 597–601.

11 Coverage of Moscow revolt: Arthur Bullard [Albert Edwards], "An Eye-witness's Story of the Russian Revolution," *Harper's Weekly* 50 (17 and 24 February, 3 March 1906): 228–29, 232, 258–61, 294–96. "After two hours": "Eye-witness's Story," 260.

12 "At last I am in a position": WEW to parents, 3 January 1906, folder 266, ASWY.

13 Appointments: AS diary-notebook, folder 301, ASWY. *New York American*: Hearst's secretary to Wilshire, 7 December 1905, folder 237, ASWY. Sedgwick note: Sedgwick to ASW, 24 January 1934 (second page only), enclosing a copy of Sedgwick to Birchall, 9 December [1905], folder 143, ASWY.

14 *Baltic* sails: NYT, 5 December 1905. "'Little girls'": Herbert M. Baer to AS, 15 December 1905, folder 32, ASWY. "I have resolved never to travel": AS to Katia, 18 December 1905, folder 113, ASWY. "You & Rose had better get passports": King to AS, 1 December 1905; he also wrote on 4, 18, and 29 December 1905, folder 73, ASWY.

15 "If pounds be the price of foolishness": "If blood be the price of admiralty, / Lord God, we ha' paid it in!" from "The Song of the Dead," in Rudyard Kipling, *Complete Verse* (Doubleday/Anchor ed., 1989), 173. A parody of the poem, set to music, later became a hymn of the Industrial Workers of the World: "If blood be the price of your cursed wealth / Good God! We have paid it in." See "We Have Fed You All for a Thousand Years," in *Rebel Voices: An I.W.W. Anthology,* ed. Joyce L. Kornbluh (1964), 29.

16 Went to Geneva: AS diary, December 1905, folder 301, ASWY. Exiles returned to Russia: ASW, autobiographical fragment, folder 363, ASWY. "I am sure I can make a success": AS to Dr. Max Strunsky, 24 December 1905, box 5, ASWH.

17 "When my book comes out": AS to father, 28 December 1905; "I promise you it is *not* the last money": AS to father, 29 December 1905, box 5, ASWH.

18 "Note for article": AS diary, 29 December 1905, folder 301, ASWY.

19 "Malicious and wicked newspaper reports": James H. Hamilton to Dr. Henry M. Leipziger, 23 September 1905, box 17, University Settlement Papers, State Historical Society of Wisconsin. Incident on train: Kellogg Durland, *The Red Reign: The True Story of an Adventurous Year in Russia* (1907), 5–6.

20 "Professional newspaper writer": WEW to father, typescript dated 24 February 1906, probably earlier, folder 266, ASWY.

21 Invitation to Caucasus: Durland, *Red Reign,* 23.

22 "About midway to the station": Durland to WEW [January–February 1906], box 2, ASWH. "Worst smelling train": Bullard to WEW [January–February 1906], box 1, SWB.

23 "The clever California girls": WEW to parents, 3 January 1906, folder 266, ASWY.

CHAPTER 15

1 "Come some way": WEW to AS, telegram [1 January 1906], folder 210, ASWY.

2 Passports: AS to father, 22 January 1906, box 5, ASWH.

3 "I sat in the train": ASW, "Revolutionary Lives," 10–11.

4 "He met us at the train": AS diary, 14 September 1906, folder 301, ASWY.

5 "That we should be here": ASW, "Revolutionary Lives," 11.

6 "On the streets": ASW, "Revolutionary Lives," 11–12.

7 "All day long": ASW, "Revolutionary Lives," 13.

8 "We were not suspected": ASW, "Revolutionary Lives," 13.

9 "Rosie always writes some news": Morris Strunsky, quoted in Cameron King to AS, 20 January 1906, folder 73, ASWY. "Dearest heart": AS to father, 28 December 1905, box 5, ASWH. Letter from frontier: noted in King to AS, 22 January 1905, folder 73, ASWY.

10 "I could tell you of letters": Hyman Strunsky to AS [April 1906], folder 156, ASWY. "Jolly your mother": King to AS, 14 February 1906, folder 73, ASWY.

11 New Year's Eve incident: ASW, fragments of "Revolutionary Lives" manuscript, folder 387, ASWY. The incident is mentioned in John Bushnell, "The Tsarist Officer Corps, 1881–1914: Customs, Duties, Inefficiency," *American Historical Review* 86 (October 1981): 753–80 (760n).

12 Arrest report: "Russian Police Arrest William E. Walling," *NYT,* 19 January 1906. Captain English: "Uncle Not Surprised," article in Chicago newspaper, 19 January 1906, clipping, box 2, WEWP; William E. English to Willoughby and Rosalind Walling (WEW's parents), 18 January 1906, and Senator Beveridge to Captain English, telegram, 18 January 1906, folder 282, ASWY. Hibben message: telegram to Captain English, 19 January 1906, box 1, WEWP. Cleared up: "Mr. Walling Not Arrested," *NYT,* 20 January 1906.

13 "Real and unreal": ASW, "Revolutionary Lives," 15.

14 "Forced our love": AS to father, undated fragment, box 5, ASWH. "Then New Year's Eve": AS to Hyman Strunsky, 3 March 1906, box 5, ASWH.

15 "The moment I discovered": WEW to parents, 29 January 1906, folder 266, ASWY.

16 "We refused to believe our hearts": AS to Rosalind Walling, 21 February 1906, folder 194, ASWY.

17 Mistress: RS, quoted indirectly, Gillmore diary, 12 April 1908.

18 "We are in the city": AS to father, 19 January 1906, box 5, ASWH.

19 "If Mr. Walling had not cabled": AS to father, 22 January 1906, box 5, ASWH.

20 Article in *New York World*: [January 21, 1906] fragment, folder 384, ASWY.

21 "A really very serious heart affair": WEW to parents, 26 January 1906, folder 266, ASWY.

22 "Henceforth I am no longer alone": AS diary, February [1906], folder 301, ASWY.

CHAPTER 16

1 Homel pogrom: "Cossacks Massacre Jews," *NYT*, 31 January 1906; *New York World*, 30 January 1906.

2 Pogroms: Ascher cites estimates that 690 incidents of anti-Jewish violence occurred in October 1905 alone; *Revolution of 1905*, 1:255.

3 "My heart has watched": AS to WEW, 19 January [1 February Western] 1906, box 5, ASWH.

4 "Slavonic indolence": RS to AS [February 1906], folder 86, ASWY.

5 Letter from Vilna: AS to WEW, 22 January [4 February] 1906, box 5, ASWH.

6 "Love and Kisses": AS to WEW, telegram [February 1906], folder 210, ASWY. "I feared that the spell": ASW, *The Homel Massacre*, pamphlet, New York Section, Council of Jewish Women (1914).

7 First day in Homel: Account is quoted or summarized from ASW, *Homel Massacre*.

8 "Nasha Zhizn": St. Petersburg newspaper sympathetic to the Social Revolutionaries; Ascher, *Revolution of 1905*, 1:383.

9 "I had altogether a terrible time": AS to RS, 25 January [7 February] 1906, folder 86, ASWY. "The sister of charity": undated fragment, box 6, ASWH.

10 "If they should come here tonight": ASW, *Homel Massacre*.

11 Photographs of victims: prints in box 7, ASWH.

12 Interview with Orlov: ASW, *Homel Massacre*.

13 Departure from Homel: ASW, *Homel Massacre*.

14 "I am too broken up": AS to Katia, January [February] 1906, folder 113, ASWY.

15 Homel article: For example, "Soon you will read a long article of the Hommel pogrom," in AS to father, [February 1906], Box 5, ASWH.

CHAPTER 17

1 "Only a question of time": quoted in WEW to parents [February 1906], folder 266, ASWY. "I thank God": mother to AS [translated by AS], 15 February 1906, box 4, ASWH.

2 "If he is the best": father to AS, 15 February 1906, folder 150, ASWY; father to AS, 16 February 1906, folder 153, ASWY.

3 "Surprised and anxious": Father to WEW, cablegram, 17 February 1906, folder 266, ASWY.

4 "The greatest laugh": WEW to father [February 1906], folder 266, ASWY. "The sudden news": mother to WEW, fragment [February 1906], folder 266, ASWY.

5 "Nothing done": WEW to father, cablegram, 19 February 1906, folder 266, ASWY. "Had your two cablegrams": WEW to father [20 February 1906], folder 266, ASWY.

6 "A queer time to fall in love": AS to Rosalind Walling, 24 February 1906, folder 194, ASWY.

7 "I haven't been a fool": WEW to mother [February–March 1906], box 1, WEWP.

8 Grunspan revelation: confirmed in ASW testimony, *New York World*, 4 March

1911. "Thank you for that *wicked, cruel* letter": Grunspan to WEW [February–March 1906], quoted in *New York World*, 24 February 1911.

9   "Tell me exactly": King to AS, 14 February 1906, folder 73, ASWY. AS's cable is quoted in this letter.

10 "I wanted you for my wife": King to AS, 15 March 1906, folder 73, ASWY.

11 "You write of fearing": King to AS, 4 April 1906, folder 73, ASWY. "I will speak thy speech": Browning, "A Woman's Last Word" (1855).

12 "I ought to be satisfied": King to AS, fragment [April 1906], folder 73, ASWY.

13 "As to Cammie": Jane Roulston to AS, 26 July 1906, box 1, WEWP.

14 Know her better: Durland to AS, undated, box 1, ASWH. "I thrive and grow fat": Durland to WEW, 7 March 1906, box 2, ASWH. Hole up in Moscow: Bullard to WEW [March 1906], box 1, SWB.

15 Going to Moscow: WEW to father, 1 April 1906, folder 266, ASWY. Always remembered: ASW diary, 20 April 1935, box 1, SWB. Snapshots: a print is in the Melville Anderson Papers, Stanford University, copy sent by Patricia White of the university libraries; other prints are owned by AWH.

16 "Too much excitement": AS to Katia, 12 April 1906, folder 113, ASWY.

17 Moscow newspaper office: manuscript fragment, probably written in English by a Russian, box 7, ASWH. "We can conveniently return": AS to family, cablegram [25 April 1906], folder 153, ASWY; "suspense terrible": AS to Max Strunsky, cablegram, 29 April 1906, folder 157, ASWY. Cables to St. Petersburg: King to AS, 13 May 1906, folder 73, ASWY.

18 Cable: AS to Katia, 2–3 May 1906, folder 113, ASWY. Letter from father: noted in AS to Hyman Strunsky, 18 May 1906, box 5, ASWH. "The chief sufferer": AS to Rosalind Walling [20 May 1906], folder 194, ASWY.

19 Postcards: King to AS, 13 May 1906, folder 73, ASWY. "I am weary": JL, quoted in AS to Max Strunsky, 11 May 1906, box 5, ASWH. Cameron King sent an account of the earthquake to AS; the original is in box 2, ASWH; it was printed in Mary McD. Gordon, "Earthquake and Fire in San Francisco," *Huntington Library Quarterly* (1985): 69–79.

20 "We did not think": AS to Rosalind Walling [20 May 1906], folder 194, ASWY.

CHAPTER 18

1   British royalties: JL to AS, 22 February 1906, box 3, ASWH. "You see, how my love": AS to JL [spring 1906], folder 82, ASWY.

2   "We will never have a home": AS to Hyman Strunsky, 31 March 1906; A Club: AS to Hyman Strunsky, 3 March 1906, box 5, ASWH.

3   "I adapt myself so easily": AS to Rosalind Walling [April 1906], folder 194, ASWY.

4   "We are equals": AS to Rosalind Walling [April 1906], folder 194, ASWY. "English and I will write a book": AS to parents [?], fragment [March 1906], box 7, ASWH.

5   "English doesn't trust me": AS to parents [?], fragment [March 1906], box 7, ASWH. "She cant sew very well": WEW to father [spring 1906], folder 266, ASWY.

6   "Everyone loves her": WEW to parents, fragment [spring 1906], folder 266, ASWY.

7   AS's standing as writer: WEW to father [March 1906], folder 266, ASWY.

8   "A marvellous psychological romance": WEW to father [March 1906], folder 266, ASWY.

9   "Anna and I begin to see our lives": WEW to Elias Strunsky, 22 April 1906, folder 259, ASWY.

10 Wedding plans: AS to father, 19 March 1906, box 5, ASWH.
11 "A religious ceremony would be farcical": AS to Rosalind Walling [April 1906], from Moscow, folder 194, ASWY.
12 "Full harvest time": WEW to parents [May 1906], box 1, WEWP.
13 "We are together": WEW to parents [23 March 1906], folder 266, ASWY.
14 "Historic procession": ASW, "Revolutionary Lives," fragment, folder 387, ASWY.
15 "We will go around the corner": AS to Max Strunsky, 13–14 May 1906, box 5, ASWH.

CHAPTER 19

1 "The spiritual isolation": AS diary [May 1906], folder 301, ASWY. Conversation with Tolstoy: RS, "Tolstoi and Young Russia," *Atlantic* 107 (April 1911): 490–97. Copy of *The Kempton-Wace Letters*: Vil Bykov, "Anna Strunsky's Parcel," *Ogonek* 4 (January 1965), typescript translation lent by AWH.
2 "Great resort of Jewish families": Karl Baedeker, *Paris and Environs*, 18th rev. ed. (1913), 397. "Wonderful and perfect accord": WEW to parents, 24 June [1906], box 6, ASWH.
3 Incident at Place de l'Opéra: WEW's account reported in *New York World*, 3 March 1911; ASW's in *New York World*, 4 March 1911. See also materials on Grunspan in box 2, WEWP.
4 Coverage of engagement: *Chicago American* [June 1906], clipping lent by AWH. "Socialism Finds Bride": newspaper article [June 1906], clipping; "William English Willing": *San Francisco Call*, 16 June 1905, clipping, folder 435, ASWY.
5 Account of wedding: AS to family, 1 July 1906, box 5, ASWH.
6 *Livret de famille*: folder 437, ASWY.
7 "We got legally married": AS to Max Strunsky, 9 July 1906, box 5, ASWH.
8 "That is why he has refused": AS to unknown correspondent, fragment [probably April 1906], box 5, ASWH.
9 "Momma does not seem to understand": AS to Max Strunsky, 9 July 1906, box 5, ASWH.
10 "It was an authoritative note": AS diary, 11 July 1906, folder 304, ASWY.
11 "Neither English nor I": AS to Wallings, 29 July 1906, folder 194, ASWY.
12 "I know that my criticisms": Dr. Walling to AS, 20 July 1906, box 6, ASWH.
13 Revolution: Ascher, *Revolution of 1905*, 2:227–63. "Reaction is in full swing": AS to Wallings, 29 July 1906, folder 194, ASWY.
14 Travel without Rose: WEW to parents, postcards [August 1906], folder 266, ASWY. Long letter explaining: WEW to parents, 19 August 1906, copy lent by AWH. Durland undercover: Durland, *Red Reign*, 209–22.

Part Four

CHAPTER 20

1 RS-Bullard romance: RS to AS, 27 February 1908, folder 86, ASWY.
2 Peasant revolt: Abraham Ascher, *The Revolution of 1905*, 2 vols. (1988, 1992), 2:111–28.
3 Marriage unconsummated: AWH, interview with author, 15 June 1992.
4 "English is standing at the desk": AS diary, 12 [25] August 1906, folder 302, ASWY.

5 "I am bankrupt of all ideas": AS diary, 12 [25] August 1906, folder 302, ASWY.

6 "Terrible finalities": AS diary, 16 and 17 [29 and 30] August 1906, folder 302, ASWY.

7 "Every day I discover": AS diary, "Kazan to Simbirsk" [1 September 1906], folder 302, ASWY.

8 "The book with English": AS diary [September 1906], folder 302, ASWY.

9 "I have to take from him": AS diary, "On board to Saratoff" [September 1906], folder 302, ASWY.

10 "There are two forces": AS diary [October 1906], folder 302, ASWY.

11 "The other who praised me": AS diary, Paris, 25 October 1906, folder 302, ASWY.

12 "He is torn with impatience": AS diary, 29 October 1906, folder 302, ASWY.

13 "My dear Anna is distressed": WEW, untitled document, folder 276, ASWY.

14 "Russia's desperate struggle": "The Peasant Gives His Orders": *Independent* 61 (18 October 1906): 905–10.

15 "Beautiful passage": WEW to father, telegram, 13 November 1906, folder 266, ASWY.

CHAPTER 21

1 Gorky visit: Ernest Poole, "Maxim Gorki in New York," *Slavonic and East European Review* 22 (1944): 77–83; M. R. Werner, "L'Affaire Gorky," *New Yorker*, 30 April 1949, 56. American distaste for revolution: Arthur W. Thompson, "The Reception of Russian Revolutionary Leaders in America, 1904–1906," *American Quarterly* 18 (Fall 1966): 452–76.

2 "Charmed fathers soul": WEW to RS, fragment [November 1906], box 1, WEWP. "Dear beautiful woman": AS to Katia, 11 December 1906, folder 113, ASWY.

3 "Not only private": WEW to RS [November 1906], folder 257, ASWY. *Chicago Examiner* interview: 23 November 1906, clipping lent by AWH.

4 "Scorns the Name of Wife": *Chicago Daily News*, 1 December 1906, clipping lent by AWH.

5 Indianapolis coverage: "She Marries, But Keeps Own Name," article in Indianapolis newspaper, 6 December 1906, clipping lent by AWH. "Sense & dignity": RS to AS, 11 January 1907, folder 86, ASWY.

6 Hull-House appearance: handbill, box 3, WEWP. WEW articles: "Will the Peasants Act?" *Independent* 61 (6 December 1906): 1315–23; "The Call to the Young Russians," *Charities* 17 (1 December 1906): 373–76.

7 Visit to Indiana: AS to Katia, 11 December 1906, folder 113, ASWY.

8 "Driven to despair": "The A Club's Object," *New York Tribune*, 11 February 1906; also "Slum-Workers to Live in Fifth Ave.," *New York Tribune*, 8 February 1906.

9 Settlement associates: Ernest Poole, *The Bridge: My Own Story* (1940), 171–73; Holt: Warren F. Kuehl, *Hamilton Holt: Journalist, Internationalist, Educator* (1960), 46; Vorse: Dee Garrison, *Mary Heaton Vorse: The Life of an American Insurgent* (1989), 36–37. Gorky sheltered: Poole, "Maxim Gorki in New York," 81.

10 Reminiscences of A Club: Poole, *The Bridge*, 171–73.

11 Christmas ball: WEW to parents, 4 January 1907, folder 267, ASWY.

12 WEW articles: "Ominous Russian Famine," *Charities* 17 (2 February 1907): 785–88; "The Village Against the Czar," *Independent* 62 (7 March 1907): 587–94; "How Is It with the Russian Revolution?" *Outlook* 85 (9 March 1907): 564–67. Simeon Strunsky comment: reported in AS to Rosalind Walling, 22 April 1907, folder 194, ASWY.

13 "So sensitive is the Government": WEW, "How Is It with the Russian Revolution?" 566–67.

14 "How badly he looks:": AS to Katia [November–December 1906], folder 113, ASWY.

15 Sorrento activities: WEW to parents, 3 March 1907, folder 267, ASWY; AS to RS, postcard [March 1907], folder 149, ASWY.

16 Perlman: AS to Rose Strunsky, postcard [March 1907], folder 149, ASWY; Selig Perlman in *Walling Symposium*, 89.

17 New lovers: Mark Perlman, interviewed by Leon Fink, "A Memoir of Selig Perlman and His Life at the University of Wisconsin," *Labor History* 32 (Fall 1991): 503–25 (508). Medical counsel: AWH, interview with author, 15 June 1992. "Buon giorno": note [March 1907], folder 149, ASWY.

18 "Twice in my life": AS diary, 22 March 1907, folder 301, ASWY.

19 Travel: WEW to RS, 7 March [1907]; WEW to Strunskys, 31 March [1907], box 6, ASWH; AS to Rosalind Walling, 18 March 1907, folder 194, ASWY. "For the first time I can see": WEW to father, 10 June 1907, folder 267, ASWY.

20 "Still writing the Pogrom": AS to Katia, 10 June 1907, folder 114, ASWY. "I have a rather bad headache": AS to Anderson, 9 May 1907, box 5, ASWH.

21 "We did not dare lose time": AS to Katia, 20 July 1907, folder 114, ASWY.

22 Attendance at Stuttgart: WEW to father, 10 June 1907, folder 267, ASWY; Bullard, "The Revolutionist," manuscript on letterhead of Hotel Silber, Stuttgart, box 2, Arthur Bullard Papers, Seeley G. Mudd Manuscript Library, Princeton University. Delegates and resolutions: Barbara W. Tuchman, *The Proud Tower: A Portrait of the World before the War, 1890–1914* (1966), 446–50.

23 Odessa mutiny and pogrom: Ascher, *Revolution of 1905*, 1: 170–74, 255, 258. WEW, "The Real Russian People," *Independent* 63 (26 September 1907): 728–35 (735).

24 "Our trip among the peasants": AS to Rosalind Walling, 10 October 1907, box 5, ASWH.

CHAPTER 22

1 Scotts: RS to AS, 21 November 1906, folder 86, ASWY.

2 "Sitting open-eyed": RS, "An American Girl in a Prison of the Czar," *Independent* 65 (1 October 1908): 772–78 (773). "La jeunesse": RS to AS, 19 December 1906, folder 86, ASWY.

3 "Life has been rather exciting": RS to WEW, 28 October 1906, folder 257, ASWY. "Nick's leg": RS to AS [November 1906], folder 86, ASWY.

4 "Now, Anna, I know you": RS to AS [November 1906], folder 86, ASWY.

5 "Shelters all kinds of students": Gillmore diary, 12 April 1908.

6 "Big Fat Friend": RS to AS, 21 November 1906, folder 86, ASWY.

7 "The 'jeunesse' seem to be the only ones": RS to AS, 19 December 1906, folder 86, ASWY.

8 "Mouse-trap in Finland": Gillmore diary, 12 April 1908.

9 "Oh God I am so happy": RS to AS [1907], folder 86, ASWY. " 'Little Darling' ": *Forum* 45 (January 1911): 31–43. "Little Darling" was the translation of a Russian nickname that RS transliterated as *Maljutka*.

10 "Kissing the spies": RS to AS, 17 January 1907; "cartilage in your nose": RS to AS, 8 February 1907, folder 86, ASWY. "Walrusing": Michael R. Gordon in *NYT*, 14 March 1996. Helping Morris in Paris: RS to "Dear Children" [AS and WEW] [May 1907], box 3, ASWH. Murmansk run: Morris Strunsky obituary, *NYT*, 10 January 1977.

11 "They are connecting her with the young people": AS to Katia, 10 June 1907, folder 114, ASWY. "Wonderful months": RS to AS [April 1907], folder 86, ASWY.

12 Father's criticism: RS to AS, 4 and 6 October 1907, folder 86, ASWY. "Too much is enough": probably from William Blake, "Enough! Or too much," in "The Marriage of Heaven and Hell" (1790–93).

13 Malmberg incident and subsequent narrative: ASW, "Our Arrest," in "Revolutionary Lives," 310–24.

14 "When I opened the door": ASW, "Revolutionary Lives," 314.

15 Williams's wife: Ariadna Tyrkova-Williams wrote for the newspaper of the Constitutional Democrats (Kadets); Louise McReynolds, "Female Journalists in Prerevolutionary Russia," *Journalism History* 14 (Winter 1987): 104–110.

16 *Tovarisch* article: "About Wallings arrest" [October 1907], handwritten manuscript, folder 146, ASWY.

17 "Every face": ASW, "Revolutionary Lives," 317.

18 Durland's release: Kellogg Durland, *The Red Reign: The True Story of an Adventurous Year in Russia* (1907), 410–432. "No cause for anxiety": "William E. Walling Arrested in Russia," NYT, 21 October 1907. "I wish you could have seen your mother": Royal Freeman Nash to AS, 5 November 1907, box 4, ASWH.

19 "Arrest of Wallings": *Chicago American*, 21 October 1907, clipping, box 3, WEWP; "Harvard Men": *Boston Herald*, 24 October 1907, clipping, box 75, James Graham Phelps Stokes Papers, Columbia University. Root intercession: *Chicago Daily News*, 21 October 1907, clipping lent by AWH.

20 "The arrest worried me": AS to Katia, 31 October 1907, folder 114, ASWY.

21 "It is all talk about Rose": AS to Dr. Walling, 5 November 1907, folder 194, ASWY.

22 Materials returned: AS to Dr. Walling, 5 November 1907, folder 194, ASWY. "Departure voluntary": cable quoted in AS to Rosalind Walling, 31 October 1907, box 5, ASWH.

23 "Gives him the whip-hand": WEW to parents, 2 November 1907, folder 267, ASWY. RS, "An American Girl in a Prison of the Czar," 777.

24 "Idiots had no business": AS to Rosalind Walling, 31 October 1907, box 5, ASWH.

25 "I have now about three months": AS to Rosalind Walling, 31 October 1907, box 5, ASWH.

CHAPTER 23

1 Hôtel de la Trémoille: Karl Baedeker, *Paris and Environs*, 18th rev. ed. (1913), 7; Gillmore diary, 2 April 1908. Max Strunsky: WEW to father, 27 December 1907, box 1, WEWP; AS to Rosalind Walling, 27 January 1908, folder 195, ASWY.

2 "I hesitate to mention": WEW to Brett, 30 November 1907, folder 179, ASWY.

3 Contacts with Brett: Brett to WEW, 13 December 1907, box 3, ASWH; Brett to WEW, 20 December 1907, box 1, WEWP. "I took two days off": AS to Dr. Walling, 27 December 1907, box 1, WEWP. "I shall telegraph you": WEW to parents, fragment [January 1908], folder 267, ASWY.

4 Davitt: Irish writer and nationalist, sent by Hearst in 1903 to cover the Kishinev pogrom; Moses Rischin, *The Promised City: New York's Jews, 1870–1914* (1962), 229.

5 "English and Rose like it very much": AS to Dr. Walling, 27 December 1907, box 1, WEWP.

6 "If I don't bring you": AS to Dr. Walling, 27 December 1907, box 1, WEWP. Sarah

Plumb: AS to Katia, 2 January 1908, folder 114, ASWY; AS to Rosalind Walling, 3 January 1908, folder 195, ASWY.

7   Cable from Hyman: AS to Wallings, 10 January 1908, folder 195, ASWY. Brett's letter: "Copy of Mr. Brett's letter," with notations on back by Hyman Strunsky [January 1908], folder 156, ASWY.

8   "In spite of your urgeing": WEW to father, fragment [January 1908], folder 267, ASWY.

9   "Lincoln's Birthday": manuscript copy, folder 358, ASWY. "When I found the baby & Anna both so well": WEW to parents, 16 February 1908, box 1, WEWP.

10 "When our First-born died": ASW diary, 13 September 1936, folder 365, ASWY.

11 "We trusted our darling": AS to parents, 18 February 1908, box 1, SWB.

12 "It is twelve days": AS to Wallings, 25 February 1908, folder 195, ASWY.

13 Family legends: AWH and Rosamond Walling Tirana, interviews with author, 15 June 1992. Plan to investigate: WEW to parents, 16 February 1908, box 1, WEWP. "Went to her house": AS to Rosalind Walling, 3 May 1908, folder 195, ASWY.

14 Headstone: author's visit, 24 April 1993.

15 "I could not recognize Paris": AS to Wallings, 7 March 1908, folder 195, ASWY.

16 "I must say that it pains me": Hyman Strunsky to AS [February–March 1908]; "lack of strength," Hyman Strunsky to AS, [March–April 1908], folder 156, ASWY.

17 Irked at mother: AS to Rosalind Walling, 22 April and 3 May 1908, folder 195, ASWY. "Not exceed all other human ties": Katia to AS, 15 April 1908, folder 114, ASWY. Durland remark: quoted in AS to Wallings [September 1908], folder 195, ASWY.

18 "Father, dear heart": AS to Dr. Walling, 25–26 February 1908, folder 195, ASWY.

19 Gershuni's death: ASW, "Andrei Gregorewitz Gershuni," in "Revolutionary Lives," 44–78 (78).

20 "She unable to see us": Gillmore diary, 3 April 1908. See the discussion of Gillmore as a feminist in Christopher Lasch, *The New Radicalism in America, 1889–1963: The Intellectual as a Social Type* (1965, 1986), 57–60.

21 "She very charming": Gillmore diary, 5 April 1908.

22 "Anna is very beautiful": Gillmore diary, 9 April 1908; "not terrific athleticism": Gillmore diary, 14 April 1908.

23 "E.W. curiously impersonal": Gillmore diary, 19 April 1908. "E.W., a dynamo": Gillmore diary, 14 April 1908.

24 Boyce and Hapgood: Gillmore diary, 19 April 1908. Farewell dinner: Gillmore diary, 1 May 1908.

25 "I must get my book out": ASW, probably to Dr. Walling [August 1908], box 1, WEWP.

26 "A mere mechanical arrangement": ASW to RS [August 1908], folder 86, ASWY.

CHAPTER 24

1   "An honor to them": ASW to Wallings, 27 March 1908, folder 195, ASWY.

2   Doubleday, Page: early history in F. N. Doubleday, *The Memoirs of a Publisher* (1972), 90–96; Christopher P. Wilson, *The Labor of Words: Literary Professionalism in the Progressive Era* (1985), 76–79. Scott editing: WEW to parents, 1 August 1908, folder 267, ASWY.

3   "Good journalism makes bad books": George Rice Carpenter, "Mr. Poole's Articles on Russia," 15 August 1905, box 105, MACM.

4   "Red Rain": NYT, 21 October 1907. Spiradovna: Durland, *Red Reign*, 155–76; photograph in WEW, *Russia's Message: The True World Import of the Revolution*

(1908), opposite 65; photograph and brief account in Scott, "The Terrorists," *Everybody's Magazine* 16 (May 1907): 609–18.

5 Late changes: Durland, *Red Reign*, 489. Praise from Kropotkin: RS to AS, 27 February 1908, folder 86, ASWY. Review of *Red Reign*: Amy C. Rice, *Arena* 38 (December 1907): 671–74.

6 Reference to Bullard and Durland: "Bibliographical Note," WEW, *Russia's Message*, 469. Bullard role: signed outline with note attached: "Please Note: Outline of Book RUSSIA'S MESSAGE by William English Walling 1907"; draft of concluding section, quoting Maeterlinck, box 5, Bullard Papers. "Myself and wife": WEW, *Russia's Message*, x.

7 "I have not dwelt on personal experience": WEW, *Russia's Message*, ix; Trotsky: 365–66; Lenin: 369–70. "Appalling": Howard Brubaker in *Walling Symposium*, 41.

8 Opposition by father and uncle: WEW to father, fragment [February 1908], folder 267, ASWY. "To build prisons": WEW, *Russia's Message*, 414–15.

9 "In every social progress": quoted in WEW, *Russia's Message*, 451.

10 Thirty reviews: WEW to parents, 1 August 1908, folder 267, ASWY; also *Independent* 65 (10 September 1908): 610–11; *Outlook* 89 (1 August 1908): 764–66; *Nation* 87 (6 August 1908): 120–21. John Reed: introduction, *Ten Days That Shook the World* (1918).

11 "To us it seemed so unwise": Captain English to WEW, 1 July 1908, folder 255, ASWY.

12 Criticism of Beveridge: WEW, *Russia's Message*, 148–50. "The Russian masses are devoted": Albert J. Beveridge, *The Russian Advance* (1903), 332–36. Beveridge's trip to Russia: Claude G. Bowers, *Beveridge and the Progressive Era* (1932), chap. 4, "An Imperialist in Russia," 146–57. "Condemned out of his own mouth": WEW to parents, 1 August 1908, folder 267, ASWY.

13 References to Beveridge ("conscience-stricken"): WEW to parents, 1 August 1908, folder 267, ASWY; "funny" and "discreet": ASW to RS, [July 1908], from Cork, folder 86, ASWY.

Part Five

CHAPTER 25

1 Return to America: WEW to parents, 1 August 1908, folder 267, ASWY.

2 Trip to Chicago: ASW to Katia [August 1908], from Twentieth Century Limited, folder 113, ASWY.

3 Springfield riot: Roberta Senechal, *The Sociogenesis of a Race Riot: Springfield, Illinois, in 1908* (1990), 15–54.

4 "After talking it over": WEW to parents, 15 August 1908, box 1, WEWP.

5 Incidents of August 15: Senechal, *Sociogenesis*, 40–46.

6 "Springfield had no shame": WEW, "The Race War in the North," *Independent* 65 (3 September 1908): 529–34 (531).

7 "Negroes' own misconduct": *Journal* quoted in WEW, "Race War in the North," 531; Political League: 532–33.

8 "Call himself a Socialist": ASW in *Walling Symposium*, 9.

9 Springfield commentary: "Atlanta Outdone," *Independent* 65 (20 August 1908): 442–43; "The Springfield Riots," *Independent* 65 (27 August 1908), 456.

10 "Political League": WEW, "Race War in the North," 532.

11 "The spirit of the abolitionists": WEW, "Race War in the North," 534.

CHAPTER 26

1 New apartment: AS or WEW to Wallings, 3 October 1908, folder 195, ASWY; Leonard Abbott to ASW, 24 October 1908, folder 2, ASWY. Hempstead house: ASW to Wallings, 7 October 1908, folder 195, ASWY.

2 Labor Day weekend: WEW to parents, 4 September 1908, folder 267, ASWY.

3 Joint lectures: WEW to parents, 4 September 1908, folder 267, ASWY; Washington trip: ASW to Wallings, 7 October 1908, folder 195, ASWY. Debs campaign: invitation to event of 14 October 1908, folder 439, ASWY.

4 "Balzac's method": ASW to Katia, 15 November 1908, folder 114, ASWY. Promise to mother-in-law: ASW to Rosalind Walling, 16 November 1908, box 5, ASWH.

5 Lecture at Cooper Union: WEW, "The Founding of the N.A.A.C.P.," Crisis 36 (July 1929): 226; Charles Flint Kellogg, NAACP: A History of the National Association for the Advancement of Colored People, vol. 1, 1909–1920 (1967), 12; AWH, interview with author, 6 May 1996.

6 "English made a great speech": ASW to Rosalind Walling, 16 November 1908, box 5, ASWH.

7 December schedule: ASW to Rosalind Walling, 16 November 1908. Indianapolis visit and pregnancy: WEW to parents [December 1908], box 6, ASWH.

8 Cosmopolitan Club dinner: Warren F. Kuehl, Hamilton Holt: Journalist, Internationalist, Educator (1960), 47; James M. McPherson, The Abolitionist Legacy From Reconstruction to the NAACP (1975), 374–75; NYT quoted in Literary Digest, 16 May 1908, clipping, scrapbook 33, Hamilton Holt Papers, Rollins College.

9 "Wittingly or unwittingly": Russell in Walling Symposium, 76–77.

10 Washington and Du Bois: There are superb recent biographies of both: Louis R. Harlan, Booker T. Washington: The Wizard of Tuskegee, 1901–1915 (1983), and David Levering Lewis, W. E. B. Du Bois: Biography of a Race, 1868–1919 (1993). Ovington and Du Bois: McPherson, Abolitionist Legacy, 380–81; Lewis, Du Bois, 388–90.

11 Ovington account: Ovington, "William English Walling," Crisis 43 (November 1936), 335.

12 Walters and Brooks: Kellogg, NAACP, 12. Wald and Kelley: WEW, "Founding of the NAACP," 226. Baker: Lewis, Du Bois, 389; Ray Stannard Baker, Following the Color Line: An Account of Negro Citizenship in the American Democracy (1908).

13 "In view of the influence": WEW, "Founding of the NAACP," 226. Villard's background: McPherson, Abolitionist Legacy, 329–31.

14 Villard and Washington: McPherson, Abolitionist Legacy, 377–84. "Drafted for them": Oswald Garrison Villard, Fighting Years: Memoirs of a Liberal Editor (1939), 192–93.

15 "Literal reign of terror": Holt to WEW, 27 January 1909, box 1, WEWP.

16 "In view of his importance": WEW to Holt, 1 February 1909, box 1, WEWP.

17 Lincoln's Birthday call: text and list of signers is in Kellogg, NAACP, 297.

18 Miscarriage: ASW to Wallings, 10 February 1909, folder 195, ASWY.

19 Stay at Hotel Navarre: WEW to parents, 8 January 1909, folder 267, ASWY.

20 "Wholly unfounded prejudice": ASW to Wallings, 24 February 1909, folder 195, ASWY. Dr. Edgar: WEW to parents [late January–early February 1909], folder 267, ASWY.

21 "Survive this horror": ASW to Wallings, 10 February 1909, folder 195, ASWY. "A little wedding ring": ASW to Rosalind Walling, 23 April 1909, folder 195, ASWY.

CHAPTER 27

1 "New abolitionists": McPherson, *Abolitionist Legacy*, 385–89.

2 Liberal Club meetings: Kellogg, *NAACP*, 15–19 (Villard quotation, 18). Invitation to Washington: Harlan, *Booker T. Washington*, 60–61.

3 Participants: *Proceedings of the National Negro Conference 1909* [NNC] (reprint, 1969).

4 Ward: William Hayes Ward, "Sixty Years of the Independent," *Independent* 65 (10 December 1908), 1345–51; Hamilton Holt, "William Hayes Ward," *Independent* 87 (11 September 1916), 363–65. Primates: *Proceedings of NNC*, 14–65.

5 "The class that stands for persecution": WEW, "The Negro and the South," *Proceedings of NNC*, 98–109 (108). Labor orientation of WEW speech: Lewis, *Du Bois*, 393.

6 Georgia strike and Taft speech: sessions of afternoon, 31 May, and morning, 1 June, *Proceedings of NNC*, 110–20, 167–73. "Black mass": Du Bois, "National Committee for the Negro," *Survey* 22 (12 June 1909): 407–409. Resolutions and amendments: *Proceedings of NNC*, 22–25.

7 "Every great crusade": Villard, in *Proceedings of NNC*, 205.

8 WEW role: Lewis, *Du Bois*, 395–96. "'Able' fellow": Villard to uncle, Francis Jackson Garrison, 4 June 1909, Villard Papers, Houghton Library, Harvard University, quoted in Kellogg, *NAACP*, 22. "Advancement": Kellogg, *NAACP*, 16; McPherson, *Abolitionist Legacy*, 385.

9 Committee of Forty: Lewis, *Du Bois*, 395–96; Kellogg, *NAACP*, 21–22. Trotter: Stephen R. Fox, *The Guardian of Boston, William Monroe Trotter* (1970), 126–30. Wells Barnett: *Crusade for Justice: The Autobiography of Ida B. Wells*, ed. Alfreda M. Duster (1970), 323–27 ("chariot wheels": 323).

10 "Conference on the Negro situation": ASW to Wallings, 2 June 1909, folder 195, ASWY.

11 Telegram: referred to in WEW to Du Bois, 8 June 1909, in *The Correspondence of W. E. B. Du Bois*, vol. 1: *Selections, 1877–1934*, ed. Herbert Aptheker (1973), 147–50. Published list: *Proceedings of NNC*, 225.

12 WEW, "Science and Human Brotherhood": *Independent* 66 (17 June 1909): 1318–27. Booker T. Washington response: *New York Age*, 24 June 1909, quoted in Kellogg, *NAACP*, 28.

13 Recovery from miscarriage: ASW to Rosalind Walling, 23 April 1909, folder 195, ASWY. Springfield story: Hamilton Holt to ASW, 25 May 1909, folder 66, ASWY. Trip to Europe: ASW to Wallings, 2 June 1909, folder 195, ASWY. Pregnancy: ASW to Wallings, 9 August 1909, folder 195, ASWY.

14 "We are living economically": WEW to parents, 25 June [1909], box 6, ASWH. "Terrible winter": ASW to Wallings, 9 August 1909.

CHAPTER 28

1 "We visited Pere Lachaise," encounter with Phillips: ASW to Wallings, 8 July 1909, folder 195, ASWY.

2 "Balm for Her Heart": *San Francisco Examiner*, 27 July 1909, clipping, folder 481, ASWY. "SOCIOLOGY, NOT LOVE": *Chicago Record-Herald*, 28 July 1909, clipping, box 2, WEWP.

3 Emil Fuchs: referred to by Ernest Poole as his "young Jewish lawyer friend," in

The Bridge: My Own Story (1940), 87. "Nine cases out of ten": *Chicago Record-Herald,* 28 July 1909.

4   "I wish English could have told you": ASW to Wallings, 9 August 1909, folder 195, ASWY.

5   "There is only one aspect of the matter": WEW to parents [August 1909], from Montreux, folder 267, ASWY.

6   "Some very mean articles": Rosalind Walling to ASW, 18 August 1909, folder 195, ASWY.

7   Dr. Mende: ASW to Wallings [early September 1909], from Charlottenburg, near Berlin; ASW to Wallings, 22 September 1909; ASW to Wallings, 30 September 1909, folder 195, ASWY.

8   "We were both horribly bored": ASW to Wallings, 30 September 30, 1909.

9   Albert moved furniture: ASW to Wallings, 2 June 1909, folder 195, ASWY. Caritas: Arthur Zipser and Pearl Zipser, *Fire and Grace: The Life of Rose Pastor Stokes* (1989), 49–52. Invitation in 1907: WEW to Stokes, 19 September [1907], folder 154, Rose Pastor Stokes Papers, Yale University.

10 "We have a good colored cook": ASW to Wallings, 24 November 1909, box 5, ASWH.

11 Committee of Forty: Kellogg, *NAACP,* 32–34. Villard's complaint: Villard to Francis Jackson Garrison, 7 December 1909, quoted in Kellogg, *NAACP,* 33. David Levering Lewis sees the breach of promise suit as the real reason for WEW's resignation; *Du Bois,* 399. See also minutes, National Negro Committee, 8 November 1909, reel 2, W. E. B. Du Bois Papers, microfilm edition, University of Massachusetts, Amherst.

12 "Not only the ordinary Socialist opposition": WEW to H. M. Hyndman, 18 November 1909, box 1, WEWP.

13 Opposition to British-style party: WEW, "Laborism versus Socialism," *International Socialist Review* 9 (March 1909): 685–89. Incautious letter: Algie M. Simons to WEW, 19 November 1909, printed in "A Labor Party," *International Socialist Review* 10 (January 1910): 594–96.

14 "Near-riot": John Spargo to Algie Simons, 29 November 1909, box 17, John Spargo Papers, Wilbur Collection, University of Vermont. "Shocked and pained": Simons to WEW, 1 December 1909, quoted in Kent Kreuter and Gretchen Kreuter, *An American Dissenter: The Life of Algie Martin Simons, 1870–1950* (1969), 112.

15 "Mentally unbalanced": Spargo to Stokes, 3 December 1909, James Graham Phelps Stokes Papers, Columbia University, quoted in Stuart, "William English Walling," 69. "Mental and moral irresponsibility": Hunter to Simons, 3 December 1909, quoted in David A. Shannon, *The Socialist Party of America: A History* (1955, 1967), 66.

16 Stokes as WEW's supporter: Stuart, "William English Walling," 68–69.

17 Letter of defense: WEW to Eugene V. Debs, 14 December 1909, in *The Letters of Eugene V. Debs,* ed. Robert J. Constantine, 2 vols. (1990), 1:311–313. Debs's reply: Debs to WEW, 7 December 1909, printed in *International Socialist Review* 10 (January 1910), 609.

18 "A large part of the rank and file": WEW to Debs, 12 February 1910, *Letters of Eugene V. Debs,* 1:343–44.

19 Joined the party: WEW to George H. Shibley, 9 March 1910, box 1, WEWP. Letters of advice: unidentified writer to WEW, 2 January 1910, folder 279, ASWY; unidentified writer to WEW [1910], folder 281, ASWY. The writer(s) may have been either Gra-

ham Stokes or WEW's brother-in-law Hyman Strunsky. "The most grievous thing": father to WEW [1910], from Jacksonville, folder 267, ASWY.

CHAPTER 29

1   "Your grand daughter": WEW to parents, 29 January 1910, telegram, folder 267, ASWY. Anxiety: WEW to parents, 1 February 1910, folder 267, ASWY; ASW to Wallings, 1 March 1910, folder 196, ASWY.

2   "Everyone seemed possessed": Frances Blascoer to "Dear Lady," 26 March 1910, reel 2, Du Bois Papers, microfilm edition. Lewis points out this letter in his *Du Bois*, 402.

3   "Very Russian Mrs. Walling": Lewis, *Du Bois*, 402. "I have seen a good deal of Mrs. Walling": Blascoer to "Dear Lady," 26 March 1910, reel 2, Du Bois Papers, microfilm edition.

4   "The whole thing": WEW to mother, 7 May [1910], box 1, WEWP. Meetings of 12–14 May 1910: Kellogg, *NAACP*, 44; Lewis, *Du Bois*, 404–6; McPherson, *Abolitionist Legacy*, 389.

5   Du Bois's previous career: Lewis, *Du Bois*, 399–404.

6   John Brown feud: Lewis, *Du Bois*, 399–402; letters relating to the dispute are printed in *Correspondence of W. E. B. Du Bois*, 1:154–59. Villard did not mention this dispute in his memoirs, and mentioned Du Bois on only one page; *Fighting Years*, 194.

7   Recruiting letter: WEW to Du Bois, 8 June 1910, in *Correspondence of W. E. B. Du Bois*, 1:169–70. "Willing to accept": Du Bois to WEW, 10 June 1910, in *Correspondence of W. E. B. Du Bois*, 1:170–71.

8   Blascoer opposition: Lewis, *Du Bois*, 406; Blascoer to Du Bois, 15 June 1910, reel 2, Du Bois Papers, microfilm edition. Meeting of 28 June: minutes of NNC; Maclean to Du Bois [28 June 1910], telegram, reel 2, Du Bois Papers, microfilm edition. Du Bois resignation from Atlanta: Lewis, *Du Bois*, 386. On the early NAACP, see August Meier and John H. Bracey, Jr., "The NAACP as a Reform Movement, 1909–1965," *Journal of Southern History* 59 (February 1993): 3–30.

9   *The Crisis*: Lewis, *Du Bois*, 409; WEW told the same story in "The Founding of the N.A.A.C.P.," 226.

10 "He did not change viscerally": ASW to Louis Kaplan, 30 June 1962, box 1, WEWP.

11 "Fair, broad, and just": B. F. Lee Jr. to WEW, 8 September 1910, box 2, ASWH.

12 Villard's snub: *The Autobiography of W. E. B. Du Bois* (1968), 256.

13 Summer correspondence: Du Bois to WEW, 16 and 24 August 1910, reel 2, Du Bois Papers, microfilm edition. First issue of *Crisis*: Lewis, *Du Bois*, 409–410.

14 Organizing trip with baby: ASW, "Diary of a Mother," folder 303, ASWY. Cleveland meetings: Washington to Myers, 25 October 1910; Myers to Washington, 31 October 1910, in *The Booker T. Washington Papers*, ed. Louis R. Harlan and Raymond W. Smock, vol. 10, *1909–11* (1981), 418, 433–34.

15 Obligations of motherhood: ASW, "Diary of a Mother," folder 303, ASWY.

CHAPTER 30

1   "Leave myself behind": ASW to WEW [January 1911], folder 210, ASWY. "Wholly out of the question": ASW to WEW [January 1911], box 5, ASWH.

2   "It is a remarkable tale": *New York Evening Journal,* 21 February 1911.

3   "For the first time": *New York World,* 24 February 1911.

4   Grunspan cross-examination: *New York World,* 25 February 1911.

5   "Her dark hair fell": *New York World,* 27 February 1911.

6   Juror No. 5: *New York World,* 1, 2, and 3 March 1911; "rasping insistent voice": *New York World,* 3 March 1911.

7   WEW testimony: *New York World,* 2 and 3 March 1911. "Did you have to take your oath": *New York World,* 3 March 1911.

8   "For heaven's sake": *New York World,* 3 March 1911.

9   "I wanted to be just as friendly": *New York World,* 3 March 1911.

10   "It seems rather strange": Washington to Fortune, 20 January 1911, *Booker T. Washington Papers,* 10: 555–56.

11   "Burn Walling up": Washington to Anderson, 3 March 1911, *Booker T. Washington Papers,* 10: 614.

12   "We hope that no colored man": *New York Age,* quoted in Harlan, *Booker T. Washington,* 32–33. Washington incident: Harlan, *Booker T. Washington,* 379–404; Lewis, *Du Bois,* 428–34.

13   "This isn't a point of law with me": *New York World,* 4 March 1911.

14   ASW testimony: *New York World,* 4 March 1911.

15   Last phase of trial: *New York World,* 4 March 1911.

16   Verdict: *New York World,* 5 March 1911.

17   Post-trial interviews: *New York World,* 6 March 1911.

18   "We saw the testimony": Rosalind Walling to WEW, 11 March [1911], box 6, ASWH.

19   Attendance at NAACP meetings: minutes of NAACP executive committee, 7 and 21 March, 11 April 1911, reel 4, Du Bois Papers, microfilm edition.

Part Six

CHAPTER 31

1   "The house may burn around me": RS to ASW [January 1911], folder 87, ASWY.

2   "Albert comes and borrows": RS to ASW, 6 February 1911, folder 86, ASWY. Necklace: RS to ASW, 6 February 1910, folder 86, ASWY.

3   *Forum* article: RS, " 'Little Darling,' " *Forum* 45 (January 1911): 31–43. *Atlantic* article: RS, "Tolstoi and Young Russia," 107 (April 1911): 490–97. "He said I write like Tolstoy": RS to ASW, [January 1911], folder 87, ASWY.

4   "He is showing them to everybody": RS to ASW [January 1911]. see also Phillips to WEW on the photographs, in Isaac F. Marcosson, *David Graham Phillips and His Times* (1932), 292. RS visit: mentioned in ASW to Wallings, 1 February 1911, folder 196, ASWY. Phillips's death: Louis Filler, *Voice of the Democracy: A Critical Biography of David Graham Phillips* (1978), 156–63.

5   "English and I shed bitter tears": ASW to Wallings, 1 February 1911, folder 196, ASWY.

6   "Did it ever occur to Phillips": ASW, "A Socialist Conversation with David Graham Phillips," *New York Call,* 29 January 1911, clipping lent by AWH.

7   "Falseness and inanity of our society": ASW, "David Graham Phillips: The Last Years of His Life," *Saturday Evening Post,* 21 October 1911, clipping, folder 373, ASWY.

8   "A Tribute to the Yellow Press": ASW, *Collier's Weekly* 47 (22 April 1911): 27–28.

9   Judge's reaction: L. A. Giegerich to ASW, 1 May 1911, box 2, ASWH.

10 Triangle Shirtwaist fire: ASW, "Fire Peril in Factories," *National Post*, 6 May 1911. The standard account is Leon Stein, *The Triangle Fire* (1962).

11 Rejection of fire article: Sidney Rogers Cook, *Collier's*, to ASW, 28 March 1911, folder 44, ASWY. *Success* and *National Post*: Brubaker to ASW, 1 April 1911, folder 34, ASWY; Samuel S. Merwin to ASW, 5 April 1911, box 4, ASWH; Frank Luther Mott, *History of American Magazines*, vol. 5, *Sketches of 21 Magazines, 1905–1930* (1968), 290. "Completely ruined": ASW to Rosalind Walling, 6 May 1911, box 5, ASWH.

12 WEW's manuscript: acknowledgment, Edward C. Marsh, Macmillan, to ASW, 1 April 1911, folder 107, ASWY. "I could not easily take such a trip": ASW to Brett, 3 April 1911, box 19, MACM.

13 "The writer is sometimes wrong": quoted in Brett to ASW (who was handling the correspondence for WEW), 4 April 1911; "Of course I do not believe": WEW to Brett, 5 April 1911; "Revolutionary Socialism" and "Organized Socialism": WEW to Brett, 5 April 1911; Brett to WEW, 6 April 1911, box 19, MACM.

14 "There have been several heavy expenses": WEW to Brett, 29 June 1911, box 19, MACM.

15 Demanded opinion: WEW to Brett, 24 July 1911; "attempting to hasten the work" Brett to WEW, 27 July 1911; "Please inform your readers": WEW to Brett, 29 July [1911]; promise to rewrite: WEW to Brett, 3 August 1911, box 19, MACM.

16 Neuritis: ASW to Rosalind Walling, 6 May 1911, box 5, ASWH. "The mss. I am now mailing": ASW to Brett, 29 June 1911, box 19, MACM.

17 "I should have brought it in person": ASW to Dr. Walling, 5 July 1911, folder 196, ASWY.

18 "The manuscript is charming": Brett to ASW, 25 July 1911, folder 107, ASWY.

19 "I regret now that I had not waited": ASW to Brett, 25 July 1911, box 19, MACM.

CHAPTER 32

1   *The House of Bondage*: discussed in Mari Jo Buhle, *Women and American Socialism, 1870–1920* (1981), 255–56. Invitation from Kauffmans: ASW to Wallings, 28 July 1911, folder 196, ASWY. RS research and household: RS to ASW, 22 December 1911, folder 86, ASWY. RS's return: ASW to Wallings, 23 and 29 April 1912, folder 197, ASWY.

2   Bullard's visit: ASW to Wallings, 12 September 1911, folder 196, ASWY. *A Man's World*: Albert Tridon, "The Novels of Albert Edwards," *New Review* 1 (May 1913): 535–37. For a recent evaluation of Bullard's novel, see Mark Pittenger, *American Socialists and Evolutionary Thought, 1870–1920* (1993), 213–18.

3   Durland's career: Albert J. Kennedy notes, box 17, University Settlement Papers, State Historical Society of Wisconsin. "I can only hope that his old mother": ASW to Rosalind Walling, 20 November 1911, folder 196, ASWY.

4   "Last night I slept out": ASW to Rosalind Walling, 27 September 1911, box 1, SWB.

5   "We are living in a civilized manner": ASW to Rosalind Walling, 20 November 1911, folder 196, ASWY.

6   Account of birth: ASW to Wallings, 10 January 1911 [1912], folder 197, ASWY. "Your experience as an accoucheur": father to WEW, 4 January 1912, folder 268, ASWY.

7 "At last I learned the fate": ASW to JL, 8 January 1912, box 5, ASWH.

8 JL's month in New York: Clarice Stasz, *American Dreamers: Charmian and Jack London* (1988), 233–36.

9 "As if he had never been away": ASW, London MSS. "We had a beautiful visit": ASW to Rosalind Walling, 29 February 1912, folder 197, ASWY. "She must be quite forty years old": Charmian London was thirty-eight at the time of the visit.

10 "I am so wholly cut off": ASW to RS, fragment [March 1912], folder 86, ASWY. "Something very temporary": RS to ASW, 28 March 1912, folder 86, ASWY.

11 "Too many of the chapters," "The writer has tried to journalize": readers quoted in Brett to WEW, 11 January 1912, box 19, MACM.

12 "Have just signed my contract": WEW to parents, 30 January 1912, folder 268, ASWY.

13 Croly and Weyl: Walter Lippmann, "As a New Republic Editor," in *Walter Weyl: An Appreciation,* ed. Bertha Poole Weyl (1922), 84–94. See also Daniel T. Rodgers, "In Search of Progressivism," in *The Promise of American History: Progress and Prospects,* ed. Stanley I. Kutler and Stanley N. Katz (1982), 113–32.

14 Rebuttal: WEW, *Socialism As It Is: A Survey of the World-Wide Revolutionary Movement* (1912), preface, vi; Lawrence strike: 366.

15 Critique of Spargo and other moderates: WEW, *Socialism As It Is,* 210–30.

16 State socialism: WEW, *Socialism As It Is,* 46–65, 117. "Equality of opportunity": see chapter of that title, 97–106. "The most anti-social aspects of capitalism": 105. See discussion in Brian Lloyd, *Left Out: Pragmatism, Exceptionalism, and the Poverty of American Marxism, 1890–1922* (1997), 212–18.

17 Form letter: WEW to recipient, 20 April 1912, box 1, WEWP. Letters from prominent persons: ASW to Rosalind Walling, 29 April 1912; diffidence: ASW to Rosalind Walling, 22 May 1912, folder 197, ASWY.

18 Publicist defined: Francis Hackett in *Walter Weyl: An Appreciation,* 103. See also John A. Thompson, *Reformers and War: American Progressive Publicists and the First World War* (1987), 23. "Publicist as opposed to the mere journalist": WEW, *Socialism As It Is,* 110. "He was interested in reaching those specialists": ASW in *Walling Symposium,* 14.

19 Sales of book: WEW to parents [April 1913], folder 268, ASWY; Rosalind Walling to ASW and WEW, 4 May 1914, folder 198, ASWY.

20 WEW and syndicalism: Christopher Lasch, *The True and Only Heaven: Progress and Its Critics* (1991), 332–40.

21 "Walter is getting great help": Bertha Poole Weyl to ASW, 28 April 1912, box 6, ASWH. "Working through Walling's book": quoted in Charles Forcey, *The Crossroads of Liberalism: Croly, Weyl, Lippmann, and the Progressive Era, 1900–1925* (1961), 162.

22 "Larger aspects": WEW to father, 10 July 1912, box 1, WEWP.

CHAPTER 33

1 "A will to beauty": Walter Lippmann, *A Preface to Politics* (1913), quoted in Buhle, *Women and American Socialism,* 292. Shortcomings of capitalism: Contrary to the perception that muckraking declined after President Roosevelt's "Man with the Muckrake" speech in April 1906 *Readers Guide to Periodical Literature* shows that magazines continued to print hundreds of articles exposing

the social effects of the American industrial and economic system. On this "language of social bonds," see Rodgers, "In Search of Progressivism," 113–32.

2 "Socialism is the answer": Ellis O. Jones, "Magazines, Morgan and Muckraking," *Masses*, April 1911: 10.

3 *International Socialist Review*: Herbert G. Gutman article *The American Radical Press: 1880–1960*, 2 vols., ed. Joseph R. Conlin (1974), 1:82–86; Pittenger, *American Socialists and Evolutionary Thought*, 120–21.

4 Writing for *International Socialist Review*: for example, RS, "The Strike of the British Transport Workers," 12 (October 1911): 199–202; WEW, "Capitalistic 'Socialism,' " 12 (November 1911): 303–308. *New Review*: David E. Brown in *The American Radical Press*, 1:139–40; statement of ownership, *New Review* 1 (12 April 1913). The author is indebted to Rick Seto for research in the files of *New Review*.

5 Family preserve: RS, "The Truth About Lincoln and the Negro"; WEW, "Roosevelt's 'Socialism' "; ASW, "Giovannitti's Poems," *New Review* 2 (May 1914): 258–69, 269–75, 288–92.

6 WEW articles in *New Review*: "The Socialist Party and the Farmers," 1 (4 January 1913): 12–20; "Industrialism or Revolutionary Unionism," 1 (11 and 18 January 1913): 82–91, 174–81; "Woodrow Wilson and State Socialism," 1 (15 March 1913): 329–35; "Woodrow Wilson and Business," 1 (22 March 1913): 364–69; "Woodrow Wilson and the Class Struggle," 1 (29 March 1913): 399–405.

7 WEW and pragmatism: Stuart, "William English Walling," 84–93; James Gilbert, "William English Walling: The Pragmatic Critique of Collectivism," in his *Designing the Industrial State: The Intellectual Pursuit of Collectivism in America, 1880–1940* (1972), 200–239.

8 "Maintaining the masses in ignorance" and "never voluntarily pay": WEW, *The Larger Aspects of Socialism* (1913), 256, 297. Leslie Fishbein, *Rebels in Bohemia: The Radicals of the Masses, 1911–1917* (1982), presents *Larger Aspects* as representative of the era's radical socialist thought and quotes it extensively.

9 Key and Gilman: Buhle, *Women and American Socialism*, 292–94; WEW, *Larger Aspects*, 325–59, 365–72.

10 "The art of love": WEW, *Larger Aspects*, 336.

11 "Problem of rearing children" and "sports, heavy drinking": WEW, *Larger Aspects*, 353 and 372.

12 "The most clumsy landlubber": La Monte, "The Apotheosis of Pragmatism," *New Review* 1 (July 1913): 661–64.

13 WEW reply to La Monte: "Pragmatism and Socialism," *New Review* 1 (August 1913): 718–19. Lippmann: Ronald Steel, *Walter Lippmann and the American Century* (1980), 45–57. "An extremely significant book": Lippmann, "La Monte, Walling and Pragmatism"; La Monte, "Pragmatism Once More," *New Review* 1 (November 1913), 907–9, 909–11.

14 Salon: Mabel Dodge Luhan, *Movers and Shakers, Volume Three of Intimate Memories* (1936), 88; Steel, *Walter Lippmann*, 50–51.

15 Haywood-Goldman-Walling debate: Luhan, *Movers and Shakers*, 89–90.

16 Rarely in the city: ASW to Rosalind Walling, 26 July 1912, folder 197, ASWY.

17 Early *Masses*: Fishbein, *Rebels in Bohemia*, 17–18; article by Richard Fitzgerald in *American Radical Press*, 2: 532–38. Young drawing: *Masses*, October 1911, 12. Eastman as editor: William L. O'Neill, *The Last Romantic: A Life of Max Eastman* (1978), 29–53.

18 Editorial meetings: Brubaker in *Walling Symposium*, 42; John Sloan diary, 15 January 1913, in *John Sloan's New York Scene: From the Diaries, Notes, and Correspondence, 1906–1913*, ed. Bruce St. John (1965), 633. "Grey-haired potbellied deliberative old men": RS to ASW, 28 March 1912, folder 86, ASWY.

19 WEW work for *Masses*: "Class Struggle Within the Working Class," January 1913, 12–13. Department: "The World-Wide Battle Line" made its first appearance in February 1913 (18).

20 "Max Eastman mailed you": ASW to JL, 18 January 1913, folder JL19864, JLH.

21 "I have been frightfully, dangerously ill": ASW to JL, 1 April 1913, folder JL19866, JLH.

22 All was well: WEW to parents [May 1913]; Cooper Union debate: WEW to parents [15 May 1913], folder 268, ASWY. Last book: ASW to Dr. Walling, 26 March 1913, folder 197, ASWY. "Only one person deeply interested": WEW to parents [March 1913], from Brevoort, folder 268, ASWY.

23 "Dont think of Anna and the babies": WEW to parents [25 May 1913]; "I have to superintend *everything*": WEW to mother, 7 June 1913, folder 268, ASWY.

24 "Hermit existence": WEW to ASW [August 1914], box 1, WEWP.

25 "It's this way about my writing": ASW to WEW [September 1913], folder 210, ASWY. "*Do* keep your promise": WEW to ASW [September 1913], box 1, WEWP.

26 "Tolstoi is right": WEW to ASW, [September 1913], box 1, WEWP.

CHAPTER 34

1 "With Anna every minute": WEW to parents, Monday [13 October 1913], folder 267, ASWY. "Her name is Georgia": WEW to parents, Wednesday [15 October 1913], folder 268, ASWY.

2 "Anna is well": WEW to parents, 18 November [1913], folder 268, ASWY.

3 "Knitted undershirts": WEW to ASW [January 1914], box 1, WEWP. "Georgia is three months old": ASW to WEW, 13 January 1913 [1914], folder 210, ASWY.

4 "Letter II": ASW to WEW, 13 January 1913 [1914], folder 210, ASWY.

5 JL at thirty-eight: Charmian London to ASW, 11 November 1913, quoted in Andrew Sinclair, *Jack: A Biography of Jack London* (1977), 196; Charmian London to ASW, 14 November 1913, quoted in Stasz, *American Dreamers*, 263. "Another Scandal": JL to Charmian London, 29 January 1914, LJL, 3:1294.

6 Reading at hotel: ASW to WEW, fragment [26 January 1914]; ASW to WEW, 28 January 1913 [1914], folder 210, ASWY. The editors of LJL (3:1307) indicate that the manuscript may have been a portion of JL's *The Star Rover* (1915).

7 Taxi accident: Stasz, *American Dreamers*, 278. Rosamond's birthday: ASW to WEW, 30 January 1914, folder 210, ASWY.

8 Lunch at the Astor: ASW to WEW, fragment [29 January 1914], folder 210, ASWY; ASW to WEW, 30 January 1914.

9 "This visit with my old friend": ASW to WEW, 30 January 1914.

10 "If you think I do not fully appreciate Jack": WEW to ASW, [February 1914], box 1, WEWP.

11 JL and Charmian in Veracruz: Stasz, *American Dreamers*, 280–83. Reed in Mexico: Robert A. Rosenstone, *Romantic Revolutionary: A Biography of John Reed* (1975), 149–69; Reed, *Insurgent Mexico* (1914).

12 "Preparing the ground for a race war": WEW, "Jack London in Mexico," *New Review* 2 (July 1914): 422–25.

13 JL and Charmian in New Orleans: Stasz, *American Dreamers*, 282–83. Request for support: WEW to JL, 28 January 1915, box 6, ASWH.

14 Spring Lake: Father to WEW, 21 April 1914; WEW to father, 2 June [1914], folder 268, ASWY.

15 "Very powerful": Robert Sterling Yard, *Century*, to ASW, 19 December 1913, box 6, ASWH. "The very extremity of the suffering": *Atlantic* to ASW, 13 February 1914, box 1, ASWH. Pamphlet: ASW, *The Homel Massacre*, New York Section, Council of Jewish Women [1914].

16 Lippmann's challenge: Lippmann, "Walling's 'Progressivism and After,'" *New Review* 2 (June 1914): 340–49.

17 "The most colossal and extraordinary blunder": WEW, "Why A Socialist Party?" *New Review* 2 (July 1914): 400–403.

18 "Impossibilist to the last degree": Lippmann, "Why a Socialist Party?" *New Review* 2 (November 1914): 658–60. "Gross misstatements": WEW, letter, *New Review* 2 (November 1914): 660–62.

19 "This fell on me": WEW to parents, 2 June [1914], folder 268, ASWY.

20 "I will be all right": AS to RS, 30 July 1914, folder 87, ASWY.

21 Fifty years later: ASW to Louis Kaplan, Wisconsin State Historical Society, 30 June 1962, box 1, WEWP.

Part Seven

CHAPTER 35

1 War with Japan: Lippmann, "Walling's 'Progressivism and After'," *New Review* 2 (June 1914), 345; WEW, "Why a Socialist Party?" *New Review* 2 (July 1914), 403.

2 Role of crowds: Modris Eksteins, *Rites of Spring: The Great War and the Birth of the Modern Age* (1989), 55–70.

3 "The War in our souls": Hutchins Hapgood, *A Victorian in the Modern World* (1939), 385.

4 Poole and Bullard in Europe: Bullard to Leonora Bagg, 20 March 1914, box 8, Arthur Bullard Papers, Seeley G. Mudd Manuscript Library, Princeton University; Ernest Poole, *The Bridge: My Own Story* (1940), 212. Bullard's "The Story of the War," started in *Outlook* 107 (22 August 1914). "The issue seems to boil down": Bullard to Bagg, 30 November 1914; Bullard in Paris: Bullard to Bagg, 8 February 1915, box 8, Bullard Papers.

5 "For we shall stop this war": quoted from Poole's handwritten draft; the published version, five paragraphs from the end of *The Harbor*, differs slightly. See folder 3–2, Ernest Poole Papers, Baker Library, Dartmouth College. Poole to Europe: *The Bridge*, 240–53.

6 "Dry salad and rice": RS to ASW [August 1914]; "I have promised to march": RS to ASW, 21 August 1914, folder 87, ASWY.

7 Criticism of British and German socialists: WEW, *Progressivism—and After* (1914), esp. chap. 15, "Nationalistic Socialism," 272–96. Crucial break: RS to ASW, 18 November 1937, folder 94, ASWY.

8 "Not only the ordinary Socialist opposition": WEW to H. M. Hyndman, 18 November 1909, box 1, WEWP. "The Socialist parties . . . have done nothing": WEW, "The Socialists and the Great War," *Independent* 79 (24 August 1914): 268–70. "Irre-

spective of *color*": WEW, "British and American Socialists on the War," *New Review* 2 (September 1914): 512–18 (512).

9   Shoot its own officers: WEW, "Socialists and the Great War," 268. "Advocate of plutocracy": WEW, "A 'Socialist' Advocate of Plutocracy," *New Review* 2 (August 1914): 471–77. "Will have amply repaid": WEW, "British and American Socialists on the War," 518.

10 WEW's magazine articles: "Socialists and the War," *Harper's Weekly* 59 (3 October 1914): 319; "The Socialist View: II. The Real Causes of the War" *Harper's Weekly* 59 (10 October 1914): 346–47. "The ablest thinker": WEW to parents [November 1914], box 1, WEWP. "Are the German People Unanimous?": WEW, "Are the German People Unanimously for the War?" *Outlook* 108 (25 November 1914): 673–78.

11 "Ultra-optimist": WEW to JL, 28 January 1915, box 6, ASWH.

12 House in Greenwich: Rosalind Walling to WEW and ASW, 30 September 1914; WEW to parents [November 1914]; ASW to Dr. Walling, 25 November 1914, folder 198, ASWY. "A room to work in": Heath to ASW, 3 November 1914, folder 63, ASWY.

13 "I have a deep-seated feeling": ASW, address, 22 November 1914, typescript, folder 374, ASWY. Helen Gurley Flynn invitation: Flynn to ASW [December 1914], box 1, WEWP.

14 Letters from St. Augustine: see file on the Alcazar letterhead, box 6, ASWH.

15 "Buried so long": ASW to WEW, 18 February 1915, folder 211, ASWY. "Dearest in the World": ASW to WEW, 28 February 1915, box 1, SWB.

16 "Jane Addams group": ASW to WEW, 15 March 1915, box 1, WEWP. Peace alliance: Barbara J. Steinson, *American Women's Activism in World War I* (1982), 27; Warren F. Kuehl, *Hamilton Holt: Journalist, Internationalist, Educator* (1960), 108–109. "Bourgeois pacifism": WEW, "The Remedy: Anti-Nationalism," *New Review* 3 (February 1915): 77–83 (80). See also WEW, "The Great Illusions," *New Review* 3 (1 June 1915), 49–50.

17 "When I told Rosamond where I was going": ASW to WEW, 5 March 1915; "Rosamond made up this speech": ASW to WEW, 10 March 1915, box 1, WEWP.

18 "Artistic misery": ASW to WEW, 12 March 1915, box 1, WEWP. Goldman invitation: Goldman to ASW, 17 March 1915, folder 58, ASWY. Grand Rapids lecture: William B. Feakins to ASW, 19 March 1915, box 1, SWB; ASW to Wallings, 26 March 1915, folder 198, ASWY. Rebuke from Lippmann: Lippmann to ASW, 31 March 1915, box 2, ASWH.

19 Foreword of 1913: manuscript dated 1 February 1913, folder 375, ASWY.

20 "They did take 'Pere Lachaise'": ASW to JL and Charmian London, 27 April 1915, box 5, ASWH. "Freed from within": ASW to Wallings, 6 April [May] 1915, folder 198, ASWY.

21 "The book waited till now": page proof, foreword, 18 May 1915, folder 375, ASWY.

22 "Story of an inner life": Sedgwick to William Morrow, Frederick A. Stokes Company, 6 May 1915, folder 108, ASWY. Title for novel: ASW to Wallings, 12 May 1915, folder 198, ASWY.

23 Dedication to Rosalind Walling: ASW to Wallings, 27 April 1915, folder 198, ASWY. "A delicate and original idealization": dust jacket, box 1, SWB.

24 "An excellent specimen of book making": Brett to ASW, 29 October 1915, box 1, SWB. Notice in *New York Herald*: 26 November 1915; Eastman in *Masses*, December 1915, clippings, folder 435, ASWY. Rose Pastor Stokes review: *Intercollegiate Socialist*, February–March 1916, 30. Reports from bookstore clerks: ASW to Dr. Walling, 22 December 1915, folder 198, ASWY.

CHAPTER 36

1 "Stars & stripes flying": RS to ASW, 20 May 1915, folder 87, ASWY.

2 "We had a wretched time with Mrs. Ellis": RS to ASW, 20 May 1915, folder 87, ASWY.

3 "A bit jealous": RS to ASW, 20 May 1915; asking prices: RS to ASW, 24 June 1915, folder 87, ASWY.

4 "As the Tribune treated me": RS to ASW, 31 July 1915, folder 87, ASWY. Competing articles: Bullard, "Zeppelins over Paris," *Outlook,* 18 August 1915; RS, "July 14," both noted in RS to ASW, 31 July 1915.

5 "A hard American face": RS to ASW, 5 September 1915, folder 87, ASWY.

6 RS moved out: RS to ASW, 30 September 1915, folder 87, ASWY. Return to America: RS to Louis Levine, 28 September 1915, Louis Levine/Lorwin Papers, held by his son, Boris Lorwin.

7 Compilation of documents: WEW, ed., *The Socialists and the War: A Documentary Statement of the Socialists of All Countries, with Special Reference to Their Peace Policy* (1915).

8 Criticism of Hillquit: WEW, *The Socialists and the War,* 380, 419. "If Germany repeats her insanity": WEW to parents, [June 1915], box 1, WEWP.

9 "We talk of war": ASW to Charmian London, 25 April 1915, box 5, ASWH.

10 "Rabid on the war question": Goldman to ASW, 2 June 1915, box 1, SWB.

11 "The Great Illusions": *New Review* 3 (1 June 1915): 49–50. "The Futility of Bourg[e]ois Pacifism," *New Review* 3 (1 September 1915): 208–9.

12 "A Washington friend on the inside": WEW to father, 22 August [1915], folder 269, ASWY.

13 Woman's Peace Party: Steinson, *American Women's Activism,* 27, 122–31. Role of socialists: Mari Jo Buhle, *Women and American Socialism, 1870–1920* (1981), 312. Listed on letterhead: for example, Margaret Lane to Rose Pastor Stokes, 8 January 1917, folder 62, Rose Pastor Stokes Papers, Yale University.

14 Dr. Walling's accident: Rosalind Walling to ASW and WEW, 14 June 1915, folder 198, ASWY. "Socialism leads to suicide": ASW to WEW, 26 June 1915, folder 211, ASWY. Nietzsche review: *New Review* 3 (1 August 1915): 166–67. "The show was not as anti-Negro": WEW to ASW [June 1915], box 6, ASWH.

15 "I am not excited, dearest": ASW to WEW, 5 July 1915, folder 211, ASWY.

16 Thank-you note: Rosalind Walling to ASW and WEW, 4 October 1915, folder 198, ASWY. Golden wedding: announcement, folder 153, ASWY.

17 Lecture tour: WEW to parents, 1 February 1915 [1916], folder 269, ASWY; ASW to Wallings, 22 February 1916, folder 199, ASWY.

18 "Assistance of my comrades and friends": Goldman to ASW, 27 February 1916; "It is alright dear": Goldman to ASW, 4 March 1916, folder 58, ASWY.

19 "What a strange girl you are": Goldman to ASW, 8 July 1916; Goldman to ASW, 16 April and 29 May 1916, folder 58, ASWY.

CHAPTER 37

1 *Whitman and Traubel:* WEW reported from Florida that he was working on the book, WEW to ASW [March 1916], folder 210, ASWY; WEW to ASW [March 1916], box 6, ASWH. Whitman dinner speeches: ASW to Wallings, 2 June 1915, box 1, WEWP; WEW to parents [June 1913], folder 268, ASWY. *The Socialism of To-Day:* WEW, J.G.

Phelps Stokes, Jessie Wallace Hughan, Harry W. Laidler et al., eds., *The Socialism of To-Day: A Sourcebook of the Present Position and Recent Development of the Socialist and Labor Parties in All Countries, Consisting Mainly of Original Documents* (1916).

2   "Data or reality or substance": ASW to WEW, 25 March 1916, folder 212, ASWY. "The sex question": ASW to WEW, 31 March [1916], folder 211, ASWY.

3   Ethel Bagg: Bullard to Leonora Bagg (Ethel Bagg's mother), 28 February and 25 June 1916, box 8, Bullard Papers. Levine's early history: Louis Levine/Lorwin, "Family Chronicle" (manuscript lent by his son, Boris Lorwin), chaps. 12–14.

4   Peace Ship and Neutral Conference: Steinson, *American Women's Activism*, 78–94. "Why don't you think I ought to go?" RS to Levine, 27 April 1916, Levine/Lorwin Papers.

5   "I dance and go motor-boating": RS to ASW [7 July 1916]; typing translations: RS to ASW [9 July 1916], folder 87, ASWY.

6   "I feel and think just as you do": ASW to RS, 18 July 1916, folder 87, ASWY.

7   "The brainiest woman in the country": WEW to mother, 12 July [1916], box 1, WEWP.

8   "Rather mechanical and theoretical": ASW to Wallings, 26 August 1916, folder 199, ASWY. "Mrs. Gilman writes so easily": ASW to RS, 28 August 1916, folder 87, ASWY.

9   "While dressing": ASW diary, 9 September 1916, folder 303, ASWY.

10   "The last remark English made": ASW diary, 12 September 1916, folder 303, ASWY.

11   Departure from Nantucket: ASW diary, 20 September 1916., folder 303, ASWY; last entry is 28 September 1916. "Defensive Warfare": 22 September 1916, program for Intercollegiate Socialist Society summer conference, 19–26 September 1916, box 25, James Graham Phelps Stokes Papers, Columbia University. Infantile paralysis and laundry: WEW to ASW, 26 and 27 September [1916], box 1, WEWP.

12   "Second vote": ASW to WEW, 29 September 1916, box 5, ASWH. Statement in *New Republic*: draft with WEW's name listed, 21 September 1916, box 25, Stokes Papers; published as "The Case for Benson," *New Republic* 7 (7 October 1916), 243–45. "Hughes is completely surrounded": WEW to father, 2 October 1916, box 6, ASWH.

13   "Effective votes": WEW, in *New York World*, 14 October 1916, quoted in Stuart, "William English Walling," 129. Supply ship: WEW to father [14 October 1916]; "an arrant fool": father to WEW, 16 October 1916, folder 269, ASWY.

14   Contribution from Wallings: Father to WEW, 21 October 1916, folder 269, ASWY. "Babinotz to Greenwich": ASW to Wallings, 26 October 1916; "overdid in New York": ASW to Dr. Walling, 4 November 1916, box 1, WEWP.

15   Dr. Walling's stroke: ASW in *Walling Symposium*, 9; father to WEW [November 1916] folder 269, ASWY; Rosalind Walling to ASW and WEW, [after 7 November 1916], folder 199, ASWY. "Read this over a second time": WEW to ASW, Wednesday [22 November 1916], box 1, WEWP.

16   JL's death: Clarice Stasz, *American Dreamers: Charmian and Jack London* (1988), 318–320. Condolence letters: ASW to Charmian London, telegram, 23 November (telegram), 30 November and 27 December 1916, Jack and Charmian London Collection, Merrill Library, Utah State University.

17   "Being so comfortless myself": ASW to WEW, 27 [28] November 1916, folder 212, ASWY.

18   "*House Notes Important*": WEW to ASW, [late November–early December 1916], box 1, WEWP; WEW to ASW, 4 December [1916], folder 212, ASWY.

19 "I know what that terror is": Rosalind Walling to ASW, 22[–25] December 1916, folder 199, ASWY.

20 Memorial article on JL: ASW to Charmian London, 9 January and 4 April 1917, box 5, ASWH. "Indescribably virile": ASW, "Memoirs of Jack London," *Masses*, July 1917, 13–17; repr. in *Echoes of Revolt: The Masses, 1911–1917*, ed. William L. O'Neill (1966), 117–22.

21 Controversy over *Sunset* story: Rose Wilder Lane, "Life and Jack London," *Sunset* magazine, November 1917, 27–30. "White beautiful friendship": JL to AS, 26 December 1900, copy with Charmian London's notations, folder 82, ASWY. The Lane article did not include the "white beautiful friendship" letter, but quoted JL to AS, 31 July 1900 (the previously unpublished "Comrades!" letter), which ASW must have lent her; see *LJL*, 1:198. Telegram: ASW to Charmian London, 18 December 1917, box 5, ASWH.

CHAPTER 38

1 "It was Miss Dixon who told me": ASW to WEW, 27 January 1917, folder 212, ASWY.

2 "Will we have a war": ASW to WEW, 5[–6] February 1917, folder 212, ASWY.

3 "The war would now be over": WEW to mother, [February–March 1917], folder 270, ASWY.

4 Operation at Polyclinic: WEW to mother, 23 February 1917; WEW to ASW and her mother [February–March 1917]; WEW to Rosamond Walling (daughter), box 6, ASWH. The new edition of *Russia's Message*—a condensation rather than a revision—was reviewed in *NYT*, 22 April 1917. Trip to St. Augustine: Mother to WEW, 21 March 1917, folder 270, ASWY; ASW to Charmian London, 4 April 1917, box 5, ASWH.

5 "Darling, it is enough": ASW to WEW, 19 March 1917, folder 212, ASWY. Emergency Peace Federation: Steinson, *American Women's Activism*, 220–45; ASW's connection: Joint Legislative Committee Investigating Seditious Activities [Lusk Committee], New York State Senate, *Revolutionary Radicalism: Its History, Purpose, and Tactics, with an Exposition and Discussion of the Steps Being Taken and Required to Curb It* (April 24, 1920), part 1, *Revolutionary and Subversive Movements Abroad and At Home*, vol. 1, 998–99.

6 "Criminal to the last degree": WEW to ASW, [March 1917], box 1, WEWP. Stuart, in "William English Walling," 138, says that Morris Strunsky told him that WEW had threatened that ASW herself might be hanged for treason.

7 "Not being a Junker": ASW to WEW, 21 March 1917, folder 212, ASWY.

8 "I have capitulated to your point of view": ASW to WEW, 26 March 1917, folder 212, ASWY.

9 WEW's prowar activity: Stuart, "William English Walling," 132–37. "THESE SOCIALISTS AMERICANS FIRST": *New York Evening Post*, 21 March 1917, clipping, box 26, Stokes Papers.

CHAPTER 39

1 "Tiny twisted unscared ghost": John Dos Passos, *U.S.A.* (3 vols. in 1, 1931), vol. 2, *Nineteen-Nineteen*, 105. Bourne and *New Republic*: Charles Forcey, *The Crossroads of Liberalism: Croly, Weyl, Lippmann, and the Progressive Era, 1900–1925* (1961), 280–83. "An apathetic nation": Randolph S. Bourne, "The War and the

Intellectuals," *Seven Arts*, June 1917; repr. in his *The War and the Intellectuals*, ed. Carl Resek (1964), 4–7; Christopher Lasch, *The New Radicalism in America, 1889–1963: The Intellectual as a Social Type* (1965), 204–11.

2　"In terms that might have emanated from any bourgeois journal": Bourne, "The War and the Intellectuals."

3　Bullard and Poole: Truman Frederick Keefer, "The Literary Career and Literary Productions of Ernest Poole, American Novelist" (Ph.D. diss., Duke University, 1961), 258–61; Stephen Vaughn, "Arthur Bullard and the Creation of the Committee on Public Information," *New Jersey History* 47 (Spring 1979): 45–53. Stokes activities: Stuart, "William English Walling," 140–46; Ronald Radosh, *American Labor and United States Foreign Policy* (1969), 35. Weyl: Forcey, *Crossroads of Liberalism*, 278, 283; Martin Schutze in *Walter Weyl: An Appreciation*, ed. Bertha Poole Weyl (1922), 72.

4　Root commission: Radosh, *American Labor*, 73–77; John A. Thompson, *Reformers and War: American Progressive Publicists and the First World War* (1987), 181–82.

5　Newspaper support for WEW: *New York Globe*, 30 April 1917, quoted in Stuart, "William English Walling," 147; a similar editorial appeared in the *Chicago Evening Post*, 9 May 1917, clipping, box 2, WEWP. "I know of no Socialist": William B. Wilson to President Wilson, 30 April 1917, in *The Papers of Woodrow Wilson*, ed. Arthur S. Link, vol. 42, *April 7–June 23, 1917* (1983), 165–66.

6　"Pro-Hyphen New York Socialist": *New York Globe*, 1 May 1917, cited in *Papers of Woodrow Wilson*, 42:197. "Ultra-pacifist, American-born group": WEW to William B. Wilson, 2 May 1917, *Papers of Woodrow Wilson*, 42:197–98. Debs on *Whitman and Traubel*: Debs to Horace Traubel, 27 June 1917, *The Letters of Eugene V. Debs*, ed. J. Robert Constantine, 2 vols. (1990), 2:312–13. "Engineered in Berlin": WEW to William B. Wilson, 2 May 1917.

7　"Very possibly the man": Lansing to President Wilson, 4 May 1917, enclosing Root to Lansing, 3 May 1917, *Papers of Woodrow Wilson*, 42:216. Invitation to serve: President Wilson to WEW, 5 May 1917, box 1, WEWP; Radosh, *American Labor*, 77–78.

8　"Geranium pot": AWH, interview with author, 3 May 1996.

9　Plan for alternative organization: Stuart, "William English Walling," 140–52; Radosh, *American Labor*, 35, 50–58. Talk at State Department: Frank Lyon Polk to Lansing, 7 May 1917, *Papers of Woodrow Wilson*, 42:240.

10　"I hope to be of real service": WEW to President Wilson, 10 May 1917, copy in box 1, WEWP; also in *Papers of Woodrow Wilson*, 42:267.

11　"Immediate renunciation:": WEW to Lansing, telegram, 16 May 1917, *Papers of Woodrow Wilson*, 42:318; " 'No Annexations, No Indemnities,' " *Independent* 90 (19 May 1917): 327–28.

12　Appointment with president: Ray Stannard Baker, *Woodrow Wilson: Life and Letters*, 8 vols. (1927–39), 7:73. Memorandum in French: WEW to President Wilson, 21 May 1917, *Papers of Woodrow Wilson*, 42:364–65.

13　*NYT* appearances: WEW interviewed on 24 May 1917; letter, 26 May 1917; statement on resignation, 3 June 1917.

14　"The black scourge of war": *Mother Earth* 12 (June 1917): 101–2.

15　Saved in memorabilia: *Mother Earth* page, folder 481, ASWY. Hapgood letter: Hapgood, *Victorian in the Modern World*, 244–45.

16　Arrest of Goldman and Berkman: Richard Drinnon, *Rebel in Paradise: A Biogra-*

phy of *Emma Goldman* (1961), 187–99; Drinnon, "Mother Earth Bulletin," in *The American Radical Press, 1880–1960*, ed. Joseph R. Conlin, 2 vols. (1974), 2:392–99.

CHAPTER 40

1   WEW writings in *NYT:* on Stockholm conference, 19 June 1917; on German Socialists, 8 July 1917; attack on Stockholm peace plan, 18 July 1917. Message to Workmen's Council: WEW to mother, [summer 1917], box 6, ASWH. American Alliance for Labor and Democracy: Stuart, "William English Walling," 154; Thompson, *Reformers and War*, 181–82; Radosh, *American Labor*, 58–70 (comparison to CIA subsidies, 70). "To fight treason": WEW to mother, 26 October 1917, folder 270, ASWY.

2   Revision of "Revolutionary Lives": ASW to WEW, 14 July 1917, folder 212, ASWY. "Kind of crazy about it": RS to ASW, 14 July 1917, folder 87, ASWY.

3   RS plan to go to Russia: RS to ASW, 14 July, 23 and 30 August 1917, folder 87, ASWY; also RS to WEW [August 1917], postcard, folder 257, ASWY; RS to Levine, 7 August 1917, Levine/Lorwin Papers.

4   "Opposed to the whole business": RS to ASW, 23 August 1917, folder 87, ASWY.

5   "It is rather a pity": unsigned critique of "They Who Freed Russia," box 1, SWB. "Seized upon certain political views": Morrow to ASW, 24 August 1917, folder 108, ASWY.

6   Haggling with Stokes: Stokes to WEW, 3 August 1917; Stokes to Spargo, 16 August 1917, box 27, Stokes Papers. Differences with Spargo: Radosh, *American Labor*, 43.

7   Stokes's mediation: Stokes to Spargo, 16 August 1917; "terribly hard for your friends": Stokes to WEW, 29 August 1917; "I regret more deeply": Stokes to WEW, 11 September 1917, box 27, Stokes Papers.

8   League for National Unity: WEW to mother, 16 and 26 October 1917, folder 270, ASWY. Vigilantes: WEW to mother, 2 January [1918], folder 270, ASWY. Hillquit campaign: WEW to mother, 26 October 1917, folder 270, ASWY; Morris Hillquit, *Loose Leaves from a Busy Life* (1934), 180–210. Resignation from ISS: Stuart, "William English Walling," 158.

9   "Socialists: The Kaiser-Party": *Independent* 91 (10 November 1917): 301–303.

10 "Now look what you've done!": AWH, interview with author, 3 May 1996.

11 "High-Brow Hearstism": *New York Globe*, 24 November 1917, quoted in Thompson, *Reformers and War*, 187. Hearst and subsidies: W. A. Swanberg, *Citizen Hearst: A Biography of William Randolph Hearst* (1961), 315–17.

12 "A great deal of sense": President Wilson to Creel, 30 November 1917, *Papers of Woodrow Wilson*, 45:162. Lippmann and The Inquiry: Ronald Steel, *Walter Lippmann and the American Century* (1980), 128–30, 134–36.

13 Swope story in *New York World*: Stuart, "William English Walling," 177–81; George F. Kennan, *Soviet-American Relations, 1917–1920*, vol. 1, *Russia Leaves the War* (1956), 264–67; Christopher Lasch, *The American Liberals and the Russian Revolution* (1962), 81–82.

14 *NYT* article: "Move to Recognize the Bolsheviki?" 14 January 1918. "Strangely authoritative tone," "most revealing and important single reflection": Kennan, *Russia Leaves the War*, 267 and 269.

15 Bullard's role: Kennan treats Bullard as a key American figure in Russia during

and after the October Revolution; see *Russia Leaves the War*, 47–58, 125–27. "Remove the misunderstanding": Swope, *New York World*, 11 January 1918.

16 Bullard's clipping: box 15, Bullard Papers.

17 Bullard and anti-Francis group: Kennan, *Russia Leaves the War*, 125–26; Edgar Sisson (head of CPI in Russia) to Creel, 4 December 1917, *The Papers of Woodrow Wilson*, ed. Arthur S. Link, vol. 45: *November 11, 1917–January 15, 1918*, 216–17. "I find it desperately hard": Bullard to Maddin Summers (American consul general), 24 January 1918, quoted in Kennan, *Russia Leaves the War*, 270.

18 "The pro-Bolshevik attitude": WEW to Lane, 17 January 1918, quoted in Kennan, *Russia Leaves the War*, 271–72.

19 Memorandum for Gompers: "The Chief Danger of Revolutions and Revolutionary Movements in Eastern Europe: Revolutions in Western Europe," enclosed with Gompers to President Wilson, 9 February 1918, *Papers of Woodrow Wilson*, 46:310–13.

20 "An unusual amount of truth": President Wilson to Lansing, 13 February 1918, *Papers of Woodrow Wilson*, 46:334; the communication is quoted in Kennan, *Russia Leaves the War*, 272–73; Radosh, *American Labor*, 126; Thompson, *Reformers and War*, 191; and Lasch, *American Liberals*, 84.

21 Disappointment with Wilson: WEW to mother [February 1918], folder 270, ASWY.

22 "Fright" during pregnancy: WEW to ASW, 2 February 1918, folder 213, ASWY; WEW to mother [February 1918], folder 270, ASWY. "Of course there is danger": mother to WEW, 18 February 1918; WEW to mother, 21 February [1918], folder 270, ASWY.

23 Miscarriage: WEW to mother, 18 March [1918]; "Anna's attitude": WEW to mother [22 March 1918], folder 270, ASWY.

CHAPTER 41

1 "Don't give him the letter": RS to ASW [summer 1918], folder 87, ASWY.

2 "Don't bother English": RS to ASW [August 1918], folder 87, ASWY.

3 Bullard reassignment and marriage: Kennan, *Soviet-American Relations, 1917–1920*, vol. 2, *The Decision to Intervene* (1958), 196–203; James R. Mock and Cedric Larson, *Words that Won the War: The Story of the Committee on Public Information 1917–1919* (1939), 306–12; Bullard to Leonora Bagg (mother-in-law), 26 August 1918, box 8, Bullard Papers. "Arthur married Ethel Bagg": RS to ASW [August 1918], folder 87, ASWY.

4 "Monday I had dinner with Levine": RS to ASW [fall 1918], folder 87, ASWY.

5 "I am young and strong again": RS to ASW [fall 1918], folder 87, ASWY.

6 WEW and Social Democratic League: Stuart, "William English Walling," 163–64. Thompson, *Reformers and War*, 196, 214. Ninety-nine dues payers: Stuart, "William English Walling," 164.

7 Taft invitation: Taft to WEW, 23 March 1918, box 1, WEWP. "Training camp": Stuart, "William English Walling," 162; WEW, "The Socialists of Europe in the War," in *What Every American Should Know About the War*, ed. Montaville Flowers (1918), 132–49. National Security League: Thompson, *Reformers and War*, 261–62; Robert D. Ward, "The Origins and Activities of the National Security League, 1914–1919," *Mississippi Valley Historical Review* 47 (June 1960): 51–65.

8 Spargo and Gompers mission: Radosh, *American Labor*, 170–220.

9 "Recall Spargo immediately": quoted in Spargo to WEW and others, 18 September 1918, box 30–31, Stokes Papers.

10 "Wroth at the simple reporting of facts": Spargo to WEW and others, 18 September 1918, box 30–31, Stokes Papers.

11 Reflection of Wilson administration policy: Radosh, *American Labor*, 220. Spargo role: Ronald Radosh, "John Spargo and Wilson's Russian Policy, 1920," *Journal of American History* 52 (December 1965): 548–65.

12 SDL conference: Stuart, "William English Walling," 170.

13 Letters from New London: ASW to WEW, 19 July and 11 August 1918, folder 213, ASWY. "How have you kept yourself": RS to ASW, [July 1918], folder 87, ASWY.

14 Confiding letter: Rose Pastor Stokes to ASW, quoted in Arthur Zipser and Pearl Zipser, *Fire and Grace: The Life of Rose Pastor Stokes* (1989), 198; her prosecution: 179–97.

15 "The War is practically over": ASW to Charmian London, 4 November 1918, box 5, ASWH.

CHAPTER 42

1 WEW's departure for Europe: WEW to mother, telegram, 8 January 1919, box 1, WEWP; Stuart, "William English Walling," 171.

2 "The logic of the emotions": ASW to WEW, 10 January 1919, folder 213, ASWY.

3 "Splendid intelligent and sympathetic men": WEW to ASW, 16 January [1919], folder 213, ASWY.

4 "My time has been exceptionally absorbed": WEW to ASW, 24 February [1919], box 6, ASWH.

5 "The opportunity came a few days ago": WEW to ASW [11 March 1919], folder 213, ASWY.

6 Herron, Gompers, and WEW: *The Autobiography of William Allen White* (1946), 563–64.

7 Memoir: ASW to Charmian London, 17 January 1919, folder 81, ASWY; manuscript is dated 22 January 1919. The memoir ultimately appeared in Charmian London, *The Book of Jack London*, 2 vols. (1921), 1:319–22.

8 "A bitterness courses": *New York Call* magazine [August 1919], clipping, box 2, SWB.

9 Brett and "Revolutionary Lives": ASW to WEW, 6 February 1919, folder 213, ASWY; also Thomas Wells, Harper & Brothers, to ASW, 6 May 1919, box 6, ASWH.

10 "Curiously far away": unsigned critique for Frederick A. Stokes Company of "They Who Freed Russia" [August 1917], box 1, SWB.

11 "Revolutionary Lives" manuscript: The author has read the microfilm version at the Bancroft Library. ASW sent the original to Vil Bykov, a Russian scholar who had interviewed her and was writing a book about Jack London. See Bykov, "Anna Strunsky's Parcel," *Ogonek* 4 (January 1965), typescript translation lent by AWH.

12 WEW's return from Paris: RS to ASW [spring 1919], folder 87, ASWY. "Starvation of innocent millions": WEW, "The Parting of the Ways," NYT, 19 April 1919.

13 "I find *every day* evidence": WEW to Willoughby Walling, 19 May 1919, box 1, WEWP.

14 WEW and Gompers: Gompers referred only briefly, albeit warmly, to WEW in his memoir, *Seventy Years of Life and Labor: An Autobiography*, 2 vols. (1925), 1:490; 2:400–401.

15 Gompers mission: WEW to mother, 17 July [1919], folder 271, ASWY; Stuart, "Wil-

liam English Walling," 224–25. "I sit next to Gompers": WEW to ASW, 30 July 1919, folder 213, ASWY.

16 Learning to drive: ASW to WEW, 31 July 1919, box 5, ASWH; ASW to WEW, 4 August 1919, folder 213, ASWY; the Marmon: Willoughby Walling to WEW, 8 October 1917, box 1, WEWP. "A negro burned": ASW to WEW, 31 July 1919, box 5, ASWH. Russell: ASW to WEW, 5 August 1919, folder 213, ASWY.

17 "My next job": WEW to mother, 16 September [1919], folder 271, ASWY.

CHAPTER 43

1 Lippmann and Baker complaints: Thompson, *Reformers and War*, 259.

2 Division of Socialist Party: David A. Shannon, *The Socialist Party of America: A History* (1955, 1967), 139–49.

3 Rose Pastor Stokes in Chicago: Zipser and Zipser, *Fire and Grace*, 211–13.

4 A. Mitchell Palmer and anti-subversive campaign: Stanley Coben, *A. Mitchell Palmer, Politician* (1963). Raids in November, December, and early January: Robert K. Murray, *Red Scare: A Study of National Hysteria, 1919–1920* (1964), 196–213. Goldman-Berkman letter: Goldman and Berkman to "Dear Friend," 1 November 1919, folder 58, ASWY. *Buford* deportation: Murray, *Red Scare*, 207.

5 Berger expulsion: Murray, *Red Scare*, 227–29. Expulsion of five Socialists: Hillquit, *Loose Leaves*, 246–51; Murray, *Red Scare*, 236–37.

6 "The seating or unseating of the Socialists": WEW, in *New York Tribune*, 26 January 1920, quoted in Stuart, "William English Walling," 189. "My aid has been sought": WEW to mother, 18 January [1920], box 1, WEWP.

7 Spargo response and resignation: *New York Tribune*, 29 January 1920, quoted in Stuart, "William English Walling," 189; Radosh, *American Labor*, 49–50. Sinclair comment: Upton Sinclair to WEW, 17 February 1920, Stokes Papers, quoted in Stuart, "William English Walling," 191.

8 "Camouflaged Communists": WEW letter, *NYT*, 3 March 1920. "In the case of any one else": Spargo to Sinclair, 14 March 1920, box 19, John Spargo Papers, Wilbur Collection, University of Vermont.

9 Palmer and Harding criticism of expulsion: Murray, *Red Scare*, 243. Hardly knew himself: WEW to mother, [March 1920], box 1, WEWP.

10 Lusk Report: Joint Legislative Committee Investigating Seditious Activities, *Revolutionary Radicalism*, part 1, 1: 845, 1000; WEW's contribution (1:99–106) was on socialism in France and his authorship credited in the index.

11 "Parlor Bolshevism": WEW, *Sovietism: The A B C of Russian Bolshevism—according to the Bolshevists* (1920), 30.

12 "English's book against the 'Dirty Bolsheviks' ": RS to Levine [summer 1920], from Watch Hill, Rhode Island, Levine/Lorwin Papers.

13 "Antiseptic against the bolshevist poison": *American Journal of Sociology* 26 (September 1920): 250; *Outlook* 126 (15 September 1920): 111. Alleged misquotation: Harold Kellock in *Freeman* 1 (8 September 1920): 620. "Anti-bolshevist hysteria": Gregory Zilboorg, *Nation* 111 (13 October 1920): 424.

14 Collaboration with Gompers: Samuel Gompers, with the collaboration of WEW, *Out of Their Own Mouths: a Revelation and an Indictment of Sovietism* (1921); Stuart, "William English Walling," 184–85.

15 Rejection of Weyl essay: Forcey, *Crossroads of Liberalism*, 296–97.

16 "Tired Radicals": Walter Weyl, *Tired Radicals and Other Papers* (1921), 9–15

(excerpt on 9–10); see also Francis Hackett in *Walter Weyl: An Appreciation*, 102. Weyl died of cancer in November 1919 at the age of forty-six.

Part Eight

CHAPTER 44

1 Scott and *The Masses*: Scott was listed as a "literary editor" from December 1912 into 1914. "Sick of the Socialist Party": Scott to Stokes, 30 April 1917, James Graham Phelps Stokes Papers, Columbia University. "I fought for *Peace!*": questionnaire for University Settlement who's who, box 27, University Settlement Papers, State Historical Society of Wisconsin.

2 Graham and Rose Pastor Stokes divorce: Arthur Zipser and Pearl Zipser, *Fire and Grace: The Life of Rose Pastor Stokes* (1989), 259–64; "puritanism": Rose Pastor Stokes to ASW, 28 October 1925, quoted in Zipser and Zipser, *Fire and Grace*, 263–64.

3 "The McGinn offer": ASW to Charmian London, 14 April 1920, box 5, ASWH.

4 Errors: ASW's undated document correcting Charmian London, *The Book of Jack London*, 2 vols. (1920), is in box 4, ASWH. "Booful": annotation on copy of JL to AS, 26 December 1900, folder 82, ASWY.

5 "His desire": RS to ASW [summer 1920], folder 88, ASWY; RS to Levine, from Watch Hill, 19 (two letters), 22, and 23 June 1920, Levine/Lorwin Papers.

6 RS's marriage and departure: Louis Levine/Lorwin, "Family Chronicle" (manuscript lent by his son, Boris Lorwin), 188; Levine to ASW, 11 October 1920, folder 84, ASWY; ASW to Rosalind Walling, 15 April 1921, box 1, WEWP.

7 RSL's pregnancy: ASW to WEW, 28 September 1921, box 5, ASWH. Aino Malmberg: RSL to Levine, 12 July 12 [1921]; birth of son: ASW to Levine, 12 October 1921, Louis Levine/Lorwin Papers, held by his son, Boris Lorwin. Magazine articles: "Twilight Sleep—Chronicle of an Experience in the Maternity Hospital at Freiburg," *McClure's*, May and June 1922, clippings, folder 379, ASWY.

8 ASW in Paris: scattered correspondence in box 1, WEWP; and ASW to WEW, 8, 11, 22, and 31 December 1922, 19 January 1923, box 5, ASWH. "We were treated as guests": Lorwin, "Family Chronicle," 211. Elias Strunsky's death: ASW to WEW, 6 and 25 February, 4 March 1923, box 5, ASWH; condolence letter, Jean Longuet to ASW, 17 February 1923, box 1, SWB.

9 Charmian London visit: WEW to ASW, 6 April 1923, box 6, ASWH.

10 "A trying guest": Lorwin, "Family Chronicle," 209. Subversion in *Book Review Digest*: Stuart, "William English Walling," 187.

11 Congressional campaign: Stuart, "William English Walling," 199–209; "Why Not Send a Progressive to Congress?", campaign flier, box 3, WEWP.

12 "While prosperity lasts": Keith Hutchinson in *The Nation* 125 (13 July 1927): 42–43, quoted in Stuart, "William English Walling," 235.

13 A Club reunion: ASW to Rosalind Walling, 16 March 1926, box 1, WEWP.

CHAPTER 45

1 "Despair! Despair": ASW diary, 17 December 1925, folder 356, ASWY.

2 "I stand in a singular relation": ASW to Henry E. Huntington [January 1925], box 5, ASWH. "If you could place upon these letters": ASW to Leslie Edgar Bliss, acting

librarian, 25 January 1926; Bliss to ASW, 30 January 1926; "I had three or five thousand dollars in mind": ASW to Bliss, 17 February 1926, box 5, ASWH.

3   "I am simply aghast": Willoughby G. Walling to WEW, 1 October 1926, folder 278, ASWY.

4   "If I had the twenty years": ASW to Rosalind Walling, 16 November 1926, box 5, ASWH.

5   "The arrangement was made" and name change: Lorwin, "Family Chronicle," 244 and 288.

6   Travel in Mexico: Stuart, "William English Walling," 191–96. Money-losing book: WEW, *The Mexican Question: Mexico and American-Mexican Relations under Calles and Obregon* (1927). Al Smith campaign: Elisabeth Israels Perry, *Belle Moskowitz: Feminine Politics and the Exercise of Power in the Age of Alfred E. Smith* (1987), 192–205: "no intellectual": WEW to Willoughby G. Walling [August 1928], box 6, ASWH. La Guardia campaign: Stuart, "William English Walling," 213–16.

7   "To assuage the fever": ASW to WEW, 13 February 1929, box 5, ASWH. "So we start out": ASW diary, 30 July 1929; "constructive plan," 7 September 1929, 3:45 A.M., folder 358, ASWY.

8   "Minor or defective": WEW to mother [October] 1929, box 1, WEWP. Children's situations: ASW to Charmian London, 5 December 1932, box 5, ASWH. "All was over" ASW to Rosamond Walling Tirana, 22 May 1932; "stunt," ASW to Rosamond Walling Tirana, 28 October 1932, folder 168, ASWY. Move to Washington Square: Hyman Strunsky obituary, *NYT*, 13 April 1942; ASW diary, 7 January 1934, folder 359, ASWY.

9   "English promised me": ASW to Rifat Tirana, 14 November 1932, folder 163, ASWY.

10   "The stage of coma": ASW diary, 13 February 1933, folder 359, ASWY. Death of Anna Hourwitch (Horowitz) Strunsky: obituary, *New York Herald Tribune*, 12 February 1933, clipping, folder 474, ASWY.

11   "I was wrong": ASW diary, 27 September 1933, folder 359, ASWY.

12   "We walk across the Square": ASW diary [1934 or 1935], box 1, SWB.

13   Leonard Abbott: Abbott to ASW, 16 May 1933, box 1, ASWH; ASW diary, 10 June 1935, folder 356, ASWY.

14   Labor Chest position: Stuart, "William English Walling," 246–47; ASW in *Walling Symposium*, 8. "O if I were sailing with you": ASW diary, 5 June 1936, box 1, SWB.

CHAPTER 46

1   WEW in Europe: ASW in *Walling Symposium*, 18–19; Stuart, "William English Walling," 247.

2   Illness in Amsterdam: ASW in *Walling Symposium*, 18–19. Forbade notification: Rosamond Walling Tirana to ASW, 15 September 1936, cablegram, folder 171, ASWY.

3   Program for the William English Walling memorial meeting: folder 483, ASWY. Simeon Strunsky's statement: *Walling Symposium*, 54.

CHAPTER 47

1   ASW's article: *Walling Symposium*, 7–20. RSL's unwritten essay: RSL to ASW, 15, 18, and 23 November 1937; 3 January 1938, folder 94, ASWY.

2 "I have often had the feeling": Sinclair to ASW, 28 March 1938, SWB.

3 Writing in 1942: foreword dated 4 September 1942, folder 392, ASWY. Visit to San Francisco: "Collaborator of Jack London Here," *San Francisco Call-Bulletin*, 14 December 1943, clipping, box 2, SWB. Liberty ship: folder 392, ASWY. Huntington: Leslie Edgar Bliss to ASW, 6 January 1953, box 1, ASWH; ASW to Bliss, 14 July 1953, box 5, ASWH; Bliss to ASW, 20 July 1953, box 1, ASWH; Bliss to ASW, 9 September 1954, box 1, SWB.

4 Historical resource: for example, correspondence with Joseph Backus on Gelett Burgess, folder 35, ASWY; Howard Quint on Wilshire, folder 135, ASWY; Allen F. Davis on WEW and other settlement residents, folder 49, ASWY; Stephen Schlesinger on WEW and other "millionaire socialists," folder 139, ASWY.

5 "The most devoted and lovely children": ASW to Louis Kaplan, 30 June 1962, box 1, WEWP. Among the four children, Rosamond was an artist; Anna had been working for the International Rescue Committee; Georgia was a psychologist; and Hayden was an architect who had worked for the American Friends Service Committee, UNICEF, and the World Health Organization.

6 "Alter self": ASW notation on Emily Paley to family, 29 May 1963, box 1, SWB. ASW's death: AWH, interview with author, 15 June 1992; obituary, *NYT*, 26 February 1964.

CHAPTER 48

1 "He was a pure flame": Hutchins Hapgood, *A Victorian in the Modern World* (1939), 244–45.

2 "I never tie myself up": WEW, quoted in ASW diary, 12 September 1916, folder 303, ASWY. Brubaker remark: *Walling Symposium*, 42.

3 Annoyed: For example, WEW to mother, 22 August [1928], box 1, WEWP.

4 "Anna's intense seriousness": Hapgood, *Victorian in the Modern World*, 425.

5 "My impulses are the same": Abbott to ASW, 13 February 1926, folder 2, ASWY.

6 Historians' attention: see extended treatment of WEW in two recent works: Mark Pittenger, *American Socialists and Evolutionary Thought, 1870–1920* (1993), and Brian Lloyd, *Left Out: Pragmatism, Exceptionalism, and the Poverty of American Marxism, 1890–1922* (1997).

7 Influence and model: for example, Charles N. Watson, *The Novels of Jack London: A Reappraisal* (1983), and Jonathan Auerbach, *Male Call: Becoming Jack London* (1996). Leon Fink's substantial essays appraising the careers of WEW and ASW appeared too late for use in these pages. See Fink, "Joining the People: William English Walling and the Specter of Intellectual Class," and "A Love for the People: Anna Strunsky Walling and the Domestic Limits of Democratic Idealism," in his *Progressive Intellectuals and the Dilemmas of Democratic Commitment* (1997), 114–46, 147–83.

8 "I see the penciled words": ASW diary, 31 July 1928, folder 300, ASWY.

Index

Violette of Père Lachaise (Strunsky), 138,
183; started, 42–43; draft finished, 80;
rejected by Macmillan, 186–87; published by Stokes Company, 213, 214–
15
Vorse, Mary Heaton, 126, 197

Wald, Lillian, 158
Walling, Anna Strunsky (daughter), 189,
265
Walling, Anna Strunsky (wife). *See*
Strunsky, Anna
Walling, Frederika Haskell (sister-in-
law), 61
Walling, Georgia (daughter), 200, 265
Walling, Mary (sister), 48
Walling, Rosalind English (daughter),
138, 140, 165; death of, 139
Walling, Rosalind English (mother), 47,
103, 106, 140–41, 166, 219, 225, 226,
241, 265
Walling, Rosamond English (daughter),
186, 265
Walling, William English: characterized,
1; family background, childhood, 47–
48; at University of Chicago, 48–49; at
Harvard Law School, 49–50; inheritance from grandfather, 49; letter on
"three niggers," 50; appointed factory
inspector, 52; economic yearbook project, 53–54; at University Settlement,
55, 56, 58, 59; writing aspirations, 59,
60; role in founding of Women's Trade
Union League, 62–63; covers Cripple
Creek strike, 65, 66–67, 68; rivalry
with Baker, 65–67; labor reporting,
67–69; affair with Grunspan, 72–73,
74, 75; first letter to Strunsky, 80–81;
creates revolutionary news bureau,
81; in St. Petersburg, 86; declaration
of love for Strunsky, 95, 96–97; resistance of parents, 103–4, 108–9;
pledges equality in marriage, 109; marriage, 113–14; unconsummated, 119;
honeymoon trip to Italy, 127–28;
arrest in St. Petersburg, 133–35; death
of daughter, Rosalind English, 138; at
Springfield riot, 152; appearance with
Strunsky at Cooper Union, 155–56;

role in National Negro Conference,
158–59, 163, 167; antagonizes Booker
T. Washington, 163; Grunspan sues,
166; unstable personality of, 167;
move to Caritas Island, 167; roils
Socialist Party, 168; recruits Du Bois
for NAACP, 171–72; organizing trip
for NAACP, 173–74; testimony at
Grunspan trial, 177; verdict, 179;
defines self as publicist, 192; articles
in *New Review*, 195; at Dodge salon,
197; role at *Masses*, 197; on causes and
issues of Great War, 210–11; criticizes
peace position of Socialist Party, 211;
optimism about war, 211–12; move to
Greenwich, Conn., 212, 225; opposition to Hughes, tacit support of Wilson, 224–25; attack on wife as traitor,
229; offered place on Root commission, declines, 232, 233; opposes negotiated peace, 233; wartime propaganda
activities, 235; disputes with Spargo
and Stokes, 236–37, 243–44; attack on
Bullard, Creel, and CPI, 238–39, 240;
fading identity as socialist, 240; to
Europe with Gompers, 246, 249;
attacks Wilson administration as pro-
Bolshevik, 248–49, 250; activities in
Red Scare, 252–53; Weyl portrayal of,
254–55; candidate for Congress (1924),
defeat, 262; in Smith campaign (1928),
264–65; difficulties in marriage, 265;
separation from Strunsky, 265–66;
Mexican divorce, 265; heads Labor
Chest, 266; death of, 267; memorial
meeting, 267–68; appraisal of career,
271. *See also Larger Aspects of Socialism; Progressivism—and After; Russia's Message; Socialism As It Is*
Walling, William Hayden English (son),
226, 265
Walling, Willoughby (father), 47, 48, 138,
146, 225; analysis of son's character,
116
Walling, Willoughby George (brother),
47, 48, 53–54, 146, 165, 263
Walters, Bishop Alexander, 157
Ward, William Hayes, 161
War of the Classes (London), 81